PUBLIC SECTOR PEN

In 1952 the Royal Institute of Public Administration embarked on a series of major research projects to be carried out by study groups. This book is the outcome of the seventh project in the series. The other six are:

THE ORGANIZATION OF BRITISH CENTRAL
GOVERNMENT 1914–1956

NEW SOURCES OF LOCAL REVENUE

BUDGETING IN PUBLIC AUTHORITIES

BUILDING BY LOCAL AUTHORITIES

OPERATIONAL RESEARCH IN LOCAL GOVERNMENT

THE GOVERNMENT EXPLAINS

Other Institute Publications

ADMINISTRATORS IN ACTION
Two Volumes

FINANCIAL ADMINISTRATION IN LOCAL GOVERNMENT

NATIONALIZATION

THE TOWN CLERK IN ENGLISH LOCAL GOVERNMENT
Allen and Unwin

Public Sector Pensions

BY

GERALD RHODES

Published for the Royal Institute
of Public Administration

TORONTO: UNIVERSITY OF TORONTO PRESS

Reprinted in 2018

Published in Canada by University of Toronto Press

ISBN 978-1-4875-7259-4 (paper)

PRINTED IN GREAT BRITAIN
in 10 point Times Roman type
BY UNWIN BROTHERS LIMITED
WOKING AND LONDON

Chairman
R. S. MCDOUGALL, C.B.E.
General Manager, Stevenage Development Corporation; formerly County Treasurer, Hertfordshire

Members
L. A. ELLWOOD, Senior Solicitor, Unilever Ltd; Chairman, The National Association of Pension Funds

S. GULLY, O.B.E., lately Principal Executive Officer, Health Services Superannuation Division, Ministry of Health

W. S. HARDACRE, County Treasurer, Berkshire; Past President, Society of County Treasurers; Member of Council, Institute of Municipal Treasurers and Accountants

*H. W. NAISH, M.B.E., lately Director of Establishments (Finance), National Coal Board; formerly Chief Finance and Establishment Officer, Coal Commission

A. R. PREST, Professor of Economics and Public Finance in the University of Manchester

Research Officer
G. RHODES
* Owing to illness, Mr Naish unfortunately had to relinquish his membership of the Group.

Terms of Reference

1. To examine the salient features of the occupational pension schemes operated by central government, local government, the nationalized industries and the health services; to classify their similarities and differences; and to compare them with the provisions of typical schemes operated in commerce and industry.

2. To consider: (a) the ways in which existing schemes, both in the public services and in commerce, could be modified to simplify their administration; and (b) the extent to which the differences in the provisions of these various schemes could be eliminated with a view to securing more economical administration.

3. To review the extent to which existing schemes encourage or discourage mobility of staff, and the effect of the National Insurance Act, 1959, on this question.

4. To examine: (a) the financial and economic advantages and disadvantages of funded and 'pay-as-you-go' schemes; and (b) the basis of funded schemes, the methods by which they are operated and the investment policies followed in their management.

5. To take into account in the foregoing enquiries the other consequences of the National Insurance Act, 1959, and the effect of changes in expectation of life and of the variations in the general levels of remuneration over periods of time.

6. To make recommendations.

PREFACE

Public Sector Pensions is one of a series of major research projects undertaken by the Royal Institute of Public Administration.

Because of the growing importance of pension schemes generally and their long history in the public services, the Institute judged the time opportune to review the policies currently implicit in public sector schemes. Particular aspects of the situation which seemed to require examination were the complexities of administration and the variety of methods of financing schemes, but the study also sought to set public sector schemes in the wider context of a national pensions policy. The terms of reference are on an earlier page.

As in the Institute's previous projects, the study was undertaken by a full-time Research Officer, in this instance Mr Gerald Rhodes, with the assistance of a study group whose members are listed earlier. The Chairman of the group was Mr R. S. McDougall, C.B.E., General Manager of Stevenage Development Corporation, and formerly County Treasurer of Hertfordshire. The Institute was most fortunate that he was willing to undertake this task, and very much appreciates the time and energy which he unstintingly devoted to it. It would also like to thank most warmly all the members of the study group for their valuable assistance and expert advice so freely given.

Each member of the group served in a personal capacity, and nothing in this report should be regarded as expressing the views of any organization with which he is or has been connected. Nor, in a work of this kind, is it likely that all the members will fully support all the conclusions reached, and Mr Ellwood in particular wishes to make it clear that he does not accept some of the conclusions of Chapter 9.

When the study group was constituted Mr R. W. Abbott, a Fellow of the Institute of Actuaries, and Mr C. A. French, Chief Accountant of the Electricity Council, accepted invitations to serve on it, and attended most of the meetings. They eventually resigned because they found themselves in fundamental disagreement with the views of the other members of the study group and with the general tenor and conclusions of the study. Moreover, they felt that the conclusions of the study group on the subject of funding could not be supported without a more thorough examination of the alternative system of pay-as-you-go than the group had undertaken. The Institute is nevertheless grateful to both Mr Abbott and Mr French for their contributions to the study group discussions.

To Mr Rhodes fell the detailed research and analysis, and subsequently the writing of this book. In carrying out these duties he demonstrated rare skill and industry and, as the following pages show, an ability to master detail and at the same time to maintain a breadth of view. His ability to suffer cheerfully and without apparent distress the many suggested amendments was a notable feature of his work. For his most valuable contribution to the success of the enterprise, the Institute and the members of the study group wish to express their appreciation and thanks.

This study was financed by a grant from the P. D. Leake Trust, created under the will of the late Percy Dewe Leake 'for the benefit and advancement of the sciences of accounting and of political economy including the subject of public finance and taxation'. The Institute wishes to record its sincere thanks for this generous support.

This study would not have been possible without the co-operation of many senior officials, both in the public services and the nationalized industries, who willingly answered what must sometimes have seemed to be endless questions. The National Association of Pension Funds also most kindly assisted by putting the Research Officer in touch with a number of private sector firms who gladly consented to supply information about their pension schemes. To all these the Institute would like to express its warmest thanks for their ready and sympathetic help.

September 1964.

CONTENTS

PREFACE 9

1. *The Origin and Growth of Pensions* 13
2. *The Development of Pension Schemes* 46
3. *Public Sector Schemes: The Benefits Provided* 69
4. *Public Sector Schemes: The Financial Arrangements* 90
5. *Private Sector Schemes: The Contrasts between the Public and Private Sectors* 127
6. *Occupational Schemes and National Insurance* 158
7. *Taxation and Pension Schemes* 190
8. *The Problem of Complexity* 198
9. *Financing Public Sector Schemes: Funding and Pay-as-you-go* 212
10. *Public Sector Schemes and the Future* 240

APPENDICES
1 Occupational Pension Schemes: The General Picture 255
2 Public Sector Pension Schemes 263
3 Pensions for the Armed Forces 275
4 Main Provisions of Twelve Public Sector Schemes 280
5 Membership and Finances of Public Sector Schemes 286
6 National Insurance Retirement Pensions 291
7 The History and Purpose of Tax Reliefs 301
INDEX 315

CHAPTER 1

The Origin and Growth of Pensions

To most men and some women a pension means a regular source of income which they hope to get when they retire from work. Sometimes it will come from their employment, sometimes from the National Insurance scheme and sometimes from both. Many married women must rely on their husband's pensions in retirement and old age, and only if they are widowed will they receive a pension in their own right.

In any description of pensions at the present day, much attention will need to be concentrated on the kind of pension, its size and how it is provided. There are pension schemes and pension schemes,[1] as anyone knows who has tried to move from one pensionable job to another, and although state pensions are the same from Caithness to Cornwall, they cater for a variety of situations.[2]

Nor is the position static. Within the last twenty years not only has the vast National Insurance scheme been built up, but millions of people have for the first time become eligible for occupational pensions. One may go further: sixty years ago state pensions did not exist and only a handful of private employers had set up pension schemes. Only in the public services was there anything approaching a regular system of pension provision and even this, outside the Civil Service, was far from complete. Changes on this scale indicate great changes in public attitudes to pensions and pension schemes. To explore the origin and growth of both occupational and state pension schemes will help to account for these changes and to illuminate the present situation. In this, public sector schemes,[3] the principal sub-

[1] The term 'pension scheme' (or 'occupational pension scheme') is used here for a definite arrangement instituted in advance for the payment of pensions and operated through a particular employment or occupation. (It does not therefore cover 'ex gratia' or 'discretionary' payments where the recipient does not know in advance whether he will get a pension nor, often, how much it will be if he does get one.)

[2] 'State pensions' covers all types of pension payments made by the State, except in its capacity as an employer. These payments are mainly Old Age pensions, and National Insurance retirement and widows' pensions.

[3] For a definition of the public sector, see Appendix 2. For practical purposes it may be taken to refer here to the public services (including the National Health Service) and the nationalized industries.

ject of this study, play an important part, spanning a period of 150 years from tentative beginnings in the nineteenth century to a coverage of nearly 4 million members in 1964.

Certain social and economic changes which have occurred over the past century and a half may well be regarded as having contributed greatly, although to some degree indirectly, to the encouragement of the growth of pensions. For example, the increased expectation of life which has become marked in the last 100 years means that many more people now survive to old age. Again, changing family relationships, combined with greater scope for mobility, have made it less common for different generations to live together or for sons and daughters to support their fathers and mothers in their old age.

The object of this chapter is not, however, to examine in detail the many factors which have contributed to what amounts to a revolution in our attitudes towards retirement and old age. It has the more limited purpose of drawing attention to certain ideas and motives which at different times led men to advocate (and oppose) pensions. The aim is therefore to give perspective to the detailed examination of public sector schemes which follows in later chapters.

But first it will be useful to clear up a confusion in terminology. The terms 'pension scheme' and 'superannuation scheme' are now practically interchangeable, and the former is generally used in this study in preference to the more cumbersome 'superannuation scheme'. Nevertheless, there was originally an important distinction so that civil service pensions were known as superannuation allowances or even as superannuations; even today such pensions are granted by virtue of the Superannuation Acts, and the term 'superannuation' is similarly used in the local government and teachers' schemes. The present position may best be understood by seeing briefly how the word 'pension' has become more restricted in meaning.

To the eighteenth century and earlier a pension was simply a source of income; it might be given after long and faithful service but equally it might be no more than a regular payment or subsidy for current services; it might be given to a worthy official but equally it might be given to a royal favourite or mistress. Dr Johnson in his dictionary of 1755 caustically remarked: 'In England it is generally understood to mean pay given to a state hireling for treason to his country.' A modern historian who has carefully analysed the recipients of pensions and annuities payable at the Exchequer or 'per Paymaster' in the middle years of the eighteenth century found in the lists not only retired officials but also some of 'the first dukes of the Kingdom' to whom a pension was 'a welcome and useful recognition of their importance' and 'a necessary help to keep up the appearances of strength and splendour required from men placed so near the Throne'; this was in addition to the many women, parasites and foreigners 'of a less dignified character' who received lesser pensions.[1]

This more general use of the word still survives (in, for example, Civil List Pensions), but the granting of a pension for life on retirement from work was adopted in the first civil service scheme designed to deal with the problem of superannuated civil servants, that is, those who were too old to continue work, and has remained ever since as the main, although not the only way of dealing with this problem. It is perhaps worth noting that even on retirement most public servants now receive a lump sum of money in addition to a pension, and that most schemes, even if they are called 'superannuation schemes', also make provision for widows' pensions or death benefits. The distinction has therefore grown very blurred in practice.

PENSIONS FOR CIVIL SERVANTS

The establishment of a pension scheme for civil servants illustrates some of the motives which contributed to the origin and subsequent growth of public service schemes. The first Act of Parliament to be concerned with the provision of pensions generally in the public offices was passed in 1810, and the first Act devoted exclusively to this problem was the Superannuation Act of 1834. These are landmarks in pension history because they attempted for the first time to establish a comprehensive and uniform scheme for all whom we should now call civil servants (or to be more accurate, for 'established' civil servants; unestablished staff are not eligible for pensions).

Even before the nineteenth century, the problem of providing for public servants who were unable, through old age or incapacity, to continue working, had been recognized, but methods of dealing with the problem varied from department to department. Two departments, Customs and Excise, had indeed established superannuation funds by the early eighteenth century to which the men paid contributions and out of which they could expect to receive pensions at the end of their careers.[2] Such schemes were no doubt inspired partly by the desire to secure efficiency through the retirement of those who were no longer fit to work and partly by humanitarian motives. There were also cases where departments had discretionary power to grant pensions financed by various means, including the sale of old stores.

---

[1] Sir Lewis Namier, *The Structure of Politics at the Accession of George III*, Macmillan, 2nd ed., 1957, pp. 185–7.

[2] They had, however, no claim to a pension. For a detailed account of the Customs Scheme, see Marios Raphael, 'The Origins of Public Superannuation Schemes in England, 1684–1859'. Unpublished Ph.D. thesis, London School of Economics, 1957.

There were in any case formidable obstacles to the establishment of any general pension scheme. To begin with, no precise line can be drawn in the modern sense between salaries paid to those who were at work and pensions paid to those who had retired from work. Some civil servants were remunerated by fees as well as or instead of salaries; some held sinecures providing an income with no duties; others again held office for life but paid a deputy part of the remuneration to perform the actual duties of the office. The confusion of arrangements for appointing and paying public servants was reflected in the confusion of arrangements for providing for both old age and retirement. Those who held sinecures, for example, were not necessarily retiring in the modern sense, although the acquisition of a sinecure might well serve as a means of providing an income in retirement. But apart from sinecures and offices performed by deputies, there were other means of making the necessary provision, as in the Post Office where public servants 'were generally allowed to make private bargains for annuities with their successors'.[1]

The political issues raised by a system of public offices which was both corrupt and wasteful led to the appointment in 1785 of three Commissioners to inquire into the 'Fees, Gratuities, Perquisites and Emoluments' of various public offices. The preamble to the Act appointing the Commissioners made it clear that their aim was to be the examination of abuses and the making of recommendations to ensure 'the better conducting and managing of the business transacted in the said offices'.

It was from the examination of abuses that the idea of a proper system of superannuation first arose. For it was natural that in their ten reports between 1786 and 1788 the Commissioners should make frequent reference to the desirability of abolishing the numerous sinecure offices which then existed. Apart from other reasons they were 'a description of office which we can only consider as a bad substitute for pensions, less open to public control and more liable to abuse in their application'.[2] They recognized that such sinecures, as well as offices which were not performed in person but by deputies, had served a purpose in providing an income in retirement, but 'we think that an establishment may, and ought in wisdom to be formed, in which such a species of Emolument would be superfluous and redundant: An establishment, by which every Public Officer should be paid for his services, not under false pretences, and in uncertain measure, but openly, and in proportion to the service he performs: An establishment too, which should entitle him to a provision upon retirement, not dependent upon caprice or accident, or arising from

---

[1] Kenneth Ellis, *The Post Office in the Eighteenth Century*, University of Durham Publications, 1958, p. 22.

[2] First Report of the Commissioners, Parliamentary Paper 309, 1806, p. 12.

the perpetuation of abuses, but known and certain, free from the competition of individuals, or the animadversion of the public'.[1] They further thought that the pension should be enough 'to afford them a decent provision' and that it 'should be charged with the salaries and other payments upon the Fee Fund'.[2]

Thus the Commissioners were only concerned with superannuation to the extent that deficiencies in the existing arrangements gave opportunities for abuse and corruption. Since in their view it was the irregularity of the existing salary system which chiefly led to abuse, their main concern was to put salaries on a regular and proper footing, but in doing this they were inevitably led to deal with the problem of superannuation because of its close connexion with the salary problem. This did not mean that there were not opportunities for abuse even where pensions were granted; a striking example was unearthed by the Commissioners in the case of William Fraser, Under Secretary of State in the Foreign Department, who was granted a pension on going out of office in 1761 and had continued to draw it although in 1785 he had been back in office 'upwards of twenty-two years'. But very largely one can see the first moves towards a system of civil service superannuation as incidental and subordinate to a much wider concern and movement to check corruption and reduce cost in the public service.

Nevertheless, progress towards a definite system of pensions was slow. A Treasury Minute of 1803 laid down a scale of allowances for certain officers of the Customs who had served 'with diligence and fidelity' and were 'absolutely incapable' from infirmity of mind or body to perform their duties. The Act of 1810 (50 Geo. III, c. 117) left a good deal unsettled and the Superannuation Act of 1834, the first measure to deal with the subject as a whole, may be regarded as providing the base for the civil service scheme of today. It is important to note too that, largely because of the historical circumstances which gave rise to a system of pensions, Parliament has always intervened more directly in the case of pensions than in the case of other conditions of service. The series of Superannuation Acts from 1834 to the present day is thus unique.

One factor which soon assumed importance in pension arrangements was the question of cost. A Committee of 1808, charged with the task of recommending reductions in public expenditure without detriment to the public service, approved the 1803 superannuation arrangements 'as uniting a due consideration towards long and meritorious service, with a just attention to economy'.[3] This atten-

---

[1] First Report of the Commissioners, Parliamentary Paper 309, 1806, p. 14.
[2] Second Report (on the Treasury), p. 58.
[3] Third Report from the Committee on the Public Expenditure, Parliamentary Paper 331, 1808, p. 271.

tion to economy was a feature of much of the debate on civil service pensions in the early part of the nineteenth century; it was very largely responsible for the introduction of a contributory system in 1822.[1]

But if the attention to economy emphasized that it was more the method than the principle of providing pensions which was now under discussion, it also became clear that ideas about the purpose of pensions were changing. Already in 1828 a Parliamentary Select Committee was reporting that heads of departments were using the provisions relating to infirmity 'to hasten the removal of the less useful of their clerks', but although this might be a good thing sometimes there were also cases where 'persons superannuated as unfit for public service have enjoyed health and strength long afterwards, and have discharged active duties in other public offices, or in private business'.[2] To this fact in particular the Committee attributed the rise in expenditure on superannuation.

Nevertheless, the advantages of a proper system of pensions in promoting efficiency, even if not quite in the form stigmatized by the 1828 Committee, became increasingly emphasized. When, in 1856, a Royal Commission was set up to consider whether any changes were needed in the system established by the Superannuation Act of 1834, they were not strictly concerned with whether there ought to be pensions for civil servants but nevertheless felt that they ought to state the general principles on which a system should be based. They thought that there were good reasons in the public interest alone why civil servants should be superannuable, and the strongest of these reasons was that otherwise civil servants might be retained in their posts after they had 'become incompetent to perform their duties' since to dismiss them might cause hardship; but 'the evil consequences of retaining a single Civil Servant in an important post for which he has become incompetent, cannot be estimated in money and may be much more than an equivalent for the expense of the superannuation of a whole department'.[3]

The emphasis on the need for efficiency was in keeping with much current thought. Nothing illustrates this better than the following extract from the Northcote–Trevelyan Report published a year or two earlier: after suggesting that the Civil Service had become a place for the indolent 'in which they are secured against the ordinary consequences of old age, or failing health, by an arrangement which provides them with the means of supporting themselves after they

---

[1] See Chapter 2, page 48. There was vigorous opposition by civil servants to the payment of contributions, cf. Raphael, op. cit. pp. 254–5.

[2] Third Report from the Select Committee on the Public Expenditure of the United Kingdom (on Superannuations), Parliamentary Paper 480, 1828, p. 13.

[3] Report of Commissioners appointed to inquire into the Operation of the Superannuation Act (1857), p. xi. The Report contains a great deal of information about the early working of the 1834 Superannuation Act.

have become incapacitated' the Report continues: 'It may be noticed in particular that the comparative lightness of the work, and the certainty of provision in case of retirement owing to bodily incapacity, furnish strong inducements to the parents and friends of sickly youths to endeavour to obtain for them employment in the service of the Government; and the extent to which the public are consequently burdened, first with the salaries of officers who are obliged to absent themselves from their duties on account of ill health, and afterwards with their pensions when they retire on the same plea, would hardly be credited by those who have not had opportunities of observing the operation of the system.'[1]

Among the arguments against providing pensions was one which was to prove a formidable obstacle to teachers, among others. It was put by the 1857 Commissioners in this way: 'It has sometimes been argued that the only duty of the Government is to offer due remuneration, in the shape of salary, for the services performed, and that it ought to be the business of the Civil Servant to make provision out of that salary for his own future wants or those of his family.' To this the Commissioners replied, first, that 'with a view to the due performance of his duty, it is important that a Civil Servant should feel himself in a safe and independent position' and not be worried about the future, and, secondly, that public opinion would not allow a man who had given long and faithful service to starve, even if he ought to have made provision in advance. Perhaps one should not put too much stress on the Commissioners' views since they had not been asked to inquire into whether there ought to be a system of pensions, but it is interesting to note how the main emphasis seems to have shifted away from the idea of pensions as a means of checking abuse and moved towards the need for efficiency; and how an increasing variety of reasons is now put forward in favour of a pension scheme.

This second point may be seen again thirty years later in the report of the Ridley Commission. This body, which was given the whole field of the Civil Establishments for inquiry, devoted a small amount of space to the question of superannuation, and found itself broadly in agreement with the 1857 Commission. It added, however, two other suggested reasons why civil service pensions were a good thing: 'Pensions help to retain in the service men who might otherwise ·be tempted elsewhere' and 'The growing practice, too, of railway companies, banks, and other large commercial undertakings, is to establish systems of superannuation'.[2] This idea of the competitive nature

---

[1] G. M. Young and W. D. Handcock (ed.), *English Historical Documents*, Eyre and Spottiswoode, 1957, vol. XII (1), Pt. VII, No. 173, p. 568.

[2] Royal Commission appointed to inquire into the Civil Establishments, Second Report, C. 5545, 1888, paras. 81 and 82.

of pensions is perhaps more familiar now than it was then, but when combined with the reasons advanced earlier it seemed to provide an unanswerable argument for a system of pensions. As yet another Royal Commission put it: 'It is advantageous to the State . . . as there is thus secured an inducement to maintain continuous service on the part of the servant and a facility on the part of the State to dispense with further services if age or infirmity renders them less efficient.'[1]

These seemingly unanswerable arguments did not, however, ensure that other public servants were able to win an easy acceptance of their claims for a proper system of pensions. The difficulties which the teachers encountered are discussed in the next section, but it is noticeable how in the case of civil servants the emphasis is for the most part on the advantage to the State of a system of civil service superannuation and the advantage to the individual civil servant is either ignored or mentioned as only an incidental or secondary advantage. Certainly, there is reference to the granting of pensions as a 'just and adequate compensation' for faithful services, as the 1785 Commissioners put it, but the tone of the various discussions may be gathered from the 1857 Report, and from the evidence of witnesses to the Ridley Commission. Mr Frank Mowatt, for example, agreed that 'pensions exist not so much for the benefit of the public servant himself as for the benefit of the public'; the same witness too echoed the views of Sir James Graham that one should not talk about giving pensions as a matter of compassion, but rather as something which could not be resisted. Other witnesses spoke of the fact that 'it would be extremely difficult to work the Government Service at all' without some system of pensions; and that it was impossible to exaggerate the importance of the government's being able to 'get rid of men who are either worn out or for any other reasons are incompetent'.[2]

Such views indicate also how far retirement from work was coming to be accepted as part of the normal pattern, at least for civil servants. For although the civil service scheme, unlike some others, did not have a formal compulsory age of retirement, but only a minimum age, this soon came to be regarded as the normal age at which a man should retire, and it was this fact as much as any other which made the system so convenient for getting rid of men who had reached an age when their usefulness was diminishing.

However, the further growth of the scheme seems to show increasingly the influence of humanitarian considerations, inspired partly no doubt by the fact that civil servants themselves were better able

[1] Royal Commission on Superannuation in the Civil Service (Courtney), Report, Cd. 1744, 1903, para. 10.
[2] Ridley Commission, questions 14,762, 14,765, 15,583 and 20,009. Mowatt is described as 'the permanent officer at the Treasury, principally responsible for granting pensions'.

to press for improvements which they thought desirable. But as time went on there was also less insistence on the part of those responsible for running the scheme on the purely utilitarian aspect of pensions, and this too no doubt reflected to some degree a change in general public attitudes. Thus the many changes which have been made in the civil service scheme since the 1859 Superannuation Act consolidated the earlier stages of its growth, seemed designed much more to bring advantage to individual civil servants than to give increased efficiency. It is not surprising that in the process the scheme ceased to cater only for the problems of superannuated civil servants.

The first decisive move away from superannuation in the narrow sense was the provision of a benefit on death. In terms of the original purpose of the scheme, there could of course be no room for a death benefit, and it was mainly agitation by civil servants themselves which led to the appointment in 1902 of the Courtney Commission to look particularly at this question. The gist of the civil servants' argument was that it was unfair that one man might live to enjoy a pension for many years, whereas another might die just before he was due to retire and neither he nor his dependants would receive anything from the scheme.

The Commission were, however, instructed that any recommendations which they made should not increase the burden on the taxpayer, and although they did in fact recommend that a lump sum should be provided at death, the cost of this concession was to be met by a reduction in the scale of pensions. Their report indicates that this conclusion was only reached after much discussion, and was not agreed to by two of the members. In view of the importance of this extension of the purpose of pension schemes, it is worth stating the principle which the majority of the Commission favoured: 'The utmost that can be done by the State is to offer a moderate provision for the commonest contingencies of life, leaving to the individual the duty of supplementing the provision either by single action or in concert with his fellows.'[1] As against this, the minority of two (including Mr E. W., later Sir Edward, Brabrook) put the view that the only way to provide against death was by life insurance which needed 'but a little self-denial in the early years of life', whereas the scheme proposed by their colleagues 'seems to offer a premium on improvidence'; they concluded that there was no need to change the present excellent system 'in order to substitute a benefit which the vast majority of those who require it can and do already provide for themselves, and which is of no value to those who do not, because they need not provide it'.[2]

[1] Report, Cd. 1744, 1903, para. 25.
[2] Ibid., pp. xvii and xviii (for E. W. Brabrook's views see also p. 34 below). He was Chief Registrar of Friendly Societies.

It was the majority view which was accepted and led in 1909 to the introduction of lump sum benefits in the civil service scheme, both on retirement and at death, but although what chiefly influenced this decision was a desire to settle a particular practical problem which had arisen, two points in the Courtney Commission report have wider implications. If the aim is to be 'a moderate provision for the commonest contingencies of life' then superannuation is no longer the only aim, since it is only one of the contingencies to be provided for. The protests of the two minority members, on the other hand, can be seen as the last appeals to the Victorian tradition of self-help. In this sense, the Report of the Courtney Commission is of great significance in marking a point of transition to the more characteristically twentieth-century view that a man's own efforts can rarely be adequate without help.

The broadening of the view of the purposes which the civil service pension scheme should serve has continued. One can trace a continuous line, for example, from death grants in 1909 to voluntary pensions for widows provided out of a further reduction of the husband's pension in 1935, and to regular widows' and other dependants' pensions, financed in part by contributions, in 1949. But even apart from these important extensions designed to give some protection to a civil servant's family, other benefits came to be associated with the pension scheme. Gratuities given to women civil servants who marry, for example, although not provided under the Superannuation Acts, are generally included now as part of the benefits of the scheme.[1] In a different way, the right which a civil servant now has to take his accrued pension rights with him on taking up employment in other parts of the public sector, although subject to various restrictions and limitations, also represents a broader view of the object of the scheme. It is also relevant to mention here other changes which have greatly extended the scope of the scheme. One may note in particular the granting of established status to many industrial civil servants in 1948, thus making them eligible for pensions, and the counting of unestablished service, subject to a number of limitations, for pension purposes.

PENSIONS FOR TEACHERS AND OTHER PUBLIC SERVANTS

Teachers' Pensions: Difficulty of Gaining Entitlement

By the middle of the nineteenth century, not merely pensions, but a regular scheme of pensions had become an established part of the

---

[1] It should be pointed out that in most schemes there is no specific marriage gratuity, but a girl can always get back the contributions which she has paid. This is not possible in the non-contributory civil service scheme; nevertheless, the marriage gratuity in the latter scheme is more generous.

terms on which civil servants were employed. Other public servants were not so fortunate; many were for long dependent on the goodwill of their employers for the hope of a pension.[1] Nevertheless, gradually pension schemes were established for teachers, policemen, poor law officers and other groups of public servants. The case of the teachers is a good example of the difficulties which the progress from ex gratia payments to pension schemes could bring. In considering it here, the object will be not to give a complete history of teachers' pensions, but to suggest some of the motives and ideas which were important.

In December 1846 the Committee of the Privy Council on Education, the forerunner of the Board of Education, issued a Minute under the heading: 'Retiring Pensions to Schoolmasters and Mistresses for long and efficient services.' The Minute made provision for the granting of pensions after at least fifteen years' service to schoolmasters and mistresses who were 'incapable by age or infirmity of continuing to teach a school efficiently', but before a pension could be granted a report on the character and conduct of the teacher had to be made.

The emphasis is very noticeably on both the need for efficiency and the reward for service, but it seems clear that it was the first motive which primarily induced the central department to act. The position was put in this way by the Rev. H. Moseley, H.M. Inspector of Schools, in 1849. 'In old age', he said,[2] 'the schoolmaster is continued in his office when he has ceased to be equal to the discharge of its duties, because there is no other means of providing for his support.' In other words, the choice was often between inefficiency and sending the teacher to the workhouse. However, quite consistently, Moseley pointed out that from the point of view of efficiency it was the bad schoolmasters who ought to be got rid of just as much as the good ones who were covered by the 1846 Minute; he therefore proposed a universal contributory system of pensions with a fund sufficient (with interest at 4½ per cent) to provide a pension of £20 p.a. at the age of 60.[3]

A universal and contributory system of pensions was at that date in operation for the Civil Service and had been in operation for

[1] Even now, there is no compulsory scheme for manual workers in local government (see Appendix 2). For the sake of accuracy it should also be pointed out that, in law, a civil servant has no entitlement to a pension; in practice, however, this limitation is only of academic significance, except in particular circumstances such as the determination of estate duty.

[2] See Report from the Select Committee on Elementary Schools (Certificated Teachers), H.C. 344, 1872, App. 2, p. 113.

[3] His proposals went further than this in providing for a return of contributions at death and, more ambitiously, in hoping to use the surplus from the fund to build almshouses for widows of schoolmasters.

twenty years. That some similar system was not adopted for the teachers may well have been due to the desire to keep costs down and also to encourage self-help. It seems to have been felt that unless some restriction was placed on the giving of pensions, the virtues of providence and thrift would not receive their due honour. But this could only be done if pensions were discretionary and not embodied in a general scheme. Less than five years after the original Minute of 1846, school inspectors were being told by the Committee that teachers should not rely on pensions 'as affording a substitute for the economy which is incumbent upon them, in common with all other workers, while their strength lasts'.[1] And the point was put more bluntly in a letter of 1857: 'It has never been proposed that the Government should make a general offer of pensions. In one form or another, it has always been assumed that the teachers were to make provision for themselves.'[2]

In pursuance of this doctrine, the number of pensions in payment to teachers at any one time was in 1851 restricted to 270 and, even when granted, a pension was liable to be withdrawn if the pensioner was discovered to have 'sufficient means of livelihood from other sources'.[3] It is impossible to say how far this attitude was due to a desire for economy as an end in itself and how far to a genuine belief that it would be wrong to do anything to discourage thrift, but the importance of such ideas as a negative influence on pensions is very great.

Soon, however, teachers themselves began to demand pensions as a right, to the cost of which they were prepared to make some contribution, and this aim proved to be a central point in the long debate on teachers' pensions. The aim was itself compounded of a number of motives, notably humanitarian, the desire to do something at least for 'the most wretched and pitiable cases', the poor destitute schoolmasters and mistresses; and the motive of ambition, the desire to improve the status of the teaching profession generally. What lent extra fervour to the debate was the fact that the teachers claimed that the 1846 Minute had been generally understood to mean that teachers would get a pension provided that they gave long and faithful service,[4] whereas the central department maintained not only that this had never been the intention of the Minute but that it had always been made clear that pensions were to be discretionary and exceptional.

[1] Committee of the Council on Education, Memorandum to Inspectors, October 1851.
[2] Circular letter to Inspectors, June 12, 1857.
[3] Committee of the Council on Education, Minute of August 6, 1851.
[4] For example, a witness to the 1872 Select Committee gave as the reason why teachers should have pensions 'simply because I was distinctly promised the chance of one when I entered the profession'. H.C. 344/1872, Question 711.

In keeping with the official view, Inspectors were exhorted in 1853 to 'remember carefully' that pensions and gratuities were intended only as 'the means of reconciling the claims of an individual with *the good of a school*'.[1] Stress was laid on the need for 'positive deserts' in the applicant; as for the good of a school, 'it would afford reasons for granting a pension that the successor was to be certificated; the floor . . . to be boarded; the desks and benches to be properly arranged', etc.

By 1857,[2] in addition to the usual exhortations that 'young schoolmasters and schoolmistresses should not spend the whole of their earnings, but should learn to put by a sufficient portion' there is a distinct threat that 'It might hereafter be a reason for not admitting any particular teacher to the benefit of the Minute of August 6, 1851, that he had, without special reasons, neglected to make proper provision for himself'. These views were warmly endorsed by the Royal Commission on Popular Education of 1861, which was distinctly hostile to all the teachers' 'alleged grievances'; for example, to teachers' complaints that their salaries did not rise sufficiently in the course of their careers, they proposed the simple solution of reducing salaries for young schoolmasters, for 'if the emoluments of the young schoolmaster were smaller, those of the older schoolmaster would appear greater'.[3] In such an atmosphere it is not surprising that in 1862 even the limited granting of pensions under the 1851 Rule came to an end, and for over thirty years those who entered the teaching profession had no expectation at all of a pension.

Nevertheless, or perhaps because of this fact, the agitation for teachers' pensions grew stronger. It was not simply confined to the teachers themselves but appeared also in some of the reports of the Inspectors of Schools; increasingly they began to urge a proper pension system as a means of attracting the right people into teaching. In 1872 the House of Commons appointed a Select Committee to consider whether provision could be made for a pension scheme, and although the Committee came to no positive conclusion, they collected a great deal of evidence and said that they had looked at a number of suggestions which were 'worthy of further consideration not only in the interests of teachers, but on grounds of public policy'.[3] The public policy was not only the by now familiar argument that some means must be found of getting rid of inefficient teachers, but the wider issue of the need to improve the quality of those who entered the profession and to stop qualified people from leaving it. Several witnesses from the teachers' side urged that a

1 Committee of the Council on Education, Memorandum to Inspectors, 1853.
2 Circular letter to Inspectors, June 12, 1857.
3 See Command Paper 2794, 1861, Vol. 1, p. 164.
4 See Report of the Committee, H.C. 344, July 29, 1872.

pension scheme would both 'attract a better class of teachers, and keep them longer'.[1]

But perhaps the Committee found more impressive the evidence of Sir James Kaye-Shuttleworth who had been secretary of the Committee on Education in 1846, and who now advocated a compulsory system of pensions. He justified the spending of public money very largely on the following grounds of public policy:[2] there would be 'a more contented class of public officers' in schools; the government would 'escape from the embarrassment consequent on the absence of any provision for the old age of 30,000 teachers'; the profession would be better able to attract 'persons belonging to classes enjoying more of the common advantages of modern civilization'; and such people would be induced to stay longer once they had taken up teaching. In face of such arguments and the statistical evidence about the 'wastage' of certificated teachers one might have expected the Committee to have come down more positively in favour of pensions, but to many people the idea of State interference in such a matter was still repugnant. The Master of the British School at Leicester wanted better salaries and not charity and did not see why teachers ought 'to be protected because we have not exercised common prudence',[3] and, as counterweight to Sir James Kaye-Shuttleworth, was the evidence of his successors, Mr Lingen and Sir Francis Sandford, who thought that all that was needed was to encourage teachers to buy annuities through the National Debt Commissioners.[4]

And so the debate continued for another twenty years. When, again, the House of Commons appointed a Select Committee to look into the question in 1892, it was no longer whether a system was possible but 'the best system of providing for the superannuation of public elementary teachers' which they were instructed to consider. Armed with a mass of actuarial data and left in no doubt that the teachers 'attach the utmost importance to the making of provision for superannuation' the Committee quickly came to the conclusion that the solution was for the Education Department to set up a fund supported by contributions from teachers and by allowances from the Exchequer.[5] By this time too the official view had moved from the position that a pension scheme was unnecessary to at least acknowledging the need for provision of a basic pension; the awk-

[1] Mr Charles Mansford, Secretary of the Wesleyan Teachers' Association, London (Question 796); the point was also put by the Secretary of the National Union of Elementary Teachers (Questions 33 and 34) among others.
[2] See Minutes of Evidence, p. 100.
[3] Ibid., p. 54.
[4] Ibid., pp. 73 ff.
[5] Report of the Select Committee on the Elementary Education (Teachers' Superannuation), H.C. 231, May 27, 1892.

ward question of state 'interference' was got over by the ingenious argument that since the State put limits on teachers' salaries 'there might be some claim on the State for dealing with them in the way of pension'.[1]

In 1893 the House of Commons resolved that a scheme 'should be established at an early date'. But it was not until 1898 that a Bill was introduced and passed setting up a universal, compulsory scheme for elementary school teachers; other school teachers had to wait still longer. Once more in the debates on the 1898 Bill much stress was laid on the need for efficiency, but the cry for efficiency had been raised for many years without success. How did it succeed in 1898 where it had failed twenty or thirty years earlier? Mainly perhaps because of the increasing recognition of the justice of the teachers' claims to some form of pension scheme, and the weakening of the strict views on self-help which had so characterized the middle years of the century. Thus although it was something of an exaggeration to say, as one Member of Parliament did, that teachers were the 'only public body in this country working for the State who are without any provision to benefit them in their old age',[2] nevertheless the debates on the Teachers' Bill did reveal quite a strong feeling that teachers *ought* to have some provision made for them.

No doubt it is more characteristic of the twentieth than the nineteenth century to regard the provision of pensions, at least for public servants, as an accepted part of what a good employer should do. It is significant, for example, that twenty-five years after the 1898 Act, when it was no longer the principle of teachers' pensions but the manner in which they should be provided (and particularly who should pay for them) which was in dispute, another Committee should say 'all of us feel, some of us feel very strongly, that there is much in the past to be atoned for'.[3] Such thoughts would not have occurred to the members of the Royal Commission on Popular Education of 1861 and are a measure of the change in attitudes to the idea of pensions which had occurred in sixty years.

Perhaps the teachers suffered more than others from the rather unusual position in which they found themselves in the latter part of the nineteenth century; employed by local bodies, they yet formed a vital link in the essentially national problem of education and one which was constantly and increasingly a matter of national debate. Superannuation, because it involved the central government in its connexion with the promotion of an efficient educational system,

[1] Evidence of Mr G. W. Kekewich, Secretary of the Education Department, especially questions 1607 and 1715.

[2] Mr W. Jones, H.C. Deb., August 1, 1898, col. 730.

[3] Report of the Departmental Committee on the Superannuation of School Teachers, Cmd. 1962, 1923, para. 40.

was a subject which was bound to recur; but for that very reason it also proved difficult to solve since any system, even the limited discretionary grants of 1846, meant expenditure by the central government. Apart from the Civil Service, for other public servants who received some measure of superannuation provision in the nineteenth century, the costs of making that provision fell, as did their salaries, on local rates and the like. As a corollary of this, the discretion to award superannuation allowances lay in local hands: with the Justices in the case of the police, with the Committee of Visitors in the case of officers of lunatic asylums, and with the Guardians in the case of poor law officers,[1] before they all succeeded in getting a contributory and non-discretionary scheme.

The later history of teachers' pensions shows a similar tendency to that of the Civil Service for the scope of the scheme to be extended. It is true that the teachers' scheme still, in 1964, remains one of the few major schemes in the public sector not to provide widows' pensions but this is not because of any opposition to the idea, but simply because of disagreement about how the pensions are to be paid for. But although there are now close similarities between the teachers' and the civil service schemes, the preceding narrative illustrates something of the different circumstances in which they arose.

Pensions for Other Public Servants

Widely differing circumstances also affected the uneven growth of pension schemes for other public servants. As with the teachers, it often took a long time to get pension schemes established. Thus, as early as 1829 in the Metropolis and 1840 elsewhere, pensions could be granted to policemen who were disabled or 'worn out by length of service', but not until 1890 was a police pensions scheme established. Again, although a scheme of contributory pensions for poor law officers was mooted in 1850, the discretionary pensions provided for by the 1864 Act were clearly aimed at the problem of the officer 'who shall become incapable of discharging the duties of his office with efficiency', and a formal scheme was not established until 1896.

One factor which is noticeable is the changing emphasis which was given to the motive of efficiency. This is perhaps most clearly brought out in the case of those employed in local government. Here, a principal cause of the delay in establishing a single local government scheme was the piecemeal way in which schemes were set up by individual local authorities. The result was that it was not until 1922 that a general local government pension scheme was introduced,

[1] See, for example, Police Act 1840: Asylums Act 1853: Poor Law Officers' Superannuation Act 1864.

and even this was not universal since it was left to individual local authorities to decide whether to adopt the scheme or not.

Nevertheless, the 1922 scheme followed the report of an official committee set up in 1919, which saw its main task not as being to decide whether there ought to be a pension scheme, but as how to devise a workable scheme in place of the existing chaos of arrangements. For the advantages of superannuation were 'too well known and too widely recognized to require much argument'. For example, schemes 'tend to secure a good class of entrants to the service to which they apply'. They also promoted efficiency by relieving employees of anxieties for their future, and because the employer 'secures a more contented staff', and 'no longer has to keep, out of compassion, men who are no longer fit for work and merely block the road to promotion for younger men'.[1]

Here efficiency is not given as the only or even as necessarily the main reason for a pension scheme, and in any case efficiency now has a much wider meaning, seeming to include the idea of contributing to good working relations. This idea and also the view that a good pension scheme helps to attract, and keep, staff have been increasingly emphasized in recent years when there has been a great growth of pension schemes in the private sector. Some account of the motives which have led to the establishment of private sector schemes is given in a later part of this chapter, but first the development of the provision of pensions by the State, not for its own employees, but for old people generally, will be considered.

STATE PENSIONS

The Aged Poor and the Old Age Pensions Act 1908

The later years of the nineteenth century were the occasion of a considerable public debate about the need for pensions to be provided by the State for the old. The reasons for this increased interest in pensions are complex and need to be studied against the changing social and economic background of later Victorian Britain. What is here attempted is an illustration of some of the main features of the debate and of the subsequent development of state pensions.

The basic problem which ultimately had to be faced was how those who had grown too old to work, and even more their widows when they died, were to live. The choice for most people in the nineteenth century was either to rely on their own resources, which for the most part meant insurance, savings or the family, or to go to the workhouse—or to starve. Occupational pension schemes were for the few

[1] Report of the Departmental Committee on the Superannuation of Persons Employed by Local Authorities in England and Wales (Norman), Cmd. 329, 1919, para. 27.

and those mostly in the middle rather than the working class. What happened to the mass of the population, the miners, factory-workers and rural labourers when they grew too old to work? The question suggests that we are here concerned with the aged poor, and this is indeed the case, but it is important to note that until there was realization that the aged poor formed a distinct class, and presented distinct problems which might well be capable of being solved separately, it was poverty generally on which public attention was directed. Accordingly something must be said about general attitudes to and ideas about poverty before considering the specific problem of poverty in old age.

The problem of the poor had been a preoccupation of government from before the time of the Elizabethan Poor Law; then it was the distinct threat to law and order presented by large numbers of poor and desperate people which chiefly formed the motive for action. However, to understand the nineteenth-century approach to the problem it is necessary to stress how strong had grown by then the belief that in some way poverty was the result of either vicious or idle habits, or both. The roots of this belief may well go back to the Puritan movement of the seventeenth century. 'The Puritan', as Professor Tawney put it, 'sees in the poverty of those who fall by the way, not a misfortune to be pitied and relieved, but a moral failing to be condemned.'[1] No doubt other motives influenced public thought and action, particularly the desire on the part of those who were paying for them to keep in check the cost of poor law measures, but the fundamental attitude was what shaped public policy. For if no man need be poor, then no sympathy need be wasted on the poor, and no elaborate provision need be made for them. True, there might be some unfortunates who had fallen into poverty through no fault of their own; but such cases would be rare and could be provided for by private charity.

This, essentially, was the characteristic attitude of Victorian, and, more particularly, mid-nineteenth-century England. But already in the reform of the Poor Law in 1834 can be seen the practical effects of this approach. For that reform laid stress on the use of poor law measures purely for relieving temporary distress, and it was in no sense designed to get rid of poverty. In particular, conditions in the workhouse were to be made as unattractive as possible so that there should be no inducement to forsake honest toil for idleness. By this means, so it was thought, only those who had incurred poverty through their own fault would find a home in the workhouse. For the

[1] R. H. Tawney, *Religion and the Rise of Capitalism*, Penguin, 1948, p. 229. Cf. Christopher Hill, *The Century of Revolution*, Nelson, 1961, p. 207, who points out that the assumption behind the Act of Settlement of 1662 was that 'a pauper was idle, vicious and rightless'.

rest, there was always work to be found by those who genuinely wanted it; granted that the misfortunes of sickness and unemployment and the inevitability of old age needed to be provided against, but to many people in the nineteenth century all that was needed was that a man when he was in work should exercise thrift.

Here then was the simple picture which dominated public attitudes; on the one side, the thrifty, honest toiler, putting aside his weekly pennies or shillings and able in sickness or old age to provide for himself; on the other, the vicious, the idle, the wastrels falling into poverty, a burden on the community for whom the workhouse was a just reward. The force of such a view has already been encountered in connexion with the campaign for teachers' pensions; the difficulty it presented to those who took a different view was that it did not even recognize a problem of old age. There might be a need to encourage saving for the future, but beyond that there could be no reason for taking any action. Nassau Senior, described by Elie Halévy as 'the luminary' of the Royal Commission on the Poor Law of 1832–34 and later Professor of Political Economy at Oxford, expressed this view quite simply: 'Old age is so much the general lot of human nature that it would strike too much into the providential habits of the poor to make anything like a regular and systematic provision for it.'[1]

In extreme form, the simple picture led to what can best be described as a horror of the poor; Malthus, for example, believed that 'the quantity of provisions consumed in the workhouse, upon a part of society that cannot in general be considered as the most valuable part, diminishes the share that would otherwise belong to the more industrious and more worthy members'.[2] In the face of such attitudes those who wished to see more positive action taken could follow two lines of argument; that the opportunities for saving open to the poor were inadequate, and that it was not true as a fact that those who were compelled to take refuge in the workhouse went there because of their own fault. It is this second line of argument in particular which first brought out the specific problem of old age.

For the most part regular saving on a small scale was dependent on the Friendly Societies. Through them a man might put aside regular sums, chiefly to provide benefits in sickness and also to meet the cost of funeral expenses. Although the provision of old age pensions was not the object of these societies, many old people were able to draw as sickness benefit what was in effect a pension. Some Friendly Societies had come into existence in the seventeenth century, but there was a great increase in their number during the

[1] Quoted in Maurice Bruce, *The Coming of the Welfare State*, Batsford, 1961, p. 94.

[2] Cf. Harold E. Raynes, *Social Security in Britain*, Pitman, 2nd ed. 1960, p. 134.

eighteenth century. However, because of incompetence or dishonesty, many societies failed, and when this happened those who had put their money into them were clearly made worse off through no fault of their own and less able to provide for their own future.

Partly because of this, there were, even in the eighteenth century, suggestions that the friendly societies idea might be applied nationally, perhaps with compulsion; in 1786 the Rev. John Acland advocated universal subscriptions of 2d a week to secure a pension, and a similar idea was behind an unsuccessful scheme for 'coal-heavers working upon the Thames' which was embodied in an Act of 1757. Such ideas could make little headway against prevailing opinion, which was more inclined to attempt to put the Friendly Societies on a sounder basis. This was indeed the aim of the first Friendly Societies Act of 1793. Cases of mismanagement and fraud continued, however, to appear in the nineteenth century and led to fairly frequent bankruptcies among Friendly Societies. Evidence given to the Royal Commission on Friendly Societies, which reported in 1874, suggested that this was a positive discouragement to thrift, and although by that time the Friendly Societies themselves had strong reasons for not wishing to see any intervention by the State into the field of sickness benefit or old age pensions, the situation did provide some encouragement to those who felt that something more was needed.

Clearly, however, the fact that some Friendly Societies failed and that this might prove discouraging to thrift, was not in itself sufficient to lead public opinion to change its views on the problem of poverty. For on the other side it could be shown that many Friendly Societies were flourishing and that they were being increasingly used; in part this latter fact was due precisely to that fear of the workhouse which the 1834 Act had encouraged.

One thing which contributed to a change of view was a question of fact—was it true that poverty by and large was a man's own fault? For if it were not true, then society must accept a more positive approach to the problems of poverty, and exhortations to thrift were not sufficient. Furthermore, if it were shown that poverty could not always be avoided by those who tried to avoid it, might it not also be that other assumptions needed questioning: for example, might not one disadvantage of relying on voluntary saving through Friendly Societies be that just those people who ought to save, would not do so? To say that giving them the opportunity to save was enough, was precisely to avoid the problem altogether, not to solve it.

Increasingly, arguments were heard on both those points. As evidence accumulated that poverty existed on a scale hitherto unsuspected, it became more and more implausible to argue that the cause lay in individual shortcomings; at the same time, more people were beginning to suspect that if poverty were to be reduced, a much more positive approach was needed. The particular need for action was seen most clearly in the case of poverty in old age, because evidence accumulated that old age was one of the prime causes of poverty.

Many people contributed to the new knowledge, but among the most important was Charles Booth, a Liverpool shipowner, who, between 1887 and 1903, published the results of an enormous and painstaking survey of *Life and Labour of the People in London*. His case is instructive; in 1885, F. D. Hyndman, of the Social Democratic Federation, had published an inquiry into conditions in a working-class district in London in which he claimed that 25 per cent of the people were living in extreme poverty. Booth, in common with many others, believed that these claims were exaggerated and undertook his survey in order to establish, in the most thorough manner possible, what were the true facts about poverty. The results were as much a shock to him as to other people; no less than one-third of the people in the areas which he surveyed were living at or below the level of poverty. Yet the thoroughness with which he had carried out his work could not be disputed; and 'after his work had become available to the general public a new era was inaugurated, in so far as the causes of the prevailing miseries were demonstrated to have arisen in large measure out of deficiencies in the conditions of industrial employment and, in general, in social organization'.[1]

When he came to examine why people should be poor, Booth was struck by the frequency with which old age appeared as the only cause; in Stepney he found that one-third of those who were poor were poor because they were old; and in his book, *The Aged Poor* (published in 1894), he estimated that between 40 per cent and 50 per cent of those over the age of 65 were living in poverty. Nor was he content simply to produce his figures. He became convinced that society for its own sake must do something to help those who, through no fault of their own, had fallen into poverty. His solution was simple—the State should provide a pension of 5s a week for all at the age of 65, even though this might cost, on his own estimates, £17 million a year. This suggestion he put in a paper in 1892 to the Royal Statistical Society, but was met there and elsewhere by a hostile reception. Nevertheless, he continued to advocate old age pensions as the only reasonable solution of the problem of the aged poor.

Meanwhile, others were tackling this same problem, though not necessarily advocating quite the same solution. The Rev. William Blackley in 1878 asserted that the only way to ensure thrift was to

[1] T. S. Simey and M. B. Simey, *Charles Booth: Social Scientist*, Oxford University Press, 1960, p. 4.

make it compulsory; he too was impressed by the growing evidence that old age was the main cause of poverty and until his death in 1902 he constantly urged the need for what we should now call contributory old age pensions. But probably the most eloquent advocate in the 1890's of pensions for the aged was Joseph Chamberlain; a member of the Royal Commission of 1893 on 'Poor Law Relief and People Destitute from Old Age' (of which Charles Booth was also a member), he gave extensive evidence to the Commission, pointing out among other things that although pauperism was only 8 per cent among those under 65, it was 25 per cent among those over that age.

He showed how difficult it was for working men to save, however thrifty they might be, but perhaps still more convincing was his counter to the extreme forms of advocacy of self-reliance: 'Some economists', he said, 'expect from the poor a virtue which we do not feel in ourselves. It is too much to expect from them the extremely penurious lives which would be necessary if they were to make sufficient provision for old age by their own efforts alone. I do not think they are called upon when in active work to deny themselves everything in the nature of luxury.'[1] Nothing could be further from the views of men like Nassau Senior, yet it must be remembered that Chamberlain was in advance of much public opinion; in his Annual Report for 1891 the Chief Registrar of Friendly Societies (Mr E. W. Brabrook), wrote: 'I remain of the opinion that there is no way of providing for old age than by thrift, self-denial and forethought in youth. . . . It is better for the State, that is, the general body of taxpayers, that he should be paid suitable wages for such service as he renders, than that it should make up for a deficiency of wages by doles of any kind.' And there is little doubt that such views were commonly held. Nevertheless, by the 1890's some movement of opinion towards the idea of old age pensions provided by the State had taken place.

But though the facts and the advocacy of eloquent men ensured that the problem of the aged poor was constantly under public debate, the need for old age pensions and the manner in which they should be provided remained matters of dispute. From 1885, when the House of Commons appointed a Select Committee to report on 'the best system of national provident insurance against pauperism', until 1899, when a similar committee was charged with recommending 'the best means of improving the conditions of the aged deserving poor', discussion was practically continuous, but only the last committee came down finally and conclusively in favour of a non-

---

[1] See Sir Arnold Wilson and G. S. MacKay, *Old Age Pensions*, Oxford University Press, 1941, p. 26. The authors quote extensively from Chamberlain's evidence.

contributory system of old age pensions; and even then it was another nine years (with the South African war intervening) before legislation was passed. Slow though this progress seemed to the advocates of old age pensions, a number of factors helped the development of the idea.

Not everyone might agree with Bismarck that 'anyone with the prospect of a pension in old age or infirmity is happier, more content with his lot, and more tractable . . . the chief cause of anxiety among artisans is uncertainty as to their future. Remove that and we shall remove their hatreds, and avert more serious troubles'.[1] But the example of Germany in providing pensions and other measures of social insurance in the 1880's was bound to influence feeling in other countries which were affected by the social and economic problems associated with modern industrial development. At the same time, the extensions of the franchise in this country in 1867 and 1885, and the increasing strength of the trade unions, which by 1895 included about one-fifth of all adult male workers,[2] gave those who stood to gain most from social insurance measures an added voice in political terms. This no doubt played a part in Joseph Chamberlain's advocacy of old age pensions, although in his evidence to the Royal Commission of which he was a member, he was careful to base his plea on self-interest, echoing the words of Bismarck: 'The foundations of property are made more secure when no real grievance is felt by the poor against the rich.' A further motive in some men's minds was the desire to treat separately the problem of the aged poor so that tighter control could be imposed on the administration of the remainder of the Poor Law. Charles Booth thought that it would be possible to effect economies by abolishing out-relief if old age pensions were instituted; and most people expected that the cost of pensions would be partly offset by saving on poor law expenditure, although this did not prove to be so.

When, finally, in 1908 Lloyd George, as Chancellor of the Exchequer, introduced the Old Age Pensions Bill, the debates seemed almost to epitomize everything which had been argued about old age pensions for the past thirty years or more. The Bill itself was on a limited scale, partly for financial reasons, but partly too in keeping with many traditional ideas; for example, pensions were not to be paid to those who had habitually failed to work when given the opportunity. As Lloyd George explained, the object was to exclude

[1] Speaking in 1881 on his first Workmen's Compensation Bill. See Wilson and MacKay, op. cit. p. 14.
[2] E. Halévy, *History of the English People in the Nineteenth Century*, Benn, Paperback ed. 1961, Vol. 5, p. 211. Some unions provided a system of benefits, including pensions, for their members, for example, the Amalgamated Society of Engineers. See Report of the Royal Commission on the Poor Law, 1909, pp. 311–12.

'loafers and wastrels' and to use the resources of the State 'to make provision for undeserved poverty'.[1]

Such sentiments were echoed by many speakers in the debate, and not least by those who emphasized that it was the duty of everybody to provide for his own old age; universal pensions, it was said, would 'simply be glorified outdoor relief'. In the House of Lords, the Bill was opposed by those who thought that it would demoralize the working classes and abolish thrift. Lloyd George himself, outside the House, was prepared to go much further than the Bill, and to advocate that 'the State should step in to the very utmost limits of its resources' to help those in unavoidable poverty.[2] Nevertheless, to many people state 'interference' in providing pensions could only be justified if it was kept to what was absolutely necessary; and to those people the idea of pensions was only acceptable with the recognition that existing ideas and means of dealing with the poor and especially the 'aged deserving poor' were inadequate.

Contributory Pensions and National Insurance

To ensure that only those who were in need were included, the 1908 Act imposed a means test on applicants for pensions. Nevertheless, the number of people who qualified for pensions was far higher than had been expected. Instead of the half-million pensioners expected, there were already by 1911 over 900,000, and instead of an annual cost of £6 million, nearly double that amount had to be provided by 1911. In view of the restrictions imposed by the Act, this could only mean that the extent of undeserved poverty in old age was even greater than had been supposed.

In future, much less was heard of the argument that forethought and prudence were all that was needed to provide for old age; nevertheless, the old age pension was designed only to supplement whatever other provision could be made—5s a week even in 1908 was scarcely enough to live on. The pensions were financed entirely by the Exchequer and payable at the age of 70, but the effect of the means test was that those who, whether inspired by the duty to be thrifty or the desire to avoid the workhouse, had been able to save enough to live on in their old age, received nothing from the State.

To this non-contributory system of old age pensions was added in 1925 a contributory system; it did not supersede the earlier system entirely but it did change the whole basis of state pensions; in place of the concept of a pension as a reward on certain conditions to the deserving poor who had failed or been unable to make provision for

[1] H.C. Deb., June 15, 1908, cols. 565–86.
[2] See A. Bullock and M. Shock, *The Liberal Tradition*, A. & C. Black, 1956, p. 211.

themselves, was substituted an entitlement to a pension in return for making contributions. The position is analogous in some ways to that of poor law officers and others in the nineteenth century who had originally been granted pensions only at the discretion of their employers but who subsequently gained entitlement to pensions on a contributory basis. But there are significant differences which illustrate different approaches to occupational and state pensions.

In the case of poor law officers and others, the change was entirely due to recognition of the inadequacy of the existing arrangements as a matter affecting conditions of employment; the officers themselves were dissatisfied because they could not be sure of a pension and because conditions varied from one part of the country to another; the employers interested in efficiency (whether widely or narrowly interpreted) were hampered by the limitation of a system which depended so much on chance factors. Old age pensions fell into a different category; what began as an attempt to deal with the problem of poverty became more and more bound up with general questions of social policy. One aspect in particular of the non-contributory system aroused much discussion, and that was the means test. Not only was it disliked by those who had to submit to it, but it was held to discourage thrift because a man who conscientiously saved in his youth might find himself ineligible for an old age pension whereas his neighbour who had not the will to stint himself and his family might qualify on the means test.

But what kept the discussion alive and made it a political issue was the increasing importance which questions of social policy generally assumed from the time of the measures taken by the Liberal Governments of 1906 and 1910, including the Old Age Pensions Act of 1908, and the National Health Insurance Act of 1911. One may mention the rise of the Labour Party and the great extension of the franchise in 1918 as examples of political changes which influenced the position. The Labour Party consistently advocated the abolition of the means test; the enfranchisement of women in 1918 more than doubled the electorate, and perhaps even more significantly from the present point of view, far more than doubled the number of old age pensioners in the electorate.

Moreover, the war of 1914–18, which greatly increased the cost of living, also drew attention to the inadequacies of at least the scales of old age pensions. So much so that the majority of a Departmental Committee appointed in 1919 to inquire into this very question (the Ryland Adkins Committee) recommended not only the doubling of the scale but also the abolition of the means test. Although the Government at the time accepted the first but not the second of these recommendations, there was continued discussion of the need for a new approach to old age pensions. These were much influenced by the examples of National Health Insurance and Unemployment Insurance; if schemes of insurance could be devised for sickness and unemployment, why not also for old age? Furthermore, if there were a system of insurance, all those who were insured would be thrifty by compulsion, the means test could be abolished and all insured persons would be certain of some source of income in old age.

But if this general shift of public opinion was inspired chiefly by changing attitudes towards social questions, and in particular by a feeling that there ought to be more general provision for the old, on the Government side too there were powerful reasons for making a change, quite apart from any questions of social justice. The cost of old age pensions was nearly £18 million in 1919 and had risen to £27 million by 1925; simply to abolish the means test and pay pensions to everybody at the age of 70 would double that cost, and even if no change at all were made in the system the cost of pensions was expected to increase greatly simply through the combined effect of increased numbers of old people in the population living longer.

The Minister of Health (Mr Neville Chamberlain), in moving the Second Reading of the Widows', Orphans' and Old Age Contributory Pensions Bill of 1925, made the point quite explicitly by saying that the country could not afford a non-contributory scheme. Thus a fundamental change in the state scheme was justified primarily in terms of finance, although in addition it brought great benefit to many people. For, with the passing of the 1925 Act, all those who had previously been insured under the National Health Insurance Acts became entitled to a pension, even though they only began to pay contributions towards pensions from 1926. Furthermore, these pensions became payable at 65 instead of 70. No doubt many of those insured would in any case have been able to get a pension by satisfying the means and other conditions under the non-contributory system, but the fact is that with the two systems running together many more people received pensions than before. For example, between 1911 and 1925, the number of non-contributory old age pensioners was about 950,000 a year, and by 1938 had dropped only to just under 600,000; but by 1938 there were in addition over 2 million contributory pensioners, of whom 1¼ million were over 70, and nearly 21 million people were insured.

But although many more people gained pensions after 1925, there was one sense in which the system remained the same. The amount of the pension, 10s a week, was not and was not intended to be sufficient to live on by itself. Mr Chamberlain, in introducing the Second Reading of the 1925 Bill, had laid stress on the fact that the pension was intended only to provide a basis, to be supplemented by other means; one of those means, he suggested, might be the provision of additional pensions by employers for their employees.

Of more significance was the change from a system of pensions, which because it was financed by the Exchequer still had an air of charity about it, and whose emphasis was on pensions for those who deserved them, to a system which, because at least in part it was financed by contributions from those who were to benefit, was thought of as a system of insurance. It differed from private insurance in that it was compulsory and applied to practically the entire poorer half of the community, and the element of insurance was weakened by the large Exchequer subsidy; contributions never were anything like sufficient to meet the cost. But it also differed fundamentally from pensions in the public service and in many private schemes which, after a life-time of service, could provide as much as two-thirds of the salary which a man was receiving at the date of his retirement. There still remained in the state scheme the main element of basic protection from complete poverty; for this reason, perhaps, as much as any other, it was not thought necessary to make universal provision for pensions even under a contributory system, although by the outbreak of the 1939–45 war the great majority of employed men were insured.

The system of National Insurance established by the 1946 Act, which came into force in 1948, marked a further stage away from the 1908 principles. The Beveridge Report, on which the 1946 Act was based, had laid stress on the principle of universality. But equally important was the proposal in the Beveridge Report that rates of benefit should be 'sufficient without further resources to provide the minimum income needed for subsistence in all normal cases'.[1]

This proposal was not fully accepted in the 1946 Act, but it was accepted that there should be some attempt 'to give a broad sub-sistence basis' within the limits of a contributory insurance scheme, according to the statement of the Minister of National Insurance on the Second Reading of the 1946 Bill.

Universal pensions and a pension with at least some relation to the basic cost of living of the old are far removed from the idea of a pension to prevent the deserving from having to go to the work-house, just as marriage gratuities and pensions for widows are far from the idea of a pension as a means to check corruption in the Civil Service. The situation is still changing; the system of contribu-tions and pensions varying according to income introduced by the National Insurance Act of 1959, whatever the motive behind it, means that the State is doing in part what employers are doing. In the words of the White Paper of 1958, *Provision for Old Age*, it is instituting 'provision for employed persons who cannot be covered by an appropriate occupational scheme to obtain some measure of

[1] Social Insurance and Allied Services, Cmd. 6404, 1942, para. 307.

pension related to their earnings'. Here is no new idea of the purpose of pensions; what is new, and what has given rise to prolonged, and sometimes bitter, controversy, is the idea that the State rather than the employer should provide something more than the bare minimum (whether subsistence or less) for the old. It is true that the scale of the graduated scheme is modest; a man earning £10 a week would have to contribute for three years before he gained an extra 6d a week on his ultimate pension; but the principle once introduced will inevitably tend to blur what was originally a distinction between the purpose of a pension provided by an employer and one provided by the State. Some light may be thrown on how this situation has come about by considering how some private employers have viewed the question of pensions.

PENSIONS IN THE PRIVATE SECTOR

For some at least of the pension schemes which have been set up in the public sector, there is a good deal of evidence about what men thought was the purpose of having pension schemes, and, sometimes, why they opposed even the granting of pensions, let alone the setting-up of schemes. But the evidence about the origin and growth of schemes in the private sector is much more scanty, particularly for the earlier years of such development, and the history of private sector pension schemes still remains to be written. For this reason no more is attempted here than a brief sketch of some of the principal developments.

Ex gratia payments of pensions to old employees or their widows have had a long history in the arrangements made by private employers. Thus in 1899 Charles Booth wrote: 'There are many old people in receipt of industrial superannuation allowances more or less charitable in their character, though very often given as an acknowledgment and recognition of past services.'[1]

But as teachers and poor law officers had found, there was a world of difference between a pension given as an act of grace and a regular scheme giving an entitlement to a pension. Before the end of the nineteenth century a number of private employers had taken this further step and established schemes.[2]

It is, however, impossible to say either how many employees were covered by such schemes by the end of the nineteenth century or what inspired their employers to institute them. Motives of efficiency

[1] In *Old Age Pensions and the Aged Poor*, quoted in M. Pilch and V. Wood, *Pension Schemes*, Hutchinson, 1960, p. 17.

[2] Among them the Gas Light and Coke Company (1842), Prudential Assurance (1866) and Siemens Brothers (1872). See E. H. Phelps Brown, *The Growth of British Industrial Relations*, Macmillan, 1959, p. 78.

must have played their part, but the evidence of some early twentieth-century schemes suggests that benevolent paternalism may also have been at work.[1]

An interesting example of a case where schemes were set up not simply by a single employer but by practically all employers in an industry is that of the railways, most of which had by the end of the nineteenth century established superannuation funds for their salaried staff. As early as 1854 the London and North Western Railway had taken power to establish a contributory scheme and the other companies on the whole followed their lead. A witness before a Departmental Committee in 1908 thought that the companies' actions were 'in imitation of the State' and it may be that the railways were among the first to realize the advantages of a pension scheme in promoting efficiency, in the narrow sense in which this term was understood at the time. However, some qualification of this statement needs to be made in the light of the following evidence.

In 1908 before the same Departmental Committee, the General Manager of the North Eastern Railway stated the position as he saw it quite bluntly. 'Surely a pension is an act of grace', he said.[2] 'I do not quite see where the obligation to pension comes in. My view of the pension is that it is an act of business common sense . . . not as philanthropy . . . Unless you have something like an efficient pension fund, the directors would be under a constant compulsion to keep on the men. It is a choice between keeping them on and sending them to the workhouse, and they could not resist keeping them on.' Ideas of this kind had also been a powerful motive to the establishment of some public service schemes; they were endorsed (with embellishments) by the Committee[3] and there seems little doubt that the growth of railway schemes in the previous fifty years had been primarily due to this desire to be able to 'place upon the retired list those men who from any cause have become permanently unfit for duty, without being embarrassed by claims for compassionate allowances in respect of servants so retired'.

However, it seems necessary to look a little more closely at this argument. Why, for example, should the directors of a railway company find any difficulty or embarrassment in retiring a man who had

---

[1] Cf. C. Wilson, *History of Unilever*, Cassell, 1954, Vol. 1, p. 158. 'Standard wages, a pension scheme and a score of welfare schemes, were an attempt to embody enlightenment in a system.'

[2] A. Kaye Butterworth. Evidence to the Departmental Committee on Railway Superannuation Funds. Cd. 5484, 1911, Questions 466, 1451 and 1452.

[3] From the point of view of the railway companies not only was the purpose of the arrangement 'to keep the whole service in an efficient condition', but it helped to speed promotion and 'has the further advantage of identifying the interest of the staff with those of the Company, and so binding the men to the service' (Report of the Committee, Cd. 5349, 1910, para. 56).

B*

grown too old to work? Why should they not say to him that he ought to have made provision for old age and that if he had not, then it was his fault if he had to go to the workhouse? This after all was what for a long time the teachers had been told and what they had had to fight against.

Some part of the explanation must lie in a gradual change in attitude to problems of poverty and old age, part perhaps in the fact that, as the General Secretary to the Railway Clerks' Association put it to the 1908–10 Committee: 'The men like to have their old age provided for, and they are willing to subscribe for that purpose.' But it does not of course follow that the views expressed in 1908 necessarily represented the motives of those who had instituted schemes fifty years earlier.

Nor is it likely that the railway companies were typical of commerce and industry generally at that time. If it is true, as a recent author has put it, that 'half a century or more ago most employers were content to employ men and women for as long as they were useful and then to replace them with younger persons without much thought as to what means of livelihood was available to the elderly ex-servant [and] employees did not expect any other treatment'[1], then it was the more charitable employer who gave allowances such as those described by Charles Booth but it was only the most enlightened who set up proper schemes.

But enlightened here means combining a desire for efficiency with a realization that to turn a man out when he is old without making any provision for him is not enough. The railway companies did realize this even if there is some doubt and ambiguity about what really lay behind that realization, and by 1908 no less than 90,000 men were covered by staff schemes. These and the further unknown number in schemes for the wages grades represented probably a good proportion of those outside the public services who were covered by schemes.

This latter point must, however, remain somewhat speculative in view of the lack of any precise information about the number of members of schemes. What is certainly true is that there has been a steady growth of private sector schemes in the last sixty years and, more particularly, in the last twenty, and that this growth has been most marked in schemes for salaried staff as opposed to wage-paid workers.

By 1936, when the first thorough survey of occupational pension schemes was made,[2] 1½ million employees outside the public services

---

[1] Gordon A. Hosking, *Pension Schemes and Retirement Benefits*, Sweet and Maxwell, 2nd ed. 1960, p. 1.

[2] See 'Schemes Providing for Pensions for Employees on Retirement from Work' in *Ministry of Labour Gazette*, May 1938.

were covered by schemes and there were estimated to be between 80,000 and 90,000 pensioners, but only just over half these employees were classified as manual workers. Twenty years later, the figure had risen to 4,300,000 employees with about 300,000 pensioners, but still only just over half these employees were wage-earners, although wage-earners formed two-thirds of the total employees even of those firms which had pension schemes. By 1958 the number of employees covered by private pension schemes was 5 million and by now it may well exceed 6 million.[1]

What these figures indicate is that growth was fairly moderate until the 1939–45 war but has been very rapid since then; this is particularly so if it is remembered that the 1½ million in the 1936 survey included many, such as railwaymen and nurses, who in the 1956 survey were no longer included in the figures for private schemes. To some degree the growth in pension schemes represents only a change from ex gratia arrangements to formal schemes; neither the 1936 nor the 1956 survey takes account of the many employers who chose to pay pensions not as a right but at discretion, partly no doubt because it would be very difficult to obtain comprehensive information about such arrangements.

In considering the many reasons which have led to this rapid growth of private sector schemes, two points may usefully be noted. One is the increasing awareness of the need for pensions on the part of employees; and behind this awareness lies a whole complex of changes which have been taking place in our society, such as the increase in the proportion of old people and greater opportunities for leisure. Secondly, employers too have come to accept a pension scheme as being something which ought to be provided by a good employer.

To illustrate these two points: the rapid growth of pension schemes since the war has been widely attributed to the need for employers to attract and retain staff.[2] But this in turn implies that many employees or potential employees regarded it as an attraction that an employment should have a pension scheme. Even so, we must assume that this desire for pensions was either less strong before the war or that employers were then less inclined to meet the demand. In fact both may well be true; it was undoubtedly one of the attractions to some people before the war of such employments as the Civil Service or the banks that the job itself would be followed by a

1 Cf. *Occupational Pension Schemes*, H.M.S.O., 1958, paras. 13–16. See also Appendix 1.

2 See, for example, such diverse publications as *National Superannuation*, Labour Party, 1957, pp. 12–13; Pilch and Wood, *Pension Schemes*, Hutchinson, 1960, p. 25; F. W. Paish and A. T. Peacock, 'The Economics of Pension Funds', *Lloyds Bank Review*, October 1954, p. 15; A. S. Owen, 'Pension Schemes at the Crossroads', *Journal of the Chartered Insurance Institute*, 1960, p. 162.

pension, and the very existence of such employments contributed, with the desire at the end of the war to escape from the insecurity which had characterized much of the inter-war years, to make people more consciously aware of the advantages of a pension scheme. At the same time those employers who had seen no reason why they should institute pension schemes now found increasingly that others were doing so just at a time when, because of full employment, the difficulties of finding and keeping staff were becoming most apparent. Nor should one forget that almost all the newly nationalized industries quickly introduced new and comprehensive pension schemes which again helped to focus attention on this issue. It would be too simple a view to suggest that employers could in times of unemployment afford to ignore demands for pensions which in times of full employment they were forced to meet. Pension schemes would probably have grown and grown at an increasing rate, even without full employment; what full employment did was to speed up the process.

It may also be that the further growth of schemes is encouraged by deliberate acts of political policy; for example, stress is often laid now on the economic advantages of pension funds, particularly in leading to the savings needed for financing new capital investment. Governments may, therefore, seek to encourage these funds, e.g. through the provision of tax reliefs, and this will affect employers' attitudes, at least to the extent of inducing them to frame their schemes in such a way as to take advantage of the legislation.

CONCLUSION

The present situation may therefore be summarized by saying that practically all employed people in the public sector may expect to enjoy an occupational pension, and so may a large and increasing number of those in the private sector; and in addition, all employed people, practically speaking, whether in the public or the private sector, and for that matter self-employed people too, can expect a National Insurance retirement pension.

A later chapter of this study will examine some of the factors which are likely to influence future pension trends, but one striking aspect of the present situation deserves comment here. Most of the discussion in this chapter has been concerned with the provision of pensions as such, without regard to the different types of scheme or the different levels of pension provided. But in fact there is a great distinction to be drawn between schemes, such as those which are general in the public sector, which aim to provide an adequate income in retirement, often the equivalent of two-thirds of salary at retirement, and schemes, which, like the flat-rate National Insurance retirement pension, aim at the most at providing a bare subsistence income.

This distinction is likely to become increasingly important in future. At the present time, there are about 6 million people drawing National Insurance retirement pensions, but probably only about 1¾ million with an occupational pension, the majority of them in the public sector. But whereas National Insurance pensioners are likely to increase only gradually with the increase in the number of old people in the population, the growth in the number of pension schemes means that many more people are gaining entitlement to an occupational pension at the present time.

We have therefore reached a point where it is no longer the provision of pensions which is in dispute but rather their adequacy. Already in 1953 Professor Titmuss was drawing attention to the significance in terms of social policy of a distinction between those who in old age could rely on a reasonably comfortable occupational pension and those who had to rely wholly or mainly on the flat-rate National Insurance pension which often needed to be supplemented by National Assistance granted as a result of a means test.[1] This theme of the 'two nations' in old age was later translated into political terms in the Labour Party's plan for *National Superannuation* published in 1957, which aimed to give 'every man or woman who goes out to work' the same opportunity of providing for old age as, for example, the staff of nationalized industries, so that those who were not covered by an occupational scheme could within certain limits get a half-pay pension. But others were advocating precisely the opposite trend, towards universal provision of pensions by employers or through other private provision such as individual saving, with selective grants provided by the State only to those genuinely in need and the ultimate abolition of National Insurance retirement pensions. On this view: 'A pension is part of remuneration, one of the fringe benefits of a good job that should be negotiated between employer and employee. The State has no business here.'[2]

Future debate is likely, therefore, to centre round the questions 'how much pension?' and 'who should provide pensions?' But that these should now be the major questions shows how far we have come in the last 150 years. Pensions have now become a concern of society as a whole. This perhaps is the most significant aspect of their growth in the past century and a half.

[1] 'The Age of Pensions', *The Times*, December 29 and 30, 1953.
[2] Arthur Seldon, *Pensions for Prosperity*, Institute of Economic Affairs, 1960, p. 34.

CHAPTER 2

The Development of Pension Schemes

The first chapter was concerned primarily with arguments about and reasons for having pensions and, more particularly, pension schemes. But a characteristic feature of the pension situation today is the great variety of pension schemes which exist; from the point of view of the member of a scheme the most important point about this variety is probably the difference in the amount of pension which different schemes provide. For a lifetime's service, the pension may be as little as a pound or two a week or as much as two-thirds of what was being earned just before retirement.

To understand the present situation, it is therefore necessary not only to look at the growth of pensions, as was done in the previous chapter, but also to see how certain features of pension schemes have developed, particularly those which have come to be associated with public sector schemes, and to examine some of the influences which have shaped them.

Foremost among the characteristics of public sector schemes is the calculation of the pension by reference to length of service and the salary or wages being received at the time of retirement or shortly before. This 'terminal-salary' type of scheme is now probably the most common single type of occupational pension scheme, and has obvious advantages to the prospective pensioner, particularly in times of inflation, over a pension of fixed amount or one depending on the amount of salaries or wages earned throughout the whole period of service, to name two examples of other ways of calculating a pension. A main purpose of this chapter will be to trace the development of this type of scheme, particularly in the Civil Service where it early made an appearance.

CIVIL SERVICE: DEVELOPMENT OF A TERMINAL-SALARY SCHEME

There can be little doubt that the origin of the terminal-salary type of scheme derives from the attempt, described in the previous chapter, to put the pay and pension of the civil servant on an orderly and regular footing. The earliest general scheme in the Act of 1810 had three main principles: it provided for superannuation allowances to be paid only to those who were unable either through physical or mental incapacity or old age to carry on work; it recognized that the allowance should increase according to the years of service worked; and it aimed to provide in most cases an allowance somewhat smaller than the pay which the man had been receiving.

All these three principles still apply not only to the civil service scheme, but to most schemes in the public sector and many outside. But it is the third principle which developed into the chief characteristic of a terminal-salary scheme, the calculation of the pension directly from the pay or salary being received at the time of or just before retirement.

That in origin this arrangement arose simply from the fact that pay and pensions were being treated together may be judged from the fact that the 1810 scheme provided for both to be charged to the same source, that is, generally the 'Fee Fund' in any department which had one; and also that no question arose of asking civil servants to contribute towards the cost of their pensions. It was therefore perhaps natural that the scale of pensions laid down by the 1810 Act should permit (in the comparatively rare circumstances of a man having fifty or more years' service and attaining the age of 65) a pension equal in amount to the salary he was receiving, but the normal pension after forty or more years' service was not to exceed three-quarters of a man's salary.

The idea of a scale of pensions varying with the number of years' service followed naturally from the idea of rewarding long service, and the prospect of a higher pension was regarded as an incentive in that direction, but it should be noted that the scales were very simple and intended to indicate maximum amounts, although they soon began to be claimed by civil servants as a right.

The steps by which the 1810 scheme was gradually transformed into a terminal-salary scheme of the modern type where the pension is calculated as a fraction of the retiring salary for each year of service illustrates very well some of the influences which have continued to operate on pension schemes ever since. Among those influences the question of cost was extremely important.

In 1821, as part of a general inquiry into costs, all departments were subjected to a minute examination, and the cost of superannuation allowances was looked at in detail. As a result of this examination, the Treasury issued a Minute in August 1821 dealing with superannuation: 'it is essentially necessary that some new regulation should be adopted, with a view to limiting this branch of the Public Expenditure in future . . . the mode of regulation which seems in all respects most eligible, is to require that the Individuals who may hereafter enjoy the benefit of Superannuation Allowances, should be called upon to contribute to a Superannuation Fund'. This new arrangement was given statutory authority in an Act of 1822 (3 Geo. IV, c. 113), together with other limiting provisions, the whole object of which was to keep down the cost of superannuation. By far the most important of them was the introduction of contributions; even so, the rate of contribution (2½ per cent of salaries between £100 and £200 p.a. and 5 per cent of salaries over £200) was not, and was not intended to be, sufficient to pay the whole cost, but only to meet half of it, the rest being provided in the same manner as before. Thus, just as the scheme for civil service superannuation had begun as non-contributory simply because of the particular circumstances out of which it arose, so it changed to being a contributory scheme because of the need for economy; in neither case was there any attempt to decide on the merits of two systems. Indeed, the question could not have arisen in this way since the problem of how to finance superannuation benefits was scarcely yet recognized as a distinct problem.

There was soon opposition to the paying of contributions on the grounds that to impose them on existing civil servants was a violation of the terms on which they had entered the service. And this opposition succeeded in getting a further Act passed in 1824 (5 Geo. IV, c. 104) abolishing contributions and returning those which had already been paid. This was the position when in 1828 a Select Committee came to consider ways of reducing public expenditure; they attributed the 'rapid and undue growth' of the cost of superannuation to 'some Acts of erroneous legislation of a recent date' and their main remedy was to suggest re-introducing a fund supported by deductions from salaries. They were optimistic enough to suppose that eventually the deductions alone would be enough to meet the cost of superannuation, but to help in keeping the costs down they recommended that no pension should exceed two-thirds of salary 'because it is expedient to establish a marked distinction between the actual performance of official duties and the non-performance of them from whatever cause that cessation may arise'. Finally, to overcome the opposition which had led to the abandonment of the 1822 contributory system, they suggested that contributions should only be paid by future entrants and that the 'existing interests and well-grounded expectations' of those already serving should be respected.[1]

The proposals for re-introducing contributions were put into effect by means of a Treasury Minute of 1829; the scales were steeper than those under the 1822 Act (2½ per cent on salaries up to £100 p.a., 5 per cent otherwise), but the money was not accumulated in a fund, and indeed the emphasis was very much on reducing current

[1] Report from the Select Committee on the Public Income and Expenditure of the United Kingdom, Parliamentary Paper 480 of 1828, pp. 3, 4, 15 and 16.

costs rather than providing for the future—the term 'deductions' was used and not contributions—although the Treasury Minute did state that the intention was 'to reduce, at a future period, the heavy charge which is now annually incurred in providing Superannuation'.

The other proposals of the 1828 Committee, however, were not dealt with until the Superannuation Act of 1834 (4 & 5 Will. IV. c. 24), which repealed the earlier Acts and made a fresh start; in the meantime the House of Commons had appointed a Select Committee to look into the whole matter because, as the Chancellor of the Exchequer said in moving the motion for such a Committee on April 26, 1830, 'It was not right to enact a law one Session and repeal it the next; and it would be equally beneficial to the public and just to the individuals to settle the principles on which every man entering the service hereafter should receive his salary and his superannuation'. What happened to this Committee is something of a mystery; it contained such eminent members as Lord Palmerston and Sir James Graham, but, in the words of the later committee of 1857, 'Unfortunately, no report was presented, and no trace of the proceedings of the Committee has been discovered'.

Parts of the 1834 Act are still in force today. It introduced further principles which were later to become part of the established pattern of public service pensions; in particular, the distinction introduced by the 1829 Treasury Minute between new entrants and existing members was carried a stage further. Not only did new entrants after August 4, 1829, have to pay contributions but they also got a less generous scale of pension, rising by twelfths of final salary to a maximum of 8/12 or 2/3 after forty-five years' service or more.

The principle embodied in these arrangements was that nobody who was already a member of a pension scheme should be made worse off against his will by changes made in the scheme. It is a principle, the acceptance of which as the 'no detriment' rule has had far-reaching consequences on the administration of public sector schemes, but it is unlikely that anyone foresaw this in 1829, when all that was being looked for was a solution to a particularly awkward problem of the time.[1]

A further provision of the 1834 Act was the limitation of the maximum pension which could be awarded to two-thirds of salary. Although the main reason for introducing it was to limit the cost of pensions, there is no evidence that the Committee had given a great deal of thought to the precise figure of two-thirds which they recommended, but it did have the advantage of fitting in well with a scale in twelfths.

This limitation of maximum pension to two-thirds of salary may seem to be a matter of detail, but both the principle behind it, as

[1] See Chapter 8 for a discussion of 'no detriment'.

stated in the Committee's Report, and the precise figure have since become established as cardinal points in the pension arrangements of this country. Only in recent years has it been possible in practice to get a pension income going beyond two-thirds; and only in recent years has it been seriously suggested that a higher maximum pension, perhaps up to 80 per cent, should be aimed at.

The scheme established by the 1834 Act thus had in it some of the main elements of a modern terminal-salary scheme. It also began to fill in some of the details left open by earlier enactments; thorny problems such as the amount of pension to be paid to re-employed pensioners had to be dealt with; and it is perhaps not surprising that the 1834 Act needed three times the amount of space of the 1810 Act to deal with pension matters.

However, the scheme did not work completely smoothly and in 1856 the Royal Commission to which reference was made in Chapter 1 was appointed to examine its workings. In its Report of May 1857 it drew attention to numerous anomalies in the system, some of which were due to the state of administration generally rather than to the superannuation system itself; for example, 'officers in Post Office establishments of London, Edinburgh and Dublin are charged with deductions and are entitled to superannuation. The similar officers in the Post Offices of Liverpool, Manchester and Glasgow neither pay deductions nor receive superannuation.'[1] But naturally the main anomaly was in the different treatment of those who had been appointed before August 1829 and those appointed after; the system of contributions in particular produced a great many complaints by civil servants to the Commission. On this point the Commission thought that a serious objection to the existing contributory system was that it implied the maintenance of a fund, although there was none. Without a fund it seemed to them that all that the 1834 Act had done was to reduce salaries but, as they severely remarked, if that had been the intention it ought to have been done straightforwardly.

Their words are worth quoting because the problem with which they were concerned is one which will need to be examined later in this study. 'It appears to us,' they said, 'that the most natural and proper course in all such transactions is, to call things by their right names. . . . If it is intended that the salary actually paid to a Civil Servant shall be of a certain amount and that in addition to this salary, he shall, under certain circumstances, be entitled to a retired allowance according to a prescribed scale, it seems prima facie to be the most correct course to describe the remuneration of the Civil Servant as consisting of a certain salary, with a prospect, under certain circumstances, of a retired allowance, rather than to add to

[1] Report, p. vii.

the salary a certain nominal amount which is supposed to be an equivalent for the chance of a superannuation allowance, and thus to describe the salary as being of a larger amount than it really is, without mentioning the superannuation.'[1]

With other arguments, such as that contributions provided a moral check or that they were a protection against interference by Parliament, the Commission dealt briefly; they could not understand why civil servants should be less secure in their pensions than in their salaries nor 'how their case is strengthened by making a nominal addition to their salaries, which is never paid to them, and calling this nominal addition a deduction or abatement paid by them for the purpose of providing their superannuations'. In 1857 a Private Member's Act was passed abolishing finally the payment of contributions by civil servants, and although at intervals (e.g. by the Ridley Commission in 1888 and the Tomlin Commission in 1931) arguments were put forward for re-introducing them the civil service scheme has remained non-contributory, the only major public sector scheme to be so.

Abolition of contributions may fairly be regarded, however, as a triumph for civil servants. The Government opposed the 1857 Act, and in 1859 introduced a Bill of its own to give effect to other recommendations of the Commission. This Superannuation Act of 1859 marked the final step in the establishment in all essentials of the modern civil service scheme. The pension scale, after the various fluctuations of earlier years, was firmly fixed in sixtieths of final salary for each year's service, thus giving a maximum pension of two-thirds after forty years' service. Similarly the minimum retirement age was, again after earlier fluctuations, fixed at 60, an age when, according to the 1857 Commission, 'bodily or mental vigour often begins to decline', and this is still the minimum age in the scheme.

In fact since 1859 the many changes which have been made in the civil service scheme may be regarded as modifications and adaptations, and in some cases additions, rather than attempts to devise afresh a system of pensions. No major change was made at all for fifty years until the 1909 Superannuation Act introduced death benefits into the scheme. Even then the change was made by reducing the amount of the annual pension in order to provide both a pension and a sum of money. Thus instead of being calculated in sixtieths, the pension was, and still remains, based on eightieths for each year of service, giving a half-pay pension after forty years' service; in addition, a lump sum is payable.

Among other changes of importance have been the introduction in 1949 of pensions for widows and other dependants, and in the same year the raising of the maximum limit for pensionable service

[1] Report, p. xii.

from 40 to 45 years. Both these changes were, however, subject to limitations; in the case of widows' pensions, part of the cost (roughly half) was to be put on the civil servants themselves either through a reduction in the amount of lump sum received at retirement or through special contributions made expressly for this purpose. In the case of the extension of the years of service, this was only to apply to those who had both reached the minimum retiring age (generally 60) and completed forty years' service.

Apart from this latter provision, which was specifically designed to encourage civil servants to remain at work, it is obvious how powerful a factor cost has been in limiting the growth of the scheme since 1859. This point can perhaps be seen even better by comparing the development of the civil service scheme with that of other public service schemes, notably that for local government employees.

LOCAL GOVERNMENT: DIFFICULTIES OF ESTABLISHING A UNIVERSAL SCHEME

Local government officers today, like civil servants, receive a pension calculated in eightieths of terminal salary for each year of service, together with a lump sum. This surface similarity conceals a very different pension history. To begin with, eightieths for sixtieths came into the local government scheme not in 1909, but in 1953, and it is therefore only true to say of local government officers joining the scheme since 1953 (and of those already serving then who chose to change) that they receive a pension plus a lump sum.

One obvious reason for the different development of pensions in local government was that the modern system of administration dates only from the Local Government Act of 1888. Nevertheless, local administration was carried on before that date by a variety of different bodies and institutions, among them, after the reform of the Poor Law in 1834, the Boards of Guardians and those whom they employed, the poor law officers.

It was not, however, until thirty years later, in 1864, that poor law officers were able to get even a footing on the pension ladder, although there had earlier been one or two abortive attempts to establish a scheme. What was done in 1864, however, was not to set up a scheme but to give the officers' employers, the Boards of Guardians, the power to grant pensions at their discretion. No scale of pensions was laid down, but, as in the civil service scheme (and probably borrowed from it), the maximum pension was limited to two-thirds of salary, and the minimum retiring age on grounds of age (as opposed to ill-health) was 60.

An interesting point about these pensions was that no money was specifically set aside to pay for them, and they were to be paid out of the same fund as the officers' salaries. Whether this indicated that pensions were not expected to be very frequent is uncertain, but the fact that there was no guarantee that a pension would be paid nor how much it would amount to if it were paid was a source of discontent among poor law officers.

Something was done by the Local Government Board in 1880 about the second point when they laid down that if a pension were paid it should be on the sixtieths scale which was then in force in the civil service scheme. But from the officers' point of view this did nothing to solve the first and principal grievance which was aggravated by the fact that in some parts of the country the Guardians refused to give pensions at all.

Part of the difficulty was undoubtedly cost. In a sense civil servants were lucky to get their pension scheme established before it was generally realized how expensive a regular system was, although it may well have been that in the particular circumstances of the position of the Civil Service in the early nineteenth century some scheme, even if not as generous as the one established, would have been regarded as not too high a price to pay. And it has already been seen how attempts were made to reduce the direct cost, both by cutting down the level of the benefits and by deducting contributions from civil servants' salaries, once it had been realized how expenditure on pensions was increasing.

In the case of poor law officers, the question of cost was for a long time an obstacle in the way of the establishment of a proper scheme. They themselves, through their Association, proposed a single central fund for pensions, but this was rejected, and it was left to a Private Member to introduce in 1896 a Bill which finally gave poor law officers an entitlement to pensions, in return for paying contributions.

These pensions, like those for civil servants, were based on sixtieths of final salary for each year of service, but the scheme differed from both the civil service scheme and the earlier arrangements for discretionary pensions in making 65 the normal age of retirement. Retirement at 60 or between 60 and 65 was possible but only, generally speaking, for those who had done forty years' service; and 65 became effectively the age of compulsory retirement.

The reason for this change in the age of retirement is not certain. Partly it may reflect changing ideas on the age at which men ceased to be capable of effective service. But it seems equally likely that it was in part connected with the desire to limit the cost of pensions. It is worth noting, however, that this particular provision has been carried through to the present-day local government scheme, and distinguishes that scheme from other public service schemes, such as those for the Civil Service and teachers.

In other ways, the question of cost was prominent in the arrangements for poor law officers. The contributions which they were to pay, generally of 2½ per cent of their salaries, would, so it was claimed by the sponsors of the 1896 Bill, be sufficient 'in all probability' to cover the whole cost of pensions without putting any additional charge on the rates. This claim was based on the experience of certain large cities which had instituted pension schemes for their employees, but although it was no doubt a good way of winning support for the measure, the claim was unsound. By 1913–14 pensions under the 1896 Act were costing £220,000 against an income from contributions of £63,000; the difference was a charge to the rates.

The method of financing the scheme was thus very simple; the only specific income which was available to pay pensions in any particular year was the money contributed by those who happened to be serving in that year. This was indeed precisely the system which the 1857 Commission on the Civil Service had criticized because no attempt was made to set aside money in a separate fund, and because, in the absence of a fund, the main result was that salaries were lower than they otherwise might have been.

Whether the criticisms of the 1857 Commissioners were justified or not, the fact remains that Parliament had adopted different attitudes to the question of financing pensions in the case of civil servants and poor law officers.[1] Basically the same method as for poor law officers was later adopted in, for example, the teachers' scheme, but local government generally adopted yet a third method, a contributory scheme in which the contributions were set aside and accumulated in a specific pension fund. This development will be considered next.

To some extent poor law officers, like teachers, were in a position somewhere between central and local government. They were certainly locally employed and paid, but the problems and policies of the Poor Law, as of education, were very much a concern of central government. And, as is well known, it was not until the Local Government Act of 1929 that the local poor law administration was taken over by the counties and county boroughs.

The position of those employed either by the municipal corporations or, after the Local Government Acts of 1888 and 1894, by counties, county boroughs and county districts was very different. For one thing, it was a long time before one could speak of 'local government officers' as a body in the way that one could talk of civil servants or teachers or poor law officers. This particular historical situation has affected the development of, among other things, salaries and pensions. It is only comparatively recently that there

[1] Of course it might be argued that the two cases were only apparently different if the fact that civil servants' pensions were non-contributory was taken into account in fixing their salaries. This point will be considered later.

have been generally accepted uniform salary scales in local government, and for similar reasons a general system of pensions was slow to develop.

The emphasis in early days, therefore, was on individual action by particular local authorities, and this naturally took a variety of forms; later development was to some degree conditioned by the resulting patchwork of provisions. To begin with, one must except certain general categories of employees; the police have always been separately provided for in the way of pensions, and some rather special problems of police pensions are considered later in this chapter. Similarly, those who worked in lunatic asylums were for long treated separately for pension purposes, rather in the manner of poor law officers. For the general body of local government employees, apart from these special categories, pensions in the nineteenth century were generally dependent on the promotion of individual local Acts. As with other public servants, the first arrangements generally provided only for discretionary payments, as in the Wallasey Improvement Act of 1864, and in an Act of 1866 to make superannuation provision for 'officers of Vestries and other Boards within the Area of the Metropolis Local Management Act'. The usual arrangement was for such pensions as were granted to be paid from the same funds as salaries.

The lack of any entitlement to pension led to other arrangements which were little more than substitutes for pensions; for example, thrift funds in which contributions by both employer and employee were accumulated. Such a fund was instituted by the Manchester Corporation in 1891 but because the benefits were small, Manchester found itself retaining in service a large number of elderly employees, thus defeating part of the object of setting up the fund. The solution which a number of local authorities found to the problem of lack of entitlement to pension was to set up superannuation funds supported by contributions from both employers and employees. These differed from the thrift funds, from which an individual could only draw the amount accumulated in his name together with interest, by being intended to be built up to amounts which would guarantee the payment of pensions; there was also provision for actuarial assessments and for the making of deficiency payments into the fund (out of the rates) if necessary in accordance with that guarantee.[1]

Liverpool in 1882, Southport in 1900 and Newcastle upon Tyne in 1904, among others, promoted local Acts for this purpose; contributions varied from 2 per cent to 4 per cent of salary from each side and the pension scale was the by now usual one in sixtieths.

But although these arrangements might be satisfactory for local government officers working in the places which had set up schemes,

[1] For a discussion of what is involved in funding see Chapter 4.

a great many officers were not included in any pension arrangements at all and, not unnaturally, this caused dissatisfaction. In June 1914 they were promised an inquiry into the whole question by the President of the Local Government Board (Mr Herbert Samuel), but because of the war this inquiry was not carried out until 1919. However, this was by no means the beginning of the story; the first Minister of Health, Dr Addison, is recorded as having said that he was not surprised that after thirty-five years of talk and nothing done local government officers should feel that they had a legitimate grievance. Mainly, this delay was due to the difficulty of tackling the existing chaos of arrangements; when the Norman Committee did look into the matter in 1919 they found the legislation 'incomplete, overlapping and conflicting'. It was not only that there were anomalies reminiscent of the early years of civil service superannuation ('a librarian may be superannuated in Poplar but not in East Ham'), but there were no common principles behind the legislation so that, for example, 'in different localities different rates of contribution are charged for the same benefits, and different benefits are given for the same rates of contributions'.[1]

To deal with this situation the Committee recommended a compulsory, universal contributory scheme with a limited number (about 200) of separate funds; they rejected the idea of a single fund for all employees, largely because of the great variations which then existed between different authorities in such matters as salary scales and conditions of service, but also because of the dangers of accumulating so large a fund.[2] No action was taken by the Government on this Report, although nobody disputed that local government employees ought to have a proper system of superannuation. It was left to a private member to introduce a Bill in 1922, but despite the recommendation of the Norman Committee, the Bill allowed local authorities the option to adopt the superannuation scheme proposed in it, and (in its final form) only imposed one restriction on the number of funds, namely, that each fund must cater for at least fifty employees.

What prevented those in local government from getting what civil servants, teachers, police and others enjoyed was simply the cost. The promoter of the Bill (Sir Herbert Nield) bluntly said that he disagreed with the Committee and that a compulsory scheme was out of the question because of the financial position of the country. The Government spokesman (Sir Alfred Mond, Minister of Health) said that the Government had at one time intended to introduce a Bill providing compulsory superannuation but had dropped it for the same reasons of financial stringency; and although at least one supporter of the Bill queried whether the additional financial burden

[1] Report of the Norman Committee, Cmd. 329, 1919, para. 26.
[2] Ibid., paras. 74–90.

was quite so great as had been maintained, since many employees were already covered by local Act schemes, it was clear that local government employees must accept either a voluntary Bill or nothing. After so many years of waiting it is not surprising that they chose the former.

Yet only three years later a Departmental Committee, under the chairmanship of Sir Amherst Selby-Bigge, once more examined this question of compulsory superannuation and reported in 1927, with only one dissentient, in favour of this principle, at least so far as local government officers were concerned. One of the difficulties of the situation in local government was that manual workers (or 'servants' as they are called to distinguish them from 'officers', i.e. salaried staff) were far more numerous than salaried officials; to have a universal, compulsory scheme might therefore be much more expensive than simply to bring in all the salaried staff. When, eventually, in 1937 legislation was passed establishing a compulsory scheme, the compulsion only applied to officers and not to servants, and though in fact many authorities have included all or some of their servants in their superannuation schemes, local government superannuation is still not universal.

The scheme laid down by the 1922 and 1937 Acts was essentially similar to the 1896 scheme for poor law officers, that is, it was a terminal-salary scheme in sixtieths with a compulsory retiring age of 65 (except for certain special groups, such as female nurses, who were compulsorily retired at 60). But the scheme differed greatly from that for the poor law officers in its financial arrangements. The contributions to be paid by employees were 5 per cent (increased to 6 per cent for officers under the 1937 Act), and these contributions (together with equivalent payments by the employers) were to be accumulated in funds. Thus Parliament approved, in the case of local government employees, yet a third means of financing pension benefits; the money to pay for pensions was to come not simply from contributions by employees, but from employers' contributions as well and from the investment of surplus income from these two sources.

Funding of this kind has generally been adopted both in nationalized industries' schemes and in the private sector. But because of the way in which pension provision developed in local government, the scheme presents the unique spectacle of a single, uniform scheme for all local government officers (and a good many servants too) which is nevertheless financed by a large number (over 500) of individual funds; each county and county borough, and many county districts maintain their own funds.

One further development in local government pensions should be mentioned; a major change was made in the scheme in 1953 to provide for the granting of pensions to the widows of members who died. In order to finance this additional benefit, lump sums were introduced into the scheme and married men were required to give up two-thirds of their lump sums on retirement to meet the prospective cost of widows' pensions.

Thus the change from pensions in sixtieths to pensions in eightieths plus a lump sum which was introduced into the civil service scheme in 1909 reached the local government scheme in 1953. In both cases, the reason for the change was the same, a rearrangement of existing benefits to make possible an additional benefit without increasing the total cost, although the additional benefit was not the same in both cases.

POLICE PENSIONS: THE PROBLEM OF SPECIAL CONDITIONS OF SERVICE

In many ways the civil service and local government schemes represent the two extremes in the development of the older public sector schemes.[1] The Civil Service early developed a single, uniform scheme, whereas local government exhibited a lengthy, piecemeal development. Again, in the matter of financing, there could not be a greater contrast than between the unfunded, non-contributory civil service scheme and the funded, contributory local government scheme, with its multiplicity of separate funds. Later chapters in this study will compare and contrast the provisions of these and other schemes as they exist at the present time, but it is as well to bear in mind that identity of provisions now may well conceal vastly different historical developments.

The development of other public sector schemes on the whole falls somewhere between the two extremes. The rather special case of the police is, however, interesting for the light it throws on another important problem of pensions, the adjustment of schemes to take account of different conditions of service. Pensions for the police date back to the establishment of regular police forces. There were first a number of local Act arrangements, beginning with that for the Metropolitan Police in 1829. Where county police forces were established under the County Police Act of 1839, they were, by an Act of 1840, required to set up superannuation funds, although it was not until 1856 that the establishment of county police forces was made obligatory. In the case of borough forces, superannuation funds were not made obligatory until 1859.

The pensions payable under these various provisions were at the discretion of the Justices of the Peace (in counties) or the Watch

[1] That is, excluding the newer schemes for the National Health Service and the nationalized industries.

Committees (in the boroughs) and policemen had no entitlement to a pension. The Acts merely specified the limits to the granting of pensions; for example, no pension could be more than two-thirds of pay or granted before the age of 60, except on grounds of ill-health.

But of more significance than these similarities with civil service pensions currently in force were some characteristic differences. The maximum pension could be gained after twenty years' service and not forty-five as under the 1834 civil service scale; a constable disabled because of an injury received in the course of his duty might have his pension raised to equal the whole of his pay; and if he died in service his widow might be granted a gratuity not exceeding the amount of one year's pay. Such provisions clearly indicate the more arduous and hazardous conditions under which the police have to work, and they have continued to be a feature of police pensions ever since.

The manner of financing these early police pensions is also interesting. Despite the fact that constables had no entitlement to a pension, they were required to make contributions of not more than $2\frac{1}{2}$ per cent of their pay. These contributions were to be placed in funds which were also to be supported by the proceeds of certain fines, stoppages of pay and sales of worn or cast-off clothing supplied for the use of constables. The proceeds of certain other fines, e.g. for selling beer on Sundays, could, at the discretion of the Justices, also be used in part for the benefit of the funds.

The object was by these means to accumulate sufficient money to be able to invest part of the funds and thus to cover the cost of paying pensions; but if nevertheless the fund was insufficient, the deficiency was to be made good out of the police rate. These police funds were thus among the earliest attempts to set up true superannuation funds. It is noticeable, too, that like the later local government scheme, these were truly local funds, one for each police force. However, both the state of the funds and the unsatisfactoriness of the discretionary system of pensions led the House of Commons to appoint a Select Committee in 1877 to consider whether any changes were needed in the law.

The Committee were assisted in their examination of the funds by a detailed analysis supplied to them by Dr William Farr, the first statistical expert of the General Register Office. He reported that most of the funds were either exhausted or soon would be, and the Committee found some difficulty in deciding whether it would be better to amalgamate them into a single or a few large funds, or to charge the cost of pensions directly onto the rates; on the whole, they favoured the latter course.[1] The Committee also thought that

[1] Report of a Select Committee on Police Superannuation Funds, H.C. 158, 1877, especially pp. viii–xi.

in place of the existing system of discretionary payments there should be a more uniform and regular system, and that there should be entitlement to a pension after twenty-five years' service when a constable 'had practically given all his best years and energies to the force and was, as a rule, no longer thoroughly efficient'.

This latter recommendation of the Committee illustrates very well the fundamental dilemma of police pensions, or indeed of any other pension system for men in particularly hazardous occupations, such as the Armed Forces. Their conditions of service are such that it seems reasonable that they should be able to draw a pension earlier than men in less physically exacting occupations. But it had already been demonstrated to the 1877 Committee that even the existing pension arrangements were inadequately provided for by pension funds based on contributions of 2–2½ per cent of pay by policemen themselves. Any further extension of the arrangements was therefore bound to prove costly and to raise the question of who was to pay.

An eloquent comment on the situation is provided by the fact that, following the Committee's Report, private members introduced Bills dealing with police pensions in each year from 1882 to 1885 but they made no progress because, in the words of the Home Secretary in 1890, they were opposed by 'Hon. Members who represented the views of the ratepayers, and who thought that the burdens of local taxation were sufficiently heavy already, and that Imperial resources should be used to assist the local rates'.[1]

In 1890 the Government itself promoted a Bill which, although it retained the existing superannuation funds, proposed to overcome the difficulty about the heavy charge falling on the rates by allocating an annual sum of £300,000 from the yield of certain customs and excise duties to be distributed to the funds. Apart from this, the financial arrangements remained as before, with contributions from the police, not exceeding 2½ per cent, being paid into funds for each area which were also supported by fines, sales of clothing, etc. Some possible further sources of income were added, such as 'the net sums received in the police area for pedlars' and chimney sweepers' certificates', but if there was a deficiency on the funds the balance of cost was to be met from the money allocated to general police purposes in the area (the 'police fund').

In the case of the police, however, unlike the poor law officers, it was difficult after 1877 to be optimistic about the solvency of these funds. The Home Secretary in 1890 himself asserted that the contributions paid by the Metropolitan Police 'if capitalized and invested would not pay one-tenth part of the proposed pensions', an assertion which, despite the greater cost of police pensions, contrasts strangely with the optimism of the sponsors of the Poor Law Officers' Super-

[1] H.C. Deb., June 27, 1890, col. 230.

annuation Bill six years later. In 1921 the attempt to keep separate police superannuation funds was abandoned, and the cost of police pensions was henceforth met in part by the contributions paid by the men themselves and in part by the general police fund in each area, which itself is now composed partly of money derived from the rates and partly of an Exchequer grant for police purposes. Thus in the case of the police, Parliament, after trying to devise a system of financing akin to what was later done in local government, abandoned it for something very like the poor law officers' system. It seems, however, that the only way in which police superannuation funds could have been kept solvent would have been by much greater annual contributions, whether from the men, the local police authorities or the central government, and this was never tried.

In other ways, too, the 1890 Police Pensions Acts (there were separate ones for England and Wales, and for Scotland) differed from the pattern which was developing for other public service schemes. For example, although the policemen now had an entitlement to pension, the rate of pension was, within certain limits, left to the discretion of individual police authorities. Thus after twenty-five years' service (the minimum qualification for an ordinary pension), he might get as little as half-pay pension or as much as 31/50ths; and the maximum (two-thirds) pension might be gained after as much as thirty-five or as little as twenty-six years' service. There were also variations in the extent to which minimum retirement ages were fixed.

It was not therefore until 1921 that, following the report of a committee set up to consider police affairs (the Desborough Committee), a uniform pension scheme for the police throughout Great Britain was instituted under the Police Pensions Act of that year. The main features of this scheme were that the sixtieths pattern of other schemes was adapted to give a half-pension after twenty-five years and two-thirds after thirty years, that widows' pensions and not just gratuities were introduced,[1] and that prominence was given to injury and disablement awards.

These have been characteristic features of the police scheme ever since, although many changes have been made in detail, notably in improving widows' pensions and in raising the contribution rate, first to 5 per cent and then, to meet part of the cost of the improved widows' pensions, to 6¼ per cent. It is an interesting reflection on the way in which pension developments take place that although awards to widows were a unique feature of the earliest police arrangements, the present level of widow's pension, dating only from 1956, is no higher than that in the civil service and similar schemes, and lower

[1] To be precise, widows' pensions began in 1918, the police being the first public service to have them.

than that in many of the nationalized industries' schemes. What was originally designed as a special award for special circumstances has in course of time come to be regarded as a normal part of a public sector pension scheme.[1]

The varied course of public sector development has been illustrated from the civil service, local government and police schemes. Other public sector schemes, although differing greatly in detail of their development, can generally be regarded as having an affinity with one or other of the examples. A brief note on the major schemes is given below.

Teachers

The first teachers' scheme under the 1898 Act seemed to owe nothing to other public service schemes of the time. Its basis was a contribution of fixed amount (£3 a year for men, £2 for women), with a pension varying according to the number of years for which contributions had been paid, but not according to the salary earned just before retirement. In addition, teachers received an annual allowance of 10s for each year of service, provided entirely by the Exchequer. This type of scheme, often known as 'money-purchase' because the pension depends on the amount of contributions paid, has not been adopted in any other major public sector scheme. It lasted only from 1898 to 1918 for teachers, and may fairly be regarded as an anomaly in terms of general public sector development. In 1918 a non-contributory, unfunded scheme based closely on that of the Civil Service, was introduced for teachers. This was soon modified to make it contributory but in essentials the scheme has since been and remained of the same type as that of the Civil Service, although with certain variations in detail.

Firemen

A separate pension scheme for firemen as a whole, as opposed to local Act schemes, dates only from 1925. Many of the details of the current scheme are identical with that of the police scheme, and in the same way depend upon the peculiarly hazardous conditions of employment of firemen. Under the 1925 Fire Brigade Pensions Act, funds were established in each fire area supported by contributions

---

[1] It should be added that the high cost of police pensions (which itself depends on the particular circumstances of police employment) has been a particularly potent factor in restricting the pace of extension of the scheme. For the lengthy discussions preceding the improved widows' pensions see H.C. Deb., March 13, 1956, cols. 271–2.

from both firemen and their employers, but these, like the police funds, have now been abolished.

Newer Schemes

The schemes so far considered (with the exception of the firemen's) have all had a long history of development. In the last twenty years an entirely different situation has arisen; the creation of the National Health Service and of the new nationalized industries brought within the public sector at one stroke many men and women who had either not been members of schemes or had been members of private sector schemes.

In this situation, the problem of pension provision has generally been resolved by the institution of completely new schemes, at least for new entrants, but such schemes were not created out of the void. The National Health Service, for example, was staffed by people many of whom were already members of existing public sector schemes, particularly the local government scheme, and this was one of the factors tending to create an affinity between the NHS and local government schemes.

On the other hand, the Airways Corporations and the Railways were not so closely linked with existing public services, and their schemes diverge rather more from existing schemes.

Nevertheless, most of the new schemes were of the terminal-salary type and based their pensions on sixtieths (or eightieths with a lump sum). Only in methods of financing was there a marked divergence; this showed itself principally in the difference between the National Health Service scheme, contributory and unfunded, and the nationalized industries, which were for the most part both contributory and funded.

DEVELOPMENT IN THE PRIVATE SECTOR

The development of public sector schemes has been traced in some detail and over a fairly long period of time. But in the case of the private sector, there is no means of making a similar analysis, partly because there is no information readily available about the development of individual schemes, and, more particularly, because it is not possible to select a few schemes as typical of the private sector in the same way as for the public sector.

For the one most obvious distinguishing feature of the main public sector schemes is their size. The membership of the civil service scheme, for example, is near 700,000, but a scheme in the private sector with even one-tenth of this membership would be very large, and there are many thousand schemes which are much smaller than this.[1] This means that an account of the development of private sector schemes must be in much broader terms than that for the public sector. At the same time, it must deal with a much wider range both of types of scheme and, partly corresponding to this, of levels of pension benefit provided.

The point was made in discussion of the development of public sector schemes that by and large they all accepted the need for a pension based on final salary and one which, at least for a man who had done a lifetime's service, did not represent a startling fall in income. In the case of private sector schemes there was no such general basis, although a number of schemes have in the course of time changed to the public sector pattern.

In one way, however, the development of private sector schemes did parallel that of the public sector. In many cases, the first pensions were not guaranteed by means of a scheme but were ex gratia payments made by the employer at his own discretion. How far such arrangements were widespread at different times, and how far they were converted into formal schemes remain matters for speculation in the absence of any detailed study of the subject. It is reasonable to assume, however, that in many cases the change from discretionary to formal pensions was not made for a long time, one reason being that, even if the need for a formal scheme was seen, the cost of instituting one was a powerful factor against doing so. This sequence was evident in the case of public servants, such as the police and teachers, and there is reason to believe that cost was an even stronger limiting factor in the case of private sector schemes.

If the State undertook to pay pensions to its retired servants, the main guarantee that money would be available to pay those pensions lay in the Act of Parliament setting up the scheme, which in turn depended on the willingness of later governments to honour the obligations of their predecessors. A private firm or undertaking needed to go further if it was to guarantee such payments; it needed to establish a fund specifically for the purpose which would be of sufficient size to ensure that in the event of bankruptcy, or other similar catastrophe, the pension fund alone could meet the obligations for pension rights already incurred.

This need for establishing adequate funds may well have served to limit the growth of pension schemes. Nevertheless, it is well to remember that a number of private undertakings did set up funded schemes before many public servants were covered by schemes. The police, as has been seen, had to wait until 1890, teachers until 1898 (some longer) and local government officers until 1922, or in some cases, 1937, before they gained an entitlement to pension. But even

[1] For further discussion of the contrasts between public and private sector schemes, see Chapter 5.

before 1890 there were schemes in the private sector, not only in the rather special case of the railway companies, but also among the banks, insurance companies and some industrial firms. The important questions, however, are not only what schemes there were but of what sort and what pensions they paid. Here there is very little evidence, except for the railway companies' schemes, but for the reasons given in Chapter 1, these are not necessarily typical.

One distinctive feature of the railway schemes which was certainly characteristic of the private as against the public sector was that there were different schemes and different types of scheme for the salaried staff and the wage-paid manual workers. Generally, staff paid a contribution fixed as a percentage of salary, and received pensions calculated as a fraction per year of service of the average salary earned during their entire career on the railways; and manual workers paid a fixed amount in contributions and received a fixed or flat-rate amount of pension.

That separate schemes for manual workers are not characteristic of the public sector may be partly due to accident, in the sense that on the whole the public services either did not employ large numbers of manual workers or, that where they did, all or many of them were not brought within the superannuation arrangements. Thus in local government, 'servants' were not made compulsorily superannuable even by the 1937 Act; and in the Civil Service it was not until after the 1939–45 war that any appreciable number (and still by no means all) of the industrial staff were brought into the scheme.

However, in both these cases (as also in the case of the National Health Service) the benefits enjoyed by manual workers who were covered by the schemes were identical with those enjoyed by salaried staff. Only with the new schemes for the nationalized industries have there appeared in the public sector separate schemes for manual workers of a markedly different kind, notably for railwaymen and mineworkers.

In the private sector, on the other hand, although the sequence of events has been the same, that is, on the whole salaried staff received pensions before the manual or wage-paid workers, the railway pattern has been the one most often followed, in which manual workers have enjoyed a more modest and restricted scheme than the staff.

As far as the amount of pension is concerned, it will be clear that the 'average-salary' basis of the original railway companies' schemes for salaried staff was likely to produce a smaller pension on the whole than a terminal-salary scheme of the civil service type, unless the fractions used were high; and that a 'flat-rate' scheme will produce a pension which may be high in relation to earnings for the lowest-paid workers but low for higher-paid workers.

C

But if the flat-rate type of scheme is modified so that either contributions or pensions or both are variable, the former according to age on entry to the scheme and the latter according to the number of years' service, the resulting scheme approximates to yet another type found in the private sector, the 'money-purchase'. The basis of such schemes is that the amount of pension is directly determined by the amount of contributions paid, allowance being made for the fact that contributions paid at younger ages earn interest for a longer period. Thus, each £1 paid in contributions at age 20 might give entitlement to a pension of 15 shillings a year at retiring age, whereas the same amount contributed at the age of 40 would give an annual pension of only six shillings.

As with the average-salary type of scheme, the money-purchase is likely to give a lower pension than a generous terminal-salary scheme, except perhaps where, in times of stable currency, a man reaches his maximum earnings early in his career. A great deal, however, depends on the precise arrangements of each type of scheme and the precise circumstances of the individual.

Apart from the range of types of scheme and differences in the level of benefits provided by them, yet a third factor must be mentioned which has contributed to the diversity of development in the private sector. This concerns the means of administering schemes. It was stated above that it was a necessary part of private sector pension scheme arrangements, though not of the public sector, to establish a fund, primarily as a guarantee that money would be available to pay the pensions.[1] But the setting-up and administering of such a fund could involve a firm, and especially a small firm, in a good deal of extra work and expense. An obvious example is the need for skill and expert management in the handling of investments.

For many smaller firms, therefore, an alternative was needed to the 'self-administered' method of instituting a fund to serve only the purposes of the scheme. One means of doing this was for the employer to arrange with an insurance company for each of his employees to take out an individual policy. Where such policies were for deferred annuities, the arrangement served the purposes of a pension scheme; where they were of the endowment assurance type they provided cover against the risk of death, and might also provide a pension if the lump sum payment at maturity could be converted into an annuity.

Nevertheless, individual policies could be a rather cumbersome method of providing for the retirement of employees, especially where there was a large turnover of staff. Furthermore, it restricted the type of benefit to money-purchase or variants of it. The method

[1] For other reasons for establishing funds and for a discussion of what is involved in funding, see Chapter 9.

is still in use today, particularly for some large schemes where particular circumstances may make it more suitable than for the ordinary situation; a notable example is the universities scheme (FSSU).

But the great development of insured schemes has taken place in the last thirty years or so with the introduction (from the USA) in the late 1920's of what is termed the Group Life and Pension Scheme. The basis of this is an agreement between the employer and the insurance company setting out the terms on which all employees are covered. Thus administration is immediately simplified by doing away with the necessity for individual policies and the substitution of what is in effect a single policy for the whole group of employees.

Whether arranged through individual or group policies, there are two main characteristics of insured schemes. One is that in most cases the major part of the burden of administration falls on the insurance company and not the employer, and the other is that they tend to be of the money-purchase type, as opposed to the self-administered scheme which is characteristically of the terminal-salary type.

In considering how development has taken place over the private field as a whole, particularly in such matters as the number of employees covered and the level of pension benefit provided, we are really reduced to two 'snapshot' portraits by official observers, one taken in 1936 and one in 1956. An earlier attempt in 1907 by the Local Government Board to assemble some basic information proved abortive.[1]

In the twenty years between 1936 and 1956 the number of members of private sector schemes trebled, but the proportion in insured schemes increased from about 20 per cent to just over 50 per cent. In both years the range of types of scheme and of benefits provided was wide. Thus in 1936 terminal-salary schemes were fairly common among the self-administered schemes and the pension was commonly based on a fraction of 1/60 or 1/80, but the range was from 1/50 to 1/120. In 1956 the position was similar, but 46 per cent of members of self-administered schemes had their pensions calculated in some way other than the terminal-salary basis. Again, in 1936 a flat-rate pension of £1 a week was a fairly common type of scheme, especially for manual workers, and in 1956 there were still 10 per cent of those in self-administered schemes and 7 per cent of those in insured schemes with pensions of this flat-rate type.

Merely to pick out one or two examples of this kind, however, fails to do justice to the immense variety of arrangements which have grown up in the private sector. Whether employees pay con-

---

[1] See Old Age Pensions: Memorandum and Tables, Cd. 3618, 1907, Section V; *Ministry of Labour Gazette*, May 1938; and Government Actuary's Survey of Occupational Pension Schemes, H.M.S.O., 1958.

tributions and if so on what basis, whether the main benefit is a pension or a lump sum or both combined, whether there are death, ill-health or widows' benefits, or what happens if a member leaves a scheme are all matters which, within certain limits, permit innumerable variations.

Even to trace the development of a selection of private sector schemes to indicate how and why particular features of those schemes were introduced would be beyond the scope of this study, but the sketch of events outlined in this chapter should be sufficient to indicate that there is a fundamental difference between the way in which public and private sector schemes have developed. In the public sector, and more particularly in that part of it which may be more accurately specified as the public services, it is possible to trace an underlying unity of purpose which has resulted in a certain pattern of pension provision, but no pattern can, except in the very broadest terms, be traced in private sector arrangements.

This sweeping generalization needs to be qualified in detail. It is therefore the purpose of the following five chapters to examine more fully the present situation of public sector schemes, what benefits they provide, how they are financed and the effect on them of the existence of the National Insurance scheme and of the present taxation system; and to see how they compare with a number of private sector schemes. It should then be clear how far the generalization is justified. Meanwhile these first two chapters will have served their purpose if they give the reader some idea of the background and general setting of the present situation.

CHAPTER 3

Public Sector Schemes: The Benefits Provided

The aim of the present and succeeding chapters is to describe the main features of pension provision, and particularly public sector pension provision, as it exists at the present day. There are, however, a number of general problems in giving an account of public sector schemes,[1] and these will be discussed first.

Closed Schemes. Because of the way in which pension development has taken place, there may at any given moment be a number of schemes in existence for those employed in a particular part of the public sector. A fairly common situation is that when a new scheme is introduced, for example on nationalization, it becomes the scheme for all new employees, but those who are already in service may have the choice either of coming into the new scheme or of remaining members of the schemes to which they already belong. These old schemes will then continue but will be closed to new members. Such closed schemes are not examined in this study since their membership is not generally large in relation to that of current or open schemes, and it will of course decline over the years. Nevertheless, the fact that there are these schemes and that in some cases they diverge considerably from the pattern of current schemes needs to be kept in mind in considering the present position.

'No Detriment.' To some extent, closed schemes represent only one example of the result of applying what, for convenience, is here termed the 'no detriment' rule. It is an almost invariable rule of public sector schemes that changes in schemes are only applied to existing members with their consent, and they are therefore given the option of remaining subject to the terms of the scheme before the change was made. This rule has been shown in Chapter 2 to have a long history; but its effect is to make it impossible to describe accurately the provisions of a scheme applying to present members except by making lengthy qualifications to every statement. When,

[1] The problem of what constitutes the public sector for this purpose and the reasons for excluding some schemes, such as that for the Armed Forces, are discussed in Appendix 2.

for example, the Superannuation Act of 1949 introduced a contributory scheme of widows' and dependants' allowances for civil servants, married men civil servants at the time could choose not to come into the new arrangements. This means that in describing the civil service scheme as comprising among other things a comprehensive system of allowances for dependants, only part of the picture is being given, and strictly speaking one should add that it only applies to a proportion of civil servants. This difficulty naturally affects most those schemes which have been running for some time because they are the ones where in the course of a number of years one would expect to find that a number of changes had taken place. Indeed it is essentially because of the long-term nature of pension arrangements that this difficulty becomes important; an option exercised by a member now may continue to form part of the scheme until he dies, which could be 65 or more years from now. Many options are not in fact exercised by more than a small proportion of existing members. Where a large number do choose to remain under the old conditions, it is usually because there are particular advantages in doing so; for example, when contributions and benefits were modified in 1948 to take account of the new National Insurance scheme, nearly everybody then serving chose to retain existing contribution rates and benefit scales since these were more advantageous. But as most changes are improvements, it is not surprising that many members do not exercise the option to remain as they are.

It is also relevant to note that in comparing different schemes, it is necessary to have regard to the dates at which similar provisions have been introduced, since this will be one of the main factors in determining what proportion of current members of schemes do in fact come under the latest provisions. For example, whereas all civil servants[1] now serving may expect to receive both a lump sum and a pension when they retire, quite a number of local government officers will receive only a pension; lump sums date back to 1909 in the civil service scheme but only to 1953 in local government.

Special Classes. Many public sector schemes are very large and special terms may apply to particular groups of members, usually because their conditions of service generally are different. Prison officers in the Civil Service, for example, and women nurses in the local government and NHS schemes may retire at an earlier age than is usual in these schemes.

Manual Workers. A difficulty of a rather different kind concerns

---

[1] Women civil servants did not get lump sums until the Superannuation Act of 1935, and it is therefore possible that some serving women civil servants who chose not to come under the new terms then will receive only a pension—a further illustration of the difficulty of generalizing.

schemes for manual workers. In some schemes manual workers are included on the same terms as other staff, but in other cases they either have separate but similar schemes or separate and quite different schemes. The facts are set out in Appendix 4, but manual workers' schemes are not examined in detail in the study since they raise a much wider problem of pensions which is not confined to the public sector; that is, whether there ought to be separate manual workers' schemes on a different basis from salaried staff schemes. This problem is referred to in Chapter 10, but meanwhile it should be remembered that the picture of public sector schemes presented here, although it applies broadly to many manual workers, does not apply to either the mineworkers or to the wage-paid staff of British Railways.

The four problems which have been discussed above all raise difficulties for anyone who is trying to give a complete guide to public sector schemes. This is not the object of this study which seeks rather to pick out the essential features of those schemes. Such an approach must therefore be selective and must, if necessary, sacrifice strict accuracy for clarity. The basic standpoint has been to concentrate attention on those provisions which apply to the majority of new entrants at the time of writing (1963–64). Thus options granted to existing members before that date are largely ignored as are the special terms applying to particular classes of members. For reasons already given the effect in what follows is to present a picture which by and large is applicable to the great majority of those employed in the public sector.

CHIEF CHARACTERISTICS OF TWELVE SCHEMES

Twelve schemes have been selected for detailed examination in this and the following chapter. Their membership (excluding pensioners) amounts to about two-thirds of the total membership of public sector schemes, including the Armed Forces, most of the remaining members being in the two large schemes for mineworkers and the male wages grades of British Railways. (For further details of membership see Appendix 5.) The twelve schemes with figures of approximate membership are:

Scheme	Members
Civil Service	700,000
Local Government	600,000
Teachers	370,000
National Health Service	400,000
Police	90,000

Scheme	Members
Firemen	25,000
National Coal Board Principal Scheme	95,000
Electricity Supply (England and Wales) Staff Scheme	55,000
Gas Industry Staff Scheme	35,000
British Railways Staff (LNER) Scheme	25,000
Airways Corporations Scheme (provisions affecting General Staff)	30,000
United Kingdom Atomic Energy Authority Principal Non-industrial Scheme	20,000

The plan of this chapter is first, to consider what are the main characteristics of these twelve schemes, taken as representative of the public sector, from the point of view of those matters which mainly affect the members, that is, contributions and benefits; secondly, to compare the different schemes with one another from the same point of view; thirdly, to consider what arrangements are made in the public sector for preservation of pension rights on change of employment; and lastly, to consider the effects of inflation on the benefits provided.

Details of the main provisions of the twelve schemes are set out in the table and notes forming Appendix 4 of this study. Their chief characteristic is that, with the partial exception of the Railways scheme, and of some doctors and dentists in the NHS scheme, they are all terminal-salary schemes, that is, the pension is expressed as a proportion of final salary. It is a further characteristic of these schemes that, with the exception of the Railways, the pension is calculated at 1/80 of final salary for each year of service with a lump sum equivalent to three years' pension; or, in those schemes where no lump sum is payable, the pension is based on 1/60 of final salary for each year of service. In the case of police and firemen, however, the calculation is so designed that a pension of one-half (30/60) is payable after twenty-five years' instead of thirty years' service, and two-thirds (40/60) after thirty years' service.

This characteristic terminal-salary pension basis in sixtieths or its assumed equivalent in eightieths plus a lump sum is found elsewhere in the public sector, and not simply in the twelve schemes considered here in detail. Notable exceptions to it are the two large schemes based on a fixed amount of pension for each year of service (Mineworkers' and Railways' Male Wages Grades), the scheme for the Armed Forces, and that for manual workers in the Gas Industry, but even so approximately two-thirds of the members of public sector schemes are in schemes of the eightieths/sixtieths type. There is also a close similarity among the twelve selected schemes in the range of

principal benefits offered, extending in many cases, as can be seen
from Appendix 4, to the precise manner in which the calculations
are made. The position may be summarized as follows:

1. Pension (or pension and lump sum) for retirement on age
   grounds, usually at 60 or over, and usually based on a maximum of forty years' service, though with the possibility of
   extension under certain conditions to a maximum of forty-five
   years' service.
2. Pension (or pension and lump sum) for retirement on grounds
   of ill-health—this is generally calculated as for retirement on
   age grounds provided that there has been a minimum period
   of ten years' service, and usually with a provision for a minimum
   payment.
3. Specific provision for the payment of a sum of money to the
   personal representative of a member who dies.
4. Widow's pension, usually at either one-third or one-half of the
   amount of the husband's pension.

This in broad terms is the general range of benefits to be found in
public sector schemes. Not all these benefits will be found in all these
schemes, and on the other hand a number of benefits which are to
be found in many of the schemes are not included in the list. But
taking these public sector schemes as a group, there is no doubt that
so far as the principal benefits are concerned and the manner in
which they are calculated, there is a close similarity in spite of the
many divergencies and despite the wide range of lesser benefits
which will be discussed later.

Two important points need to be stated here: in the first place,
both in money terms and in terms of the purpose of schemes, the
most important benefit is the pension (or pension and lump sum)
which the member expects to receive on retirement;[1] on the manner
of calculating this benefit there is very close agreement between the
schemes. In the second place, the divergencies between these different schemes are far less than between a group of private sector
schemes because in the latter there is no common pattern, a point
which is considered in more detail in Chapter 5.

It is this factor more than any other which makes it possible to
treat public sector schemes as a group in spite of differences between
them, and in spite of the fact that two very large schemes, the Mineworkers' and the Male Wages Grades of the Railways, do not fit
into this classification. The measure of uniformity which exists at
present is the result of a number of factors, among which may be

[1] As an illustration, in the N.C.B. Principal Scheme, 1962–63, out of a total
expenditure of nearly £9 million, over £6¼ million went on retirement pensions
and lump sums.

C*

mentioned the historical development of these schemes, and the watchful eye kept by the Treasury on schemes which may involve the expenditure of public money. The first accounts for the fact that a new scheme tended to build on the pattern of ones already established, as was illustrated in Chapter 2. The second has grown increasingly important as the size of the public sector has grown, so that, for example, any considerable increase in benefits secured by any one scheme would tend to lead to similar demands from members of other schemes. There is thus a very direct interest from the Treasury point of view in securing as great a measure of uniformity between the different schemes as possible.

COMPARISON OF TWELVE SCHEMES

If it is true, as was suggested above, that some kind of standard pattern can be discerned in public sector schemes, it is also true that anyone who reads through the various Acts, Regulations and Rules relating to the different schemes would be immediately struck by the apparent dissimilarities between them. This is partly the effect of the different language and presentation, from the numerous Acts of Parliament stretching from 1834 to the present day, which form the basis of the civil service scheme, to the slim booklet which constitutes the rules of the staff schemes of the Gas Industry. How far these outward dissimilarities conceal true differences between the twelve selected schemes is the subject of the detailed comparisons in this section.

1. *Membership*. Most public sector schemes are compulsory for full-time employees, the only exception in the twelve schemes being local government servants. Part-time employees are not generally covered by superannuation arrangements except where they combine two or more part-time posts within the public service (some teachers, for example), or where special circumstances arise; for example, part-time firemen may be eligible for injury awards but do not come under the general provisions of the scheme. A point to be noted is that membership of a scheme does not necessarily correspond to the numbers employed in a particular service; for example, although established civil servants, whether clerks, administrators, engineers or postmen, generally come under the Superannuation Acts, some civil servants for special reasons are superannuable under the Federated Superannuation System for Universities; in the case of police and firemen the schemes on the whole cover only full-time regulars; and in the case of some of the nationalized industries, notably Transport, many people remain in closed schemes. Normally, membership begins at the date of becoming employed in the parti-

cular service or industry, although in some cases a minimum age or a waiting period is specified.

2. *Contributions.* Contributions paid by members vary widely from scheme to scheme. Civil servants do not pay contributions except for the 1¼ per cent which some married men pay under the 1949 Superannuation Act to secure that if they should die their widows and children will receive benefits.[1] Teachers and non-manual workers in local government and the National Health Service pay 6 per cent (manual workers in these two schemes pay 5 per cent). Firemen pay 5 per cent and policemen 6¼ per cent (the police scheme is unusual in that policewomen pay a lower contribution of 4½ per cent), but the higher rate for policemen is related to better widows' pensions.

In the nationalized industries, the range of contributions is from 4 per cent (National Coal Board) to 8¼ per cent (for late entrants to the Railways' scheme), but the most common rates of contribution are 5 per cent or 6 per cent. The Gas scheme, like the police, provides for lower contributions from women, and with the introduction of widows' pensions in the Airways' scheme in 1963 a similar differentiation was introduced. The Railways' scheme is unusual among public sector schemes in providing for different rates of contribution according to the age of the member when he joins, the lowest rates being paid by the youngest entrants.

Important as the rate of contribution is to the members of schemes, the significance of variations in these rates between schemes can only be fully appreciated in the context of the costs of different schemes and the means which have been adopted for financing them. What the member pays is one aspect of this. These points are discussed more fully in Chapter 4.

3. *Age of retirement.* In the civil service, teachers' and National Health Service schemes, retirement may take place at 60, although the qualifying conditions vary in the different schemes, particularly for teachers. In local government, for the general body of members retirement at 60 or between 60 and 65 is only possible if the member has had forty years' service, and there is a compulsory retirement age of 65. In the police and firemen's schemes, retirement after twenty-five years' service is possible, although the pension cannot be drawn until the age of 50 unless the member has had thirty years' service; effectively, therefore, 50 is the minimum retiring age. In the nationalized industries, the most usual ages at which retirement may take place are 65 for men and 60 for women; the Railways' and Airways' schemes have different ages, but keep the distinction of an earlier retiring age for women.

[1] There is an alternative arrangement whereby some civil servants have their lump sums reduced instead of paying contributions.

The lack of uniformity in the age at which retirement may take place seems to be due principally to two factors. In the case of the police and firemen, the lower ages of retirement are part of the distinctive conditions of employment in these two services. But the distinction between the older central and local government schemes (with which, by analogy, goes the National Health Service), and the newer nationalized industries' schemes seems to be largely historical. In particular, the latter were influenced by the National Insurance scheme and newer ideas of what is a reasonable age for retirement. It is the older schemes which now seem out of step in permitting general retirement at 60, on the basis of what was fixed for the Civil Service a hundred years ago. The question has gained more prominence in recent years, particularly in relation to the need to encourage older people to remain in employment, and because of the increased expectation of life, although attention has perhaps been directed more to the National Insurance scheme than to public sector schemes.

4. *Qualification for Age Pension.* This is normally ten years' service in addition to any age restriction (as in 3 above) and the only significant variations are in the police and firemen's schemes where at least twenty-five years' service are usually necessary before a pension is payable, and the teachers' scheme where, except for married women, a total of thirty years' service (but not necessarily continuous) is required.

5. *Benefits on Retirement at or after Normal Pension Age.* The point has already been made that the pension, or pension and lump sum, payable on retirement is calculated in a very similar way in all of these schemes with the exception of the Railways' (LNER Staff) scheme. The most striking variation is in the police and firemen's schemes where effectively what happens is that calculation is 1/60 of pensionable pay for each year of service up to 20 and for each half-year of service from 20 to 30 years when the maximum of two-thirds (40/60) is reached.

The Gas scheme appears to have a peculiar variation but in fact the different way of calculating pension is simply due to the so-called 'modification' for National Insurance which is discussed in Chapter 6. Only the Railways' scheme departs from the normal in having the pension based in part on average salary throughout years of service; effectively this is a sixtieths scheme but related partly to average earnings during whole career, together with a lump sum in fortieths (which is based on final salary). This tends to emphasize the fact that unlike the other schemes, this is not an entirely new scheme introduced since nationalization, but an existing scheme which has been continued, though with modifications.

Another point of variation is in what constitutes final or terminal salary for the purpose of calculating the pension. Generally, this is now standardized as the average of the last three years' salary, but in the nationalized industries' schemes only Gas and AEA keep strictly to this method of calculation. In the remainder, there are variations (e.g. the average of the highest paid four or five consecutive years in the last twenty), often as alternatives to the last three years' average.

One may say that broadly speaking in these schemes at normal or minimum retiring age the maximum pension is equivalent to two-thirds of pensionable salary; this means that even in those schemes where it is possible to serve more than forty years by normal retiring age, the pension will only be calculated on forty years' service. This position arises particularly in those schemes where normal retirement is at age 65, and accounts for the fact that some schemes provide for contributions to cease after forty years.[1] However, it is general now in most schemes to permit a higher pension to be earned if work is continued beyond normal or minimum retiring age. This usually takes the form of adding one year to the calculation of pension (and lump sum where it exists) for every year served up to a maximum of five. The Gas scheme is more generous in adding 1½ per cent to the pension for each quarter of a year served beyond normal retiring age, although it may not be as common as in some other schemes to continue in service. The rather special arrangements in the police and firemen's schemes are in a separate category.

Finally, one important point must be made about the lump sum payments in those schemes which have them. In a number of schemes these lump sums are reduced for married men in order to meet the cost or part of the cost of providing widows' (and in some cases also children's) benefits, so that although it is true that the lump sum is generally calculated as 3/80 of average salary for each year of service, what the member actually receives if he is a married man and a member of the local government or National Health Service schemes will be reduced to one-third of this amount. The position, which is somewhat complicated, is discussed in Chapter 4.

7. *Benefits on Retirement before Normal Retiring Age because of Permanent Ill-health.* The usual provision is for a pension (or pension and lump sum) to be paid on exactly the same basis as for ordinary retirement provided that the member has ten years' service, but there is provision for a minimum payment in most schemes, the effect of

---

[1] One consequence is that in some schemes (e.g. police and firemen's) contributions might be paid for thirty-two years (age 18–50) and secure no higher pension than contributions paid for thirty years (i.e. a policeman or fireman joining at age 20 and retiring at age 50).

which is to make it unlikely that anyone except comparatively late-age entrants would receive as little as a pension calculated on ten years' service. Nevertheless, the precise formula by which the minimum payment is calculated does vary from scheme to scheme.

Provision for retirement because of ill-health after less than ten years' service shows much more variety in the different schemes: for example, in the Gas scheme no special provision is made; in the Airways' and Railways' schemes a pension is payable (though only of £20 per annum in the latter); and in the other schemes there is a lump sum grant but the amount and the qualifying period are far from being standardized.

8. *Benefits Payable on Death* (*excluding widows' pensions*). Generally speaking a death grant is payable to the personal representative of the dead member. The main distinction to be drawn here is between those schemes in which nothing is paid if some other award is payable (usually a widow's pension) and those where some payment is made, provided that the qualifying conditions are fulfilled, whether there is a widow's pension or not. To the first category belong the police, firemen's and Gas schemes; in these schemes if no widow's or other award is payable, a return of contributions is made. In the second category the award generally takes the form of a lump sum, but there are several different ways of calculating the amount in different schemes; furthermore, there are often one or even two alternative means of calculating the amount within a single scheme, and the recipient gets whichever provides the greatest sum of money. For example, the lump sum may be on the usual 3/80ths basis for each year of service, with an alternative or minimum amount of the equivalent of the pensionable salary. This means that the alternative will be greater unless the member has done twenty-seven or more years' service (i.e. $27 \times 3/80$ gives a fraction of 81/80 of pensionable salary).

Sometimes the amount of contributions paid by the member (with compound interest) provides a second alternative. It should be emphasized, however, that it is a characteristic feature of contributory schemes that unless some specific benefit is payable, contributions are refunded; this is not therefore a specific death benefit but rather the usual provision operating where death benefit cannot be claimed. As with the lump sum payable on age retirement the amount is sometimes reduced to meet the cost or part of the cost of the widow's pension, and this provides a further alternative calculation for the death benefit.[1]

[1] For example, in local government the death grant for a married man is either the reduced lump sum based on eightieths or, if greater, the excess of the death grant which would have been payable but for the widow's pension liability over the capital value of the widow's pension.

These are benefits payable when death occurs before retirement. If the member dies in retirement, the grant is usually limited to making up payments already made to him to some specified sum (e.g. five years' pension or the amount of death benefit as calculated above), so that the effect is that there is no death benefit except where death occurs within a few years of retirement. Finally, mention should be made of the special arrangement in the Railways' scheme for a joint annuity payable either after age 60 for death in service or on death in retirement.

9. *Widows' and Children's Pensions.* Widows' pensions are a comparatively recent feature of most public sector schemes and, before they developed, practically the only way in which members could make provision for their widows in the event of death was by the allocation of part of their own pensions for this purpose; even this provision does not have a long history, dating, in the case of the Civil Service, only from the Superannuation Act of 1935. Perhaps as a consequence of this comparatively late growth, both the level of widows' pensions and the means adopted for financing them vary a good deal from scheme to scheme. The latter point, which considerably affects comparisons, is considered in more detail in Chapter 4. Here it may be useful to note the following:

(i) Only two schemes make no provision for these benefits (teachers and Railways), but the 1956 Teachers' Superannuation Act made it possible for a scheme to be provided for teachers; so far no arrangement has been made, the chief obstacle being the problem of how the cost is to be shared.[1] In the case of the Railways, there is, as already mentioned, a provision for joint annuities.

(ii) The amounts of children's pensions show great variety, whether expressed as a fraction of the widow's pension or as a flat rate; furthermore in some schemes where there is a widow's pension there is no provision for children (e.g. local government).

(iii) To get the full effect of the difference in provisions it is useful to compare the two extremes of local government and NCB. Both schemes provide very similar principal benefits, but an officer in local government who is married pays 6 per cent in contributions and has his lump sum on retirement reduced by two-thirds to provide for a widow's pension of one-third of his pension and no children's pension, whereas the NCB

[1] The teachers would have been happy to share the cost 50–50 (as in the Civil Service and A.E.A.) but neither the Government nor the local authorities would agree to this.

officer in return for contributions of 5 per cent gets his lump sum in full, the same widow's pension and pensions for any dependent children if he dies. The implications of these different arrangements are considered in connexion with the finances of schemes in Chapter 4, but from the point of view of the employee it does seem that the important comparison is not simply of the amount of widow's pension but of what he gets for his money as a whole.

The above are some of the main points in these twelve schemes as seen by the members. There are many other benefits in these schemes, some of which concern perhaps a handful of members. There are also other matters which concern members, notably what service is counted in the different schemes towards a pension. It is difficult to make comparisons between schemes as a whole in the sense of weighing the value to the member of benefits in one scheme against benefits in another; for one thing it depends to a certain degree on the individual—to some members the fact that a scheme has a generous pension arrangement for widows may not be of such importance as whether it has a lump sum payment on retirement. Nevertheless, in terms of what he may receive for what contributions, the member of the NCB scheme on the face of it has the best bargain, apart from the police and firemen, as compared with older schemes such as teachers and local government. The Civil Service stands apart because nobody really knows what the civil servant is paying for his benefits.[1] Electricity is in all essentials like NCB except for the higher contributions. NHS and local government go closely together, and AEA, apart from the question of contributions, goes, as one might expect, very closely with the Civil Service. Gas and Airways have a number of distinctive features and Railways, for reasons already mentioned stands rather apart from the other schemes.

So far as the member of a scheme is concerned who hopes one day to benefit from it, it cannot be too strongly emphasized that what really counts is what he is going to get in the way of a pension in his old age, or if he is unfortunate, when his health breaks down; and here, if one excepts the Railways, the only significant differences are between the schemes which provide a pension only and those which provide a pension and a lump sum, significant that is in the sense of what a member is hoping to receive in cash terms. This is not to ignore the importance of death benefits, widows' pensions and other lesser benefits but merely to emphasize that most people

[1] In evidence to the Priestley Commission on the Civil Service, Treasury witnesses conceded that but for the fact of superannuation, civil service rates of pay might be higher; see Royal Commission on the Civil Service 1953–55, Minutes of Evidence, 17th Day (September 28, 1954), Q. 2585, also Q. 2588.

expect to and do live a normal period of working life, followed by some years of retirement. For roughly similar benefits, however, a man may have to pay a different proportion of his income in different schemes; his employer may pay as much as, twice as much as, or more than twice as much as he does (including deficiency payments). Why this should be so is discussed in the next chapter.

PRESERVATION OF BENEFITS ON CHANGE OF EMPLOYMENT

An important element in pension schemes is the extent to which the provision of benefits is dependent on service in the particular employment to which the scheme is related. This question has assumed greater importance as the number of pension schemes has grown, largely because of its connexion with the subject of mobility of staff. If a scheme makes no provision for the preservation in some form of the entitlement to benefit already earned when a member moves to other employment, then this fact may in itself act as a deterrent to movement which on other grounds is desirable. This section describes something of the history of and present arrangements for preserving pension rights on change of employment in public sector schemes.

To some degree the arrangements adopted in different schemes depend on the view taken of the purpose of the scheme. For example, it is clear that if a pension is regarded as the end secured by a contract between employer and employed; and if the employee's side of the contract is to serve his employer for a certain number of years until a certain age, then if the employee leaves before his time he is strictly in breach of the contract and forfeits all his rights. This view of the matter was the one put by the Treasury to the Priestley Commission on the Civil Service.[1] No doubt in the case of the Civil Service there are two special features which help to reinforce this view; one is that the scheme is nominally non-contributory, the other that the civil servant has no legal entitlement to a pension. If a scheme is contributory, it is hard not to say that a man who leaves is entitled at least to the return of what he has put in, even though strictly on the Treasury view there is no reason why he should be entitled to it; and in fact all contributory schemes do make provision for at least the return of contributions.

But perhaps even more important than the general view of pensions in influencing attitudes to the question of preservation of pension rights has been the view taken of the nature of a career in the public service. For if the public service, or still more a particular part of it such as the Civil Service, is regarded as being a career for life this

[1] See especially evidence of Treasury Witnesses, 17th Day (September 28, 1954), Q. 2574 and 2590.

will reinforce the view that a man who leaves before his time is breaking his part of the bargain and cannot therefore complain at losing, among other things, his pension rights or expectations. It was this view, that 'the Civil Service is a career service and transfers should be exceptional rather than frequent', which chiefly influenced the Priestley Commission in recommending no change in the arrangements for transfer of pension rights.[1] In doing so they accepted, at least by implication, both the importance of transfer of pension rights in affecting mobility, and the unwillingness of some civil servants to subscribe to the life service doctrine. For those who did would neither want to move nor be much affected by any extension of transfer arrangements.

But whatever the reasons for treating preservation of pension rights as something exceptional, it is of interest to see how far modifications have been made in practice to the strict contract view of pensions. This can best be done by noting the various stages at which the Civil Service has departed from the strict view, and then describing what the present situation is. The reasons for treating the subject in this way are that it is in relation to the Civil Service that discussion of the question has been most explicit and that, generally speaking, where changes have been made, other schemes have followed a pattern laid down for the Civil Service. This does not necessarily reflect the relative interest in preservation in the different schemes but rather the importance of the Treasury in influencing the way in which such matters are treated.

(1) *Preservation in the Civil Service, 1911–1948*

Apart from some earlier arrangements of minor importance, the Public Office Rules, 1911, first established a procedure for paying either a single pension to a man who had served in more than one employment, the cost being shared between the two or more employers, or two or more separate pensions calculated for each period of employment and paid separately by each employer. The choice of method depended on what superannuation arrangements each employer had, the first method being used where the arrangements were either the same or very similar. These two methods correspond to the two main ideas which have ever since dominated thinking on this question, namely the outright transfer with the second or final employer taking responsibility for payment of the whole pension or the 'cold storage' or 'frozen' pension. So far as the Civil Service is concerned, although the Treasury told the Priestley Commission that the use of the Public Office procedure is quite common, this does not represent in practice a very wide field since the arrangements apply

[1] See in particular Report, Cmd. 9613, 1955, paras. 700–707.

either to semi-civil service bodies such as the Forestry Commission or to service with Colonial governments.

A further extension based on the 'frozen' pension idea was made possible by the Superannuation Act of 1914.[1] Employment could be approved by the Treasury and the department in which a man was serving, and if it was approved he could transfer to that employment knowing that his pension, calculated on the number of years he had spent in the Civil Service and his salary at the time he left, would be paid him when he reached retiring age, provided that he remained in an (though not necessarily the same) approved employment. If, meanwhile, he returned to the Civil Service, he could count his earlier years of Civil Service towards his final pension. In theory, there is no limit to the employment which might be approved in this way, but in practice the criterion of public interest has been applied and employment 'of a private or commercial character' has not been approved. In the years 1952 and 1953 transfers to approved employment were about eighty a year, to such places as NATO, the British Sugar Corporation and the Commonwealth Institute of Entomology, and even this modest amount of movement is probably more than in pre-war days. In 1960–61 there were 200 transfers to approved employment.

(2) *The 1948 Arrangements and After*

Apart from one or two other special arrangements to meet particular circumstances,[2] this was the situation in the Civil Service until 1948 and it cannot be said that any great breach had been made in the concept of the Civil Service as a life career. The post-war situation raised new problems; not only did large numbers of people come into the Civil Service as a result of the extension of the activities of central government but many of the new public bodies such as the National Health Service and the nationalized Electricity industry took a large part of their staff from the existing public service, notably from local government but also to some degree from the Civil Service as in the case of the U.K. Atomic Energy Authority set up in 1954. One result was that employment which had been commercial (e.g. Coal) now became public and this in itself would have needed some change in the existing arrangements. What happened in 1948 under the Superannuation (Miscellaneous Provisions) Act was that it was made generally possible to transfer between two public employments, under certain conditions, without loss of pension rights.[3]

[1] Strictly speaking, one should regard this as an extension of an idea which first began to operate in a limited way under the 1859 Act.

[2] E.g. with local government for people with special qualifications and with the FSSU for scientists (some scientists were able to remain under FSSU when they became civil servants).

[3] It should be noted, however, that transfers to and from the National Health Service are dealt with mainly under Regulations made under the National Health Service Act 1946.

The pension was paid by the second (or final) employer and a financial adjustment made between the two employers in the form of the payment of a 'transfer value' by the first employer. The matter is not quite as simple as it sounds because each separate 'interchange rule' is the subject of one or more statutory instruments so that there are separate rules for interchange between the Civil Service and local government, Civil Service and teaching, etc.; in the case of the nationalized industries and other parts of the public sector outside central and local government, a single set of rules generally covers the transfer arrangements, e.g. from the Civil Service to what are known collectively as 'Public Boards'. The main reason for these rules is that the various pension schemes, although similar, are not identical. All the major parts of the public sector (except, at present, Transport and the police) are fully covered by these arrangements and the ramifications extend to such bodies as the Sugar Board, the Commonwealth Institute and the Jersey Civil Service, but not to any private commercial or industrial undertaking.

Finally, mention should be made of an arrangement peculiar to the Civil Service and in part deriving from the fact that voluntary retirement normally means loss of everything, whereas in most schemes there is at least the entitlement to return of contributions. Since the 1949 Superannuation Act it has been possible for a civil servant to retire at any time after the age of 50 and to have his pension from the age of 60. This provision is not conditional either on what his department or the Treasury says or on how the civil servant proposes to spend his time once he has left the service. It is not, of course, specifically a provision for preservation of pension rights on transfer from one employment to another, but it may operate in this way for those who are able to get another job at the age of 50 or more, and this has been of particular benefit to senior civil servants. For example, a Second Secretary in the Treasury resigned at 50 to become a Director of Vickers, and a Permanent Secretary of the Board of Trade left at 56 to become a Director of English Electric.

Recently, too, there have been signs that at least in relation to senior civil servants government policy on preservation may be still further modified. The Joint Permanent Secretary to the Treasury, in evidence to the Estimates Committee in March 1964, said, 'I think it is good for the life of the nation that people should move out. We do not, in general, I think, lose severely through people moving out to industry.'[1] Although this view was accepted only with reservations by the Committee, it was followed in June 1964 by a government announcement relaxing the rules to permit members of the Higher Civil Service to leave the service before the age of 50 with a frozen

[1] Fifth Report from the Estimates Committee, 1963–64, Treasury Control of Establishments, H.C. 228, Q. 1109.

pension in order to take posts in private industry. This proposal was linked with another proposal to recruit annually a small number of higher civil servants from industry, thus demonstrating the influence of views on the desirability of encouraging greater mobility of senior staff in the narrower field of preserving pension rights. Both the wider and the narrower points will be examined in Chapter 10 in relation to the future of public sector schemes.

In other public sector schemes before 1948 the doctrine of life service was practically complete. There were a few exceptions, notably in the teachers' scheme where 'approved external service' operated on similar lines to approved employment in the Civil Service, but generally speaking those who started their careers in a particular branch of the public service had to remain in that branch if they wanted a pension. The effect of the 1948 Act has been to modify this to the extent that by and large a pension is granted after a career spent in the public sector and not simply in a particular branch of it.

For those, however, who wish to move from the public sector to the private very little opportunity exists for preserving pension rights. It is true that, apart from the Civil Service, public sector schemes are generally contributory and therefore a member leaving may get a refund of the amount of the contributions which he has paid, usually with compound interest; this refund he may be able to use to buy some credit in the pension scheme of his new employment. Even if he can do this he will inevitably lose something, chiefly because his employer's contributions will remain in the public sector fund, incidentally contributing to the profit of that fund.

Apart from the special civil service arrangement outlined above, only the nationalized industries offer opportunities of transferring to the private sector without loss of pension rights. In all the main nationalized industries' schemes considered here there is provision for reciprocal arrangements to be made with private schemes for the receipt and payment of transfer values. These provisions may be subject to qualifications (e.g. the member may have to have done a minimum period of service, or the private scheme may have to have been approved by the Inland Revenue for tax purposes), but they are fairly general in the nationalized industries and a number of other public boards (e.g. the BBC). It is also usual in these schemes to make it possible to have a deferred (i.e. 'cold storage') pension payable at normal retiring age (or occasionally, as in the Airways' scheme, at an earlier age at a reduced rate); and a further alternative is provided in some schemes (e.g. NCB, Electricity, AEA) so that the member's 'actuarial reserve', i.e. his entire interest in the fund at the date of departure and not simply the amount of his own contributions, may be used for the purchase of an annuity payable from normal retiring age. It might be thought that a member of those schemes was completely safeguarded by these provisions, but everything turns on how they are used in practice. In the case of the NCB scheme, transfer to other employment has to be with the consent of the employer, but even where this is not so, it may often happen that the member himself prefers to receive his own contributions back and this is an important factor when considering how much transfer of pension rights actually takes place.

(3) *Transfers in Practice*

There is little in the way of comprehensive information about how the transfer arrangements and, particularly those under the 1948 Act, work in practice. Some evidence was presented to the Royal Commission on the Civil Service by the Treasury and showed that in the year 1952–53 about 560 civil servants transferred under the 1948 and similar transfer rules, of whom most went to the National Health Service (230), local government (150) and teaching (20).[1] More recent figures for 1962 supplied by the Treasury show that in that year there were about 1,250 transfers, exclusive of those to the National Health Service, and that of these, most (about 480) were to local government and 250 to teaching, with about 430 to 'public boards'. Voluntary retirements after the age of 50 with entitlement to a deferred pension have increased sharply in recent years, from an average of around 350 a year in the period 1951 to 1955 to around 950 a year in 1958 to 1961.[2]

Figures supplied by the Ministry of Education show that about 730 people transferred to teaching in 1962–63 and rather more than half that number transferred from teaching to other parts of the public sector; movement into teaching was mostly from local government (293) and the Civil Service (195), and movement out largely to local government (204) with a much smaller number (84) going to the National Health Service. There is a comparatively large amount of movement between the National Health Service and local government, over 3,000 people going from the first to the second in 1962, and nearly 2,000 in the opposite direction, but this probably reflects the close link between the two services for certain functions (e.g. nursing and midwifery).

In the Electricity scheme in recent years an average of about 350 members a year have been joining from other public sector schemes, mostly local government and to a lesser extent the Civil Service and

[1] See Royal Commission Report, Cmd. 9613, 1955, p. 230.

[2] See *Whitley Bulletin*, July 1963, p. 108. In a few cases immediate rather than deferred pensions may be granted. It appears from the figures that the increase in recent years has been largely among industrial staff; corresponding figures for non-industrial staff only are 250 and 380.

National Coal Board, and about 270 have been leaving, mostly to local government. On the other hand there has been only a handful of transfers either to or from private schemes. These figures relate to a total membership of around 55,000 and compare with annual figures of approximately 3,000 withdrawals with refunds of contributions. In the NCB principal scheme, 320 members transferred to other schemes in 1961–62 out of a total membership of nearly 100,000 and this compares with withdrawals of 4,500. Again, from figures supplied by the U.K. Atomic Energy Authority, it is possible to estimate that transfers into their schemes have averaged about 275 a year in the last 6½ years, transfers out about 160 a year, and withdrawals with return of contributions about 2,000 a year.

Fragmentary as this information is, it does suggest two things: first, that even with the fairly elaborate and comprehensive arrangements for transfers within the public sector which now exist the amount of regular movement is not large, that is, excluding such special movements as the large-scale transfers from local government to the National Health Service when the latter was created. This may mean that there is little opportunity to move; or that most people still regard the particular employment which they join as a life career; or simply that even where there is an opportunity to transfer they prefer to take the cash represented by their accumulated contributions. Secondly, in terms of numbers, withdrawals are greater than transfers, but it must be remembered that a great many withdrawals, e.g. of girls on marriage, have nothing to do with the question of change of employment. Perhaps of more significance are the amounts paid in the respective cases. For example, on average each transfer value paid out of the Electricity scheme in recent years amounted to about £500, and each refund of contributions about £100. Admittedly, transfer values include an element for the employer's contributions which would tend to increase their average value, but even so these figures are at least consistent with the commonly held view that many lower-paid employees are less concerned with maintaining their pension rights than with obtaining a cash payment when they leave.

It is therefore not easy to assess what transfer arrangements mean to those who are members of schemes as opposed to merely describing what those arrangements are. We do not know whether there would be much more movement of staff if, as in the National Insurance scheme, there was no refund of contributions but automatic preservation of pension rights in occupational (including public sector) schemes. It might well be that because employees of different ages and status took different views the total amount of movement might not change much, although it might be distributed in a different manner. It is perhaps surprising that in view of the recent interest in preservation of pension rights in relation to mobility, no thorough inquiry has been undertaken to assess what the likely effect would be of extending such arrangements.

EFFECTS OF INFLATION

Description of the benefits provided by public sector schemes would not be complete without some reference to a problem which has become increasingly important in the last twenty years: however generous a pension may be when awarded, its true value will, in a period of inflation, soon diminish unless steps are taken to maintain it. The position in public sector schemes is that without exception they lay down the scale of benefits to be awarded but make no provision for varying the amount of pension once a member has retired. The basic principle was stated by Mr Amory when Chancellor of the Exchequer to be that 'pensions are directly related to length of service and pay on retirement and, once awarded, are not normally altered'.[1]

Such a principle presupposes that in the normal state of affairs the value of money remains stable or at least declines only slowly, but certainly in the period since the war this assumption has not proved very satisfactory to employees in practice. Adjustments have been made from time to time to pensions being paid from central and local government schemes by means of a series of specific Pensions (Increase) Acts.[2] These have tended to become more extensive in scope, perhaps under the realization that inflation, if not the normal state of affairs, is at least not quite so abnormal as had been assumed; but so far there has been no indication that the principle stated by Mr Amory is likely to be superseded.

However, one consequence of the long-continued decline in the true value of pensions, for which periodic Pensions (Increase) Acts have provided only a partial answer, is that there has been an increasing demand for more positive and regular measures to maintain the value of pensions. This demand has taken two forms; that pensions should be automatically linked to current salary scales for similar service ('parity') or that there should be an automatic review of pensions every two years. The first, which has been pressed by, among others, the National Union of Teachers, would mean abandoning the principle that the amount of pension is calculated on final salary earned, and so far has been met with the answer that 'Her Majesty's Government, like all previous Governments, are unable to accept such a fundamental and costly change in the principles

[1] H.C. Deb., June 2, 1959, col. 40.

[2] In 1944, 1947, 1952, 1954, 1956, 1959 and 1962; the 1954 Act was, however, very limited in scope. There were also earlier Acts in 1920 and 1924 following the First World War.

governing public service pensions'. The second, which has been supported by the Civil Service Staff Side, was extensively discussed during the debates on the Pensions (Increase) Bill, 1962, in the House of Commons. In April 1964, however, the Staff Side proposed to the Treasury a modified form of parity which, like earlier suggestions, was rejected.

An interesting feature of the 1962 debates was that many speakers emphasized that it was unsatisfactory to have Pensions (Increase) Acts every few years even though they did not necessarily regard a biennial review as the right solution. In reply the Chief Secretary to the Treasury (Mr Boyd-Carpenter) gave a guarded and cautious promise: 'I will endeavour to find whether some improvement in our system is possible . . . [to] enable the consideration of all these very human and important matters to be a little more smooth and a little more effective, in some ways, than is the present procedure.' The chief Opposition spokesman, Mr Houghton, was equally cautious, but dropped a hint that a long-term solution might be negotiated whereby those at present serving might have some guarantee that their pensions would retain their value, although this might involve some extra charge on serving members of schemes.[1]

There are other ways too in which the problem might be tackled, e.g. by linking pensions to a cost-of-living index or to an index of wage or salary rates. Either of these could be done in conjunction with a regular review of pensions. Clearly the application of such ideas is wider than simply public sector schemes; inflation affects private sector schemes and the state scheme too. For this reason, the wider implications will be considered in the final chapter of this study. But in view of the close connexion with the cost of schemes and the methods of financing them, this aspect will be considered in the next chapter.

[1] H.C. Deb., November 20, 1962, cols. 1162–7.

CHAPTER 4

Public Sector Schemes: The Financial Arrangements

FUNDING

As was indicated in the previous chapter, to the member of a pension scheme it is not only the benefits which are important, but also whether he will have to contribute part of his wages or salary towards their cost and, if so, how much. The contributions, if any, which a member pays form, however, only a part of the arrangements for financing the cost of pension benefits. The main object of this chapter is to describe the different methods of financing which have been adopted in the public sector, and some of the factors which influence the cost of pension schemes.

But first something must be said about the general problem of financing pensions. The distinguishing feature of a pension scheme is that the benefit outgo is small at first but will gradually rise as more and more employees retire on pension. This rising outgo will continue for very many years as new entrants to the employer's service join the scheme and thus over a long period add to the growing number of beneficiaries, i.e. employed persons and pensioners.

This well-known fact has led to the general adoption of funding as a means of making provision for the payment of pension benefits as they become due. What usually happens in private sector schemes is that an employer who wishes to provide pension benefits for his employees on their retirement executes a trust deed under which a fund is established, the trustees being under obligation to make benefit payments of defined amounts at defined intervals to defined persons.

In order to create the assets necessary to meet the obligations for benefit payments, the trust deed provides that the employer (and possibly the employee also) shall make payments to the fund for the purpose of ensuring (so far as possible) that the benefits can be paid. This is the process of funding, and the payments into the fund are, especially if they are made regularly and by employees, known as contributions.

But although this is the essential outline of funding, there are many different methods of funding which could be devised. To take an extreme case—for example, if an employer decided to pay into the fund just as much as was needed to meet the outgo and paid it into the fund one day before payment became due, he could still be said in theory to be funding, but in such a way that he would gain none of the advantages of funding. For the whole object of funding is, by paying into the fund more than is immediately required for meeting the cost of benefits, and especially in the early years when payments out are small, to have a current surplus which can be invested. This helps to build up the fund and to produce an investment income which in the long run will be needed to pay for the ultimately much larger annual outgo.

In this process, perhaps the three most important elements are the total cost of the benefits, the rate of funding adopted, and the division of the cost between employer and employee. All these three points will need to be examined in relation to funded public sector schemes, but it may be useful to state here that the method of funding which is of most importance so far as these schemes go is what may be termed the 'new entrant contribution' basis. The object of such a method is to determine a total rate of contribution which would be sufficient if paid by and on behalf of the average new entrant to the scheme throughout all his years of service to support the benefits provided by the scheme. For those already in service when the scheme starts there is generally provision for the payment into the fund of regular annual sums which should be sufficient to meet these 'back-service' liabilities over a fixed and stated number of years. It will be clear, therefore, that a most important part of such schemes is how the total contribution rate is determined and how it is decided what proportion, if any, of it is to be paid by the employee.

Although it was said above that funding in some form has generally been adopted to finance the payment of pension benefits, the first and most characteristic point to be made about public sector schemes is that this statement is not true about them. Over 50 per cent of the members of public sector schemes (and practically 60 per cent if the Armed Forces are included) are in schemes where there is no accumulation at all of surplus income, and therefore no fund in the generally accepted sense of the term. These schemes are genericallly described here as 'pay-as-you-go' because benefits have to be met currently out of whatever income is available.[1]

Thus a major distinction between the private and the public sectors is that in the former all schemes, practically speaking, are funded, and in the latter many are not. But just as there are different

[1] The technical term 'assessmentism' is applied to pay-as-you-go schemes in which the contribution income in a limited period is adjusted so that it always balances expenditure in that period. The National Insurance scheme is run on this principle.

methods of funding, so there are different ways of arranging pay-as-you-go schemes, depending chiefly on how the liabilities of the scheme are assessed and what contributions, if any, members pay. These points will be examined later, but in terms of the main distinction the principal public sector schemes may be classified as follows:

Funded	*Pay-as-you-go*
Local Government	Civil Service
National Coal Board	Teachers
(Principal and Mineworkers')	National Health Service
Electricity	Police
(Staff and Manual Workers')	Firemen
Gas	Railways' Male Wages Grades
(Staff and Manual Workers')	Atomic Energy Authority
Railways' Staff	(Non-industrial and Industrial)
Airways	

As far as the funded schemes in the classification are concerned, the general principle followed is that for each scheme there is one fund. Thus a single fund has been established for the whole of the Electricity Supply industry's staff scheme and a separate fund for the Manual Workers' scheme. The major exception to this principle is the local government scheme, in which, as was described in Chapter 2, there are over 500 separate funds. These funds are financially autonomous, that is, the responsibility for their investment lies entirely with the administering authority, subject to the limitations imposed by Act of Parliament; and each is individually assessed by means of periodical actuarial valuations, as described below.

The Gas industry also has a unique arrangement; there are formally thirteen separate schemes and correspondingly thirteen separate funds, covering the Gas Council and each of the twelve Area Boards in Great Britain. Since the schemes for staff and manual workers are also separate, this means in theory twenty-six schemes and twenty-six funds. In fact there is machinery to ensure that the rules of the thirteen staff schemes are identical, and similarly with the thirteen manual workers' schemes. There is separate management for each of the schemes and therefore of the funds, which may operate in a similar way to the separate local government funds. However, the rules of the schemes provide also for the establishment of a central fund managed by a central committee consisting of representatives of the separate schemes, and the management of the schemes may choose to invest their funds through the central fund.

As will be clear from the first two chapters of the study, the past history of public sector schemes does not provide any clear-cut answer to the questions whether schemes should be funded and whether they should be contributory. The civil service scheme, for example, was once contributory and, for a brief period, funded; the police scheme had funds until 1921; and at least one of the precursors of the local government scheme, that for poor law officers, was contributory but not funded.

The implications of this situation will be examined more fully in Chapter 9, but the classification shown above seems to indicate a tendency for schemes to be non-funded where the central government has a direct interest either in the financing or the administration (or both) of the scheme. This would apply to the first three pay-as-you-go schemes listed and, to some degree, to the Atomic Energy Authority whose finances come mainly, although not entirely, from the Exchequer; but it applies much less to the police, firemen's and railways' male wages grades schemes. It is also noticeable that all the funded schemes are in the nationalized industries with the (very large) exception of the local government scheme.

It was suggested above that, apart from the method of funding, important differences between funded schemes lay in the total cost of the benefits and how that cost, in terms of contributions, was shared between employer and employee. Again, before considering the situation in funded public sector schemes, it will be useful to see how in general the cost of funded schemes is assessed.

Assessment of the cost of schemes is carried out by the actuary of the scheme, but since, for reasons which will become clearer later, cost is not a fixed item for all time but is related to a number of factors which may vary over a period of time, his task is really twofold. He must first assess, when a scheme is started, what the proposed scale of benefits is likely to cost and, for the 'new entrant contribution' basis of funding which is usual in the public sector, this means expressing the cost as a total rate of contribution, generally in terms of a percentage of wages or salaries. But, secondly, he must also, by means of periodical valuations, assess the progress of the fund to see, among other things, whether the original contribution rate is still correct. And as a corollary of the first task, he must also assess the cost of any changes proposed to be made in the range or scale of benefits of the scheme.

For the first task he needs to take into account a number of variable factors, among them:

(i) the *age-distribution* of the members of a scheme (for example, if on the whole the average age of entry is high there will be less time for the members' contributions to accumulate in the fund, as well as less money paid in by way of contributions);[1]

[1] I.e. on the assumption (which is general in public sector schemes) that members pay the same rate of contribution whatever their age on joining; but note that the Railways' staff scheme is exceptional in having different rates of contribution according to age on entry.

(ii) the *mortality, ill-health* and *withdrawal* rates which are likely to apply to these members (for example, a high withdrawal rate may benefit the fund which will probably only have to pay out the member's accumulated contributions in most cases);

(iii) the *salary-scales* applying to members—obviously, in a terminal-salary scheme the most important factor is the salary which a man will be earning just before he retires; the actuary must therefore calculate the progression of salaries with age; but there is also the important question of whether the salary-scales themselves are likely to be increased;

(iv) the *rate of interest* which is likely to be earned on the fund's investments—the higher the rate of interest which can be assumed, the less (other things being equal) the contribution rate which will be needed to support the benefits.

It is fairly obvious that no two schemes are likely to have exactly the same experience in relation to all these factors and the result will be that even where schemes have very broadly the same scale of benefits, the total rate of contribution will not necessarily be the same. And where the total rate of contribution differs, there is also likely to be a difference in the rate paid by the employee.[1]

In making his initial assessment of the total cost, then, the actuary is projecting the situation which he finds into the future, and trying to assess what value should be attached to the contribution element if the fund is to be just sufficient to meet the cost of all the benefits which are likely to have to be paid to a typical member of the scheme. It is important to make clear that in making his assessment the actuary is not directly concerned with what in fact may happen to the fund; it may, for example, receive a sudden large influx of young new members, the effect of which will be to increase the total of contributions immediately at a far greater rate than the increase in pensions, and thus the fund will build up more rapidly. What the actuary is concerned with is to ensure as far as possible that if his assumptions are correct the contributions which those members make will be adequate to meet the benefits which eventually will need to be paid to them, taking the scheme as a whole.[2]

It will be clear that the actuary in performing his first task has to

[1] There is of course no necessary connexion between the two; if the total contribution for one scheme was assessed at 12 per cent and for another at 14 per cent, the employee might in both cases pay 6 per cent. But the wider the difference in total cost the less likely that the employee will pay exactly the same.

[2] It is of course unlikely that any particular individual member will pay just enough in contributions to meet his own benefits; the typical member is an abstraction, and the fund is more like a pool in which over the long term the inflow equals the outflow.

make a number of assumptions as a basis for his calculations, and these assumptions need to be tested from time to time. For example, if, after a period of time, interest rates fall and the fund cannot earn the rate of interest used in the initial calculations, contributions may need to be increased to fulfil the funding plan originally adopted. This is one reason why in all funded schemes there is provision for an actuarial valuation to be made, often every five years, and this is the second main task of the actuary indicated above.

In making his periodic valuations the actuary needs, of course, to take into account the same factors as in making his initial assessment of cost. But his point of view is rather different; he is now trying to establish whether, on the necessary assumptions, the fund is likely to be sufficient to pay the prospective and current benefits of existing members and pensioners. Again, it is important realize that he is not concerned with predicting the actual progress of the fund, but only with ensuring that if the fund were immediately closed to new members it would not be exhausted until the last surviving pensioner (or his widow) from among the present members had died, perhaps sixty or more years ahead from the date of the valuation.

The point of the valuation is thus to provide a criterion for the solvency of the fund. For clearly if the actuary's assumptions are correct, then the fund will be able to meet all its liabilities, whatever happens. For this purpose, he compares the capitalized value of the benefits with the capitalized value of future contributions plus the value of the existing fund. If all his assumptions prove exactly right, or if the variations in practice cancel out, no action need be taken following the actuarial valuation, but of course this is not likely to happen very often.

Take, for example, the question of interest rates; £1,000 invested annually at an average rate of interest of 3 per cent will have accumulated in forty years to £75,000 but at 4 per cent to £95,000, that is, an amount over 25 per cent higher. Most pension funds have a fairly wide range of investments, and it is not easy for the actuary to select a rate of interest which is likely to be a reasonable approximation to what the investments will, on average, earn. At the same time a difference of $\frac{1}{2}$ per cent, or even $\frac{1}{4}$ per cent in the rate assumed at the valuation will make an appreciable difference to the result of the calculations. In practice, the actuary will try to ensure that the balance of the various assumptions accurately reflects the progress of the fund, but nevertheless the individual assumptions are important. If the capitalized value of the benefits exceeds the capitalized value of future contributions plus the existing fund, there is said to be a deficiency at the valuation, and if the reverse is the case, there is a surplus. Generally speaking, action will be taken following the declaration of a deficiency or a surplus, often by an increase in the contribution rate in the former case (for the employer if not for the employee), and by a reduction in contributions or, sometimes, an improvement in the benefits in the case of a surplus.

FUNDED SCHEMES IN THE PUBLIC SECTOR

In considering the finances of funded schemes in the public sector in detail, the first point to examine is the question of total cost and how it is shared between employer and employee. The question is complicated by the fact that the financing of family benefits (that is, widows', children's and other dependants' allowances) varies a good deal from scheme to scheme. This in turn may reflect the different experiences of the schemes, particularly in comparison of the local government with the newer nationalized industries' schemes.

The bare facts, taking only the funded schemes of those which were selected for detailed comparison in Chapter 3, may be summarized as follows:

Contributions in Funded Schemes

Scheme	Woman or Single man		Married man contributing for family benefits	
	Employee	Employer	Employee	Employer
Local Government	6% (5% servant	6% 5%)	As for a woman, but the lump sum on retirement is reduced by two-thirds	
NCB Principal	4%	8%	5%	10%
Electricity Staff	5%	10%	6%	12%
Gas Staff	5½% (women only)	*	6½%	*
Railways' Staff	5% (varies with age at entry)	5%	No family benefits	
Airways' General Staff	5% (women only)	*	6½%	*

Notes: (1) Widows' pensions are normally one-third of the husband's pension in local government, NCB and Electricity but one-half in Gas and Airways.
(2) The asterisks indicate that no specific contribution is payable by the employer and he meets the balance of cost (in fact this comes to about double the employees' constributions at the moment).
(3) In Gas and Airways all men pay 6½ per cent but bachelors get a refund of part of their contributions on retirement.

As the notes to this table indicate, it is not easy to indicate even the bare facts without a certain amount of qualification, but one or two general points may be made. The first and most obvious is that the local government officer is paying a higher proportion of the total cost of the benefits than the member of the NCB and Electricity schemes, the two schemes which are most directly comparable with that for local government. The second is that, although for the general reasons given earlier the total cost of schemes providing similar benefits is bound to show variation, the range of variation is fairly small; excluding family benefits (and excluding also the rather different Railways' scheme), the range is between 12 per cent (local government, NCB) and 15 per cent or a little over (Electricity, Gas, Airways).[1] The third point is that there are two main ways of paying for family benefits, either through a reduction in some other benefit (local government) or through additional contributions, the latter being again subdivided according to whether the contributions are voluntary (NCB, Electricity) or compulsory (Gas, Airways).

What he pays and how he pays it are naturally important matters for the member of a scheme, and it is worth drawing attention to the fact that much of the variation between schemes arises from a deliberate decision about how the cost is to be shared. If, for example, in the NCB scheme the cost of the benefits had been shared equally at $7\frac{1}{2} + 7\frac{1}{2}$ per cent for a married man, the gap between what the member pays in local government and NCB would have been very much reduced. There would, however, have remained the very real difference in the form in which contributions were made and benefits received.

The effect on the member is of course only one aspect of the financing of benefits. From the employer's point of view, it is just as important to look at the total amounts which he is paying into the scheme and what proportion they bear to the total cost. In the following table based on the detailed figures in Appendix 5, four of the six schemes are compared to show the proportion of income coming from different sources (the Railways' and Airways' schemes have been omitted since they do not have, or have only recently had in the case of the Airways, provision for family benefits).

Again, such figures must be used with caution and need to be interpreted in the light of the different stages which the schemes have reached; the nationalized industries' funds, for example, are still building up rapidly, whereas many local government funds have been in existence for thirty years or more. Furthermore, the relatively

[1] The lower rates for local government servants are almost entirely due to their much smaller progression of salaries with age, and they are therefore more comparable with manual workers in nationalized industries (not shown in the table).

D

large amounts contributed to the income of the Electricity and Gas schemes by transfer payments (in 'Other' column) again make comparisons difficult; the figures given in brackets show what the position would be if the 'Other' column were omitted.

Proportions of Annual Income from Different Sources

	Employees' contributions	Employers' contributions Normal	Back service deficiency, etc.	Investments	Other
Local Government (1960–61)	25% (27)	25% (27)	15% (16)	29% (30)	6% (—)
NCB (1962–63)	20% (20)	38% (39)	½% (1)	39% (40)	2½% (—)
Electricity (1961–62)	20% (23)	39% (43)	Negligible (—)	30% (34)	11% (—)
Gas (1960–61)	21% (25)	40% (45)		26% (30)	13% (—)

Nevertheless, certain points may be made; the relatively high income from investments in the NCB scheme means that less is needed in contributions and, particularly, given the 2:1 division of the total cost, in employee contributions.[1] The 1:1 division of the cost in local government disguises the fact that if the employers' very large payments for back service and deficiencies are included, the actual ratio of annual payments is more like 8:5 between employer and employee. It is indeed a noticeable feature of the table how similar all four schemes are in terms of the proportion of the total annual payment made by the employer.

In comparing schemes in this way, the importance of income from investments is obvious, and one factor which deserves mention is the policies which have been followed on investment. Partly, this is a question of restrictions; thus, before the Trustee Investments Act of 1961 local authorities were very largely restricted (under Section 21 of the 1937 Act) either to investing in gilt-edged securities or to borrowing money from the fund for other capital purposes, and paying interest to the fund equivalent to what they would have had to pay on a loan raised on mortgage. Under the 1961 Act, local authorities (like other trustees) may now invest up to 50 per cent of their funds (on certain conditions) in equities.

[1] The recent valuation surplus on the scheme (due largely to higher interest rates) shows that the total contribution rate of 12 per cent is now in excess of what is needed, but the 12 per cent is being retained as a precautionary measure.

But even within what is permitted, variations arise over the policies followed; thus at the end of 1960, 47 per cent of local authority funds was on loan to the authorities administering the funds and 33 per cent in British Government (or Government guaranteed) stocks, but these average figures concealed wide variations among individual funds; in some cases 80 per cent or more of the fund has been lent to the administering authority. In the case of the Railways' staff scheme, there is provision for the British Railways Board to use the surplus fund moneys for their own capital purposes and to guarantee interest on it at 4 per cent; about 80 per cent of the assets of the fund now consist, therefore, of rolling-stock, stations, etc.

By contrast the majority of the nationalized industries' funds have not been restricted to trustee investments and under certain conditions have invested in equities, and also in property; some of them had invested 30 per cent of their funds in ordinary and preference shares alone even before they were authorized to raise the amount so invested to 50 per cent of the total to bring them in line with trustee investments following the 1961 Act. It is likely that there will be an increasing trend towards investment in equities and property.[1]

Moreover, many local government funds were being built up at a time when the rate of interest on gilt-edged securities was comparatively low. From what was said earlier, it will be clear that not only actual earnings from investments, but prospective earnings as seen by the actuary, will play a large part in whether a surplus or a deficiency is shown at valuation. For many years it was the common experience of local authorities to have to meet the cost of deficiencies at successive valuations, and this was generally done by making an annual payment (the so-called 'equal annual charge') to the fund which, over a period of forty years, was sufficient to discharge the deficiency. Since valuations were made every five years, it can be seen that the equal annual charge could soon rise quite rapidly. In the Bedfordshire fund, for example, which was established in 1934, deficiency payments at the first valuation (1940) were over £15,000 a year, and by the time of the third valuation (1950) had reached over double that amount.

On the other hand, more recently, thanks primarily to higher interest rates, local government funds have generally been able to show surpluses and, with the greater opportunities for investment which are now open to them, this trend may well continue. The nationalized industries' funds which, on the whole, have been built up during a period of high interest rates, have consequently from the

---

[1] As an example, nearly 80 per cent of the investment of new money in the Mineworkers' scheme in the eighteen months to September 30, 1963, went into ordinary shares and real property.

start generally shown surpluses. Of course, how well a fund does depends a great deal on the skill and foresight of those responsible for the investment of the fund, but chance, if only in the form of general economic factors, may play its part as also in public sector schemes does government policy in, for example, restricting the range of possible investments.

The emphasis on investment earnings is not intended to suggest that this is the only factor affecting the performance of funds and hence, in general, differences between local government experience and nationalized industries' experience. But it is a most important factor and one, moreover, which does not have any direct relation to the experience of the members of the fund. Of those factors which do depend on the members' experience, one in particular has had a profound influence on the performance of funds in the last twenty years; that is the rate at which salaries have increased in money terms.

Here one should perhaps distinguish two ways in which the effects of different factors may be brought into the valuation picture. The actuary may try to assess as accurately as he can how the particular factor is likely to operate and will then adjust the allowance to be made for this factor, if necessary, at each valuation, so that all the time there is an interplay between the assumptions made by the actuary and the way in which the assumptions work out in practice. The valuation then reflects the effect of the closeness of the actuary's assumptions to what in fact happens. But, alternatively, little or no attempt may be made to make accurate allowance for a particular factor, and the result will be that the effect of this factor will be felt in its entirety at subsequent valuations.

This latter point is particularly important in relation to the question of salaries. Apart from the rate at which members of the scheme on average progress up the salary-scale, the rate at which salaries themselves increase can greatly affect the cost of a terminal-salary scheme. For although a general increase in salaries will automatically increase the amount of contributions paid by members where, as is general in public sector terminal-salary schemes, the contribution is expressed as a percentage of salary, it will increase even more the ultimate liability for pensions of those members and this, as has been seen, is what the actuarial valuation aims to assess. In the last twenty years especially, when salary scales between valuations five years apart have frequently been found to increase by anything between 25 and 50 per cent, this factor has become of the utmost importance.

So far as funded public sector schemes are concerned, however, the effect of this factor has emerged in rather a different way from the effect of the rate of interest. In the case of the latter, the actuary at each valuation assesses the rate of interest which, taking everything into account, may reasonably be applied to the fund's assets; but in the case of rising salary scales he frequently makes little or no direct allowance for this factor, although he may make some indirect allowance, for example, by retaining a higher contribution rate than would be strictly necessary on the assumption of constant salary-scales.

At first sight it seems strange that rising salary-scales do not always figure in actuarial valuations as a direct calculation, like mortality rates or interest rates, but it must be remembered that until comparatively recently there has been a general feeling that it was abnormal for salaries (and indeed wages and prices too) to rise constantly, and that the normal situation was one in which money-values were more or less stable. It may be that (under the influence of the NEDC for example) this attitude will become less marked in future and that this will affect the position of actuarial valuations. But there is also a practical point; employers might well be reluctant to see set down in black and white an assumption that salaries were going to rise at, say, 4 per cent per annum, since this would be tantamount to inviting the staff associations and unions to apply for at least this amount. And in the case of central and local government schemes there may be reasons of government policy for not wishing to treat inflation as a permanent feature.

Furthermore, it may be argued that in practical terms there may not be so very much difference between making a direct allowance for increasing salary-scales and, in effect, allowing inter-valuation increases to appear on the debit side of the next valuation balance-sheet. For in either case the fact of the increased salary-scales would lead either to the reduction or cancelling-out of what would otherwise have been a surplus, or to a positive deficiency, the main difference being in the timing; that is, if no allowance is made for rising salary-scales the effect will be felt at the next and subsequent valuations rather than the one which is being currently conducted.

But this argument does not apply uniquely to salary-scales. An actuary who consistently assumed a higher rate of interest earnings than was in fact earned by a fund would be inflating the credit side of the valuation balance-sheet. In practice, therefore, one must regard the situation over salary-scales as being somewhat anomalous, and probably to be explained in terms of the particular historical circumstances in which funding has developed.

The point does, however, lead to consideration of what in fact happens in a funded, public sector scheme if a deficiency or surplus is shown at valuation. Since the calculation relates only to a fund for existing members and pensioners, it follows that if their benefits are to be completely safeguarded a deficiency should be made good by the immediate payment into the fund of a lump sum for the amount of the deficiency. In practice, this is not usually done; mainly this is because there is no need to make an adjustment at one go to what is essentially a long-term operation. This is so even in terms of the actuary's hypothetical model of a fund running down to nothing which is designed to give a precise criterion and meaning to solvency in relation to a pension fund; and still more is it so, of course, if, as is usually the case, the fund in practice is a continuing entity with new members constantly taking the place of those who retire or die.

In fact, one of the objects of having funded schemes subject to periodical valuation is to achieve a more regular series of payments into the scheme than would be so in a strict pay-as-you-go scheme, where chance variations in the expenditure from year to year would require corresponding variations in the amounts paid into the scheme by way of contributions. This being so, it has usually been the practice in funded schemes to try to hold the employee's rate of contribution to the scheme constant over a long period, and indeed in many of these schemes it is not easy to change the contribution rate, at least for existing members.[1]

Surpluses and deficiencies in practice therefore affect chiefly either the employers' contributions or the benefits, or both. In order to eliminate sudden fluctuations in payments, the amount of a deficiency is thus often expressed either as a percentage contribution of salaries and wages or, as was indicated above, a level annual amount, and in both cases the payment is made by the employer for a fixed term of years. Correspondingly, a subsequent surplus may be used to reduce previous deficiency payments, but when these have all been eliminated, the way is open to provide better benefits which again will usually mean that the surplus is disbursed gradually over a period of time rather than in one sudden rush.

In some schemes, notably Gas and Airways, the employer's normal contribution is not expressed as a fixed percentage of salaries and wages, but he undertakes to meet the balance of cost as determined by the actuary. In theory this could mean that at a time of good surpluses the employer could reduce his contributions below the level of what, in comparable schemes, is a fixed percentage. In practice this is unlikely to happen, since it is a feature of the nationalized industries' schemes (though not, it should be noted, of local government) that each fund has a committee of management, with representatives of both employers and employees, in which questions such as the disposal of surpluses are discussed and form

---

[1] For example, it would require an Act of Parliament to raise contributions in local government, and in most nationalized industries' schemes contributions and prospective benefits of existing members could only be altered if two-thirds of the members voted to do so.

the subject, no doubt, of some hard bargaining before agreement which is reasonably in the interests of both sides is reached (though subject generally to Ministerial approval).

The separateness of local government in this, as in a number of other matters, draws attention to the general effect of having this particular kind of financial arrangement. One obvious effect which might be expected would be an increasing diversity in the schemes, not only in comparison with non-funded schemes but also among themselves. The initial diversity of experience would be further accentuated by the different results obtained by funds resulting in changes in the pattern of benefits and, to some degree, in the contribution rates; and this would happen in a way which would not be possible in non-funded schemes.

To some degree this may be said to be happening in the nationalized industries' schemes where those schemes which have been particularly successful in their investment policies (such as the NCB Principal scheme) will increasingly be able to offer at least as good a range of benefits as similar schemes at less total cost, and less cost to the member.[1] But the separate character of local government is nowhere more apparent than in this point. Whether an individual fund makes a surplus or deficiency can have no direct effect on the general range of benefits of the members of that particular fund,[2] because of the unique situation whereby the rules of the scheme are laid down nationally by Act of Parliament and Regulations while the financing of the scheme is achieved through over 500 autonomous funds.

The point may be brought out by considering what happened at the last major revision of the local government scheme in 1953, which was in fact only the second major revision since the institution of the original scheme in 1922. The final result as embodied in the 1953 Act and Regulations was in the nature of a 'package deal'; lump sums, for example, were provided for the first time, but on the other hand married men did not receive them in full; against this, they had the chance, which was not open to them before, of a guaranteed widow's pension. The lengthy discussions which preceded the introduction of a Bill in 1953 are an indication of the hard bargaining which must have gone on. That the final result was greatly influenced by financial considerations cannot be doubted, but equally the state

[1] There is of course a much wider issue of whether lower percentage contributions are necessarily so much more advantageous if the salaries on which they are paid are lower than elsewhere. The point is touched on later in relation to the civil service scheme, but here the qualification 'other things being equal' must be assumed to the statement made in the text.

[2] There are, however, some discretionary powers permitted to local authorities, e.g. the power to grant benefits for non-contributing service on the same terms as for contributing service, whose use might be influenced by the financial situation of the fund.

of the funds as a whole at that time was only one factor in the bargaining. In local government, the success of the individual funds is to be regarded as much more in the nature of a long-term effect on the scheme than is the case in the nationalized industries.

One further point about funded schemes in the public sector should be stressed. In keeping with the size of those schemes, the amount of the accumulated funds and the rate at which they are continuing to build up is considerable. Detailed figures for each scheme are shown in Appendix 5, the most striking feature being the very large total of local government funds. In 1962 they amounted to £635 million, that is, more than half the total of public sector funds and over one-tenth of the combined total of all pension funds in the private and public sectors. Moreover, local government funds are increasing by approximately £50 million p.a. The largest single funds in the public sector are the NCB Principal with £159 million in 1963 and an annual increase of about £12 million, and the Electricity Staff with £110 million and annual increase of £13 million. By contrast, it is rare to find a private sector scheme with a fund of more than £50 million, and most, of course, are very much smaller than this.

PAY-AS-YOU-GO SCHEMES IN THE PUBLIC SECTOR

Civil Service

The variety of arrangements for financing pay-as-you-go schemes may be reduced to three: those where the member pays no contributions; those where he pays contributions in much the same way as for a funded scheme; and those where, although he pays contributions, there is no regular assessment of the correctness of the contribution rate. To the first group belongs the civil service scheme, to the second the teachers, National Health Service and Atomic Energy Authority's schemes (and also the Railways' Male Wages Grades), and to the third the police and firemen's schemes.

The civil service scheme is unique in being non-contributory, except for the widows' and other dependants' benefits introduced in 1949. In theory, therefore, the whole cost, apart from these benefits, falls on the Exchequer, that is the taxpayer, and the civil servant enjoys a great advantage over the members of other schemes in getting his benefits 'for nothing'. In practice, this would only be true if it could be shown that, in the absence of a non-contributory pension scheme, civil servants would have exactly the same salaries. But in fact it is recognized that this is not the case, and that some allowance is made for the fact of a non-contributory pension in arriving at salary scales. The position is that 'the Government needs to pay its present servants less than it would have to if there were no non-contributory pensions. The result is that the State raises so much less in taxation to pay the salaries of its present servants, but so much more to meet the superannuation of its past servants.'[1]

Thus, although the civil service scheme is only nominally non-contributory, it might be expected that the important question was to determine exactly how much allowance was made in salary negotiations for this factor. In practice this is not possible since superannuation benefits are treated as an 'unquantifiable' factor, like annual holidays or house purchase facilities,[2] although the rate of contribution is treated as 'quantifiable' in making comparisons with outside salaries. It can be said that, in contrast to the position in local government described above, bargaining about pensions in the Civil Service has two dimensions, one in strict pension terms and one in salary terms.

Because of this unique situation, it may not always be apparent to the outside observer, and, particularly, the taxpayer, that a fair allowance has been made in arriving at civil service salary scales for the fact that no direct contribution is made by the civil servant to the cost of pensions. It is possible that this is one reason why the cost of the improved benefits of 1949 was specifically charged, in part, to the civil servant.

The point need not, however, be exaggerated. Ever since the major reform of 1859, the history of the civil service scheme has been on the whole of gradual extensions and improvements interspersed at intervals with major changes. But these major changes were made as far as possible without increasing the total cost of the scheme; this was specifically so in the introduction of lump sums and death grants in 1909, and in the provisions for allocation of pension (to provide a widow's pension) in 1935. The year 1949 was important because the new benefits introduced then represented additional cost; the Government agreed to meet half this cost and the civil servant's half was to be met by a reduction of one-third in his lump sum on retirement, or, if he specifically chose it, by the payment of contributions of $1\frac{1}{4}$ per cent of salary. Thus, in a sense this re-introduction of contributions into the Civil Service was also a benefit, because it catered for the man who wished to retain his lump sum intact, whereas in local government, for example, there is less flexibility, partly, no doubt, in the interests of administrative simplicity.

The difference between the civil service and the local government schemes also illustrates the importance of factors other than the

---

[1] J. Enoch Powell, *Saving in a Free Society*, Hutchinson for Institute of Economic Affairs, 1960, p. 69. See also Treasury Evidence to Priestley Commission, September 28, 1954, Sir Thomas Padmore, Q. 2585.

[2] See, for example, the arguments of the Civil Service Alliance and the Treasury before the Civil Service Arbitration Tribunal as reported in *Whitley Bulletin*, April 1959, pp. 56–58.

D*

purely financial in determining how the cost is to be met. Despite the increasing cost of civil service superannuation, and the lack of a fund to give security for the benefits, civil servants were not required, as were local government employees, to meet the whole cost of family benefits. It is also an illustration of the difficulty of making useful comparisons in financial terms of different schemes.

Apart from the complication which has been introduced by the family benefits' scheme, the financial arrangements of the civil service scheme are very simple. The main fact, indeed the only fact to be regularly published, is the year-by-year cost. Whatever calculations the Government Actuary may make behind the scenes, the first public indication of the financial situation of civil service pensions each year is the publication of the Civil Estimates with forecasts of the estimated cost of pensions for the coming financial year, briefly set out under headings, such as pensions, lump sums and injury awards. Furthermore, even this information has only been available for the last few years in a convenient form; previously it was split up over a number of different items in the Estimates, so that it is practically impossible for anyone to get a reliable series of statistics of the cost of civil service superannuation over any length of time. The one fact which does emerge from the published figures is that the cost is rising year by year, having more than doubled in money terms in the last ten years, if Pensions Increase is excluded, although of course this represents a much smaller increase in real terms.

This point has been emphasized to point the contrast between a fully funded scheme, such as that for Electricity, and the other extreme of the non-contributory, non-funded civil service. The essential difference is that a funded scheme puts pensions into a separate financial compartment, a fund which must be adjusted and put in balance for the purpose of paying pensions benefits alone;[1] whereas in the Civil Service no distinction is made in the annual estimates between the charge for pensions and the charge for, say, travelling expenses or printing and stationery. All are treated as inescapable items for which the Exchequer must somehow find the money currently, and if there are real differences between them (such as that pensions represent an almost certainly increasing future obligation whereas the other items may, within limits, be varied according to circumstances), this does not appear in the published figures. There are no figures, for example, projecting the cost ten or twenty years ahead as is done for the National Insurance scheme.

But although this is the essential difference between funding and non-funding, it would be wrong to imply that the peculiar nature of

[1] It must be said, however, that this strict view is somewhat weakened where, as with the Railway Staff scheme or some local government funds, a large part of the fund has been borrowed for other purposes.

pensions and their cost is completely ignored in the civil service scheme. For one thing, assessments of their cost are made from time to time,[1] but, perhaps more importantly, one part of the civil service scheme is regularly assessed in fairly precise terms. Since the method of assessment, which is usually known as 'notional funding', is also applied to the schemes in the second main group of pay-as-you-go schemes, it will be necessary to consider it in more detail.

Notional Funds

The Post Office has for many years had distinctive financial arrangements, culminating in 1961 in the establishment of a separate Post Office Fund, with the intention that it should operate on similar terms to the other nationalized industries, an important exception being that its staff continued to be civil servants. The problem, in terms of pensions, has been that whereas in the other nationalized industries with their funded schemes the annual charge for pensions has represented pension liability, the pay-as-you-go civil service scheme would normally only give a figure for the actual cost of pensions each year. The difference is of course due to the fact that in the former case the amount paid into the fund in a year is related to the future cost of pensions for service in that year, whereas the actual cost represents the charge for past services.

Thus in terms of showing in the Post Office accounts a fair charge each year for pensions, the position would at present be understated if actual cost were used, as compared with normal practice in the private sector or the nationalized industries, although in the long run the position should be reversed so that at some future date Post Office accounts would, if they showed only annual cost, begin to overstate the charge for pensions. In either case, it was felt that in order that the Post Office should make a proper charge for its services it should conform as nearly as possible to normal commercial practice.

The method of doing this has been to try to assess what the position would have been if there had been a fund. Hence the method is referred to as notional funding. It is assumed, for example, that a fund has been set up and invested in $2\frac{1}{2}$ per cent Consols, and valuations are made at intervals just as with true funds, at which surpluses or deficiencies are shown. In 1962–63, £43 million was charged to the Post Office accounts for pension liability, compared with the gross cost of pensions of just over £26 million.

It can be said, therefore, that present users of Post Office services are paying more and the general taxpayer less than would be the

[1] For example, the Treasury have quoted a figure of 15 per cent of salary as the actuarial value of civil service pension rights (Royal Commission on the Civil Service, 1953–55, Minutes of Evidence, September 28, 1954, p. 792).

case if notional funding had not been introduced. In the long run, of course, the balance should be restored, but it is fair to regard the Post Office notional fund as mainly an accounting technique for the limited purpose stated; it can have no effect on the civil service scheme itself, nor does it affect the total amount of money which needs to be raised annually to meet the cost of civil service (including Post Office) pensions. What it does affect is the distribution of that money from the various sources from which it may be raised.[1]

Perhaps of more importance, because of their effects, or possible effects, on the future of the schemes are the notional funds for the teachers', National Health Service and Atomic Energy Authority schemes. Although there are important differences of detail between these schemes, the basis of their financial arrangements is the same. Only the position of the teachers' scheme is therefore considered in detail here, as the oldest of the notional funds of these three schemes.

The important point about all these schemes, and the one which distinguishes them from pure 'assessment' schemes, is that in all the employee pays a contribution as a fixed percentage of salary, whereas pure assessmentism would require that the amount raised by contributions should vary from year to year or at least over short periods to correspond with the amounts to be paid out in benefits. Thus the schemes combine two elements, the fixed rate of contribution which, as has been seen, is normal in funded schemes, and the payment of benefits not out of an accumulated fund but out of whatever current income is available, which is characteristic of non-funded schemes.

The analogy with funded schemes has in fact been carried a stage further, for the employer also pays a fixed contribution and does not, as might be expected, simply guarantee to meet the balance of cost, if any, remaining when the employees' contributions have, in any particular year, been applied to the payment of benefits. Apart from the desire to follow the pattern of funded schemes, especially the local government one,[2] two other reasons may be suggested why this course was adopted; first to make it clear that the employers were also paying their fair share of the cost, and, secondly, and to some extent connected with this, because the employer was not the

---

[1] It is worth noting that for the first time a valuation is now being carried out for the civil service widows' and dependants' scheme to assess the position at the end of 1962. This too will use the notional fund technique, but it is not clear what effect it will have on the future of the scheme. Clearly it could provide evidence which would be used if any proposals were made to alter the scheme (e.g. for raising widows' pensions from one-third to one-half). The valuation will admittedly cause a good deal of extra work in the compilation of the necessary statistics.

[2] It must be remembered that the teachers' scheme of 1925 was established very soon after the 1922 local government scheme.

same person as the guarantor of the scheme. This at least is true of the teachers' scheme, where the scheme is administered centrally and guaranteed by the central government, but the employers are the individual local education authorities. But it is not true of the Atomic Energy Authority, unless one takes account of the fact that, perhaps to a greater degree than with other nationalized industries, the Authority is dependent in a financial sense on the central government (e.g. it is not a commercial concern in the same way as other nationalized industries). Nor is it true of the National Health Service, where, although the employers are different bodies from the central government, only to a very limited degree can they be said to be financially independent. Perhaps the truth is that the two later schemes simply followed the pattern already established by the teachers' scheme.

It is now possible to set out the facts about contributions in these three schemes in the same way as for the funded schemes:

Contributions in Notionally Funded Schemes

Scheme	Woman or single man		Married man covered for family benefits	
	Employee	Employer	Employee	Employer
Teachers	6%	6%	6% (no family benefits at present)	6%
National Health Service	6% (5% manual workers	8% 6%)	As for a woman but the lump sum on retirement is reduced by two-thirds	
Atomic Energy Authority	6% (4¼% manual workers	8% 5¾%)	As for a woman but the lump sum on retirement is reduced by one-third	

Once again it will be clear how similar contribution rates paid by the employee disguise differences between schemes, most noticeably perhaps in comparing the NHS and AEA (Non-industrial) schemes. Although the contribution rates for both employee and employer are identical, the 8 per cent contribution by the employer in the AEA scheme includes an element for part of the cost of family benefits, but this is not so in the NHS where (as in local government) the employee meets the whole cost of these benefits. Furthermore, family benefits in the AEA include children's allowances which are not found in either the NHS or local government schemes.

At first sight these variations seem to be puzzling. In funded schemes the actuary can, on the basis of his assumptions, determine with some precision the cost of particular benefits, but this does not seem to be possible where there is no fund. What in fact is done in these notionally funded schemes is to put them as nearly as possible into the position they would have been in if they had been funded.

This, briefly, is what a notional fund is; it is an attempt to treat a pay-as-you-go scheme as though it were funded.

To do this, it may be necessary for the actuary to look at the basic assumptions rather differently than he would if there were a fund. For example, at the start of a scheme, some assumption has to be made about how the cost of 'back-service' is to be met; it may be that the employer will agree to meet this cost over a period of, say, thirty years, and the actuary must therefore take these payments into the credit side of the account over the appropriate period. But the most important assumption is about the rate of interest to be earned on the notional fund's investments, because this is the chief way in which a true fund might show different results from a notional fund.

Since in these three schemes the reason for instituting notional funds is not, as in the case of the Post Office, the need to include a proper charge for pension liability for costing purposes, the reason must be sought elsewhere. Here the main evidence is provided by the scheme set up under the Teachers (Superannuation) Act of 1925; the main object of the Act was to replace the short-lived non-contributory scheme of 1918 with a contributory scheme, as recommended by the Emmott Committee. This Committee had, however, also recommended that the contributions should be paid into a fund, and this the government did not accept, largely because, in terms of Exchequer financing, there was no point in instituting a separate fund for this particular purpose.

It is quite clear, therefore, that the 1925 teachers' scheme was in the nature of a compromise; the government wanted teachers and their employers to make some contribution towards pensions, but at the same time they did not want the needless elaboration of a separate fund. The main object of the notional fund was therefore to give 'a valid account of liability as between the Treasury and the contributors'.[1] Thus the main analogy with funded schemes lies in the use of the notional fund as a means of financial control or discipline; an actuarial valuation of a notional fund will, so far as it is possible to do so, establish whether the right contribution is being paid for the benefits or whether, on the same kind of assumptions as would apply to a funded scheme, more or less needs to be paid to meet the liabilities.

The example of the civil service scheme (apart from the special case of the Post Office) shows that but for the fixed contribution rate it might not be necessary to have a notional fund. For in a pure assessment scheme it would only be necessary to show that the amount raised in contributions in a particular year or period was

---

[1] The President of the Board of Education (Lord Eustace Percy) introducing the Second Reading of the Bill (H.C. Deb., May 12, 1925, col. 1784).

just sufficient to meet the outgoings in the same period. But the whole purpose of a percentage contribution rate is to avoid such fluctuations, because, broadly speaking, such a rate will produce more than enough to meet outgoings in the early years of the scheme, but less than enough in later years. And the balance is achieved by investing the surplus in the early years, and thus having income from investments to draw on in later years.

These points about notional funds may seem to be unduly laboured, but there is a real difficulty in understanding how the actual financial working of the scheme on its pay-as-you-go cash basis is related to the theoretical concept of a notional fund. It can now be seen that there are two quite distinct ways of looking at such schemes. One is to examine how in fact the cost of benefits has been and is being met, and the other is to see what the effect would be of applying funding methods to such a scheme. The former is important for discovering how much teachers' pensions, for example, are costing and who is paying for them, but the latter, through the medium of actuarial valuations at intervals, has formed the basis of assessing and making changes in the financial arrangements of the scheme.

The position can be well seen in the case of the teachers' scheme which has now been in existence for forty years as a notional fund. One would expect that the characteristic feature of most public sector schemes in recent years, increasing membership coupled with increasing salary-scales, would serve to accentuate the difference between the two ways of looking at the teachers' scheme and this is indeed so, the main point to be noted being that whereas these two factors have the effect of immediately increasing income, which is important in pay-as-you-go terms, they have the long-term effect of increasing the ultimate liability for pensions, and this is just as important in funding terms.

Contributions to the teachers' scheme were fixed by the 1925 Act at 5 per cent for teachers and 5 per cent for their employers. In fact teachers had been making their contributions since 1922, and the notional fund therefore dates from that year;[1] the government accepted the obligation to pay pensions for pre-1922 service, that is, the cost of these pensions was excluded entirely from the accounts of the notional fund. Any surplus on current account of contribution income over expenditure in a particular year went to the Exchequer and served to reduce the net cost of the Education Estimates for that year. The rate of interest was fixed at $3\frac{1}{2}$ per cent and was intended to be 'permanently and finally laid down', according to the President of the Board of Education; it is still in force today.

---

[1] Employers did not in fact begin contributing until 1928, but for the purpose of the accounts of the notional fund, 'the contributions of both parties are deemed to have commenced on 1st June 1922', H.C. 78, 1935, para. 12.

From the three Government Actuary's reports on the scheme since it was instituted[1] and from the annual Civil Estimates for the period since 1956, it can be calculated that since 1922 teachers and their employers in England and Wales have contributed about £500 million and that in the same period rather less than that amount has been paid out for pensions and other benefits (excluding Pensions Increase). These figures disguise fluctuations in the position at different periods, but the table opposite shows that only in the early years and in recent years has income from contributions exceeded expenditure; between 1932 and 1954 the Exchequer had to meet the difference, amounting in total to approximately £46 million; against this, there was a surplus of nearly £10 million in the earlier period and of nearly £60 million in the later period (after making some allowance to exclude Pensions Increase).

However, the expenditure figures shown in the table are figures of total expenditure and make no allowance for the fact that, as indicated above, the cost of pensions for pre-1922 service was accepted as an obligation falling entirely on the Exchequer. During the period 1922–56 the cost of pensions for pre-1922 service amounted to approximately £172 million, and over the whole period 1922–63 probably to just over £200 million. Thus, as it happens, over the forty years income has balanced expenditure but the obligations of the different parties have not worked out as the 1925 Act appeared to intend. To see just how this has come about, it is necessary to look at the very different picture presented by the Government Actuary's three valuations of the scheme (again, for the sake of simplicity, taking only the position disclosed in England and Wales).

In his report on the first eleven years of the scheme the Government Actuary showed that there was a deficiency of £10 million and recommended that contributions should be raised to 6 per cent for both employers and employees, but no action was taken by the government. Thus although one of the main objects of the notional fund was to demonstrate the correctness of the contribution rates imposed, the demonstration that they were in fact incorrect did not lead to any action.[2] However, by the time of the 1948 valuation, the deficiency had risen to £102 million, mostly because of increased salaries, but including nearly £17 million which was due to the previous uncorrected deficit, and this time the government proposed

[1] H.C. 78, 1935, covered the years 1922–33; H.C. 128, 1951, the years 1933–48; and H.C. 269, 1961, the years 1948–56. The next report should be for 1956–61. (The references are to the England and Wales reports; there are similar reports for Scotland.)

[2] This incidentally illustrates the difficulties of having a notional rather than a true fund; or looking at it another way, it demonstrates the unreality of the situation; it would be unthinkable to ignore such a large deficit in a funded scheme.

to raise contributions. So great was the opposition to this course that a Bill put forward in the 1953–54 Session for the purpose had to be withdrawn, but after further argument and discussions another Bill was introduced and this became the Teachers' Superannuation Act, 1956.[1]

Teachers' Superannuation (England and Wales)

[Three-year intervals 1923–24 to 1953–54; individual years 1953–54 to 1962–63]

Year	Total contributions (£ millions)	Pensions and other benefits (excluding Pensions Increase) (£ millions)
1923–24	4·8	2·7
1926–27	5·0	3·6
1929–30	5·2	4·8
1932–33	4·9	6·2
1935–36	5·5	6·7
1938–39	5·7	7·9
1941–42	5·8	8·5
1944–45	6·8	9·6
1947–48	9·6	12·1
1950–51	11·2	15·6
1953–54	15·4	17·0
1954–55	17·1	17·1
1955–56	18·1	18·1
1956–57	23	23 *
1957–58	29	26 *
1958–59	31	26 *
1959–60	34	28 *
1960–61	38	32 *
1961–62	40	34 *
1962–63	46	36 *

* N.B. From 1956–57 onwards expenditure includes Pensions (Increase), which is not separately identified in the published figures.

Sources: Government Actuary's Reports up to 1955–56, Civil Estimates after that date.

No doubt the action of the government was partly due to the expectation of a further deficiency at the next valuation. In fact, the adverse balance disclosed by the 1948–56 Report amounted to £274 million, and would have been even higher (£330 million) but for the

[1] For the part played by the National Union of Teachers in opposing increased contributions, see S. E. Finer, *Anonymous Empire*, Pall Mall Press, 1958, pp. 65–66 and 89–91. The Act offended against the 'no detriment' rule by imposing increased contributions on existing as well as future teachers.

increased contributions. To liquidate such a deficiency in a true fund would have required an annual payment of perhaps about £14 million over twenty-five years, and this figure may be compared with the fact that total contributions were, in 1955–56, £18 million. In fact, what the government did was to make an Exchequer credit of the whole £274 million to the notional fund, but perhaps of more significance for the future was the fact that the 1956 Act provided that any deficiencies on future valuations were to be met by supplementary contributions from the employers, that is, the local education authorities.

Since these payments will be actual (unlike the Exchequer credit which does not involve any immediate transfer), the effect in pay-as-you-go terms of increasing the employers' contributions in this way will be to defer still longer the day when the Exchequer has to meet currently any part of the cost of teachers' pensions. With this point should also be noted the fact that whereas previously contributions made by employers and employees served to reduce the Education Estimates, they are now paid direct to the Exchequer, so that currently speaking any money paid in contributions in a particular year which is in excess of the cost of pensions in that year is a kind of special tax, and to that extent relieves the general taxpayer, always remembering that at some future date the position may be reversed.[1]

One of the consequences of the fierce opposition which the increase in contributions aroused was that the Minister of Education invited the teachers to 'include this extra charge upon their income as an argument in the Burnham Committee', and although this was an understandable political move, its effect could only be to weaken the arguments based on sound finance provided by the actuarial valuation of the teachers' scheme.[2] A further consequence of the Act (and probably an influencing factor in the decision to raise contributions), was that the teachers were brought into line with local government and NHS officers in paying contributions of 6 per cent.

The position of the NHS and AEA notional funds is broadly similar to that of the teachers, although it is important to note that neither has a permanently fixed rate of interest; for example, the original rate of $2\frac{1}{2}$ per cent in the NHS scheme was raised to $3\frac{1}{4}$ per cent in 1955. But to some extent this is accidental; for example, the employers pay 8 per cent in the NHS scheme, but only 6 per cent in the teachers', and it might well have been that if the rate of interest

[1] A further complication is that expenditure by local authorities on teachers' superannuation is to a considerable extent met by the Exchequer through the General Grant system.

[2] Sir David (now Lord) Eccles, H.C. Deb., December 6, 1955. Mr John Vaizey has pointed out that whereas the increased contributions from teachers were expected to amount to £1¾ million in 1956–57, the 1956 Burnham award cost £31 m. (*The Costs of Education*, Allen & Unwin, 1958, p. 178.)

in the teachers' scheme had been fixed lower, the employers would correspondingly have paid contributions at a higher rate.

The position in notionally-funded schemes is then that all the financial arrangements are as they would be in a funded scheme, except that there is no fund. Percentage contribution rates, deficiencies or surpluses, and the cost of new benefits are all assessed in exactly the same manner as for the funded schemes described earlier, but all the time the current cost of pensions and other benefits is being met in a different way. Some time has been spent on examining the position because notional funds are a unique feature of the public sector and it seemed important to establish exactly how they worked in practice as a prelude to the later examination (in Chapter 9) of how far they do achieve the best of both worlds, funding and pay-as-you-go.

Police and Firemen

Of the final group of schemes, those for police and firemen, less need be said. In a sense they stand between the first two groups; for although they are contributory on the percentage basis characteristic of funded schemes, no attempt is made in any regular systematic way to assess this contribution or the finances of the scheme generally, as is done in valuations of the teachers' scheme. In effect there is little to distinguish these schemes from the civil service scheme, except for the fact that police and firemen may claim a refund of contributions on withdrawal from the scheme.

Part of the difference between the police and teachers' schemes may be due to the different circumstances in which, at about the same time, changes were made in their financial arrangements. The problem with the teachers, as was seen above, was to change a non-contributory to a contributory scheme without going to the trouble of setting up a fund. But in the case of the police scheme in 1921, the main change was from a funded to a non-funded scheme in recognition of the *de facto* situation that generally speaking the existing funds were quite inadequate. In a sense, therefore, there was no need to put a notional fund (or, even more, notional funds) in place of the existing funds, since it was quite obvious that the contributions paid by the police themselves (only $2\frac{1}{2}$ per cent under the 1890 and 1921 Acts) were by no means excessive when account is taken of the higher total cost of police pensions resulting chiefly from the early age of retirement.

Furthermore, it was characteristic of the police scheme even when it was funded that there was no fixed contribution from the employers, but, as was shown in Chapter 2, some rather miscellaneous sources of income apart from the contributions paid by the police themselves. Thus, not only was there lacking the tradition of a shared-cost basis, but to have introduced one purely for notional-funding purposes would have meant making the employer's contribution very large, assuming that the 2½ per cent contribution by the police had been retained. Again, there is the practical point that the police scheme, unlike the teachers', had always been run on a local basis, and, although in theory it would have been possible to substitute a whole series of notional funds for the existing true funds, the confusion and possibilities of confusion of such a situation would have made this an absurd solution. A notional fund would only have made sense in terms of a single centralized scheme and from this it may well be that the government of the day shrank.

Thus, once the decision was taken to unfund the police scheme, it was perfectly reasonable not to substitute any financial control derived from true funding, but it is perhaps more interesting to speculate why the further step of making the scheme non-contributory was not taken. Partly this may have been a matter of tradition, partly the psychological value to the police themselves of having a contribution to give them a feeling of greater entitlement to a pension. But a practical reason was demonstrated shortly after the 1921 Act; the Geddes Committee, in searching for economies in public expenditure, noted that the 2½ per cent contribution rate paid by the police was low, both in relation to other public servants and in relation to the cost of police superannuation. They therefore recommended an increase to 5 per cent which was put into effect and remained until improved widows' pensions were introduced in 1956. Unpopular as the move was with the police it might have proved even more difficult if it had had to be represented as a 2½ per cent cut in police pay.

Thus the police scheme (and the firemen's scheme following it closely) has remained outside the general line of public sector schemes, both in its distinctive benefits and, to some extent following from this, in its financial arrangements. For although no regular assessment of the finances of police pensions are made, there have been, as with the Civil Service, particular assessments for specific purposes, all indicating the very high cost of police pensions. A particular example is the introduction of improved widows' pensions in 1956; this followed a recommendation of the Oaksey Committee on Police Conditions of Service (1949); they, however, pointed out that since the police contributed comparatively little towards the cost of benefits, any great improvement in widows' pensions should be accompanied by an increase in contributions.

This proved to be a difficult question; a Working Party of the Police Council failed to reach agreement either on the level of improved benefit or on how its cost should be shared. In the course of their examination of the question, it was stated that the total value at entry of the existing benefits of the scheme was about 25 per cent of pay, although at that time the contributions made by the police were only 5 per cent.[1] The basis of this calculation is not stated, but it may reasonably be assumed that it derived from an assessment in notional fund terms. The additional $1\frac{1}{4}$ per cent now paid by the police for improved widows' pensions was calculated to go a good way towards meeting the additional cost, but changing circumstances in the last ten years, and particularly improved rates of pay, have almost certainly increased still further the cost of police pensions as a percentage of pay.

There remains, however, the fundamental problem about the financing of the police and firemen's schemes that the total cost of providing benefits is bound to be relatively high, given their special conditions of service. Whether schemes are funded or not, therefore, the problem of meeting the cost is not an easy one. Whether the theoretical 50-50 basis of the local government scheme is the right one for that scheme or not, it certainly would not be a practical proposition to apply it to the police scheme if it meant, as it probably would, that instead of paying $6\frac{1}{4}$ per cent the police should pay nearer 15 per cent. But anything short of this principle means that either the rate-payer or the taxpayer (or both) must meet a heavy bill, and, furthermore, on the pay-as-you-go basis if not quite to the same extent on a funded basis, this bill will go on growing for a long time to come.

COSTS OF ADMINISTRATION

The foregoing analysis has dealt broadly with the financial arrangements of the main public sector schemes. It has been concerned for the most part with the answers to two questions: how is the cost of schemes assessed and how is the cost met. What has not been examined is what might be termed the content of the cost element. For the most part cost means simply the cost of the benefits as laid down in the rules of each scheme. Two items which fall outside this definition, the cost of administering schemes and the cost of improving benefits once they are in payment, will be considered in this final part of the chapter.

It might be thought that funded schemes in particular would make some allowance for the costs of administration, since one of the

[1] Police Pensions: Report of the Working Party of the Police Council, H.M.S.O. 1952, para. 32. It is noteworthy that the police representatives appealed to the example of the civil service scheme and were prepared to pay $1\frac{1}{4}$ per cent for a shared-cost scheme, whereas the local authority representatives wished to maintain the principle in the local government scheme that the whole cost should be met by a reduction in other benefits, although they were prepared to share the cost under certain conditions.

effects of funding is to make a scheme financially self-contained. In practice, however, most funded schemes in the public sector do not charge the cost of administration to the fund, and this cost is merged with the employer's general costs of administration. Only the Airways', Mineworkers' and London Transport Staff schemes, of the funded schemes in the public sector which are considered here, charge the cost of administration to the fund, and they do not necessarily use the same basis of calculation.

In the great majority of schemes, whether funded or not, not only does the cost of administration not fall on the scheme's finances but it is practically impossible to assess that cost without a great deal of effort. It is not, generally speaking, a separately identifiable item at all.

No doubt the main reason for this situation is, that in terms of administration, pensions are not usually separate from other 'establishment' subjects of a related kind, and there would therefore be little point in going to the trouble of separately identifying the cost of the administrative work involved. Nevertheless, the effect must be, and this applies especially to funded schemes, that both the total cost of pension schemes and in particular the cost falling on the employer are understated in the accounts of the scheme to the extent at least that additional work and costs are incurred simply through having a pension scheme.

Since a primary concern of this study is with the administrative effects of pension schemes, it would be valuable to form some idea of the costs of administration both in relation to individual schemes, and in relation to the public sector as a whole. Unfortunately, for the reasons already given, in the absence of comprehensive information, all that can be done is to piece together such information as is available and then to make as reasonable an estimate as possible for the missing parts. In what follows, therefore, the positive information is given first.

Funded Schemes. The cost of administration in 1962–63 in the Airways' scheme amounted to approximately £2 15s 0d per contributor (about £2 11s 0d if total membership, including pensioners, is taken into account). This figure includes all administrative work (e.g. that involved in investment), and not simply the cost of the staff directly employed on the keeping of records, making payments, etc. In the Mineworkers' scheme, again taking the year 1962–63, cost amounted to about 9s per contributor (7s if pensioners are included), and in the London Transport Staff scheme in the same year the corresponding figures were about 15s and 12s.

Non-funded Schemes. Only in the case of the National Health Service scheme is any information available, and that only for England and

Wales. In the Civil Estimates for 1963–64, 318 staff were allowed for in the NHS Superannuation Division at a total cost of £295,000, that is approximately 17s per contributor (15s if pensioners are included), but although this no doubt represents the main part of the cost of administration, it makes no allowance either for the cost of work done in other parts of the Ministry of Health and other government departments (e.g. the Government Actuary's Department) or for work done at Regional Board and hospital or Executive Council level, etc.[1]

This is the sum-total of definite published information. However, further estimates of cost may be added. Thus, on the basis of costs for the metropolitan police, the Home Office have made a rough estimate of the total cost of administering police superannuation at £186,000, or perhaps £2 10s 0d per contributor. In the field of local government the position is complicated by the existence of many funds of different sizes. A survey of 166 funds in 1950 carried out by the Institute of Municipal Treasurers and Accountants[2] was interesting not only for the concrete evidence on costs which it provided, but also for the variations which it revealed, larger funds, generally speaking, costing less per head to administer than smaller. Thus, although the average annual cost of all the 166 funds was 13s 6d per member, the range was from 17s 10d for funds of under 1,000 members to 12s 4d for funds with over 3,000 members, and for individual funds the range was from 3s 10d to £2 2s 7d.

In this IMTA survey, cost was limited, no doubt for simplicity, to the cost of staff directly engaged on superannuation matters, and although, as in the case of the NHS figures, this probably is the largest single item in the total cost, it may well understate quite considerably the total costs involved. In order to try to get a more complete picture, and also to bring up-to-date the 1950 figures, since costs have obviously risen a great deal since then, a number of inquiries were made among individual local authorities, although it was not possible to mount anything like so elaborate an inquiry as that of the 1950 IMTA survey.

Particular help was given by the Berkshire County Council both on the costs involved and on the effect of discontinuing superannuation work completely. Generally speaking, it seems likely that an average figure for the cost of administration of a local government fund in 1963 would be in the region of £2 to £2 10s 0d per contri-

---

[1] It has been estimated by the Association of Chief Financial Officers (NHS) that over 10,000,000 calculations are required annually at local level simply to assess the amount of employers' contributions.

[2] H. R. James and J. Massey, *Local Government Superannuation: Administration and Procedures*, IMTA, 1955.

butor per annum. This figure would make allowance not only for staff costs, both direct and indirect, but for overheads such as accommodation.

Again, as in 1950, this average figure undoubtedly conceals wide variations between individual funds. Even so, in comparison with the Airways and other schemes quoted earlier, the variations between schemes also show a considerable range, allowing for the different years used in the comparisons. This arises partly because cost per head is not necessarily the most meaningful guide. It is used here simply in order to give a basis for estimating the total cost of administration of public sector schemes.

For this purpose, certain more or less arbitrary assumptions need to be made. The first is that large flat-rate schemes, such as the Mineworkers' or Railways' Wages Grades, probably cost less to administer than the possibly more complex terminal-salary schemes which are more general in the public sector. The second is that a large centrally-administered scheme, such as the teachers', is on the whole more economical to run than one which is highly decentralized, such as the police or local government. The third is that funded schemes are on the whole more costly to run than non-funded. The fourth is that a contributory scheme is more costly to run than a non-contributory one.

Even if all these assumptions are accepted as reasonable, it is far from easy to say what they imply in precise cash terms. For the two large flat-rate schemes one might simply project forward the Mineworkers' scheme figures, and assess the total annual cost of these two schemes as somewhere in the region of £340,000.

For the remaining schemes, perhaps the best technique is to distinguish several categories, as follows:

(1) Large, unfunded centrally administered schemes (civil service, teachers, National Health Service): here the only information is that for the National Health Service of 15s 0d per member. The cost of the items not included in this figure could hardly be less than one-third as much again (£1) and might be double that figure (25s 0d). On the other hand, the cost of the civil service scheme ought, on the assumptions made, to be lower than for the other two. Perhaps something in the region of 22s 6d might give the best figure for the group as a whole, or, say, £2,800,000 altogether.

(2) Smaller unfunded locally administered schemes (police, firemen): here in the absence of any other information, it seems best to apply the rough estimate for the police scheme to that for firemen, say, £275,000 for the two schemes.

(3) Large funded decentralized (local government): using the

average figure of £2 5s 0d per member, total cost would be approximately £1,600,000.

(4) Remainder (that is, nationalized industries' schemes, other than flat-rate): here the only figure is that for the Airways' scheme which is higher than any of those used above; it may well be that the special circumstances of the Airways' scheme make the cost of administration higher than is the case with, say, the NCB or Electricity schemes. From the general assumptions made one would expect the average cost of this group of schemes to be somewhere between groups (1) and (3), that is, between £1 2s 6d, and £2 5s 0d per member, although tending to be nearer the latter than the former. If the figure was £1 15s 0d, the total cost would be approximately £790,000; if £2, it would be approximately £900,000. One might fix arbitrarily on £850,000.

The total figure for the annual cost of administration of public sector schemes derived from these estimates is in the region of £5¾ million to £6 million. For reasons already given this is clearly subject to a very wide margin of error. For example, the very large differences between even the published figures of costs for different schemes, when calculated as an amount per head, indicates that this is an uncertain base for projections for other schemes.

Another way of looking at administrative costs is to see what proportion they bear to the contribution income. On this basis, the proportion in the Airways' scheme is about 1½ per cent, and in the Mineworkers' just over 2 per cent. If the figure of 1½ per cent were applied to all contributory schemes and allowances made for non-contributory schemes, the total cost of administration would amount to about £4½ million; if 2 per cent, it would be about £6 million. Taking everything into account, it would be reasonable to assume that the cost of administration of public sector schemes is at present in the region of £5 million to £6 million annually. Since expenditure, including Pensions (Increase), is currently about £240 million, or £300 million including the Armed Forces, one may conclude broadly that costs of administration represent approximately an additional 2 per cent to the expenditure being charged to schemes.

Tentative as this analysis must necessarily be, it does indicate that the cost of administration, though small, is not negligible. Its smallness may well indeed be one reason why its study has been comparatively neglected and why in most schemes, including funded schemes, it has not been thought necessary to charge the cost to the scheme but to general administrative costs, just as the work itself is merged in with other administrative work. Again, if there were no pension schemes in the public sector, the saving in administrative costs would not be to the full extent of the £5 to £6 million indicated above.

The situation of administrative costs is thus somewhat ambiguous. For the most part they are not regarded as an appropriate charge on the scheme's finances, and yet at the same time they do represent some additional cost exclusively due to the existence of pension schemes. This exclusive additional cost may not amount to more than about 1½ per cent or so of the annual expenditure on pensions at the present time, perhaps £4½ million in the whole of the public sector.

COSTS OF COUNTERING INFLATION

The second main item which falls outside the definition of cost which is usually used in pension schemes is the cost of making adjustments to pensions already in payment. In terms of total expenditure, this is a far more important item than the cost of administration, but its exclusion from the cost of schemes is for rather different reasons.

As was pointed out in Chapter 3, the rules of public sector schemes do not make any provision for increasing (or decreasing) the amount of pension once it is in payment. The result is that where, as has been particularly the case since 1945, arrangements have been made periodically to increase pensions to take account of inflation, separate financial arrangements have had to be made.

It is necessary, in considering the situation, to distinguish between central and local government schemes (including the National Health Service) on the one hand, and the nationalized industries' schemes on the other. The former are covered by the periodical Pensions (Increase) Acts, but the latter are not, because, as was explained by a former Chancellor of the Exchequer, 'pensioners of industries now nationalized are not paid their pensions from public funds. . . . Moreover . . . the nationalized industries do not need additional statutory powers of this kind for the payment of pensions increase. The essential point, however, is that any improvement of pensions in this way is primarily a matter for the Boards concerned.'[1]

To take the first group first, that of schemes covered by the Pensions (Increase) Acts: in practice the financial arrangements are chiefly of importance in the local government scheme, since this is the only scheme which is funded. This means that the cost of pensions increase is charged to the general rate fund and not to the superannuation fund. In the other schemes, since there are no funds, pensions increase serves simply to increase the total annual charge which has to be met for pensions. But because pensions increase is

[1] H.C. Deb., June 2, 1959, col. 42.

not a scheme charge its cost is not included in the normal assessments of schemes (e.g. the notional fund valuations of the teachers' and NHS schemes).

To estimate the importance of pensions increase it is necessary to consider briefly how the provisions of the more recent Acts operate. Before the 1959 Act, somewhat complicated formulae were applied to pensions to determine the increase payable and, in accordance with the underlying principle of the relief of hardship, generally speaking the largest increases went to the smallest pensions and, as a corollary of this, to those which had been longest in payment.

The 1959 Act introduced a much simpler basis of calculation, a straight percentage increase on a scale which increased according to the length of time for which the pension had been in payment, and this principle was retained in the 1962 Act. In both cases, no increase was paid for the most recent pensions.

The effect of the two latest Acts may perhaps be seen most easily in the following table:

Year in which pension began to be paid	1959 Act	1962 Act
1961–62 and later	No increase	No increase
1960–61	No increase	2%
1959–60	No increase	4%
1958–59	No increase	6%
1957–58	No increase	8%
1956–57	2%	10%
1955–56	4%	12%
1954–55	6%	12%
1953–54	8%	12%

In considering this table, it should be borne in mind that each increase is applied to what is known as the 'adjusted rate' of pension, that is the basic pension as it was at the date of retirement plus any increases made under previous Pensions (Increase) Acts. Thus, a public servant who retired in 1956–57 would receive as a result of both the 1959 and the 1962 Acts an increase of rather more than 12 per cent on his original rate of pension and one who retired in 1953–54 might have qualified for an increase under the 1956 Act in addition to his 18 per cent plus, under the two subsequent Acts. One further point should be made about the 1962 Act; it aimed at providing rather more generous increases than earlier Acts. Not only was the year on which the lowest rate of increase was payable made more recent, but a new provision was added giving additional amounts to those who were aged over 70.

It can be seen that one effect of the present system is that the total amount of pensions increase which is paid in a year is neither constant nor constantly increasing. It is subject to considerable fluctuations, although with a tendency to increase immediately after the introduction of a new Act, and then to decline somewhat. At the same time, each Act would be expected to cost more than its predecessor in money terms, even if it were not designed to give improved benefits, simply because the increases would be applied to higher and more pensions.

Unfortunately, it is not easy to present a comprehensive picture over a period of time of the cost of Pensions (Increase) Acts since many of the annually published statistics (e.g. those for the NHS and teachers' schemes) do not separately distinguish these payments from other expenditure on pensions. For the Civil Service, however, the following figures taken from the Financial Secretary's Memoranda on the Civil Estimates indicate the fluctuations and the relative cost of Pensions (Increase) over the last ten years.

	(£ million)		
Year	Total gross cost of Superannuation	Pensions (Increase)	P(I) as % of total
1955–56	38·3	2·7	7%
1956–57	42·5	4·5	11%
1957–58	49·7	4·1	8%
1958–59	57·7	3·9	7%
1959–60	64·8	4·8	7%
1960–61	68·3	5·6	8%
1961–62	71·9	5·2	7%
1962–63	76·9	6·5	8%
1963–64	86·0	9·4	11%
1964–65	88·1	8·9	10%

Thus although the gross cost (including Pensions (Increase)) has risen steadily year by year, the relative cost of Pensions (Increase) itself has shown a tendency to a 'trough and peak' effect.

For the public services as a whole covered by the Pensions (Increase) Acts, the Treasury have estimated that currently (1963–64) the cost of pensions increase may be in the region of £40 million or perhaps about 15 per cent of the gross total of expenditure on pensions in these services. Some idea of the increasing cost of pensions increase may also be gained from the fact that whereas the initial cost of the 1959 Act was expected to be £8½ million in a year, that for the 1962 Act was expected to be £16 million.

In the case of the nationalized industries, neither the extent nor the cost of arrangements for increasing pensions is at all clear. In some cases (for example the Airways Corporations) there seem to be no arrangements at all, in other cases (e.g. the Railways) adjustments are made from time to time,[1] and in others again (e.g. the National Coal Board) rather more formal arrangements operate. In total, these arrangements probably cost little relatively to that incurred under the Pensions (Increase) Acts. On the other hand, since most of the nationalized industries' schemes are of comparatively recent origin, it is probably true to say that the problem has not yet become as acute as it is in the older public service schemes.

Leaving aside for the moment the position of the nationalized industries, the seriousness of the problem of pensions increase in financial terms is evident from the information given above. Not only does pensions increase even in its present form create a considerable extra charge for pensions, but because that charge does not fall on the finances of schemes it represents an additional charge for the employer alone. This at least is the case in funded schemes such as local government; in the case of non-funded but contributory schemes such as the teachers' or National Health Service, it remains true on the theoretical, notional funding basis, although on current account the ordinary contributions from employers and employees may, and indeed at present do, cover the cost of both scheme pensions and pensions increase.

For this reason, any proposals such as those described in Chapter 3 for putting pensions increase on a more permanent basis, and still more for linking pensions in payment in some kind of automatic way either to the cost-of-living index or to the value of pensions currently being issued, is bound to come up against the fundamental difficulty of cost, and, perhaps, equally important, of whether that cost should be shared between employer and employee as is generally the case with the cost of pensions under the scheme.[2]

For the nationalized industries with their funded schemes the problem of cost would also be particularly acute for employers, although a recent development may point the way to an easing of this problem. The latest valuation of the NCB Principal scheme disclosed a large surplus, and it is proposed to use the major part of this in a scheme to provide for the preservation of the value of pensions after retirement. This clearly would be one way of providing the improvement without a great deal of extra expense.

[1] The plight of railway superannuitants, many on very small pensions, has attracted attention in the House of Commons and elsewhere. The latest (1963) scheme for supplementing these pensions was estimated to affect over 20,000 pensioners at an annual cost of £930,000 (H.C. Deb., March 13, 1963, Written Answer, col. 168).

[2] For example, the Financial Secretary to the Treasury estimated that in 1962 the cost of raising current pensions to the level of those being awarded at that time would be equivalent for civil servants to a 4 per cent contribution, and this would tend to rise (H.C. Deb., August 2, 1962).

It remains to be seen whether other schemes will follow this example.

Both the cost of administration and, more particularly, the cost of pensions increase alter significantly the financial picture of the cost of pensions. Whether they ought to be taken into account in assessing the cost under pension schemes is not in issue here. The point which is important is that simply to look at the financial arrangements of schemes as they exist at present does not indicate how all the costs which may reasonably be associated with the provision of pensions are met. And of the total gross cost of pensions in any particular year, perhaps 15–20 per cent has to be met outside the finances of the scheme as a direct charge on the employer.

CHAPTER 5

Private Sector Schemes:
The Contrasts between the Public and
Private Sectors

To examine the whole field of pension provision within the limits of one book would be a formidable undertaking. What the present study aims to do is rather to throw light on some general problems which an examination of the present position in the public sector suggests. But the question immediately arises whether these problems are peculiar to public sector schemes or whether they are common to all schemes. It is the main purpose of this chapter to consider some schemes in private commerce and industry to see whether they can help towards an understanding of the problems and difficulties exemplified in greater detail in the account of public sector schemes, and also to draw attention to significant ways in which such schemes differ from those in the public sector.

The obvious points of contrast between public and private sector schemes should be emphasized, although some of these points have already been touched on in earlier chapters. To begin with, there is the size of the public sector and of the main schemes within it. Accurate, up-to-date figures of the number of people covered by pension schemes are not easily obtainable but a note summarizing the present position and that of recent years is included as Appendix 1. From this it can be seen that in spite of the rapid growth of private schemes in recent years, public sector schemes (including the Armed Forces) still account for perhaps 40 per cent of the membership of all pension schemes; ten years ago it may have been in the region of 55 per cent; but perhaps even more striking is the fact that within the public sector four large schemes (civil service, local government, teachers, National Health Service) together account for over 2 million members, that is, for nearly one-fifth of the total membership of all schemes, both public and private. And the smallest scheme considered in detail in Chapters 3 and 4 (the AEA Non-industrial) has 20,000 members. On the other hand, the Government Actuary's survey of the position in 1956 indicated that 75 per cent of private schemes had less than fifty members, and less than 2 per cent had 1,000 or more members.

The question of size also has a bearing on the variety of schemes. A striking point which has emerged from the consideration of public sector schemes in earlier chapters is not that there are variations from scheme to scheme, e.g. to take account (as in the case of the police and firemen) of different conditions of service, but that by and large they form a single group of schemes sharing their main characteristics. But this is certainly not true of private sector schemes as a whole, one of whose main characteristics is variety.

Such variety in the private sector as a whole does not necessarily mean that there are not distinctive patterns, for example, within particular industries or particular branches of commerce. It might well be possible to compare pension provision in, say, the banks, with that in the building industry, and to establish that a certain historical development had led to the development of terminal-salary schemes in the former but not to any great extent in the latter. But this in itself would demonstrate a difference between the public and private sectors, since in the public sector activities as diverse as that of the Electricity Supply industry and of the National Health Service support broadly similar pension schemes.

One may sum up the position by saying that on the one hand most public sector schemes are very large, and on the other that the tendency of private sector schemes is to show much greater diversity, at the same time being much smaller in terms of numbers. In these circumstances, it is quite impossible to select anything in the nature of a typical group of private sector schemes; such schemes may range from a flat-rate type providing a very small pension to schemes as generous as, or perhaps in some respects more generous, than the ordinary level of public sector schemes, up to the limit permitted by the Inland Revenue authorities.

An illustration of the extent to which schemes may differ purely in terms of the level of pension is provided by the figures in the Government Actuary's survey: of those self-administered schemes which provided pensions, in rather less than half[1] the pension was calculated as a fraction of wages or salary for each year of service, that is to say on the same basis as for public service schemes, but whereas one-third used eightieths in the calculation and rather less than one-third used sixtieths, the remainder had some other fraction; but apart from these terminal-salary schemes, there were others which had a fixed amount of pension or a fixed proportion of final salary, some in which the pension depended on the amount of contributions, and a residue of one-fifth of cases which used some other basis. One may contrast this position with that of public sector schemes which, with the two important exceptions of the Mine-

[1] To be accurate, the results are expressed in the survey in terms of the percentages of numbers of members in the different categories.

workers and the Railways Male Wages Grade (and, in a different way, of the Armed Forces), are all terminal-salary schemes. A similar situation but a different pattern is revealed by the insured schemes: of those which provided pensions, in nearly half the pension depended on the total amount of salary or wages earned throughout service; in about a quarter one or other of the means specified above was used; and in the remaining quarter some other basis was used.[1]

Such contrasts between public sector schemes as a whole and private schemes, and within private schemes between insured and non-insured schemes, run through the whole range of provisions in the schemes. For example, where employees in the public sector pay a fixed percentage contribution of wages or salary, they mostly (80 per cent) pay more than 5 per cent and the range is only between 4 per cent and 6½ per cent; but in insured schemes the majority (78 per cent) pay 5 per cent and the range is between 2 per cent and 10 per cent; and in non-insured schemes 52 per cent pay less than 5 per cent, 40 per cent pay 5 per cent and the range is even wider between 1 per cent and 11 per cent. With all this it has to be remembered that this particular method of paying contributions, as opposed to either not having contributions at all (which is quite common in private sector schemes) or using some other method, is very common in the public sector, fairly common in self-administered schemes and comparatively rare in insured schemes. Even allowing for the fact that in some cases these different approaches might be regarded as variations of one method rather than different methods, it will be seen that at the least one would need to look at two typical sets of schemes, one for self-administered and one for insured schemes in order to have a basis for comparisons.

This discussion suggests that a rather different approach will need to be made in this chapter from that in the chapters dealing with public sector schemes. First, a general survey of the position of private sector schemes will be made, based on the Government Actuary's survey; although this was made several years ago, it remains the only comprehensive guide to such questions as the range of contributions and the basis of calculation of pensions in the different schemes; nevertheless, it should be borne in mind that the position revealed by the survey may well have changed in some ways

---

[1] It is possible that the variety of private sector schemes may not be so great in terms of the amount of pension actually received. The information relates only to the provisions of schemes; but it is the practice of many employers who have installed a modest pension scheme, to supplement pensions as they become due on an *ex gratia* basis. There are obvious advantages to the employer in such an arrangement and corresponding disadvantages to the employee, but in the nature of the case it is difficult to get comprehensive information about such arrangements, and still more to say how this affects comparison of how much pension is actually received by public and private sector members.

E

since then. Secondly, a more detailed examination will be made of a number of selected schemes. Finally, a number of general topics which are of concern to all schemes will be considered.

As was indicated in footnote 1 (p. 128), the results of the Government Actuary's survey are presented in the form of percentages of members of schemes covered by the different arrangements; the effect of this is to give greater weight to the provisions of the schemes with the largest numbers of members. To the extent that the larger private schemes are more truly comparable with public sector schemes than the smaller, this may serve to bring out the points of difference between the two types of scheme, but it should be borne in mind that figures quoted from the survey are in this form and do not relate to the proportion of schemes in the different categories.

One point which the survey does illustrate is the tendency referred to in Chapter 2 to have separate schemes for salaried staff on the one hand and workpeople on the other, to a greater extent than in the public sector. It is noticeable, however, that in two of the nationalized industries which employ very large numbers of manual workers, coal and railways, there are distinct and separate schemes for these workers, although in the case of the coal industry, manual workers who are not mineworkers belong to the salaried staff scheme.

Reference was made earlier to the wide range of contributions and the differing ways of calculating them in private sector schemes, and corresponding to this is a great variety of pension calculations. It is also worth mentioning one or two other points of interest in this connexion which are brought out by the survey. In the first place, 44 per cent of those in non-insured schemes and 30 per cent in insured were in non-contributory schemes; these comparatively high figures are, however, said to be overstated.[1] Secondly, widows' benefits, though fairly general in the public sector, are not very common in private sector schemes where the usual benefit on death is a lump sum payment (this may, however, be a case where developments since 1956 have altered the picture).[2] Thirdly, all public sector schemes provide a pension on retirement for reasons of ill-health, but this is comparatively rare in insured schemes, although common but by no means universal in non-insured schemes; on the other hand, private sector schemes and particularly insured schemes commonly provide for a reduced pension for retirement within five to ten years before normal retiring age whereas only about half those

[1] The reason for this over-statement is not clear, as 'Top Hat' schemes (on which see page 308) were excluded from the survey. The figures should therefore be treated with caution.

[2] On the other hand, a recent survey of pension schemes in 180 companies seems to indicate that the trend may be in the direction of more generous lump sum payments. (Michael Pilch and Victor Wood, *New Trends in Pensions*, Hutchinson, 1964, p. 53).

in public sector schemes can take advantage of such an arrangement.

A further point of some interest is that it is very rare in private sector schemes to provide both a pension and a lump sum on retirement, although this, as has been seen, is a characteristic feature of public sector schemes. This difference is probably largely due to the different historical development of schemes in the public and private sectors and also to the influence of the provisions governing the tax treatment of pension schemes. Indeed the whole subject of lump sums on retirement is very closely bound up with the tax position and is considered further in Chapter 7 (and also Appendix 7).

DETAILED COMPARISON OF SELECTED PRIVATE SECTOR SCHEMES

So far only the general aspects of private sector schemes have been considered, particularly as they appear in the Government Actuary's survey. To balance this picture some examples of actual schemes will be given to see how far their rules and detailed working conform to the general picture already presented. With one exception (the Federated Superannuation System for Universities, on which see page 135), these schemes belong to the National Association of Pension Funds; they are all, again with this one exception, self-administered or non-insured, and they are on the whole schemes of the larger employers. From what has already been said, it will be clear that these schemes are therefore not typical in the sense that the largest class of schemes is that of the insured, small scheme. On the other hand, since the problems with which this study is concerned are mainly those of the very large public sector schemes it is perhaps more likely that light will be thrown on them by considering the larger private sector schemes.

The method chosen here has been to select for detailed study the schemes of six firms, with a further five in rather less detail, the object being partly to indicate the quite considerable range of variation even among the schemes of larger employers, and partly to see whether even so the characteristic differences between private and public sector schemes can be identified. Thus, although the selected schemes may not be typical of private schemes as a whole, they should provide a fair cross-section of a particular group of them and one which one would expect to be reasonably close to public sector schemes in level of benefits. The six firms mentioned between them run thirteen principal schemes, that is, excluding the smaller closed schemes or those specially designed to provide lesser benefits for special groups of staff. The number of staff covered by these thirteen schemes is about 100,000 and the number of pensioners about 19,000; individual schemes range from about 2,000 to about

22,000 members, so that they all come within the top $\frac{1}{2}$ per cent of the Government Actuary's distribution by size (as opposed to the 75 per cent with fewer than fifty members). Furthermore, the 100,000 members represent perhaps 1 per cent of all members of pension schemes but about 4 per cent of the total of self-administered or non-insured private schemes. The schemes of the five firms considered in less detail contribute a further 44,000 members and 12,000 pensioners.

Table A in the Appendix to this chapter (page 153) gives details of the provisions of ten of the thirteen schemes, on the basis adopted in presenting public sector schemes, that is, showing the conditions which would apply to new entrants to these schemes now. The individual firms are represented by letters and not by the names of the firm, since for the purposes of this study it is not important to identify the particular firm concerned and also because many of the details of these schemes are private to the particular firm concerned in a way which is not so in the case of public sector schemes. Table A reveals some interesting points: the tendency towards terminal-salary schemes, particularly for salaried staff; the tendency towards making the normal age of retirement coincide with the normal age at which National Insurance retirement pensions become payable; the tendency towards providing for death before retirement both lump sum death benefits and a widow's pension of half what the husband would have got—these may be said to represent common factors to these schemes.

But perhaps of more significance, particularly to the members and pensioners, are the differences. Even taking simply the terminal-salary schemes (but leaving aside for the moment the 'D' schemes) the pension after forty years may vary from less than half final salary to two-thirds. This point illustrates very well how difficult is the comparison between private and public sector schemes, particularly in any attempt to compare level of benefits. For example, a widow's pension of one-half, as is found in a number of the schemes shown in Table A, may seem relatively generous when compared with the normal widow's pension of one-third in public service schemes, particularly where that pension is provided either wholly (local government, NHS) or partly (Civil Service, AEA) by reduction of another benefit. As against this it has to be remembered that in some of the private schemes considered here the actual amount of pension may not differ so much from corresponding pensions in public sector schemes, given the differing fractions on which pensions are calculated.[1] Again in making comparisons it has to be remembered

[1] The position is even more difficult to present with accuracy for the following reason: most public sector schemes normally provide a pension *and* a lump sum on retirement but the widow's pension is based only on the husband's pension.

that a great many public servants may retire on a maximum (two-thirds) pension at the age of 60 whereas in the case of most of these private schemes, if retirement is permitted before the normal retiring age (and it generally is) the pension will be reduced.

Certain characteristic features of the schemes shown in Table A are not usually found in public sector schemes. One is the possibility of paying extra contributions to gain additional pension, a provision found only in some of the nationalized industries' schemes in the public sector. For this there may be two reasons: one is that the normal career in any case would bring the maximum permissible pension; the other that in so far as the 'life service' tradition still applies in the public service, there may be less need for a provision designed to supplement what would otherwise be a rather small pension in the case of someone joining a scheme at a later age than the minimum. The point may be illustrated by reference to the 'A' staff scheme: after forty years' service the pension would be half the final salary but without a lump sum as in most public sector schemes; on the other hand, if only twenty years' service were possible until retiring age, the drop from retiring salary to pension would be even more marked. It remains true, however, that this provision on the whole is not frequently used in these private schemes, partly no doubt because there is no employer's contribution to match that paid by the employee. As one would expect, however, it is used more often in those schemes where the normal level of contributions and benefits is relatively modest.

Another characteristic feature of these schemes is the possibility, already referred to, of retirement before the normal retiring age, for reasons other than the ones normally recognized by schemes, such as ill-health. The rule might be that retirement might take place up to ten years before normal retiring age with a pension reduced actuarially to take account of the increased number of years during which it is likely to be payable. But in fact even within these few schemes the precise conditions for this provision vary greatly. Retirement may be permitted up to five or up to ten years before retirement; it may be subject in all or some cases to the approval of the employer; it may require a qualifying period of service; or it may allow the alternative of a deferred pension at normal retiring age. This latter provision resembles that in the civil service scheme, under which a civil servant may retire at any time after the age of 50 with a deferred pension payable at 60, but only in exceptional circum-

One would need therefore to take into account any lump sum benefits payable to the widow before making comparisons. Furthermore, public sector schemes generally do and private sector schemes generally do not provide the same widow's benefit if death occurs after retirement as they do for death before retirement. Points like these serve to show how misleading isolated comparisons can be.

stances is a pension payable immediately. But apart from this rather special civil service case, this kind of provision is found only in certain nationalized industries' schemes within the public sector.

The pattern so far disclosed by these ten schemes is not markedly changed by a glance at the main points of five further salaried staff schemes which are briefly noted in Table B of the Appendix. What emerges most strikingly perhaps is the variety of ways in which the pension can be calculated in terminal-salary schemes, and this is in marked contrast to the uniformity of public sector schemes. But if one asks how these schemes compare as a whole with public sector schemes the question is really unanswerable. It is of course possible to assess the value in actuarial terms (e.g. as a percentage of salaries) of the different benefits in different schemes, but this is not necessarily the same thing as assessing the value of different kinds of benefit to members of schemes. To take just one example: is it better to have simply a pension or a pension and a lump sum even if they are actuarially equivalent?

Again, in the matter of employee contributions, comparison is even less meaningful than it was in the case of public sector schemes, without taking into account a whole range of other factors. To take just one example: staff scheme 'A' and staff scheme 'E' are similar and in both the employee pays a contribution of 6 per cent, but the former provides a smaller pension than the latter. One cannot simply conclude that 'E' is a better scheme than 'A'; for one thing, it would first be necessary to consider the schemes as a whole. It may be that a greater rate of inflation is allowed for in 'A' than in 'E' for example, and this more conservative actuarial basis would mean that a given contribution would not provide as large a benefit. But it is also necessary to take into account the general policies pursued by firms. One firm may not be as wealthy as another and may not therefore be able to afford as generous a pension scheme. Alternatively there might be two equally wealthy firms which pursued different policies in relation to pension schemes. This would be particularly liable to happen where the firms were in different industries, with different traditions and a different outlook on the part of both management and staff.

The safe conclusion seems to be that neither in level of benefits nor in the rate of contributions paid by the employee can any worthwhile comparison be drawn between these private schemes and public sector schemes. Nevertheless, this is not quite the only thing which can be said. Perhaps the most generous scheme from the member's viewpoint is staff scheme 'E' (again, leaving aside the rather complicated arrangements of 'D' which are discussed later); for a contribution of 6 per cent it provides a two-thirds pension after forty years and a widow's pension of half the husband's pension, to name the two benefits of the greatest general importance. Effectively, this is very similar to the NCB Principal scheme except that there contributions are 5 per cent, but it is perhaps rather more generous than, say, local government where the widow's pension is less and where the pension plus lump sum is also less than two-thirds for a married man. But the point is not to establish whether 'E' is or is not a more generous scheme than those in the public sector but rather to make the general point that a scheme of this kind is, taken as a whole, at the same kind of level as a public sector scheme. This takes no account of the fact that in some respects it may be more generous and in some respects less so; although, to be fair, it should be pointed out that a firm which did want to introduce a scheme which was much more generous than public service schemes would find itself in difficulties with the Inland Revenue authorities.[1]

It may be useful for comparative purposes to consider here the main features of one important insured scheme, the Federated Superannuation System for Universities (FSSU) of which brief details are also included in Table A. Again, this scheme is not typical of the majority of insured schemes, which are now based on group arrangements; and the arrangement under which a number of separate employers take part is also not typical; but it merits detailed consideration here. In the first place, it is in the nature of a borderline case between a public sector and a private scheme; secondly, it is a large scheme, comparable in size with other private sector schemes considered here (20,000 members); thirdly, although it has a number of special features it also has a number of characteristics which it shares with other insured schemes and which serve to contrast them with non-insured and particularly terminal-salary schemes.

One point of very great importance is that there is no fixed scale of benefits; this is because there are eight different types of policy and fourteen different insurance companies offering policies (although each company rarely offers more than three or four of the eight types). The member can choose the policy which best suits his needs from the various 'options' (about fifty in all). Some of the eight types of policy are of relatively minor importance and it would be true to say that the choice is mainly between an endowment assurance (with or without profits) and a deferred annuity (with or without profits). Since all the endowment assurances carry a guaranteed rate of annuity from age 60, and all the deferred annuities carry a guaranteed cash option from the same age the main difference

---

[1] For example, a scheme providing more than a two-thirds pension at the end of forty years' service would not be approved for the purpose of tax reliefs; but so advantageous are these reliefs that it is highly unlikely that any scheme would be so framed. The point illustrates the considerable influence of taxation arrangements on private sector schemes (see also Chapter 7).

between the two types is that the former provides a death benefit and the latter does not but only a return of contributions. There are no widows' benefits as such although on retirement a member may convert his annuity into a joint annuity for himself and his wife; but, to guard against the possibility of death in service, the member must either choose an endowment assurance or make arrangements outside the scheme. There is also no provision for an immediate pension for retirement on grounds of ill-health.

In this latter respect, FSSU is similar to many insured schemes; in the Government Actuary's survey, for example, 70 per cent of members of insured schemes were shown to be without the benefit of a provision for ill-health retirement compared with only 25 per cent in private non-insured schemes and none in public service schemes. Similarly, the lump sum death benefit is characteristic of insured schemes; the Government Actuary's survey showed that all the members of insured schemes were entitled to this benefit and none to a widow's pension, although nearly a quarter of members of non-insured schemes and more than three-quarters of those in the public services could claim a widow's pension.

But even more significant than the ways in which FSSU is similar to other insured schemes is the fact that in one important way it differs considerably from the great majority of pension schemes. Almost all private pension schemes give entitlement to a pension on normal retirement and only a very small number provide only a lump sum; but in FSSU the whole of the benefits can be taken in the form of a lump sum. The restriction on lump sums in most schemes, however, is not simply a question of preference for pensions as such; it derives from the fact that since pensions are taxed as income but lump sums are untaxed the Inland Revenue will not approve a scheme which provides more than one-quarter of the total retirement benefits in the form of a lump sum. FSSU was set up before tax considerations played any part in superannuation and remained exempt from later legislation on the subject.[1]

The interesting question remains of how benefits under FSSU compare with those in a typical terminal-salary scheme. The number of factors and possible alternatives to be taken into account in making such a comparison seems to make this an impossible question to answer without a great deal of labour. Fortunately, the labour has

[1] A further point about the FSSU scheme is that the whole of the lump sum benefit may be used to buy an annuity which will now, under the general provisions of the Finance Act, 1956 (section 27), be only partly taxed. The scheme is, however, 'frozen' in the sense that if any major change were made in it it would have to seek Inland Revenue approval and thus become subject to the current tax rules relating to pension schemes (on which see Chapter 7 and Appendix 7). For the specific tax position of FSSU see Report of a Committee on the Superannuation of University Teachers, H.M.S.O. 1960, pp. 38–40.

already been done; the Committee set up by the University Grants Committee and the Treasury in 1958 to consider the superannuation of university teachers was concerned with just this question from the point of view of whether it would be advantageous to university staffs to have a terminal-salary rather than the existing scheme. In order to see the relative financial advantages, an assessment was made of the relation between pension and final salary under FSSU on various assumptions about type of career, type of policy and levels of salaries; and these were compared with corresponding ratios under a terminal-salary scheme.

The interesting conclusion was reached that if annual salary increases were at the rate of about 2 per cent or less FSSU produced a more favourable pension position, but if the rate were higher a terminal-salary scheme became progressively more advantageous; this advantage was, however, considerably reduced by the more favourable tax liability of the pensioner under FSSU.[1] What is true of FSSU is of course not necessarily true of other insured schemes, nor can a straight comparison of the level of principal benefits tell us anything about the value to a member of a scheme which has a widow's benefit compared with one which has not, but certain general points can be made: one is that FSSU shows that a money-purchase scheme is not necessarily much inferior in terms of the main benefit to a terminal-salary scheme provided that there is not steep inflation; another is that a scheme of this kind is able to allow more variety in the calculation of this benefit, compared with a terminal-salary scheme where the pension must necessarily be calculated in the same way for everybody.[2] A third point, on the preservation of pension rights, is dealt with later in this chapter.

THE IMPACT OF NATIONAL INSURANCE

Before trying to sum up the position, it will be useful to consider some specific problems which affect both public and private sector schemes. Foremost among these is the problem of state pensions provided through the National Insurance system; some account of the effect generally on both public and private sector schemes will be given in Chapter 6. Here, reference will be made simply to ways in which the schemes listed in the Appendix have tackled the basic problem, that is, given a universal state scheme, whether allowance should be made for it in the terms of the occupational scheme. More

[1] This ignores some other complicating factors. For a full statement and for the impossibility of comparing the two types of scheme as a whole see the Report of the Committee, H.M.S.O. 1960, paras. 41–57.

[2] On the other hand, a terminal-salary scheme may have more scope for variety in the range of benefits provided.

E*

recently there has been the further problem of whether or not to take part in the graduated scheme.

From the Appendix Tables, it will be seen that some direct account of the existence of the National Insurance retirement pension is taken in about half these schemes, mainly those for salaried staff. This would be quite consistent with the view that it is the schemes which are already paying, as most public sector schemes do, a reasonably generous pension which naturally tend to limit these schemes to take account of the universal National Insurance benefit. There is a strong financial reason for this too; an employer who has set up a reasonably generous scheme is probably contributing to it on a generous scale. He will also have to pay the employer's share of the National Insurance contribution; he may well feel therefore that it is reasonable and justifiable to make some reduction in the total expense, and since he cannot escape the National Insurance contribution he will reduce the occupational scheme. The method most favoured for doing this is to reduce the salary by a specified amount before calculating both contributions and pensions. But the method varies a good deal from scheme to scheme: in 'A' the reduction in salary is £100, but this is an optional arrangement and was only introduced with the introduction of the graduated scheme; in 'C' there was originally a reduction in contributions of 1s per week from the introduction of National Insurance in 1948 with an actuarially equivalent reduction in pension, and the amounts have been increased at intervals since; in 'E' the reduction in salary was £200 but this was increased to £300 with the introduction of the graduated scheme in 1961; in 'D' full integration with National Insurance has taken place (this is discussed below).

The second point of interest is that in only one of these private sector schemes have the members been contracted out of the graduated pension scheme; this may seem surprising in view of the size of these schemes and the fact that nearly 30 per cent of the members of private sector schemes have been contracted out as well as most of the members of public sector schemes, but the factors influencing the decision are very complex and even in terms of cost to the employer, let alone advantage to the employee, the decision is not obvious. But on the evidence of these schemes, the graduated scheme has proved an incentive to making allowance (or in some cases further allowance) in both contributions and pensions for the effects of National Insurance. In the case of 'D', the graduated scheme has been the occasion for a new approach to the problem of the relations between the state and occupational schemes and for this reason the arrangements will be described in some detail.

There are two schemes, one for works employees and one for salaried staff, but similar terms apply to both. A single contribution of 8 per cent by the employee covers both his contribution to the National Insurance scheme for pensions, including any graduated contribution, and his contribution to the occupational scheme. Correspondingly, the scheme provides for a total pension payable on retirement, part under the National Insurance scheme and part under the occupational scheme. The effect on the scheme's finances, as compared with the more usual arrangement, is thus two-fold: first, income from contributions will vary according to changes in the rate of National Insurance contribution, and, secondly, there is no guaranteed rate of pension which the occupational scheme must pay, since this too will depend on the amount of National Insurance pension at the time of retirement. Effectively, the firm's guarantee of a total rate of pension which is related to final wages or salary depends on the maintenance of the present system of National Insurance.

This system has the advantage from the employee's point of view that whatever changes are made in the National Insurance scheme, including the graduated part, his rate of contribution and of pension will remain the same.[1] Correspondingly, the advantage to the employer is that he has no need to change the rules of the scheme for every change in National Insurance, although administratively he will still have to make adjustments each time the state scheme is altered in the apportionment of contributions and benefits between the two systems. There is also the consequence that if the state scheme grows in importance, or if it becomes more costly, correspondingly the occupational scheme will diminish in importance, unless at some point the present total contribution of 8 per cent is raised. At present, the occupational scheme accounts for the greater part of the contribution paid by the employee, particularly of course and increasingly as the salary rises above the graduated limit of £18 a week (£960 p.a.). A somewhat similar position applies to the amount of pension, although there the comparison is made more complicated by the fact that the schemes are on different bases and that there is less correspondence, in the case of National Insurance, between the amount of contribution paid and the amount of pension received. On a 'typical' career of forty years' service, with a retiring salary in the range £750–£1,000, the state pension might account (excluding the additional married man's part) for somewhere around 30 per cent of the whole, the other 70 per cent being provided by the occupational scheme.

The significance of the 'D' scheme arrangements will be more apparent when account is taken of the wider arguments concerning

---

[1] Since the state pension included in the calculation is that payable to a single person, this statement necessarily excludes any changes which may be made in the *additional* pension payable to a married man (see Appendix 6).

state pensions which are discussed in Chapter 6. But one thing may be said here; this scheme goes further in practice than most schemes, and certainly further than public sector schemes in recognizing the state scheme as an integral part of the pension provisions for retirement. In other words, it is implicit in the 'D' scheme arrangements that there is a certain optimum level of pension benefit, and that the object of the occupational scheme should be to supplement whatever provision is made by the State in order to achieve that level. This approach will need to be considered again later in Chapter 10 in connexion with the future development of public sector schemes.

PRESERVATION OF PENSION RIGHTS ON CHANGE OF EMPLOYMENT

Reference was made in Chapter 3 to the arrangements for preservation of pension rights on change of employment in public sector schemes. Evidence generally about the position on transfers between private sector schemes is not plentiful: in 1950 comparatively few privately administered schemes had power to pay transfer values and even where there was the power it was not necessarily used very much; 'cold-storage' was believed to be very rare; and in life office schemes there was not usually any provision for payment of transfer values, although either a cash surrender value or a paid-up, i.e. 'cold-storage' pension could be taken based, however, only on the employee's own contributions in most cases.[1]

Somewhat fuller information showing the same tendencies is given in the Government Actuary's survey of the position in 1956; only about one-quarter of the members of privately administered schemes were able, according to the rules of those schemes, to benefit from the payment of transfer values on change of employment, compared with 98 per cent of public sector employees. These figures do not indicate the conditions under which transfer values were payable, an important point when it is remembered that the public sector arrangements are in practice restricted almost entirely to movement within the public sector. But it is stated that in the great majority of cases payment was at the employer's discretion. Nor does the survey indicate what is almost equally important: the extent to which in practice these provisions are used. It did, however, show that where the basis of the transfer values was stated in the rules, in one-fifth of the cases it amounted to no more than the total of contributions paid, with interest. Transfer values are not explicitly provided for in insured schemes; over half the members of such schemes could, however, take the option of a deferred annuity in lieu of a return of

[1] The information is in a Report, *Preservation of Pension Rights* by F. H. Spratling, F. W. Bacon and A. E. Bromfield published by the Institute of Actuaries and the Faculty of Actuaries in 1957.

contributions, often including also the benefit of the employers' contributions, but again it is not stated under what conditions such deferred annuities may be taken.

Such is the general position so far as the available information reveals it.[1] In turning to the individual schemes shown in Table A, it is noticeable that in general there is either no specific provision for preservation of pension rights on voluntary withdrawal, or else, where a transfer value may be paid it is equivalent only to the amount of contributions paid by the employee, with accumulated interest. This situation applies to 'B' (both schemes), 'C', 'E' (works scheme) and 'F'. In 'A', a paid-up pension or transfer value equivalent to the accrued pension rights may be chosen after ten years' service; in 'D' a paid-up pension may be chosen by any employee leaving after at least five years' service; and in 'E' (staff scheme) a paid-up pension or a transfer value based on the employee's actuarial interest may be granted. In the first two cases, the choice is the employee's and therefore information about the numbers who choose either a paid-up pension or a transfer payment in preference to a return of contributions should throw some light on the value of such arrangements to the members of schemes. Through the courtesy of the Pension Officer of the 'D' scheme, the following information has been provided about staff employees leaving in 1960; of those who were entitled to take paid-up pensions instead of a refund of contributions, the proportions who did so were:

Men under age 35	Men over age 35	Women under age 40	Women over age 40
10%	25%	4%	25%

Thus even in the most favourable situation for preserving pension rights, where the employee is not restricted by having to obtain his employer's consent, no more than a quarter even of the older employees chose to do so. These figures merely serve to confirm the general experience of those concerned with running pension schemes that there is little interest on the part of employees in being able to preserve their pension rights on change of employment. It is easy to see some of the reasons which may account for this situation; a man of 40 may well feel that the 'bird in the hand' of an immediate cash payment is of more value to him than a pension payable in twenty-five years' time. He knows that he can make use of a capital sum of, say £500 representing his contributions over fifteen years plus interest, whereas the prospect of a pension for life from the age of 65 of £200 a year, although it may represent better value for money

[1] See also R. C. Sansom and N. N. B. Ordman, *Preserving Pension Rights for Professional Engineers*, Engineers' Guild, 1964.

in the long run, is not without hazards; death and inflation, to name only the two most obvious, may serve to reduce greatly the value of a prospective pension.

But a further point should be noted here: one may distinguish three categories of change of employment, and the situation is different in each. They are (1) within the public sector; (2) public to private sector or vice versa; (3) within the private sector. The point was made in Chapter 3 that in (1) there increasingly tends to be freedom of movement between one public sector scheme and another through the system of interchange rules, but as far as (2) is concerned practically the only arrangements made are between certain nationalized industries (e.g. Electricity) and individual private firms. In the case of (3) the situation is probably somewhere in between; although over large areas of the private field no effective provision exists either for frozen pensions or for transfer arrangements, in others a variety of means have been adopted including the unilateral or 'no strings attached' 'frozen pension'; among others, Unilever, Guinness, United Kingdom Provident Institution and Lloyds Bank have adopted this latter arrangement.[1]

A rather different type of arrangement operates in some private schemes. This is where a number of employers take part in the same scheme so that a change of employer makes no difference to the continuity of the pension cover. These schemes are usually limited to those employed in a particular profession or occupation and often they are insured schemes based on the 'money-purchase' system. The reason for this is clear; in a terminal-salary scheme the last employer, that is, the employer at the time of retirement, has the responsibility of meeting the cost of the pension for the whole period of service although in any particular case he may only have been the employer for the last few years of service. In an extreme case, such as local government with its large number of separate funds, this situation may even act to deter an employer from employing a man; but even where there is not the complication of separate funds, the division of cost between a number of separate employers may give rise to difficulties. All this is avoided if the scheme is based on individual or group policies of assurance, for then no transfer arrangements or preservation arrangements are necessary, the employer accepting the obligation to pay his share of the contributions precisely as he accepts his obligation to pay salaries or wages.

One of the earliest and one of the most important schemes of this kind is FSSU. Indeed, one of the main objects of the establishment of FSSU in 1913 was to make it possible for university teachers to move

---

[1] Arthur Seldon, 'Pensions, Public and Private', *The Times*, December 6, 1960. Usually, as in the 'D' scheme, there is a minimum period of qualifying service.

freely from one university to another without loss of pension rights. The particular problem in a case of this kind is that whereas the employers, the universities, are separate independent bodies, the normal career is not or is not necessarily restricted to only one employer. Indeed, no one would dispute that if, as was the case before 1913, separate superannuation arrangements in the different universities tended to discourage movement of staff this would be undesirable. FSSU, as has been seen, is based on individual insurance policies and movement from one university to another involves simply the assignment of the policy. It is, of course, true that both the teachers' and the NHS schemes also provide that change of employment within the teaching or health services should maintain the continuity of pension rights with the minimum of formality, but in these cases the continuity is achieved through a central organization which has records for the entire scheme, and more importantly, is responsible for the finances of the scheme. In this way awkward problems of adjustment between different employers are avoided.

Similar schemes to FSSU are the Federated Superannuation scheme for Nurses and Hospital Officers (a pre-NHS scheme), a scheme for Chartered Accountants' Employees (a group scheme), one for officers in the Merchant Navy and one for employees in the flour-milling industry. In all except the last case there is an obvious association between the particular occupation and movement; a nurse is no more expected to spend her working life in one hospital than a ship's captain on one ship. But the extension to flour-milling employees shows that such a system need not be confined only to the professions. Further interesting developments of this kind are the Port Employers' and Registered Dockworkers' Pension scheme which was introduced at the beginning of 1961,[1] the scheme for agricultural workers launched by the National Farmers' Union early in 1962, and the scheme put forward by the Horserace Betting Levy Board in June 1964 for jockeys and others employed in racing stables. The essence of such schemes is that a worker going from employment under one employer in the scheme to another automatically carries his pension rights with him as indeed he does under the National Insurance scheme. Another interesting arrangement is the Social Workers Pension scheme, a scheme covering any body of voluntary workers which chooses to join.

Particular conditions may apply to these particular employments, but why should not the same principle be extended, say, to other professions—engineers, for example? It was pointed out in 1960 that although almost all professional engineers had some entitlement to a pension, very few could rely on full preservation of pension

[1] For a brief account of this scheme, see *Industry and Labour*, I.L.O, August 1, 1961, vol. XXVI, No. 3.

rights on voluntary change of employment.[1] But it seems likely that such schemes are for the most part confined to employers who are in particularly close association with one another, or for whom mobility between different employers is important; moreover, it should not be forgotten that one of the motives for the setting up of pension schemes has been the desire to compete for and retain staff, a desire which is at variance with the idea of federated pension schemes. There are also obvious limitations on the idea even within the private field: for one thing, even within the particular profession or occupation it only applies to those employers who agree to take part, and although this may mean all of them (as with the universities) it is not necessarily so; secondly, the same problems arise as elsewhere for anybody who wants to move outside the particular group. This is akin to the problem of transfers between the public and the private sectors, and it emphasizes how difficult it is, both as a matter of policy and in terms of practical arrangements, to find an agreed principle on which to work.

The situation at the moment may be summarized by saying that on the one hand, a limited amount of opportunity exists within the private field of retaining pension rights on change of employment and on the other, that even where the opportunity exists it is comparatively rarely used. Many would like to see this changed in favour of some universal system of preservation of pension rights, perhaps with compulsion, and interest in the subject has also been stimulated by the National Economic Development Council's advocacy of preservation in the interests of greater mobility of staff. Clearly the whole question has a bearing on the future development of both public and private sector schemes, and further discussion of it is therefore deferred until Chapter 10.

FINANCIAL ARRANGEMENTS

Partly through history and partly through the particular experience of different schemes, public sector schemes show a great variety of financial arrangements even for schemes whose level of benefits is very similar. On the surface this appears as a distinction between contributory and non-contributory schemes and between funded and non-funded schemes, but basically perhaps the main problem is how the cost is to be met and by whom. This of course is a problem for private schemes too but there perhaps the primary decision is what level of benefits, and particularly what level of pension, is to be adopted and this will be the main factor in determining the cost of

[1] See R. C. Sansom, 'Preserving Pension Rights', *The Professional Engineer*, October 1960; also, the later study by the same author and N. N. B. Ordman referred to above.

the scheme. How that cost is to be divided between employer and employee and whether the scheme should be arranged through a life office or not are then important questions to be considered; so too is the rate of funding in the case of self-administered funds and the investment policy to be followed.

Underlying all this is a factor which is of supreme importance to private schemes but which either does not apply to public sector schemes or at least not to the same degree. This is the fact that pensions are a long-term charge on the undertaking and if this is not met as the liability arises it will to some degree distort the financial position of the undertaking. Something of the same situation may be said to arise in, for example, most of the nationalized industries or in the Post Office, but there the position is complicated by the fact that in the last resort the Exchequer accepts some obligation for the continued existence of the undertakings. In private firms, however, if the obligation is accepted to pay pensions calculated in a certain way to all or certain classes of employees, not to make some current provision for the future cost of those pensions is to run the risk of being unable to meet that cost because of the strain on the firm's resources when the time comes, quite apart from the fact that the obligation would become meaningless if meanwhile the firm went bankrupt or was taken over (and also quite apart from the taxation position). Whatever the merits, therefore, of notional fund and similar arrangements in the public sector, they are unlikely to offer much advantage to private schemes.

However, granted that current income is, in one form or another, to be accumulated to pay future pensions, it is still an open question whether contributions should be paid by the employee or not. There is something in the view that it is 'only a matter of form whether the contribution is paid entirely by the employer in the first place or whether some of it is paid first to the employee as salary and then contributed by him to the scheme. In the last analysis the difference is largely psychological.'[1] But there may also be positive disadvantages for the employee in a non-contributory scheme; for example, he may move to other employment after a number of years and find that his pension rights are not preserved; since he cannot receive a refund of contributions he gets nothing at all from the scheme—a situation paralleled in the civil service scheme. But whatever the reasons, the majority of private schemes are contributory. So are all the schemes considered in detail in this chapter, although in the case of 'E' there is a separate 'Top-Hat' scheme for senior staff which is non-contributory.

Contributions paid by the employees, as was said in the case of

[1] Gordon A. Hosking, *Pension Schemes and Retirement Benefits*, Sweet & Maxwell, 2nd ed., 1960, p. 57.

public sector schemes, are only one element in the financial arrangements. It is a striking feature of private as compared with public sector schemes that the employer pays not a specified amount, but the balance of the cost; such an arrangement is found, according to the Government Actuary's survey, in schemes for 64 per cent of members of non-insured and 86 per cent of insured schemes. In the public sector, employers' contributions as a specified percentage of salary or wages are usual even in non-funded schemes such as the National Health Service. The majority of the schemes considered in detail in this chapter do, however, specify the amount of the employers' contribution, often in the form of a sum equal to (or double, etc.) the amount of the employees' contributions.

The other important element in the income of a scheme is that derived from investments. Here there will clearly be variations for the same reasons as in public sector schemes, with the additional point that private schemes are less likely to be restricted to the same extent in their choice of investments. As a result, the investment policy adopted by a fund's management committee will have a considerable effect on the finances of the fund. This at least will be the situation so far as private self-administered funds are concerned and advice on and discussions about investment policy are a feature of the literature about these funds. Such discussions naturally concentrate on the particular factors which are of most importance to pension funds; the need to gain a good yield over a long period, and the need to maintain adequate security for the capital of the fund. With insured schemes, on the other hand, the hazards and rewards of investment are entrusted to the investment managers of the life offices and successful investment does not directly benefit scheme members or their employers, except to the extent that, as has become increasingly common in recent years, the scheme is based on 'with profits' policies. In other ways there may be an indirect effect on schemes; for example, a more successful company might offer lower premiums—but here too many factors enter into the reckoning so that it is difficult to make any firm statement.

This raises a further point of considerable importance for pension schemes. The great and growing size of the funds of these schemes, particularly if the funds of insurance companies are included so far as they relate to pension business, are an important element in the total amount of funds available for investment. The point applies to both public and private sector schemes but in the case of the former most of the largest schemes are not funded. In the analysis given in Appendix 1, it is suggested that the total of private sector funds may have reached something in the region of £4,500 million by the end of 1962. This figure may be compared with, for example, the total value of stock exchange securities which is in the region of £50,000 million. Moreover, pension funds are increasing rapidly.

The economic importance of funds of this size and, more particularly, their relation to savings, will be discussed later (see Chapter 9). As far as the progress of a particular fund is concerned, the skilful investment of the income is a matter of great importance and calls for expert management. For the schemes listed in Tables A and B, the funds vary in size from under £2 million to over £50 million and the total of funds for all the schemes listed is in the region of £175 million. One may compare these figures with those shown in Appendix 5 for public sector schemes; there, the vast amount of local government funds, totalling over £600 million, dominates the picture, although, from the point of view of investment, these represent a large number of separate funds averaging about £1 million each. But, apart from local government, three schemes (NCB Principal, Mineworkers and Electricity Staff) all have funds larger than the biggest single private scheme considered here and most of the other nationalized industries' funds are considerably larger than the majority of these private schemes.

Contributions and investments are particularly important topics which bulk large in any consideration of the finances of private sector, and especially self-administered schemes. Hardly less important is the subject of taxation; since, however, the influence of taxation extends beyond the purely financial aspects of schemes, it is here considered separately in Chapter 7. Some other matters concerning the finances of private schemes may be mentioned briefly. *Actuarial valuations* are general in private schemes, often at five-yearly intervals but sometimes more frequently; no special features of these valuations need to be mentioned here (in the case of insured schemes the valuations are carried out as part of the general valuation of the life office's funds rather than for a particular scheme). The *costs of administration* generally speaking, as in the case of public sector schemes, are borne by the company or firm and not by the fund in the case of self-administered funds; in insured schemes, the cost of administration falling on the life office will naturally be reflected in the premiums charged, although some costs, e.g. a certain amount of clerical work in deducting contributions, etc., will fall to the employer. G. A. Hosking in his book, to which reference has already been made, suggests that the charge for expenses included in life office premiums may vary from about 5 per cent in the case of group life and pensions schemes to perhaps 10 per cent in the case of endowment assurance schemes; whereas in the case of large private funds, including allowance for such items as accommodation, lighting and heating, the cost may be below 2 per cent of the contribution income.[1]

[1] Hosking, op. cit. p. 118.

In all the private schemes considered in detail, the cost of administration is borne by the employer and not by the fund except in the case of 'B' and 'C'; in the case of 'B', management expenses and professional charges amount to about £1 per member per year, and in 'C' to about twice that amount, representing about 2 per cent and 3 per cent respectively of the contribution income. But as in the case of public sector schemes, these figures mean very little without a detailed analysis of what is included in the different cases.

As in the case of public sector schemes, the question of *supplementing pensions* already in payment to counter the effects of inflation has, in recent years, grown in importance. For the most part, however, again as in the case of public sector schemes, any arrangements of this kind have been made outside the provisions of schemes and the cost has therefore fallen, not on the fund but on the employer. As a result, it is very difficult to give any precise indication of how extensive the practice is, or how much the additional expenditure on pensions amounts to. For, to the extent that this cost is met solely by the employer, it is likely, as is generally the case with the nationalized industries, to be merged with other costs and may not be readily identifiable as a separate item. In the Government Actuary's survey, no direct reference to this subject is made, no doubt largely because provision for supplementing pensions appeared rarely, if at all, in the rules of schemes. But indirectly one interesting piece of information is provided; the questionnaire sent out to the employers selected for the sample inquiry asked for information about the amounts of pension paid during 1956. In the case of information provided about insured schemes, the total figures estimated from the sample could be compared with the statistics published by the life offices. The latter showed that about £8½ million was paid to pensioners under insured schemes compared with £10 million in the Government Actuary's estimate. 'The probable reason', comments the Government Actuary (para. 19 of the Report), 'for the higher amount shown here is the payment by employers of pensions additional and supplementary to the amounts due under such schemes.'

Of course not all such additional payments will correspond to what is done in public sector schemes by means of Pensions (Increase) Acts, that is, the supplementing of pensions which, because of inflation, have declined in value. Reference was made earlier to the practice of supplementing out of the firm's resources the pensions payable under the rules of the pension scheme in order to bring them up to a reasonable figure; for example, in scheme 'J' (Table B) pensions are supplemented in this way so that after, say, forty years' service, the pension payable will be half the retiring salary although the pension under the scheme may be only about half this amount. Another reason for additional payments may be the supplementation of pensions for service before the scheme began. But even granted that there may be a number of reasons why the amounts paid out in pensions should be higher than would be provided for simply under the rules of the scheme, the effect is likely to be the same as in the case of Pensions (Increase) and similar arrangements in public sector schemes, that the total cost of pensions will be understated if only the cost falling on the pension fund is taken into account.

The interesting question is posed, as with public sector schemes, whether in relation specifically to the effects of inflation on the value of pensions, some provision should be made in the rules of the scheme. It is perhaps of some significance that the Inland Revenue now raise no objection to a rule in a scheme providing for pensions to be increased after retirement on the basis of increases in the Ministry of Labour Cost of Living Index figure; previously they had maintained that each such proposal to raise pensions in payment, if the increase was to fall on the fund, would require an amendment of the scheme.[1] This suggests that there is a greater tendency in the direction of making some more automatic adjustment of pensions to take account of inflation. Similarly, a number of life offices have now launched 'growth pension' schemes which, though varying a great deal in detail, all aim to increase the amount of pension in retirement beyond what would be expected on the basis of a normal insured scheme's rules. These are simply indications of possible trends and it is impossible to say at this stage how many schemes have adopted such arrangements or are likely to do so. But in comparing the situation in the private and public sectors, as also in attempting to assess the whole picture, it is useful to compare what is said here with the arguments put forward in the House of Commons in connexion with the latest Pensions (Increase) Act (of 1962), and particularly the strong pressure from all sides for some more regular method of dealing with the effects of inflation on pensions (see page 89 above).

CONCLUSION

From the point of view of this study two questions, or perhaps two sides of the same question, seem to be suggested by the analysis which has been made in this chapter. In what ways does it help in understanding the problems raised by the more detailed study of public sector schemes? And how far are any views expressed in this study on the future of public sector schemes likely to be at all relevant to the private sector?

The first point is that many of the wider problems of pensions are not confined simply to public sector schemes, although in detail they

[1] See 'Superannuation', *Journal of the National Association of Pension Funds*, April 1961, p. 8.

may affect these schemes in a different way. This applies in particular to the relation between National Insurance and occupational schemes and to taxation; indeed in the case of taxation, it may well be that the problems are greater for private than for public sector schemes. Again, the whole question of preservation of pension rights on change of employment is one which all schemes, both public and private, must face although it may be that different considerations and different policies have until now been applied in the two sectors. To some extent this question is also bound up with National Insurance; at least it may be that the effect of the graduated scheme or any extension of it will be to direct attention increasingly to this problem. But all these problems are common to both public and private sector schemes.

In detail it may be more difficult to make suggestions applicable to all schemes. Because there is a link, however uncertain it may appear in places, between the different schemes of the public sector they can be treated as a whole. But in the private sector it is the element of diversity which is significant, not the common elements, and this diversity reflects the fact that pension schemes on the whole are a matter for the individual employer. It follows that each employer will try to devise or choose the particular scheme which suits his own circumstances. He will therefore take into account factors such as the proportion of men and women in his employment before devising or choosing a scheme. But above all he will look to what he or his company and his employees can afford to pay towards the cost of pension benefits—and included in that assessment will increasingly be the cost of what he has to pay in any case to the National Insurance scheme, and also, one should add, the cost in terms of loss of staff or inability to attract staff in not having a pension scheme or of having a less generous scheme than his competitors.

Thus, although as was suggested earlier, certain patterns of scheme may emerge within the private sector in particular industrial or commercial fields, individual employers must often find the prospects of their own particular business the most important limiting factor in determining how generous a pension scheme is provided. Furthermore, this point has a bearing on another characteristic feature of private sector schemes; this is, that a firm's scheme may be completely re-modelled as circumstances change. Both the 'A' staff and 'D' schemes, for example, in Table A were until recently on a money-purchase basis.

This is in marked contrast with the public sector where the limitation of cost does not appear in quite the same way, and where the type of scheme has shown much less variety over the years. On questions of cost, therefore, and methods of financing generally, it may be that the particular problems of the public sector are distinct and that what is applicable there is not necessarily generally applicable to all schemes. This is not to say that a study of what goes on in one sector may not be illuminating for the other. To take one example: if it is right to make proper allowance for pension provision in determining a realistic price for a product, this must have some relevance to the price of coal as well as to the price of margarine. But perhaps the point of contrast may be said to be in the fact that whereas cost by and large determines the shape of private sector schemes, this is not so in the case of public sector schemes, simply because, apart from the nationalized industries, they are not dependent on the results of trading activities as a criterion of ability to support a pension scheme; and even with the nationalized industries, the limitation may not be so severe as for a private firm. Here, however, the argument enters the controversial field of how public sector schemes should be financed, and further consideration of this topic belongs to Chapter 9. What perhaps may be said without fear of contradiction is that financial questions do in practice appear rather differently in the public and private sectors, and that this is likely to have some influence on pension schemes.

In a similar way, questions about the desirability of standardization and uniformity of schemes may arise in the public sector simply because there already exists some measure of standardization and because it is possible to think of the public sector as a whole. But since by their very nature private sector schemes represent what individual employers, or at the most, groups of employers, think meets their particular case (and perhaps also to some degree what their employees want), any standardization is likely to come not so much from a deliberate attempt to standardize, as from similar reactions to similar influences, e.g. companies modelling their schemes on what their main competitors are doing, or trade unions in one industry trying to secure similar terms to those enjoyed in another. Such tendencies are, however, liable to be opposed by others, such as the desire to go one better than a competitor, so that it is difficult to believe that there will ever be a high degree of standardization as long as occupational schemes continue to exist in the form in which we know them.

What can happen is that certain restrictions or limitations may be put on schemes, as for example, in the case of the tax rules at present, or as might happen if, as some people have suggested, it were made a legal requirement that all schemes should provide for the preservation of accrued pension rights on change of employment. But within such limitations the possible range and variety of schemes is still large. Perhaps the only serious limitation on the scope of schemes would be a big extension of the level of benefit of a compulsory, universal state scheme, and even this, though it would limit the importance and value of occupational pension benefits, would not necessarily lead to more uniformity.

There is a sense, then, in which the public sector, because it is the public sector, raises questions about pension schemes which do not arise in the private sector. Only on broad general pension questions is there likely to be common ground between public and private sector schemes, and it is significant that such questions arise generally because of the effect of external factors on schemes, particularly the state scheme, taxation and inflation.

The following two chapters will deal with the problems raised for pension schemes, but particularly public sector schemes, by the first two factors. In later chapters an attempt will be made to look ahead to the future pattern of pension scheme development, again with particular reference to public sector schemes, but drawing attention whenever possible to points which seem to be relevant to all pension schemes. In this way it is hoped that although this study is primarily addressed to those concerned with and interested in public sector schemes, it may also prove of value to those in the private sector.

APPENDIX

Table A

Main Provisions of Ten Private Sector Schemes
(For notes, see page 156)

	Type of Scheme	Ordinary contributions by members	Ordinary retirement benefits	Normal age of retirement	Ill Health retirement	Death Benefits and Widows' pensions	Adjusted for N.I.	Contracted out	Voluntary contributions	Early retirement	Late retirement
A Works	Money-purchase (compulsory)	Fixed weekly amounts	Pension based on contributions paid	65	Actuarially reduced pension	Death: no specific. Widows: by allocation	No	No	Yes	Yes	Yes
Staff	Terminal salary (compulsory)	6%	Pension: 1/80 × average of last five years for each year's service	65 men 63 women	Pension counting all years to normal retiring age	Death: lump sum Widows: by allocation, also separate contributory scheme	Yes	No	Yes	Yes	Yes
B General	Money purchase (compulsory)	Fixed amounts according to salary group	Pension based on contributions paid	65 men 60 women	Pension based on age and contributions paid	Death: lump sum Widows: by allocation	No	No	Yes	Yes	Yes
Special	Terminal salary (compulsory)	3⅝% or 5¼% according to grade	Pension: 1/90 or 1/70 × average of last 5 years for each year's service plus additional 1% for each year (latter may be commuted to lump sum)	60	Actuarially reduced pension	Death: lump sum. Widows: half pension (also by allocation)	No	No	Yes	Yes	Yes

[continued

Table A—continued

Type of Scheme	Ordinary contributions by members	Ordinary retirement benefits	Normal age of retirement	Ill Health retirement	Death Benefits and Widows' pensions	Adjusted for N.I.	Contracted out	Voluntary contributions	Early retirement	Late retirement
C	Average salary (compulsory) (Women: money purchase)	Percentages of 3½% upwards according to age on joining and level of earnings (Women pay approx. 4–5%)	Pension: percentages of total earnings varying according to age at retirement (women: pension based on contributions paid)	60½ men 55 women	Pension: amount discretionary	Death: no specific. Widows: additional contributions of 1/3 normal contributions to provide half pension	Yes	No	Yes	No	Yes
D Works } Staff	Terminal salary (compulsory)	8% (including N.I.)	Pension: 3/200 (1½%) of final pay for each year's service plus 12½% if 30 years' service (including N.I. pension)	65 men 60 women	Actuarially reduced pension	Death: no specific Widows: half pension (excluding N.I. pension)	Yes	No	No	Yes	Yes
B Works	Flat rate (voluntary)	Weekly amount varying according to age on joining	Pension: 6d per week for every 52 weekly contributions (in addition there is a non-contributory pension of 1d per week for each month of service)	65 men 60 women	Pension as for ordinary retirement	Death: lump sum. Widows: no provision	No	No	—	No	Yes

E Staff	Terminal salary (compulsory)	6% (women 5%)	Pension: 1/60 × average of last five year's service for each year's service	65 men 60 women	Pension as for ordinary retirement but taking into account number of years to normal retiring age	Death: lump sum. Widows: half pension	Yes	No	Yes	Yes	Yes Yes
F	Money purchase (compulsory for salaried staff, voluntary for other members)	2½%	Pension based on contributions paid (but supplemented on a non-contributory basis)	65	Actuarially reduced pension	Death: return of both employer's and employee's contributions. Widows: flat-rate pension, also by separate fund for salaried staff with higher widows' pension)	No	Yes	No	No	No No
FSSU	Money-purchase (insured) compulsory	5%	Depending on type of policy	60 (minimum)	No provision	Depending on type of policy	No	No	No	No	No Yes

[Notes overleaf]

NOTES: General. In compressing the rules of such a variety of schemes into a table of this kind there is a risk of seriously distorting the picture presented. The following notes are intended as a clarification where such a risk exists. But it should be noted that apart from any other variations the precise conditions under which a benefit may be granted are not necessarily the same in all schemes.

Headings. (a) *Contributions.* No attempt is made to indicate the amount of the contribution made by employers; in any case this is not always specified in the rules of the schemes.

(b) *Ill-health Retirement.* In some cases this benefit is given only in cases of total incapacity; in other cases the schemes distinguish between, and provide different benefits for, total and partial incapacity.

(c) *Death Benefits and Widows' Pensions.* Specific death benefits are included only if they go beyond a return of the employee's contributions. 'By allocation' means that, as in public sector schemes, a man may give up part of his pension on retirement in order to provide a pension for his widow if he dies.

(d) *Adjusted for National Insurance.* This means, generally speaking, making some reduction in contributions and benefits to take account of the National Insurance retirement pension, but it also includes the unusual arrangement of 'D'.

(e) *Voluntary Contributions.* i.e. whether the scheme provides for the member to make additional voluntary contributions to increase his pension. This is not applicable to 'E' Works scheme, which is essentially a non-contributory scheme with a voluntary additional contributory part.

(f) *Early Retirement, Late Retirement.* These simply indicate whether the schemes provide for a reduced pension to be granted for retirement before normal retiring age, and for an increased pension for later service. The early retirement provision means voluntary retirement, i.e. not specifically on grounds of ill-health, redundancy, etc. Scheme 'F' has a compulsory retiring age for salaried staff.

Other Provisions. Not included here, but found in some of these schemes, are provisions for dependants other than widows, and 'alternative pensions', i.e. the option to take a higher pension until age 65 and a lower one after.

Table B

Some Comparative Features of Five Additional Private Sector Schemes

	G (Staff Scheme only)	H	I (Staff Scheme only)	J	K
Terminal-Salary	Yes	Yes	Yes	No (money purchase)	Yes
If terminal-salary, fraction used per year of service; in other cases, basis of pension	1/84 (women 1/80)	1/60	2/135 (women 1/60)	Percentage of total contributions (but supplemented by non-contributory)	1/3 of retiring salary in all cases, plus 1/100 per year of service
Contributions of employee as percentage of salary	6¼% (women 3¼%)	5% on first £450 (women first £575) 10% on remainder	5¼%	5%	3¼% + (varies with age on joining)
Normal retiring age	65 (60 women)	65 (60 women)	65 (60 women)	55	65
Whether ill-health pension provided	Yes	Yes	Yes	Yes	Yes
Death benefit	Lump sum (only for widows)	Lump sum	No specific	No specific	No specific
Pension for widows	Half pension	Half pension	Only by allocation	Only by allocation	Only by allocation
Specific adjustment for National Insurance	No	Yes	No	Yes	No
Voluntary contributions for additional pension	No	Yes	No	No	No

N.B. The notes to Table A should be read in conjunction with this table.

CHAPTER 6

Occupational Schemes and National Insurance

Modification of Schemes

As was shown earlier, the institution of formal pension schemes in this country began with certain special groups, such as civil servants and the police, and intervention by the State to provide pensions for the population generally did not begin until 1908, and then only on a limited scale. Extension of the State's responsibility for pensions and particularly the universal provision of pensions under the National Insurance Act 1946, has created a number of problems for occupational pension schemes. Underlying these problems is the fundamental question of the extent to which pensions should be provided by the State or by the employer and this question has been raised perhaps most strongly by the introduction of the graduated system of pensions under the National Insurance Act 1959, which presented every occupational scheme with the choice of either taking part in the new system or 'contracting out'.[1] In this chapter the impact of National Insurance particularly on public sector schemes will be considered first before looking at the specific problems raised by the graduated scheme.

Schemes for the public services, like the majority of public sector schemes, were designed to provide reasonable benefits for a man to live on in his retirement; to this end, after forty years of faithful service, he could look forward to a pension only one-third less than his retiring salary. The original Old Age Pensions served a rather different purpose: to preserve from destitution those who were unable to provide for themselves. There was thus no reason why the two kinds of arrangement should not exist side by side. With the introduction of a national system of contributory pensions in 1925, provision was for the first time made for a basic pension for a large part of the population. This was still not a universal system, how-

[1] A brief outline of National Insurance arrangements for retirement pensions since 1946 is in Appendix 6.

ever, and those in the Civil Service, local government and a number of other occupations in which adequate pension provision existed were exempted from taking part in it, and their employment was treated as 'excepted' under the Act.

The situation changed with the introduction of the new National Insurance Scheme in 1948 based on the Beveridge proposals. Those proposals depended on 'Six Principles of Social Insurance', of which the three most important for the present discussion were: flat rate subsistence benefit; flat rate of contribution; and comprehensiveness.[1] All were to contribute and all were to be entitled to benefits. By this means, as the government White Paper put it,[2] 'concrete expression is . . . given to the solidarity and unity of the nation'. Thus public servants were for the first time brought within the scope of state insurance, paying contributions and receiving benefits on the same terms as everyone else.

But if public servants were to be eligible for National Insurance benefits, including retirement pensions, it could well happen, especially in the case of lower paid staff, that the amount of state and occupational pension together would be not far short of retiring salary. Moreover, where the occupational scheme was contributory, the total of contributions for National Insurance and the pension scheme might be quite heavy, especially again in the case of lower paid staff.[3] Sir William Beveridge clearly recognized these points and suggested (in paragraph 149 of his Report): 'as regards pensions . . . if there are any occupations which have already made provision for these circumstances, they should do so in future in the light of the basic provision being made for all, including their members, by the national plan for Social Security. All that is needed is that they should be given time to readjust their own schemes.' The problem was of course common to all occupational pension schemes, but particularly important for public sector schemes since at that time they made better provision generally speaking than other schemes. More modest schemes might well have continued alongside the National Insurance scheme as supplements to the basic provision aimed at by the Beveridge plan.

The government accepted that some adjustment was needed to public sector schemes as a result of the introduction of National Insurance, and proposed a reduction in pensions 'so as to avoid duplication of benefit under both an occupational and the national

[1] Social Insurance and Allied Services (Beveridge), Cmd. 6404, 1942, paras. 303–9.
[2] Social Insurance, Part I, H.M.S.O., 1944.
[3] The combined stamp for an employee in July 1948 was 4s 8½d representing nearly 5 per cent of a wage of £5 a week. This of course included a small contribution towards the National Health Service.

scheme.[1] The reduction was not, however, to exceed 26s a week (which was the rate of retirement pension for a single person), and was to be accompanied in contributory schemes by an 'adjustment' of contributions.[2] It is important, in view of later developments, to emphasize that what took place was an assertion of the over-riding importance of the principle of universality in National Insurance so that the problem was purely a practical one of how far and in what manner public sector schemes were to be scaled down to take account of this situation. However, one other long-standing principle in superannuation matters was allowed to take precedence: that existing members of schemes should not have their arrangements changed without their consent. Accordingly, the new adjustments, or 'modification' as it was called, was to apply only to future entrants to schemes. Existing members were either automatically excluded (as in the Civil Service) or given the option (which scarcely any chose to exercise) of having their benefits and contributions reduced.

The practical problem of modification was how to adjust schemes based on percentage contributions and terminal salaries to a scheme based on flat-rate contributions and benefits. The problem was made more complicated because under the National Insurance scheme a married couple received a bigger pension than a single person, although the rate of contribution was the same for both single and married men (women paid a lower rate, partly because the liability for a widow's pension was carried by the men's contribution). In public sector schemes, however, not only was the scheme pension the same for both single and married people, but increasingly as widows' pensions developed married men had to pay higher contributions or suffer some reduction in their pension benefits to meet part or all of the cost of providing them. Finally, from the point of view of administration, it should be noted that National Insurance retirement pensions are not payable before age 65 (60 for women) but some public sector pensions are. Any reduced pension may therefore have to be brought in some time after a man has retired, with consequent complication for the administration of schemes.

At first sight it seems that an obvious way of modifying public sector schemes would be simply to reduce the amount of pension paid by the amount of National Insurance pension or at least, to avoid difficulties over the differential pension for a married couple,

[1] The Chancellor of the Exchequer (Mr Hugh Dalton) announcing the decision by Written Answer (H.C. Deb., August 7, 1947).

[2] Although these proposals were entirely new as far as most public service schemes were concerned, some adjustments had in certain cases been made, e.g. in some local government schemes in connexion with the Widows', Orphans' and Old Age Contributory Pensions Act 1936. Although these are not considered here, it is as well to keep in mind that they can still trouble administrators of pension schemes.

by the amount of a single person's pension. This would mean that the total of pension received would always be that laid down in the pension scheme (with the exception of the additional pension paid to a married couple under the National Insurance scheme), but that the proportion of total pension which would be received from the pension scheme would vary according to different circumstances.

This last point was undoubtedly one reason why this particular method of modification was not adopted. It was felt that some allowance should be made for the fact that in a public sector scheme the amount of pension was related to both final salary and number of years' service. Simply to reduce the amount of pension by the flat rate of the National Insurance pension would produce anomalies between those who had served different lengths of time in the public sector.

There was also the problem of how to adjust contributions. This was complicated by the fact that it was possible to draw the state pension in full in the early years of the National Insurance scheme without necessarily having paid contributions to the scheme for the full span of years from age 18 to 65, whereas public sector pensions varied directly with the number of years for which contributions had been paid.

Thus the problem of modification seems to have been seen primarily as a problem of how to achieve as far as possible a fair balance between different kinds of members and contributors to public sector schemes. This at least is a reasonable inference from the solution which was actually adopted under which there was an actuarial equivalence between the amounts by which pensions were reduced and the amounts of reduced contributions, thus permitting variations in the amount of reduced pensions to be related to the number of years for which reduced contributions had been paid.

To understand how this was done some further explanation is desirable. But since in fact scarcely any two schemes in the public sector made precisely the same calculations, the method will be outlined in general terms before the detailed arrangements in different schemes are specified. As was stated above, the maximum reduction of pension was to be related to the single person's pension which under the 1948 National Insurance scheme was £1 6s 0d per week. It was therefore natural to make this maximum reduction apply to the maximum occupational pension which in 1948 was payable at the end of forty years' service. A simple calculation showed that if the occupational pension were to be reduced by £1 14s 0d a year for each year of service from 1948, the reduction for forty years' service would correspond to the annual value of the state pension (40 × £1 14s 0d = £68; 52 × £1 6s 0d = £67 12s 0d). This reduction by £1 14s 0d per year of service therefore formed the basis of most modification arrangements.

F

The next step was to see, for contributory schemes, what reduction in contributions would give an actuarial equivalence to this reduction in pension. Since the equivalence necessarily had to depend on the experience of each scheme, it is not surprising that the calculations produced different results for different schemes. This accounts for the fact, which may seem strange on the surface, that although there is general uniformity in the reduction of pensions there is no uniformity in the reduction of contributions. But, given the situation described in Chapter 4, it will be seen that this is no more surprising than the variety in rates of contribution generally.

In considering how the twelve public sector schemes examined in Chapter 3 have applied modification in detail, the first point to be noted is that two nationalized industries' schemes (Gas Staff and Airways) have used a different method from that outlined above, as follows:

Gas. Men pay contributions of 5 per cent on the first £425 of annual salary and 6½ per cent on the remainder. (Women: 4 per cent and 5½ per cent.) Pensions are calculated for both men and women as 1/80 of the first £425 and 1/60 of the remainder of pensionable salary for each year of service;

Airways. Here modification is achieved by ignoring the first £100 of salary in the calculation of both contributions and pensions.

But although these methods appear to be different from the main method described above, in practice they come to much the same thing although the calculation operates in a different way. Thus in the Gas scheme there is effectively a reduction of 1½ per cent × £425, i.e. £6 3s 4d in the annual contribution and of 1/240 × £425, i.e. £1 15s 5d for each year of service since 1948 in the annual pension. The only people to whom this would not apply would be those earning less than £425 per annum, but although there may have been some in this category when the scheme started there are unlikely to be any now. Similarly, in the Airways scheme the reduction in contributions is 6½ per cent × £100, i.e. £6 10s 0d (for men) and the reduction in pension 1/60 × £100, i.e. £1 13s 4d for each year.

It is thus possible, by re-interpreting the Gas and Airways schemes in this way, to tabulate the modification arrangements as shown opposite.

Some of the items in the table call for comment. Most of the minor variations in the last column arise from the fact that there is not an exact equivalence between the annual value of the 1948 state pension and a calculation based on £1 14s 0d per annum. The Regulations for the NCB, Electricity and Atomic Energy schemes specify the maximum as an amount 'corresponding to 40 years' service', but 40 × £1 14s 0d = £68, whereas the state pension is either £67 12s 0d per annum (52 × £1 6s 0d) or perhaps more accurately £67 15s 0d if allowance is made for the fact that a year is 1¼ days over the 52 weeks. Most schemes have introduced this further refinement, although the effect is that at the 40th year of service the calculation in multiples of £1 14s 0d has to be abandoned.

Scheme	Reduction in Contributions	Reduction in Pension (per year of service)			Maximum Reduction		
		£	s	d	£	s	d
Civil Service	—	1	14	0	67	15	0
Local government and National Health Service	£3 0s. 8d p.a. (women £3 5s 0d p.a.)	1	14	0	67	15	0
Teachers	£2 8s 0d p.a. (women £2 19s 0d p.a.)	1	14	0	67	15	0
Police and firemen	1s 2d per week	1	14	0	51	0	0*
NCB Principal and Electricity Staff	9d per week (women 10d per week)	1 14 0 (varies with age of joining)			68	0	0
Gas Staff	£6 3s 4d p.a.	1	15	5	70	16	8
Railways Staff (modification not introduced until 1956)	Varies according to age of entry from £3 0s 10d p.a. to £11 1s 8d p.a. (women £3 13s 10d to £13 9s 6d)	1	14	0	67	12	0
Airways	£6 10s 0d p.a. (women £5 0s 0d)	1	13	4	66	13	4
Atomic Energy Non-industrial	1s 0d per week (women 1s 2d per week)	1 14 0 (varies with age of joining)			68	0	0

* Related to normal maximum of 30 years' service.

Comparison of the reduction in contributions is complicated by the fact that sometimes the amounts are expressed as weekly and sometimes as annual sums. But assuming that £3 0s 8d p.a. is 1s 2d per week and that the teachers' scale works out at 11d per week (1s 1½d for women), there are four different scales for the eight schemes which are directly comparable (i.e. excluding Civil Service,

Gas, Railways and Airways).[1] The refinement of variable rates of reduction in the Railways' scheme corresponds to the variable rates of normal contribution.

A further refinement which also complicates the comparison is that in three of the schemes (NCB, Electricity, Atomic Energy Authority) the reduction in pension varies with the age of the member at the time of joining the scheme so that the £1 14s 0d reduction applies only to those joining at the youngest ages (20 and under) and grows progressively smaller at older ages.[2]

The Effectiveness of Modification Arrangements

It may be thought that too much attention has been paid to the details of these modification arrangements, but it is worth stressing how much thought was devoted to this subject at the time of the introduction of the National Insurance scheme. The careful attention to such details as limiting the maximum reduction to £67 15s 0d rather than the easier but less accurate £68, and the precision in terms of pence per week in the reduction of contributions show how seriously the attempt was made to devise an accurate but fair system. In spite of this, however, it must be recorded that there are serious limitations on the extent to which in practice duplication of benefit is avoided now, sixteen years after the introduction of the National Insurance scheme.

There is, first, the fact that practically all those who were in service in 1948 are, through the operation of the 'no detriment' rule, exempt from modification. This means not only that most of those who have retired since 1948 have their public sector pensions in full, but that for many years to come the bulk of those who retire will also be in this position. Nor is this offset to any marked extent by the fact that not everybody who was in service in 1948 qualified for a National Insurance pension. Those who were aged between 55 and 65 in 1948 (or between 50 and 60 if they were women) could only qualify for this pension after being insured for ten years, but otherwise practically everybody who was in service in 1948 qualified for a pension at 65, or 60 in the case of women.

The practical effect is that many thousands of public servants and employees of the nationalized industries are now enjoying or looking forward to the prospect of a double pension. This year (1964) men

[1] In fact, to give a thoroughgoing explanation of these differences one would need to take into account such matters as the extent to which the total contribution in the various schemes is shared between employer and employee.

[2] These reductions are almost but not quite uniform in the different schemes; thus in the NCB scheme the reduction is 16s 0d at age 53, and age 54, and 15s 0d at age 55 and over; in the AEA scheme, 16s 0d at age 53, 15s 6d at age 54 and 15s 6d at age 55 and over. There seems no particular reason for these differences.

who were 49 in 1948 will reach the age of 65 and many will retire having paid National Insurance contributions for sixteen years which will nevertheless entitle them to the full rate of pension, in addition to their public sector pension. But for somebody who was not 49 but 19 in 1948, who was and continues to be employed in the public sector, the prospect is even more distant. He will not be 65 until 1994 but he can then retire and draw a full occupational and state pension until he dies perhaps twenty years' later. No doubt such an 'unmodified' person will be comparatively rare by that time, fifty years from now and sixty-six years after the introduction of National Insurance, but the fact that he may exist at all is a serious breach of the avowed aim of the modification procedure.

But there are two other limitations on the effectiveness of the procedure. The first is perhaps inevitable (given the different bases of state and public sector schemes): no allowance is made in modification for the fact that married couples receive a higher state pension than a single person, amounting at present to a difference of just over £2 a week or nearly £110 a year.

Far more serious is the fact that no change has been made in the rates of modification since 1948, despite the fact that both contributions and benefits in the flat rate National Insurance scheme have been raised six times, so that the single person's pension is now not far short of three times what it was in 1948. In theory, this point should mean that even the maximum modification of pension will still leave a fair measure of duplication of benefit, but the immediate situation is less serious than the long-term effects unless some change is made in the system. This is partly because of the fact that few people retiring now or in the immediate future will have their pensions reduced, and those who do will have had comparatively short service which would not in any case, given the present system, have led to anything like the maximum reduction. It is as well to remember, for example, that nobody will qualify for the maximum reduction before 1988, that is after serving for forty years from the latter part of 1948.

Perhaps an example may illustrate the position. A single man retires in 1964 after fifteen years' (modified) service in, say, local government, with a pensionable salary of £1,200 p.a., aged 65. His occupational pension would be £225 less £25 10s 0d modification, i.e. £199 10s 0d, and his state pension £175 10s 0d. As he would also get a lump sum from his occupational scheme, it might be fairer to calculate his scheme pension in sixtieths, giving a modified pension of £274 10s 0d per annum.[1] In either case the net addition to his

---

[1] 15/80 × £1,200 = £225: less modification 15 × £1 14s 0d = £25 10s 0d state pension of £3 7s 6d per week = £175 10s 0d p.a. 15/60 × £1,200 = £300 − £25 10s 0d = £274 10s 0d.

pension from the state scheme is £150; and this compares, on the sixtieths basis, with a total pension of £450 (£274 10s 0d plus £175 10s 0d). One could say, therefore, that this man has benefited from the introduction of the state scheme, in spite of modification, to the extent of a 50 per cent addition to the pension which he would otherwise have received.

There can be little doubt that the system of modification at present in force fails to achieve its intended purpose of preventing duplication of benefits. But of the two main reasons which have been suggested above for this situation, one clearly rests on a matter of principle, the preservation of the 'no detriment' rule, which goes far wider than this particular issue. The other main reason depends entirely on the method which was chosen to carry out the policy of modification. This method could have worked only if the National Insurance scheme had remained unchanged since 1948 or had perhaps changed only at long intervals. It was therefore a method designed for a stable situation, and particularly a stable money situation, and, unfortunately, the years since 1948 have been very far from stable.

To say, however, that the method was workable only in a stable situation touches on the very important question, which is of direct concern for this study of the administrative consequences of modification. In theory, modification could have been adapted to each change in the National Insurance flat-rate pension, but the result would have been to introduce a great many complications into the administration of schemes. It is not simply that there would have been one rate of reduction of contributions for the period 1948–51, another for the period 1951–52, another for the period 1952–55 and so on. Tiresome as such changes would be, the actual change in the amount to be deducted would be no more difficult than the change, made at the same time, in the deductions from salary of the National Insurance contribution, although there would of course be a certain amount of actuarial work in determining the appropriate new rates.

Nor is it simply the more difficult operation which would be involved in calculating the pension. Instead of, as at present, multiplying the total number of modified years by the single sum of (usually) £1 14s 0d and deducting that from the total pension, each separate period of modification would require a separate calculation with a different sum, so that the total modification would be something like 3¼ years at £1 14s 0d plus ¾ year at £1 18s 0d plus 2 11/12 years at £2, etc., perhaps involving over a period of forty years fifteen separate pieces of modification, if the experience of the last sixteen years is anything to go by.

This would not be impossibly difficult given the fact that there would be a kind of standard rate for each period and that most people would serve several complete periods (since so far the longest periods have been only three or four years), but it would certainly be very complicated, especially where pensioners had, perhaps thirty or more years before their date of retirement, entered modified service part of the way through a particular period or where it was possible to count towards pension periods of discontinuous service.

What would have made the system of modification unworkable if it had been adapted in this way for each change in the National Insurance scheme would have been the cumulative effect of the complications outlined above together with others arising from the need to make adjustments in many different aspects of schemes.

Consider, for example, the local government scheme. Modification transformed the existing two rates of contribution into six, viz:

5 per cent: 'unmodified' servant
6 per cent: 'unmodified' officer
5 per cent — £3 0s 8d: 'modified' male servant
5 per cent — £3 5s 0d: 'modified' female servant
6 per cent — £3 0s 8d: 'modified' male officer
6 per cent — £3 5s 0d: 'modified' female officer

It also affected transfer value calculations and record-keeping. For those who are modified, transfer values have to be reduced; for this purpose the Government Actuary has prepared tables showing the amount of reduction which varies according to the age of the person transferring.

Again, anyone serving in 1948 who did not then choose to be 'modified' can preserve this right as long as he remains in public employment, for example, if he transfers elsewhere in the public sector under the Interchange Rules. But if he leaves the public sector and accepts a return of contributions and then returns at a later date, he becomes modified from the date of re-entering service. However, he may still be able to count his earlier service (e.g. as non-contributing), and his final pension will therefore have to be calculated from records showing not only what his service has been but which parts were modified and which not.[1]

For reasons of this kind, it may easily be imagined what the total effect on the administration of schemes would have been if modification has consistently held to its original approach at each change in the National Insurance scheme. Something of this dilemma has indeed already faced those schemes which have introduced further modification in relation to the graduated state pension scheme.

---

[1] It may incidentally be pointed out that in the local government and NHS schemes there is a further refinement in that the reduction of pension for modified non-contributing service is half that for contributing service.

MODIFICATION OF THE LOCAL GOVERNMENT AND NHS SCHEMES
FOR THE GRADUATED PENSION SCHEME

The Detailed Arrangements

The National Insurance Act of 1959 not only made provision for the first time in the state scheme for some part of the contribution and pension to be related to earnings, but it also enabled members of occupational schemes to be exempted from these new provisions under certain conditions, a process generally known as 'contracting out'. For the most part members of public sector schemes were contracted out of the new graduated scheme; for them no problem arose of further modification. In the local government and National Health Service schemes, however, it was decided that some members should be contracted out and that others should participate. This has added to the problems of modification in these schemes.

The reasons why these two schemes did not follow other public sector schemes are complex, but to understand the criterion which was chosen for determining when contracting out should take place, it is necessary to draw attention to two features of the 1959 Act. One was that graduated contributions were paid only on that part of wages or salaries between £9 and £15 a week; the other that the flat-rate contribution paid by a contracted-out employee was higher than that paid by one who participated in the graduated scheme. The effect was that for lower paid employees there was an advantage in being in the graduated scheme. Thus on £10 a week a man paid less than he would if he had been contracted out and at the same time was gaining entitlement to a higher state pension.

On the other hand, it was more debatable from an employee's point of view when the advantage of participating ceased. At £11 a week, for example, a man paid 12s 5d a week if he were participating against 12s 2d if he were contracted out. The question was whether the extra graduated pension was worth paying an extra 3d a week. At £12 a week the difference was 1s 1d and so on. Furthermore the calculation was different for women. The question was even more complicated because other considerations had to be taken into account by employers. In particular, the arrangements by which 'equivalent pension benefits' had to be assured for employees who left contracted-out employment (see Appendix 6, page 294) meant that if a large number of employees were likely to leave, the employer could be involved in making quite heavy additional payments to the National Insurance scheme in the form of 'payments in lieu' of contributions, particularly if those contracted out and leaving were mostly earning well below £15 a week.

Both the local government and NHS schemes chose a certain level of salary or wages as the criterion for determining participation, but no doubt because of differing opinions on considerations such as those outlined above, they chose different levels. In local government those earning £13 a week (£12 in the case of women) or less, and in the National Health Service those earning £12 10s 0d a week (£11 in the case of women) or less participated in the graduated scheme, and the remainder were contracted out. The problem then became how to determine the further modification for those who were contributing both to the flat-rate and graduated state schemes.[1]

The problem was difficult and various suggestions were made for solving it.[2] The chief difficulty was that proposals which were actuarially precise tended to be administratively unworkable. The final result was a combined modification for both flat-rate and graduated pensions together of a 1 per cent reduction in contributions and a reduction in pension of 1/240th of pensionable salary up to £780 a year (£15 a week) for each year of service in which graduated contributions were paid. Since this was a combined modification, it doubled the number of possibilities for contribution rates compared with those resulting from the 1948 arrangements, thus:

Servants

	Contribution rate	
	Male	Female
Not modified under 1946 Act, contracted out	5%	5%
Modified under 1946 Act, contracted out	5%—£3 0s 8d p.a.	5%—£3 5s 0d p.a.
Modified under 1946 Act, participating	4%	4%
Not modified under 1946 Act, participating	4% + £3 0s 8d p.a.	4% + £3 5s 0d p.a.

Officers

	Contribution rate	
	Male	Female
Not modified under 1946 Act, contracted out	6%	6%
Modified under 1946 Act, contracted out	6% − £3 0s 8d p.a.	6% − £3 5s 0d p.a.
Modified under 1946 Act, participating	5%	5%
Not modified under 1946 Act, participating	5% + £3 0s 8d p.a.	5% + £3 5s 0d p.a.

[1] In what follows attention is concentrated on the local government scheme, but the position is similar for the National Health Service.

[2] See, for example, George H. Forster, *Graduated National Pensions as affecting Local Authorities*, Charles Knight & Co., London, 1961, p. 90.

F*

It will be seen that because the 1 per cent was a combined flat-rate and graduated reduction, it would have been too large for those who had not previously been modified but who were now participating, and these people therefore had the flat-rate modification added back.[1]

Not all these categories of contributors will be found in every local authority. Indeed, some, such as female servants modified under the 1946 Act but contracted out of the graduated scheme, must be quite rare. But the point is that each local authority must be aware of the exact contribution category of each of its employees, and the graduated scheme has introduced a further sub-division into the already-existing categories. It is fortunate that the combined modification has abandoned the refinement of a separate calculation for women.

As with the flat-rate reductions, the new 'modification' bears no relation to the amount paid in graduated contributions; the latter, being based on $4\frac{1}{4}$ per cent of earnings between £9 and £15, naturally rises more sharply than the former as can be seen by comparing columns (3) and (4) in the following table:

(1) Remuneration	(2) 1% of remuneration s d	(3) Less 1s 2d for flat-rate s d	(4) Graduated Contribution s d
£10 per week	2 0	10	11
£11 per week	2 $2\frac{1}{4}$	1 $0\frac{1}{4}$	1 10
£12 per week	2 5	1 3	2 8
£13 per week	2 $7\frac{1}{2}$	1 $5\frac{1}{4}$	3 6

What has happened is that the pension has been reduced roughly at a rate to correspond with the graduated pension, and the reduction in contributions represents (again roughly) an actuarially equivalent amount. The following table compares the reduced pensions with the corresponding National Insurance retirement pensions, assuming twenty-five years of graduated contributions and constant remuneration:

Remuneration	Reduction in pension at 25/240ths £ s d	Less flat-rate reduction at £1 14s × 25 p.a. (= 16s 4d per week)	N. Insurance graduated pension
£10 per week	1 0 10 per week	4s 6d per week	4s 0d per week
£11 per week	1 3 0 per week	6s 8d per week	8s 0d per week
£12 per week	1 5 0 per week	8s 8d per week	11s 6d per week
£13 per week	1 7 1 per week	10s 9d per week	15s 0d per week

[1] Probably only an example will make this clear. A servant earning £600 p.a. and therefore previously paying £30 p.a. in contributions would, if he were a man now pay £24 + £3 0s 8d = £27 0s 8d p.a.

That there is only an approximate correspondence between the reduction in pension and the amount of the graduated pension is not surprising. The local government scheme and the graduated scheme run on entirely different principles. In the latter, each £7 10s 0d contributed by a man earns 6d a week on his ultimate pension, and no provision is made for varying the amount of pension, whatever happens to the value of money; indeed, the only provision bearing on this in the 1959 Act was one making it possible to increase the total of contributions required for the same amount of pension so that by 1980 it may be necessary to accumulate a total of £9 5s 0d in contributions for 6d a week of pension.[1] In the local government scheme, on the other hand, there is no direct correspondence between the amount paid in contributions and the ultimate pension.

What this means is that it is extremely difficult to devise a scheme of modification which will both achieve the stated object of avoiding duplication of benefits *and* at the same time produce equivalence between reductions in pensions and contributions. But apart from the intricacies of the calculations this new 'modification' has brought with it further complications to harass administrators of the local government and NHS schemes. For example:

(1) Graduated contributions are assessed on total pay each week or month, whereas scheme contributions are assessed on re-muneration which therefore excludes, for example, overtime.

(2) Because the dividing line between those who participate and those who are contracted out is in terms of the amount of remuneration, complicated arrangements have to be made to ensure that those whose remuneration rises (or falls) are brought into the right category.

(3) In calculating transfer values as well as pensions and other benefits, separate computations need to be made for (*a*) years of service before April 3, 1961; (*b*) years of participating service after April 3, 1961; (*c*) years of contracted-out service after April 3, 1961.

(4) As with contributions, it has to be remembered that for those who were not modified under the 1946 Act but who participate in the graduated scheme the pension first has to be reduced by the 240ths formula, for the period of participation and then *increased* by the amount by which it would have been reduced for the flat-rate pension, i.e. £1 14s 0d for each year of contributing service.

(5) In addition, non-contributing service (i.e. total service minus contributing service) counts as half, and the reduction in

[1] Of course it would be possible for a future government to increase the amount of pension simply by passing a further Act, but at least in the long run, this could only be done by increasing the amount raised in contributions.

pension is 1/480th for each year of graduated contributions (or 1/480 plus 17s in the circumstances of (4) above).

(6) Not least of the headaches of administrators has been the devising of simple but accurate forms telling employees just what contributions they would have to pay and how the figures were arrived at.

Unfortunately for the administration of pension schemes, the graduated scheme, like the flat-rate scheme, has not stood still. Less than two years after the introduction of the graduated scheme in 1961, the government introduced an amending Bill to raise the upper limit of earnings on which graduated contributions were to be payable from £15 to £18 week; the main reason given by the government was that average earnings had risen since the 1959 Act proposals were made. At the same time flat-rate contributions and benefits were raised, but of particular concern to the local government and National Health service schemes was the fact that contributions payable by those contracted out went up proportionately more than for those participating.[1]

One immediate effect of this was to alter the point at which the total contribution was the same for those participating and those contracted out:

Employees' weekly contributions (men)

Earnings	1959 Act		1963 Act	
	Participating	Contracted out	Participating	Contracted out
£11 per week	12s 5d	12s 2d	13s 6d	14s 1d
£12 per week	13s 3d	12s 2d	14s 4d	14s 1d

As a result of the changes made by the 1963 Act, the arrangements for modification in the local government and NHS schemes also had to be changed, particularly:

(i) the level of earnings above which employees became contracted out was raised from £13 a week (women £12) to £14 10s 0d (women £13 10s 0d) in local government and from £12 10s 0d a week (women £11) to £14 a week (women £13) in the National Health Service;

(ii) the reduction in pension operating on pensionable salary up to £780 a year (£15 a week) was changed so that it operated on pensionable salary up to £936 a year (£18 a week), but only for periods of participating employment after January 5, 1964 (the date when the Regulations making these changes came into effect).

---

[1] 20 per cent compared with 14 per cent. The financing of National Insurance is a complex subject, on which some brief notes will be found in Appendix 6. The increased contributions under the National Insurance Act, 1963, began in June 1963.

One further complication which might have caused a great deal of trouble was, however, skilfully avoided. Suppose that a man in local government had been earning £12 10s 0d a week when the graduated scheme began in 1961 and had therefore been participating; by 1963 he might have been earning £13 10s 0d and would therefore have been contracted out. The Regulations under the 1963 Act coming into force in 1964 ought therefore to have put him back into the participating category, but in fact it is specifically provided that in such a case the man should remain contracted out in spite of the fact that his earnings are below the level agreed.

This bias in favour of contracting out, if one may so describe it, was also in the original 1961 Regulations to the extent that they provided that if earnings fell just below £13 a week a man would still be contracted out. Only if his earnings fell below £11 a week would he change from contracted-out to participating employment. On the whole, of course, the tendency is the other way in the sense that earnings have in recent years increased, thus leading to the contracting out of those who previously participated, but the bias described above arises mainly from the fact that certain complications arise when those who are contracted out pass to participating employment.

The Effects on the Administration of Schemes

It is not the purpose of this study to detail all the intricacies which follow from the modification arrangements resulting from the 1959 and 1963 Acts. Some idea of the problems presented to local authorities by these new arrangements may be gained from the guidance offered by *Shaw's Guide to Superannuation for Local Authorities*, the latest edition of which devotes a whole chapter to modification for those participating in the graduated scheme; from the fact that one author has devoted a sizeable book (in two volumes) simply to the subject of the graduated pension scheme as it affects local authorities,[1] or from the fact that the local authority associations set up a working party which produced three memoranda of guidance to help local authorities to cope with the problems of graduated pensions, including modification. And all these were written before the 1963 Act.

This last point is of great significance. Modification for the flat-rate National Insurance scheme is comparatively straightforward, mainly, as was described earlier, because it has not changed for changes in the National Insurance scheme and because a large number of people were excluded from its provisions. It seems that with

[1] Forster, *Graduated National Pensions as affecting Local Authorities*. A large part of the book is taken up with reproduction of the relevant Acts, Regulations, etc.

the graduated scheme modification, local government and the National Health Service are committed to an indefinite series of changes if they are to keep in line with the development of the graduated scheme.

To take just one example: if the upper limit of earnings on which graduated contributions are payable is to be raised every few years, the reduction in pension for a man who retires while contracted out but who for a good part of his career was participating is likely to involve a series of calculations. This is because to be fair to him his reduction will not simply be calculated as 1/240 of the current change-over point of earnings for graduated pensions for each year of participation, but will be calculated for each period according to the change-over point then in force. For example, a man retiring on £2,000 a year in thirty years' time when the upper graduated limit is, let us suppose, £30 a week (£1,560 a year) having had twenty years of participation would suffer too big a reduction if his modification were calculated as 20/240 of whatever was then the current point in the local government scheme at which the transition from participation to contracting out took place (perhaps £25 a week), since when he first participated his corresponding reduction in contributions may have operated only on his then earnings of £10 a week.

Points like these tend to make the subject of graduated modification seem like a particularly involved maze. But what must surely cause even more apprehension to those responsible for the local government and NHS schemes is that, having mastered this particular maze, nobody knows when they may have to thread their way through a different but equally involved maze. The 1963 Act raised the limit on which graduated contributions were to be paid. The next time the scheme is changed it may not only raise the limit again but may in addition alter the relationship between graduted contributions and pensions[1] with consequent need to reassess the 1 per cent and 1/240 formulae.

This latter point is of much wider concern to all occupational schemes. How the state scheme will develop is an open question, but, particularly since the 1959 Act, it is a question of great concern to occupational schemes. What seems evident is that, rightly or wrongly, the local government and NHS schemes have embarked on a course which cannot fail to involve ever-growing complexity as long as the state scheme develops at all.

Finally, in this lengthy consideration of modification, one may note that the ramifications of the graduated modification are so extensive that it is not surprising that the Regulations and administra-

[1] Beyond what was already provided for in the way of quinquennial increases in contributions under the 1959 Act, which were presumably allowed for in arriving at the current modification figures.

tive arrangements which were made as the result of the 1959 Act led to certain difficulties and anomalies which have had to be put right subsequently. Thus a good deal of the National Insurance (Modification of Local Government Superannuation Schemes) Regulations, 1963, is concerned not just with amending the 1961 Regulations to take account of the 1963 National Insurance Act, but with improving those Regulations for points which had subsequently come to light. This is made clear in the notes to the 1963 Regulations issued by the Ministry of Housing and Local Government (as Circular No. 71/63), from which the following points are taken:

(1) Regulation 7 was made because earlier Regulations had not dealt with how a reduction of contributions was to be made where an employee had two or more separate employments under the same authority.

(2) Regulation 8 was introduced in part because it was found that at some age and pay levels the graduated reduction under the existing regulations 'is less than it would have been if the payments (i.e. of additional contributions) had been subject to flat rate deduction only'.

(3) Regulation 9 deals in part with the (rare) circumstance in which because of modification a transfer value would be reduced to nil.

(4) Regulations 17 to 19 deal with various complications arising where employees transfer to local government from other employment.

The list could be extended and only an optimist could be confident that even without the problems presented by developments in the graduated scheme, no further anomalies or difficulties in the original arrangements will come to light. A fourth memorandum of guidance was issued by the local authorities' working party early in 1964 and there is every indication that this will need to become a permanent body. Graduated modification has indeed had far-reaching effects on those schemes which have introduced it.

THE PROBLEM OF MODIFICATION

Before considering the general implications of modification in public sector schemes, it is important to see how far this problem is specifically a concern of the public sector. For it seems likely that one reason why it was felt in 1947 that it would be wrong for public servants to continue to draw their occupational pensions in full in addition to the state pension was that the public sector should give a lead to the private sector in carrying out the 'readjustment' advocated by Sir William Beveridge in his Report.

According to the Government Actuary's survey of Occupational

Pension Schemes in 1956, however, only 8 per cent of members of non-insured private sector pension schemes were covered by arrangements for modification of contributions and no members of insured schemes were so covered. Apart from the fact that the position may since have changed, particularly following the 1959 Act, the following points should also be taken into account:

(1) Many private sector schemes do not offer so generous a pension as that which is general in the public sector; there would therefore be less need than in the public sector to make adjustments if the combined contributions and the combined pension were no higher than in 'unmodified' public sector schemes.

(2) Many private sector schemes have in any case been set up since the introduction of National Insurance in 1948, and may well, therefore, have been designed to take into account the fact that employees would receive a flat-rate state pension; in this sense there would be an indirect adjustment for National Insurance, that is, scheme contributions and pensions would be lower than they otherwise might have been.

Leaving aside the specific problems presented by the graduated scheme (which are described in the final section of this chapter) it seems likely that specific or direct modification for National Insurance is a problem which has been encountered only by a few private sector schemes, and these one would expect to be, on the whole, long-established schemes with benefits at or near the level of the civil service and other similar public sector schemes.

It is for this reason that such a comparatively large number of the schemes examined in detail in the previous chapter do make some arrangement for reducing contributions and pensions. On the whole, however, these schemes too have not generally changed their arrangements for every change in the National Insurance scheme, and they have favoured the method also used in the Airways scheme of calculating contributions and pensions on a lower salary than that actually being earned. Only the 'D' scheme, as described in detail there, has devised a scheme which automatically adjusts contributions to and pensions from the scheme in accordance with changes in the state scheme. So far, however, there are few signs that many other schemes are likely to go in the same direction.

Although, therefore, a number of schemes in the private sector have encountered some of the problems of modification, it is probably true to say that on the whole they are mainly problems of public sector schemes. And this is likely to continue to be the case in future to the extent that the universal flat-rate scheme remains at a comparatively low level of pension provision. A wholly different situation has been created by the graduated scheme because it is not a universal scheme. In what follows, modification is treated as primarily a public sector problem.

The preceding analysis of modification arrangements may seem out of proportion, first in devoting so much space to some of the details of one particular piece of administrative machinery, and secondly in giving almost as much prominence to the graduated modification, which affects only two public sector schemes, as to the flat-rate modification which is found almost universally in the public sector.

But in the first place this particular piece of administrative machinery is important because it is completely new and has resulted from external developments. The 50 to 60 pages of *Shaw's Guide* now devoted to National Insurance, and particularly to modification, would have been unnecessary before 1948. One might say, therefore, that modification is a piece of machinery which in no way contributes to the provision of pensions under occupational schemes; it is negative in a way in which the rules for calculation of ill-health pensions, for example, are not negative. Given that ill-health pensions are to form part of pension schemes, some rules for administration are necessary. In the case of modification, both the reason for its introduction and the particular form of machinery devised must inevitably be the subject of close scrutiny in a study particularly concerned with the administration of public sector schemes.

The reasons for devoting a comparatively large amount of space to the graduated modifications are rather different. First, there is the fact that even to describe adequately what the arrangements are requires a certain amount of space (and it must be remembered that a good deal of detail has been left out of the description). Secondly, to some degree the problems which the local government and NHS schemes have had to face in connexion with graduated modification are likely in the long run to face all schemes with flat-rate modification, provided that they maintain the same basic approach (and provided also that the state scheme continues to operate universally). But thirdly, and perhaps most important of all, the thinking behind modification arrangement, the problem it sets out to solve and the degree of success which it has achieved are all important and relevant factors for the future development of public sector schemes, and some of these factors are seen perhaps more clearly in the case of the graduated than in the case of the flat-rate modification.

Thus the problem has two aspects in its bearing on the administration of public sector schemes. First, there is the general problem of the need to make adjustments to those schemes to take account of the state scheme, adjustments which are bound to create some complexity simply from the irreconcilably different natures of the two kinds of scheme, if they are even approximately to avoid duplication of benefits. But secondly, granted the need, one must assess how far present arrangements achieve their purpose in the most economical administrative terms.

On this second point it is important to emphasize that administrative convenience was not the dominant factor in the original flat-rate modification, although, as suggested above, it played some part in the combined modification arrangement (e.g. the simpler 1 per cent reduction in contributions). Rightly or wrongly, it was decided in the original plan that the over-riding consideration should be to achieve a balance between reduced contributions and reduced pensions; this inevitably meant relating the reduction in pension to the number of years during which reduced contributions had been paid, thus importing a further distinction between the state and occupational schemes into the administrative arrangements.

But the crux of the matter is this: if fairness to the individual is to take precedence over administrative convenience, it must surely not be forgotten that the avowed primary aim of the whole operation is to secure that the total of contributions paid and benefits received is limited implicitly to roughly the level of the occupational scheme before the introduction of National Insurance.[1] This the graduated modification does approximately achieve, but the flat-rate modification does not. The graduated modification achieves it, however, only at the cost of greatly elaborating and complicating the administrative arrangements of schemes, particularly if, as was suggested above, one looks to the almost indefinite possibilities for further elaboration which lie in the future. And the flat-rate modification could only have achieved it if it too had become vastly more complex (and also if on this occasion the 'no-detriment' rule had been pushed aside).

In this situation, it is surely a matter of some urgency to try to establish what the essential requirements are, first by examining whether the fundamental aim is reasonable and still as valid as it seemed to be in 1947; and, secondly, by seeing whether there is any escape from the dilemma with which public sector schemes are presented at the moment, that the only way in which they can achieve both the primary aim of modification and be fair to individual members of schemes, seems to be at the cost of great and ever-growing complexity.

The reasons for urgency are two: first, a situation in which additional work is being imposed on schemes without achieving its

[1] The present flat-rate modification might of course be justified on the grounds that it prevented some overlap of pension benefits, but it seems clear from the original statement by the Chancellor of the Exchequer on August 7, 1947, that the intention was to go further than that not only 'to avoid duplication of benefit under both an occupational and the national scheme', but because there was a specific limitation of the reduction in pension to 26s a week (less if service had been less than normal working life).

object, is administratively bad, but this is precisely what is happening with flat-rate modification. The only object which is being completely achieved is to ensure that any reductions which are now being made in contributions will be matched by equivalent reductions in the ultimate pension, but this object relates to the manner of modification rather than to the end which it is designed to serve. As far as that end is concerned, modification has become irrelevant to the situation of the National Insurance scheme today. The maximum reduction in pension which can operate in 1964 is £25 10s 0d, the maximum reduction which will operate in 1988 will be £67 15s 0d; but the single person's pension in 1964 is £175 10s 0d and by 1988 might well be £400 or £500.

Moreover, the urgency for trying to put the situation right is reinforced by the fact that the longer the situation continues as at present the less easy is it to put forward a workable solution. This is not just because, as was noted in the previous paragraph, the state scheme is constantly on the move while (flat-rate) modification stands still. Even more it is because, owing to the operation of the 'no detriment' rule, all those who have been modified since October 1951 on the 1948 rate would be protected against increased reductions relating to that period.[1] It is true that one might attempt to redress the balance by increasing the reductions to something in excess of what would be required by the current National Insurance rates, e.g. by increasing the pension reduction from £1 14s 0d per year of service to £6 (i.e. £240 after forty years' service), but apart from the further crop of anomalies which this would produce it is difficult to see the staff associations and unions agreeing to such a course.

The second reason for urgency is that the longer the present situation continues, the less easy is it to justify the present system of modification to members of schemes, and the stronger is likely to grow the agitation to have the whole system swept away. It is difficult enough to explain that the 9d, 1s 0d or 1s 2d reduction in weekly contributions is related, not as the innocent member might suppose, to that part of the National Insurance contribution which is required for pensions but to the cost of providing the portion of the scheme pension which is to be given up; but when he discovers that that reduction is related not to anything in the present National Insurance benefits but to what a single person could get by way of retirement pension sixteen years ago, he is inclined to regard the whole operation as meaningless.

It is hardly surprising, therefore, that the subject of modification,

[1] October 1951 was the date of the first increase in National Insurance contributions and pensions. Perhaps it is not strictly the 'no detriment' rule but a dislike of retrospection which would prevent such action (and anomalies between those retiring in future and those already retired).

apart from being a source of headaches for administrators of schemes, has also proved a source of irritation to members of schemes who fail to see what point it has. To sweep the whole thing away would clearly be a gesture of defeat but to leave the present system as it is would be equally to invite criticism. The underlying problem is to determine what the relations between the state and occupational schemes should be, and this will be considered further in the final chapter of the study. Meanwhile, something must be said about the general effect of the National Insurance Act, 1959, on this situation.

THE GRADUATED STATE PENSION SCHEME

The Problem of Contracting-Out

If the impression has been created by the earlier part of this chapter that modification arrangements have been the chief result of the impact of the National Insurance scheme on occupational schemes, that impression needs to be qualified in detail. First, there is the fact that modification has in general been a problem for public rather than private sector schemes; second, within the public sector, modification has been practically the only problem (certainly the only major problem) presented by the flat-rate National Insurance scheme; thirdly, all occupational schemes have had problems resulting from the introduction of the graduated scheme, but only in the case of the local government and NHS schemes in the public sector has modification been a major part of those problems.

In most discussions of the effects of the National Insurance Act 1959, on occupational pension schemes attention is concentrated on the problems of contracting out. This is naturally the point which is decisive as far as the future of the particular occupational scheme is concerned, but it is also important to consider some of the general implications raised by the introduction of a scheme of graduated contributions and pensions. In particular, such a scheme, added to the already existing flat-rate system and not merely substituted for it, was bound to increase the administrative complexity of running National Insurance both for the central government departments and for employers. This would have been true even if no occupational schemes had existed; the existence of occupational schemes and of the contracting-out proposals were therefore further complications.

Although the National Insurance Act of 1946 raised administrative problems for employers, two factors on which the Beveridge Report had laid stress helped to make those problems easier:

(i) the fact that contributions and benefits were flat-rate made the system comparatively straightforward, even though different categories, such as those aged under 18, paid different rates;

(ii) a single insurance stamp per week on a single insurance document covered not only retirement pensions but sickness, unemployment, etc., and a contribution to the National Health Service.

Both these points had to be abandoned in order to provide for a sliding-scale or graduated system of both benefits and contributions covering only retirement pensions, and this in itself had immediate effects on the administrative arrangements. In their guide for employers to graduated contributions, for example, the Ministry of Pensions and National Insurance give twenty-five different rates of contribution for weekly-paid employees and twenty-seven for monthly-paid.

But apart from these general considerations, a number of difficulties arising from the particular manner in which the graduated scheme has been devised have further complicated the situation. Essentially these difficulties appear as ways in which the administration of the graduated scheme differs from that of the existing flat-rate scheme, of which the following are examples:

(i) *System of collection.* In addition to buying stamps from the post office and sticking them on an insurance card for the flat-rate contribution, the employer has to deduct the graduated contributions under the PAYE system and send them to the Inland Revenue tax office.[1] Graduated contributions are calculated on the gross pay for income tax purposes, but the amount must be calculated week by week on the sums actually paid in that week (or fortnight or month, etc., in the case of employees paid on that basis). Thus, especially in the case of employees whose actual pay fluctuates from week to week, a check and a separate calculation must be made each time. This is more rigid than the PAYE system for tax purposes where the tax is cumulative.

(ii) *Detailed points.* Married women pay graduated contributions but most of them do not pay the flat-rate contribution; the amount of graduated contributions paid by each employee has to be added up at the end of each year; complications arise when employees have more than one job or only a part-time job.

No doubt the administrative work falling on employers soon becomes reduced to a routine and the calculations will not in general

[1] This means incidentally that the employer may have to consult two offices instead of one in the case of a query—M.P.N.I. on the question of whether graduated contributions have to be paid for a particular employee and the tax office on the question of the amount of pay on which the contributions are due.

cause too much difficulty, particularly to a large and highly-mechanized employer. But the essential point is that this is all additional work and additional complication which every employer has to deal with whether or not he has instituted an occupational pension scheme, unless he has contracted out his employees. If there had been no provision for contracting out he would still have had to decide whether to continue (with or without modifications) or to abandon any occupational pension scheme he might have, but the fact that it is possible, under certain conditions, to contract out of the graduated but not the flat-rate scheme has complicated the decision what to do about any existing scheme. The mere fact of the existence of the graduated scheme with its consequent administrative work is an important factor, even if only in the negative sense that an employer may be encouraged to contract out by the realization that he is in any case faced with the prospect of increased administrative costs.

'If the government had deliberately set out to create a problem to baffle employers and the pension industry alike, they could scarcely have done better than devise the conditions for contracting out that are embodied in the National Insurance Act 1959.' So begins the chapter on 'Contracting-Out' in a book designed to help employers in designing and running pension schemes.[1] For the most part this perplexity arises from trying to assess whether it would be more advantageous to contract out than to participate; here so many factors need to be weighed that it is not surprising that according to the authors 'anyone who is interested in the subject must by now be knee-deep in pamphlets, arguing to the last extremity the finer points of whether it is a few pence cheaper to contract in or contract out.'

Other things are involved, however, apart from the question of cost to the employer; for example, the attitude of the employees has to be considered. From the note on the National Insurance Scheme in Appendix 6, it is an easy matter to see that in terms of what he has to pay and what he will get for it the employee at £9 or £10 a week will do better if he is in the graduated scheme than if he is contracted out. This has naturally meant that other things being equal lower-paid staff have generally been in favour of participating in the graduated scheme.

Nevertheless, although cost is not the only point at issue it has figured very largely in discussions of whether or not to contract out; one element in this is the administrative cost. Here, although it was clear that contracting out involved increased work, it was not so clear how far this increased work was greater or less than the increased work which would in any case result from the graduated scheme. Some employers did make up their minds quickly; Ind

[1] Michael Pilch and Victor Wood, *Pension Schemes*, Hutchinson, 1960.

Coope, for example, who hold the first Certificate of Non-participation,[1] but it is likely that in many cases this was done not just on the narrow issue of costs but on a wider question of principle.[2]

Two stages in the contracting-out process under the 1959 Act may illustrate some of the main problems involved.

Let us suppose that an employer had decided to contract out his employees who were covered by the firm's scheme. He had to apply to the Registrar of Non-participating Employments for a Certificate of Non-participation. The Registrar issued a 20-page booklet (leaflet R.1) explaining what needed to be done. The main hurdle here was to see that the occupational scheme satisfied the conditions for contracting-out or could be suitably modified for that purpose. The conditions were not onerous—among other things the scheme had to guarantee a pension of 10½d a week for men and 9d a week for women for each year of service—but many points of technical detail might need to be considered necessitating correspondence, discussion and the provision by the employer of a good deal of information about the scheme.[3] Not least, the Registrar could delay issuing his Certificate if representations were made by the employees. If, however, the Registrar issued a Certificate the employer was still under an obligation to supply him with the annual statement of accounts and balance sheet of the scheme, a copy of each actuarial valuation and any other 'information, reports, documents, accounts or statements' which he wanted.

Another set of difficult problems for an employer attempting to assess costs arose from the arrangements to be made when employees who were contracted out left for other employment. It was a fundamental part of the 1959 Act provisions that in such circumstances the employee should have a right to a pension for the period of his contracted-out employment which was at least equivalent to what

[1] Cf. British Institute of Management booklet on *Government Pension Scheme 1961*; at a conference on May 24, 1960, Mr S. R. Plant of Ind Coope gave as one of the main reasons for not participating: 'It is quite clear that it will take time and clerical effort and we cannot see that that expense is justified whilst at the same time having to bear the administrative costs of running a company pension scheme. We feel that the cost of this unproductive work which will not sell another bottle of beer, if it is not to be saved, should be used towards the provision of increased pension benefits.'

[2] As indeed was the case with Ind Coope; cf. the Chairman's letter to *The Times*, January 14, 1960: 'It is Ind Coope's view that suitable pension provisions are best made by the employer.'

[3] Public sector schemes, in common with many others, had to make some relatively minor adjustments in order to qualify for contracting out; this led to a whole series of Statutory Instruments to carry out the adjustments. See among others, S.I. 1960 No. 1270 (Civil Service), and No. 2289 (Police); S.I. 1961 No. 267 (Firemen), No. 306 (Electricity), No. 307 (Gas), No. 324 (Scottish Teachers), and No. 559 (Transport), etc.

he could have become entitled to in the graduated scheme for the same period if he had been earning £15 a week.

It can be readily seen that this provision was administratively simpler to operate than one which attempted to relate the equivalent pension benefit to the actual amounts which the employee had been earning at different periods during his contracted-out employment, but it might well lead to considerable extra expense to an employer, particularly where he had to assure the equivalent pension by means of what were termed 'payments in lieu of contributions' (PIL) to the National Insurance Fund, since these were equivalent to the difference between the contracted-out and maximum participating rates of contribution and had to be paid for the whole length of contracted-out employment.[1]

Indeed, the ramifications of equivalent pension benefits could be considerable. In the Civil Service, for example, because the scheme is non-contributory the whole cost of payments in lieu falls on the Treasury and it is not possible, as is usual in contributory schemes, for the employer to recover up to half this cost from any refund of contributions to the employee under the occupational scheme. As a consequence, the Treasury have informed the civil service staff associations that if the cost of making payments in lieu becomes heavy, it may be necessary to consider making savings elsewhere, e.g. by a reduction in benefits. Although the situation in the civil service scheme may have been peculiar, the likely cost of having to assure equivalent pension benefits was generally an important factor for employers who were thinking of contracting out.

In assessing the general financial advantages or disadvantages of contracting out, an employer could make use of the numerous analyses to which reference was made above. Many of them, such as the pamphlet issued jointly by the Life Offices' Association and the Associated Scottish Life Offices in August 1959, contained detailed calculations of the effects of different courses of action, or showed how benefits under the graduated scheme compared with benefits under a private scheme. But the essential point, and the reason for the spate of pamphlets, was that there was no simple equation which would automatically give the right answer on the question of costs; there were too many differential factors, such as the lower flat-rate contributions for those participating or the different levels of earnings at which it was clearly advantageous for a man to participate, as compared with a woman.

[1] For the various ways of assuring equivalent pension benefits, see Appendix 6. The procedures were laid down in the 13 pages of The National Insurance (Non-participation—Assurance of Equivalent Pension Benefits) Regulations (S.I. 1960 No. 1103), not the least complex of the spate of Regulations which followed the 1959 Act.

Thus even on the apparently straightforward question of costs, it was no easy matter for the employer to decide where the advantage lay. As if this were not confusing enough, other factors might have to be taken into account; one, already mentioned, was the attitude of the employees, and arising from this, the desire of the employer to maintain an occupational scheme even at some extra cost, particularly where the main motive of setting up the scheme was the desire to attract and keep staff or to promote good relations between employer and employed; and this in turn may be seen as one aspect of a general attitude which emphasizes the advantages of private, as opposed to State, provision of pensions.[1]

One way in which the problem presented itself to many employers was in the form of speculation about the future course of National Insurance, and in particular, of the graduated scheme. The 1959 Act proposed increases in contributions at five-yearly intervals from 1965 onwards without any corresponding increase in benefits. 'Would this be all that would happen?' was the question which occurred to many people. In relation to the problem of contracting out an employer might feel that if he took part in the graduated scheme and kept on his own scheme, he might be faced at a later date with a situation where the total burden of contribution payments became too heavy; he would then have the choice of abandoning the occupational scheme or contracting out, but it might be that by that time the conditions for contracting out would be less easy and more expensive.[2] On the other hand, if he decided to contract out, improvements in the graduated scheme might in course of time make contracting out less attractive, and a decision to participate then might raise problems, e.g. in having to preserve 'equivalent pension rights' for all employees who had been contracted out.

As it happened, the first change in the graduated scheme probably came sooner than most people expected, and although its main provision, under the 1963 Act, was simply to raise the upper limit of earnings on which graduated contributions were to be paid (with no corresponding increase in the lower limit), it at once created difficulties for those who had already contracted out. Perhaps the main point was that there was a consequent increase both in the level of pension which the occupational scheme had to guarantee in order to qualify for contracting out and in the amount of the PIL.

[1] Cf. the point made by the Chairman of Ind Coope, already quoted. For a useful summary of the main arguments for and against participation see Forster, op. cit. pp. 67–69. Although he lists fourteen points against and only five in favour, most of the former are general arguments in favour of occupational schemes.

[2] The assumption being that if the graduated scheme got into financial difficulties, being on a pay-as-you-go basis, the government could not afford the loss of income if too many were contracted out.

The effect of these increases was that where an employer had contracted out with a scheme which was at or only a little above the level sufficient to qualify under the 1959 Act, he was faced with the choice of either improving his scheme in order to continue to qualify for contracting out, or of deciding to participate or of deciding to contract out only part of the membership of his schemes. But in either of the last two cases he would have to take into account the fact that any employees who ceased to be contracted out would either have to be guaranteed an equivalent pension for the period of their contracted-out service or would involve the employer in the payment of PIL for the same period.

Again, an employer who had not contracted out any of his employees under the 1959 Act had to consider whether the cost of remaining in the graduated scheme was now likely to be too high; this might arise, for example, where, as a result of having a fairly high proportion of employees earning over £15 a week, the extra cost of graduated contributions under the 1963 Act was quite high. Against this would have to be balanced (as under the 1959 Act) the cost of contracting out some or all of his employees particularly if there was likely to be a high rate of withdrawal. Another possibility for an employer in this situation might be to modify his own scheme so that the combined cost and level of benefits remained at what seemed to be a reasonable level.

A third situation might be similar to that of the local government and National Health Service schemes in the public sector where certain groups of employees had been contracted out under the 1959 Act, but it was now necessary to consider whether the criteria for determining these groups needed to be revised. It need not necessarily be, of course, that level of remuneration had been chosen as the criterion, but the problem would arise in a similar way even with different criteria.

But apart from these special problems affecting employers in particular situations,[1] some adjustment in administrative arrangements must have fallen on all employers with pension schemes, even though they might not have had either to amend their schemes or to seek to change their Certificate of Non-participation, where one had been issued under the 1959 Act. Because such reconsideration and possibly changes were inevitable under the 1963 Act, it was arranged that the increased level of equivalent pension benefits and of payments in lieu would not become effective until January 6, 1964, although the increased contributions under the Act, including the

[1] The Minister of Pensions and National Insurance (Mr Macpherson) estimated that 8,000 schemes would have to be modified as a result of the decision to raise the graduated limit to £18 (H.C. Deb., February 5, 1963, col. 359).

extension of the graduated range of contributions, came into force at the beginning of June 1963.

The Significance of the Graduated Scheme for Occupational Schemes
Perhaps the main significance of the introduction of the state graduated pension scheme is that it has focused attention on a problem, which, as long as the state scheme was on an entirely flat-rate basis and at a modest level, did not seem particularly urgent, except perhaps for those comparatively few occupational schemes, such as the majority of those in the public sector, which already provided what may be termed a reasonable living standard pension. This problem was that of the extent to which pensions should be provided through a man's employment or by the State.

Clearly, such a problem goes beyond the technicalities of the graduated scheme arrangements. To many it seemed that the mere fact that the State was entering the field of 'wage-related' pensions, in however modest a way, was an intrusion into a field which properly belonged only to occupational schemes. Moreover, the reasons given by the Government (in the 1958 White Paper, 'Provision for Old Age') for introducing such a scheme, might seem to lend support to the view that its main purpose was to improve the finances of the National Insurance scheme by reducing what, under the pre-1959 arrangements, was becoming a considerable Exchequer charge.

The White Paper gave the following as the aims of the government proposals (para. 45):

'(1) To place the National Insurance scheme on a sound financial basis.
 (2) To institute provision for employed persons who cannot be covered by an appropriate occupational scheme to obtain some measure of pension related to their earnings.
 (3) To preserve and encourage the best development of occupational pension schemes.'

Thus there were two grounds on which critics of state intervention in this field might be uneasy. The first was that if the main need was to put the finances of the National Insurance scheme on a sounder basis from the Exchequer's point of view, further changes in the scheme might be expected to follow the financial needs of National Insurance and would not necessarily be related to the best development of occupational schemes. And secondly, a scheme in which contributions and benefits were related to earnings was much more capable of expansion than the flat-rate scheme in directions which might bring it directly in competition with occupational schemes.

Whether these apprehensions were justified or not, the proposal by a Conservative Government in 1958 to introduce the graduated scheme, following as it did a similar though more ambitious proposal by the Labour Party in 1957, led to a good deal of controversy, including the publication of articles and pamphlets with titles such as *National Pensions: An Appeal to Statesmanship* and 'Pension Schemes at the Crossroads: the Stewardship of the Life Offices'.[1] A Conservative back-bencher accused the Minister of Pensions and National Insurance of putting further obstacles in the way of the development of occupational schemes by proceeding 'solemnly to build up the enormous fabric of the State system'. Other critics proclaimed that 'the seeds of the ultimate conflict have already been sown', or advocated the repeal of the 1959 Act before it had come into operation.[2]

With this new and acute controversy about the graduated scheme there has also been increasing debate about what kind of provision generally should be made by the State for old age. The Beveridge principle of universal, basic provision has increasingly come under attack; what should replace it is a subject of political controversy.[3]

This controversy may have played some part in influencing the decision whether to contract out or not. Certainly the facts are that over $4\frac{1}{2}$ million people have been contracted out of the graduated scheme, against the $2\frac{1}{4}$ million provisionally allowed for in the government's estimates. This has been claimed by the Conservatives as a demonstration of the scheme's success and described by a Labour Party spokesman as 'an outrageous swindle'. But whichever view is taken it is as well to bear in mind that of the $4\frac{1}{2}$ million, 60 per cent are in public sector schemes where political considerations are unlikely to have played much if any part, and where the chief motive was probably the feeling that the level of public sector schemes was high enough in itself not to require any additional provision from the State.

In a sense, therefore, the impact of National Insurance has been different for public sector and the majority at least of private sector schemes. The former have all along been in the position that their main problem has been how to avoid excessive pension provision,

[1] The first was a memorandum published jointly by the Institute of Actuaries and the Scottish Faculty of Actuaries in 1959, the second an article by A. S. Owen in the *Journal of the Chartered Insurance Institute*, 1960.

[2] See H.C. Deb., November 15, 1960, col. 267 (Mr John Eden); Pilch and Wood, op. cit. p. 164; Arthur Seldon, *Pensions for Prosperity*, p. 42.

[3] There were of course critics of Beveridge at the time when he was writing, e.g. Sir Hubert Henderson, *The Inter-War Years and Other Papers*, Oxford University Press, 1955, pp. 200–205, but more recently criticisms have come from writers of markedly differing views. See, for example, two articles by Arthur Seldon and Brian Abel-Smith, 'Beveridge: 20 Years After', *New Society*, February 14 and 28, 1963.

assuming that the existing public sector pattern provided the right level of pension. The latter have to a far greater extent been concerned with costs, which is why the graduated scheme with its finely-balanced need to weigh one point against another, and its permitting of contracting out has made a far greater impact than the inescapable and fairly modest flat-rate scheme; but this financial question has also to some extent been complicated by questions of political principle.

We seem to have reached a stage where everyone agrees that there ought to be better, less uneven all-round provision of pensions in retirement, but few people agree on exactly how this should be achieved and what part the State should play. All three political parties, for example, have produced plans or ideas for the future of the state scheme but all differ greatly from one another.

What the future pattern of pension provision should be is not therefore an easy question to answer. What may reasonably be attempted in a study of this kind is an examination of the factors involved in its consideration and the consequences for public sector schemes. Such an approach ought to put the question of modification in its proper context, and may suggest ways out of the present impasse. For one thing which is clear from this chapter is that the system of flat-rate modification generally adopted in the public sector has not proved to be the most suitable method for its purpose in the situation which has developed since 1948.

Chapter 10 will therefore be concerned in part with this important problem of the future relations between state and occupational schemes. It is hoped that the present chapter has at least indicated why the problem is important, not least for the administration of public sector schemes.

CHAPTER 7

Taxation and Pension Schemes

THE EFFECTS ON ADMINISTRATION

Tax Reliefs

Among the many problems which confront the administrator of pension schemes, those concerned with taxation are certainly not the least troublesome. In the first place, the law and practice on income tax in particular (and income tax is what is chiefly important in this context) are very complex. In the second place, and this probably concerns private more often than public sector schemes, to take advantage of tax reliefs to the maximum possible extent may be of great financial benefit to both employer and employees. Thus some knowledge of the tax position is essential for any pension scheme administrator, and to get the fullest advantage from it he may need to be something of an expert.

Taxation is, of course, a problem which affects administration in many different fields. It is well known that: 'The tax law is already complicated and elaborate. It merits this description not merely because of the varieties of circumstance and condition in which it is applied but also because of the refined distinctions that have been grafted onto what was originally a simple structure.'[1] To the extent, therefore, that pension schemes come into contact with this general elaboration and complication of the tax laws, they are no worse or better off than, say, charitable trusts, which also need to look to the tax position in making their administrative arrangements. But it is still worth examining whether the particular difficulties of pension schemes are inevitable or whether, short of a reform of the tax laws, some at least of those difficulties might be eased.

The impact of taxation on pension schemes is partly a matter of tax law and partly of tax practice. Specific legislation relating to schemes has developed over the last forty years, but there are also provisions of the general income tax law which affect schemes. The present situation is thus a combination of a number of different factors and some account of the history and background of the

[1] *Final Report of the Royal Commission on the Taxation of Profits and Income*, Cmd. 9474, 1955, para. 22.

legislation will be found in Appendix 7. In this chapter, the intention is to concentrate on the ways in which in practice problems and difficulties arise.

The essence of the present arrangements is that a pension, being a source of regular income, is taxed in the same way as salary or wages; but that since the money required to provide the pension is often put aside beforehand, either by the person who hopes to benefit or by his employer or both, some relief of taxation is given on the payments made beforehand to secure the pension. In other words, the basic position from a taxation point of view is that a pension is treated as being remuneration deferred from earlier years, the deferred remuneration consisting of contributions to pension funds and investment income of the funds. This principle is often referred to as exempting the build-up and taxing the benefits.

In one important way, this basic principle is not applied. Lump sums, under the general income tax laws, are not taxable since they are not regarded as income. A pension scheme which provided lump sum benefits would therefore be in a more favourable position than one which provided only pensions, if some action were not taken by the Inland Revenue authorities. This action takes the form partly of limiting the proportion of benefits which may be taken in lump-sum form and partly in reversing the main principle, that is, of not granting the full tax reliefs on contributions and investment income which are related to the provision of lump sums.

This difference between the tax position of pensions and that of lump sums gives rise to many of the practical difficulties arising from taxation. A further distinction must also be drawn: compulsory contributions by employees under 'statutory superannuation schemes' (i.e. roughly corresponding to what are here called public or public sector schemes) are exempted from tax. The result is that teachers and local government officers, for example, get tax relief on their contributions even though part of their benefits are in the form of tax-free lump sums.

This latter point suggests that one should distinguish between complexities in the law and specific problems of taxation. Considered from the point of view of the administrators of individual schemes, the special position of statutory schemes does not constitute a problem. But in the wider context of an equitable tax system, there is surely a problem to be examined; an anomaly of this kind which has existed for forty years and is there only because of a particular historical situation is, in a wider sense, bad administration. Apart from this, it is a point which anybody concerned with schemes needs to be aware of.

Approval of Schemes

The next task is to consider the practical administrative consequences of the basic tax principle and of the position of lump sum benefits. The main point to notice is that in order to secure tax reliefs, pension schemes have to be submitted to the Department of Inland Revenue for approval. Since without tax reliefs a scheme would be much more costly to run, this means that in practical terms all schemes are scrutinized by the Inland Revenue. One effect, therefore, of the tax position is to limit the ways in which schemes might develop by making it necessary to frame them in accordance with the current conditions for approval.

The basic position of the Inland Revenue in looking at schemes submitted for approval is that tax reliefs should only be granted to reasonable and genuine schemes. Both points are important; it is clearly necessary to establish that a scheme is genuinely designed to make provision for superannuation and not just to take advantage of the tax reliefs. Equally, if the contributions and benefits were in excess of what is generally regarded as reasonable, the effect of giving approval might be to give excessive tax benefits to members of those schemes.

It will be seen, therefore, that the whole basis of the present system is restrictive. Schemes which pass the test qualify for tax reliefs, but the whole object of the test is to make sure that only schemes within certain limits benefit. Two things make the position more complicated: the first is that schemes may be approved in part even if they do not satisfy all the conditions in force for tax reliefs; the second that changes in schemes also require approval. This second point perhaps gives rise to most problems for the administrators of schemes.

The significance of the present approach to approval of schemes is that almost any detail in the rules of a scheme may be scrutinized by the Inland Revenue, and even the precise wording of a rule may reflect the current conditions of approval rather than exactly what the framers of the rule intended. This has come about very largely because almost anything which is put into the rules of a scheme may affect the fundamental principle. For example, for a fund seeking approval under Section 379[1] it is obvious that the conditions under which a refund of contributions during service is permitted is of great concern to the Inland Revenue authorities, since some tax at least must be paid on the refund to balance the tax reliefs given on the original payment of contributions. But apart from scrutinizing the rules, the Inland Revenue also effectively put restrictions on schemes. For example, one condition is that schemes should only be

[1] For the significance of Section 379 and Section 388 approval see Appendix 7.

approved to the extent that they provide pensions not exceeding £3,000 p.a., the point being that if larger pensions were payable, there would be the possibility of gaining considerable benefit from a return of contributions.[1]

Again, the general level of benefits must be reasonably comparable with that of public schemes, that is, a maximum pension at normal pension age and after forty years' service of two-thirds of final salary, and anything in excess of this would not be approved. For the same reason, where lump sum benefits are payable they are limited to one-quarter of the total benefits, which is conventionally taken to be the proportion in such schemes as the Civil Service.

Limitations of this kind are likely to affect the shape of a scheme when it is drawn up and to restrict its further growth. But a rather different set of problems arises when in course of time a proposal is made to change an approved scheme. The proposal may be to make some quite minor variation in the benefits, but because the scheme has already been approved by the Inland Revenue, they will want to examine the effect of the change, if any, on the position for approval. If the change is of a kind which is fairly general in schemes, the taxation position may be reasonably straightforward although the precise way in which the change is made may cause difficulty. This is because human ingenuity in devising slightly different arrangements to meet slightly different situations may lead to an almost infinite variety of provisions, the effects of which are not always easy to calculate.

The Inland Revenue do now in fact issue a certain amount of guidance on the kind of points on which they will be prepared to give approval, and, just as important, on the limits of approval. Here are some examples: an employer wishes to put a rule in his scheme making it possible to increase pensions if the cost of living goes up—the Inland Revenue will now permit this within certain limits; another scheme allows a refund of contributions to a woman member who marries—the Inland Revenue consider the situation when the woman continues in the service of the employer but ceases to be a member of the scheme, and raise no objection to the return of contributions in such a case; two employers propose to run a scheme jointly—the Inland Revenue will want to consider closely how far there is common control of the two firms before giving approval.

Examples such as these show how closely administrators of schemes must try to keep in touch with current Inland Revenue practice. For it is obviously one of the difficulties of the situation that practice may change; as ideas on what is reasonable superannuation provision

---

[1] An employee gets tax relief on payment of contributions, but the tax charged on refunds of contributions is at only one-quarter of the standard rate.

G

develop, what was not approved a few years ago may now be approved. And in many cases those who run schemes need to consult the Inland Revenue in advance about proposed changes, to find out whether they are likely to be approved, particularly if they are at all unusual. This creates difficulties for administrators of pension schemes, and is one of the principal reasons why the present system of approval is regarded as an added burden on administration. There are also difficulties of administration for the Inland Revenue; not only must they constantly adapt their working rules to changing ideas and practice, but they must also try to secure that the rules are applied uniformly to all schemes.

The Position of Public Sector Schemes

The need to secure approval has been described in a general way, but chiefly as it affects private sector schemes. Here the problem is largely a question of trying to discover and meet the precise conditions of approval within the current rules of the Inland Revenue. The situation is rather different for public sector schemes.

There are first some obvious ways in which taxation does not affect the routine administration of some of these schemes. Where there are no contributions as in the Civil Service, there are no problems about tax reliefs on contributions;[1] where there are no funds, again as in the civil service or teachers' schemes, no problems arise over tax reliefs for investment income. But perhaps a more fundamental point is that most public sector schemes do not need to seek approval through the usual means, although, as statutory superannuation schemes, employees' contributions, where they exist, get tax relief.

This last point does not mean that public sector schemes can ignore the tax position, but rather that the influence of the Inland Revenue Department is exerted in a different way, and largely through the normal machinery of inter-departmental consultation. If changes are proposed in a public sector scheme, clearly one of the questions which must be considered by the management, whether local authority or central government department is how they are going to affect the tax position.[2] Because the level of benefits of 'statutory superannuation schemes' is also the general standard of approval for all schemes, changes may have repercussions in the private sector as well.

The importance of this point largely depends on the extent of the changes proposed. To take an extreme example: an extension of the tax-free lump sum benefit in public sector schemes so that it consti-

---

[1] The contributions for widows', etc., benefits do not get tax relief, because they are calculated on a net basis (see Millard Tucker Report, para. 60).

[2] The question does not arise in this way for those nationalized industries' schemes which have been approved under Section 379.

tuted the equivalent of one-third of total retirement benefit, and not one-quarter as at present, would be of great concern to the Inland Revenue because of the loss of revenue not only through public sector schemes, but also through the higher limits which they would inevitably have to apply to private sector schemes too.

Perhaps the different impact of the tax position on public and private sector schemes may be summed up in this way: if a private sector scheme wanted to provide pensions of four-fifths instead of two-thirds after forty years' service it would not be approved; but if a public sector scheme wanted to do the same thing, the effect on the tax position would be only one of the considerations which would need to be debated, and it is likely that if the change was generally regarded as reasonable it would be introduced in spite of the tax effects.

Nevertheless, apart from this general distinction between public and private sector schemes, it remains true that all schemes have problems in day-to-day administration as long as they get tax reliefs, and this means broadly all funded or contributory schemes. Some of the complicated ways in which this happens are described in Appendix 7.

FUTURE PROSPECTS

This last point provides the starting-point for any consideration of ways in which the present situation might be improved from the point of view of administrators of pension schemes. Taxation, so far as it affects routine administration, is an additional element calling for expert knowledge. But it is not simply because the general tax laws are complicated that schemes suffer from this additional complexity. The specific legislation relating to pension schemes adds to the difficulties, partly because the distinctions which are important for tax purposes are not necessarily so in pension terms.

The main example of this is the treatment of lump sums. The basic problem is that untaxed lump sums are important largely because rates of tax, and particularly surtax, make them very attractive, especially for those with large incomes. This accounts for the growth and popularity of 'Top-Hat' schemes, about which there has been much publicity. For the same reason, the Inland Revenue cannot be expected to relax their fairly strict control over schemes as long as there is this possibility of getting large tax-free lump sums; equally the demand for equity as between different classes of taxpayers will reinforce this view.[1]

It follows that a reduction in tax rates and particularly in surtax

[1] On 'Top-Hat' schemes and generally on the arguments over tax reliefs, see page 308 ff.

would make tax-free lump sums less attractive, and hence make the strict control of schemes by the Inland Revenue less necessary. This is something which cannot be pursued here, but it serves to show the influence of quite extraneous factors on the position. Something of the same result could be achieved if lump sums were taxed, perhaps with some exemption for small amounts. Certainly the existence of tax-free lump sums is such an obvious and, from the point of view of the underlying tax principle, indefensible anomaly, that no impartial observer could fail to regard it as the first object of any reform of the present system. Both the Millard Tucker Committee and the Royal Commission of 1955 thought it essential that something should be done about it. It is true that they did not agree among themselves about the precise remedy, but even so it is not an encouraging sign for any attempt to produce a more rational system that nothing whatever has been done about lump sums in the ten years since the Millard Tucker Report appeared.

As Appendix 7 indicates, there are other anomalies in the tax position. But many of them do not produce great difficulties for administrators, although they must of course be aware of them. In the case of untaxed lump sums, however, the very existence of the anomaly creates distortions. Thus we find such oddities as partially approved funds, where contribution and investment income has to be split into two so that the part relating to pensions may receive tax reliefs and the part relating to lump sums may not. Such a device does complicate administration by introducing a distinction which is relevant in tax terms but not in pension terms.

If lump sums became less attractive, either because they were taxed or because the tax relief was less valuable, or even if both things happened, it still does not follow that pension schemes would be untroubled by tax matters. True, they ought to be less troubled in the sense that the Inland Revenue's control need not be so strict. But the basic position would remain that tax reliefs would only be granted on certain conditions and that schemes would need to be examined and, when changes were made, re-examined, to see that they conformed with those conditions. Given this fact, and given that the tendency for schemes, particularly private schemes, is to change and go on changing, there seems to be an inescapable involvement with the complicated and ever-changing rules of the Inland Revenue Department. The position is not unlike that described by the Royal Commission on the Taxation of Profits and Income in relation to the tax laws generally; the obstacle to simplification, they said, is that 'the tendency both of Parliament and of the Inland Revenue Department has been in the opposite direction. Scrupulous regard has been paid to even small differences in individual situations; and while it is comparatively easy to advance from a simple system to a more refined one by introducing qualifications and differentials, it is very much more difficult to retire from a refined system to a simpler one and, by so doing, to ignore distinctions which hitherto have been recognized and allowed for.'[1]

As things stand, therefore, some scrutiny by the Inland Revenue is the price which has to be paid for securing tax reliefs, although some lessening of the scrutiny might be obtained by reforms of the existing tax law. This suggests that it might be worth looking at other possibilities. Might it not be, for example, that the oversight of pension schemes has become too heavily biased by the tax interest involved? Now, when the government's avowed aim is to 'encourage the best development of occupational schemes',[2] might not that aim be best achieved by making other arrangements for the general oversight of schemes? Such questions raise the problem of the determination of government policy in pension matters, a big subject about which more will be said in the final chapter.

Considered purely from the angle of the administration of public sector schemes, however, the problem of taxation is not quite so formidable as for private schemes. Whereas private sector schemes are funded, some public schemes, and among them the largest, are not. The problems of taxation affect funded schemes more than unfunded; they also affect contributory schemes more than non-contributory. But the question of whether there should be funds and contributions in public schemes is among the most important of the questions to be considered later in this study. Without suggesting that the best way of avoiding the complications of taxation is to unfund schemes and make them non-contributory, it could be argued that if this course were desirable on other grounds, then the fact that it brings this advantage too should not be ignored.

This, however, is only one example of a wider approach. Since taxation is an external factor which has no essential connexion with the provision of pensions, it is probably better to concentrate on those problems which arise directly out of the nature of pension provision, in the hope that this may lead indirectly at least to a lessening or certainly no increase in the problems created by taxation. Any simplification in the tax rules would, of course, be welcome but at least for the purposes of this study taxation, though it cannot be ignored, must take second place.

1 Cmd. 9474, 1955, para. 1088.
2 Cmd. 538, 1958, para. 45.

CHAPTER 8

The Problem of Complexity

The main object of previous chapters has been to describe the important features of present-day pension schemes, particularly of those
in the public sector, and to sketch their historical background. Among
the more important points to emerge are the following:

(1) During the nineteenth and early twentieth centuries public
service pension schemes grew piecemeal. Although these schemes
were not all exactly alike, there was a tendency for later schemes to
adopt a similar pattern (e.g. the terminal-salary basis) to that which
had already been used in earlier schemes.

(2) With the acceptance of a pension scheme as a normal part of
service conditions, and also with the great extension of the public
sector, there developed a generally accepted level of pension provision in the public sector (e.g. pensions in sixtieths or in eightieths
plus a lump sum). At the same time there was much less uniformity
in methods of assessing the cost and financing schemes.

(3) The broad picture of the private sector is of a slower growth of
schemes until the Second World War, but a rapid growth since. This
growth has been accompanied by a greater variety and range of
schemes than in the public sector, the main reasons being the greater
diversity of the private sector and the need of the employer to
temper what he thinks reasonable (or what his employees would like)
according to what he reckons he can afford. The result is that the
most generous schemes, which are broadly comparable with those
in the public sector, show more variety (e.g. in the calculation of the
pension), and many schemes provide only a modest pension.

(4) Two external factors are also of great importance in considering the present situation, National Insurance and taxation. National
Insurance has affected schemes because it provides a basic pension
for all whether in an occupational scheme or not and, more recently,
because it has begun to develop in directions similar to those of
occupational schemes. A particular example of the effect of the first
point is the case of those schemes which, even before National
Insurance, were designed in themselves to make reasonable pension

provision. But for public sector schemes, which mostly fall in this category, complicated administrative arrangements have failed to come to terms with the existence of National Insurance.

(5) Taxation, although it has a longer history of involvement with pension schemes, does not raise the same questions of principle as National Insurance, in the sense that basically pension schemes are concerned with general tax law and practice, although particular problems have also been caused by the special rules for schemes. The chief importance of taxation is that it limits what schemes may do, and that it creates certain administrative difficulties. But its impact is different for public and private sector schemes, and also for different types of scheme in the public sector.

The analysis of pension schemes presented in earlier chapters was deliberately restricted; it did not attempt, for example, to include details of all the provisions of public sector schemes which apply even to all current members, but was designed only to show what a new entrant in 1963 or 1964 might expect. This followed quite naturally from the aim of giving a conspectus of the whole field and of illustrating the main principles and motives behind the present arrangements. For the details of schemes one must turn to the various Acts of Parliament, Statutory Instruments and books of rules in which they are to be found; even to have listed all these details in summary form would have been a formidable task, and would probably have led the reader to feel that he had taken up a catalogue rather than a book.

This point does, however, draw attention to a factor which is of particular concern for this study, and which it would be wrong to ignore in any description of public sector schemes. Scarcely any writer or speaker concerned with the administration of schemes has not called attention to their complexity, and, still more, to their tendency to increasing complexity.[1] Something of this complexity has been hinted at in earlier chapters, but more particularly perhaps in the chapters concerned with National Insurance and Taxation, because it is obvious that where external and additional factors (i.e. additional to the business of providing pensions through occupational schemes) have to be reckoned with, some addition to and therefore complication in the work of administration is bound to follow.

But although the influence of these external factors on the administration of schemes is of great importance, taken by themselves they do not account for all the complications which are met. The first aim

---

[1] See, among others, R. S. McDougall, *Superannuation—Present Tendencies and their Implications*, Institute of Municipal Treasurers and Accountants, June 1949, or the Prefaces to the various editions of *Shaw's Guide to Superannuation for Local Authorities*.

of this chapter will then be to see what other reasons can be suggested for complexity and then to consider the implications of this situation.

One obvious factor which has a bearing on complexity is the generally very large size of public sector organizations, which in turn means that pension arrangements may have to cater for many different groups of employees. Examples are different retirement conditions for prison officers in the Civil Service or for women nurses in the local government and NHS schemes. In the nationalized industries, the Airways' scheme provides a striking example of the need for special pension terms in the case of pilots and other flying crew. The importance of such arrangements for the administration of schemes is that different rules must be drawn up and applied in the case of these various special groups of members, who may in certain cases in fact form a significant proportion of the total membership, as in the case of the Airways' scheme.

A further noticeable element in the general complexity of public sector schemes is the great amount of detail contained in their rules. Comparatively little is left to be decided at the discretion of the employers, and the rules attempt to cover all the possibilities which are likely to occur. For the most part, this detailed approach derives from the essential nature of the public services, and, particularly, from the need to ensure that proper Parliamentary control is exercised over the expenditure of public money. Thus, Parliament has legislated for central and local government schemes either by statute or by subordinate legislation (and usually by both), and in doing so has sought to lay down the precise terms and conditions for the payment of benefits. Nationalized industries' schemes, although in general their rules are not specifically laid down by Act of Parliament or by Statutory Instrument, nevertheless tend to follow the same pattern of detailed rules; for example, the 1963 rules in the Airways' scheme for widows' pensions provide among other cases for the member who 'is lawfully married to two or more persons.'

The result is that in the course of time the accumulated rules of the various schemes amount to a formidable bulk of printed matter. In the case of local government, for example, the latest edition of *Shaw's Guide* lists seventy-two Statutory Instruments 'especially relevant to local government superannuation' from 1939 onwards, in addition to the various statutes. For the civil service scheme, the Treasury issue from time to time volumes containing 'all the principal statutory provisions and regulations' in force at the time; the 1952 edition lists 24 main Superannuation Acts from 1834 to 1950, 48 other Acts and 78 Rules, Regulations and Orders, all of which in whole or part, are relevant to the provision of pensions for civil servants.[1]

For those concerned with the running of schemes the problem is to be aware of all the various rules which may apply, and also to understand them. For the attempt to put into precise legal language (as with a Statutory Instrument) the exact circumstances under which, for example, a particular benefit is payable, is likely to make the rule more involved. The National Health Service Regulations, for example, are long and complicated and the Minister of Health at the time, a man with a reputation for an acute intellect, remarked of the 1955 Regulations that it was difficult to believe that anyone could completely master them, although they were said to be easier to follow than the previous Regulations of 1950.[2]

Moreover, the elaboration of rules makes it harder not easier to decide individual cases, one of the most difficult and time-consuming tasks which administrators of schemes have to tackle. Great difficulty may be caused by trying to decide whether Smith is entitled to claim the more favourable terms of rule X or whether his case really comes under rule Y. Furthermore, there are almost certain to be exceptional cases which seem to fall outside the rules, however carefully they are framed. And there may also be provision for appeals in disputed cases, so that here again quite lengthy administrative procedures may be involved.[3]

Although probably the main reason for the elaborate rules of public sector schemes is the need to ensure that the precise conditions for payments which may involve public money are set down for all to see, other influences are also present which tend in the direction of elaboration rather than simplicity. One of these is the part played by the demands of the staff themselves. It is an important characteristic of the public services that staff associations developed early and have a strong influence particularly in matters concerning conditions of employment. In pension terms, this may well have helped to secure that special conditions should apply to particular groups of members, and that refinements were introduced into the rules allowing as many people as possible to take advantage of the most favourable terms. Another point in which staff associations have taken a notable part, the 'no detriment' rule, is discussed separately below. In view of the aims of staff associations, which are naturally to secure the best pos-

[1] *Digest of Pension Law and Regulations of the Civil Service*, H.M.S.O., 1952.

[2] Mr Iain Macleod, H.C. Deb., July 19, 1955, col. 331.

[3] In local government the appeal is to the Minister (of Housing and Local Government) and can be on any decision 'concerning the rights or liabilities' of an employee (1937 Act, Section 35; 1953 Act, Section 21). It is illuminating to study the pages of *The Local Government Chronicle* or *Local Government Finance* to see what difficulties individual cases may cause.

G*

sible terms for their members, it is not surprising that their tendency should be towards elaborating rather than simplifying schemes.

Partly this approach derives from what, in another context, a Labour Party spokesman, himself a former civil servant, described as 'our passion for equity' which 'makes complications of otherwise perfectly simple ideas'.[1] There is a strong feeling, in the public services especially, that pension schemes should ensure that everybody is entitled to and gets at least as good terms as those in comparable situations. Since, in such large organizations as the Civil Service, the application of a simple rule to everybody is almost bound to lead to anomalies, this too tends to the further elaboration of the rules of schemes in an attempt to iron out the anomalies.

A number of these points bear directly on what many would regard as a particularly important factor in the administrative complexity of public sector schemes, the operation of the 'no detriment' rule. The effects of this rule are chiefly important because changes occur in schemes fairly frequently, but the fundamental point is that it is an attempt to be scrupulously fair to all members of schemes. This fairness is based on the fact that because of the long-term nature of pension provision, changes in schemes may affect the plans and expectations of individual members which have been laid over many years; and this is so even if the changes represent improvements in schemes. For example, if widows' pensions are introduced into a scheme where none was provided before, the improvement may not be of much value to members who had made their own private arrangements over a period of thirty years or more, and there might indeed be considerable disadvantage to them if they were compelled to upset these long-established arrangements because of changes in the pension scheme.

'No detriment' then, like the making of detailed rules generally is very much part of the public service tradition in which the emphasis is on precise terms and conditions safeguarding the rights of individuals in all circumstances. For the practical effect of 'no detriment' for the individual member is that he always has the choice of his existing or the new terms when changes are made in schemes, and he is therefore protected from arbitrary changes of policy although not, of course, from making the wrong choice.

In terms of administrative consequences, the main point about 'no detriment' is that a decision to grant a particular option at a particular time to a particular group of members has repercussions over a long period. In the first place, since that particular option may well apply to members who may not retire for thirty or more years, its effects are felt for so long that it often seems a permanent feature of the scheme. But, secondly, since schemes do not remain unchanged

[1] Mr Douglas Houghton, H.C. Deb., June 12, 1956, col. 330.

for long periods, that particular option is likely to be only one of a number which at any given moment may be being exercised by the same or different groups of members. The cumulative effect of the various options under the 'no detriment' rule combined with the desire to cover all possibilities under the rules creates a very big problem for those responsible for running schemes. The position has been described by an administrator with long experience of the London County Council scheme: there are 'multiple prescriptions, sometimes mandatory and sometimes depending on the past or present option of the individual, to cover a single contingency. Things have now reached a state in which even a superannuation specialist in a large authority must constantly refer to legislation and hope that he has recalled all provisions relevant to the particular circumstances. For an employee in a smaller authority for whom superannuation is not a full-time job the position is infinitely worse— particularly when he first takes over the work!'[1]

A particular example of this situation is the continued existence of entire schemes long after the administrative division of responsibilities which gave rise to them has ceased to exist. The nationalized transport industry, in particular, still has employees pensionable under the Great Eastern Railway New Pension Fund or the Sharpness and Gloucester Dock Company Pension and Life Assurance scheme, among others;[2] in the National Health Service, similarly, about 8 per cent of the membership was in 1955 still pensionable under the terms of schemes started in pre-NHS days.[3]

Complexity, and the reasons for it, has here been treated as a public sector problem. This is not to say that the administration of private sector schemes is not complex too, but the problems there are rather different. External factors, such as taxation and National Insurance, are as important as in the public sector, and indeed are almost certainly more so. But there is probably less need for the detailed elaboration of rules or for the extreme complexity presented by 'no detriment', to take two examples. Furthermore, private sector schemes are on the whole very much smaller than those in the public sector. In what follows, therefore, the implications of complexity will be treated as primarily a public sector problem, although with some bearing on private sector schemes too.

[1] A. C. Robb, *Shaw's Guide to Superannuation for Local Authorities*, 3rd ed., 1962, p. 4.
[2] See The British Transport Reorganization (Pensions of Employees) (No. 3) Order, 1962; S.I. 1962 No. 2758: the Schedule lists 95 such schemes, together with a further 81 insured schemes.
[3] See Government Actuary's Report on the Scheme, H.M.S.O. 1959, para. 10.

IMPLICATIONS OF COMPLEXITY

The situation in the public sector, then, is that quite apart from the influence of external factors, a number of reasons have combined to make the administration of schemes complicated. Furthermore, it does not seem to be anyone's concern at the moment to seek administrative economies on any scale. This may seem surprising in view of the emphasis which has been placed on the great and growing complexity of schemes; it might be thought that awareness of this tendency would provide sufficient incentive to do something about it. That this is not so derives essentially from the nature of the situation; for on the one side, is the fact that the first concern of members of schemes is naturally with securing the most favourable pension terms and with equity, a concern which must normally bring more not less work in administration; and on the other side, employers have not resisted very strenuously the tendency towards complexity perhaps because they have felt that many of the difficulties are more or less inevitable or that complexity can go a long way before schemes break down (witness the modification arrangements for the graduated scheme in local government and the National Health Service); above all was probably the feeling that the saving to be achieved even if one could overcome all the difficulties would scarcely justify the effort involved. On the whole the general attitude seems to be that pension administration is troublesome, but one must learn to live with it.

Against this view that complexity is not too high a price to pay for achieving the objects of pension schemes, it could be argued that it is wasteful to spend more on the administration of schemes than is necessary. Such work has no 'productive' value,[1] and ought to be kept to the minimum, even if to halve the costs of administration would have a negligible effect on public sector finances.

There is a further consequence of complexity to which attention should be drawn. However much it springs, in part at least, from an attempt to safeguard the rights of individual members, its effect is to make it very much harder for the individual member to discover what his rights are. An admirable illustration of the dilemma is provided by one of the Regulations for the local government scheme which were made following the 1953 Act. This provides that a new employee is to be asked for full details of all his previous periods of employment, and not merely for details of previous local government or similar service. The reason given by the Ministry of Housing and Local Government is that 'Experience has proved, in the growing complexity of the subject, that employees cannot be relied upon to distinguish what previous employment may count for superannuation purposes and what does not. The complete record asked

[1] Cf. the remarks made by the Ind Coope spokesman quoted on page 183n.

for should avoid difficulties arising in future over undisclosed service.'[1]

The basic problem brought out by this example and the earlier discussion is how to assess the degree of complexity which is necessary or tolerable. The obvious starting-point is to examine present administrative arrangements to see whether they achieve in the most effective and economical way the objects which they are designed to serve. This would be a useful but limited inquiry, since it would leave out of account the need to examine whether the aims and objects at present being pursued are the right ones. It may be that in some cases what is needed is not an improvement of existing arrangements but different arrangements to serve different purposes. It is difficult to assume without question, for example, that all that is needed in the case of modification is a better formula. From what has been said earlier it seems clear that one must first examine the need for having modification at all; and this can only be done satisfactorily by having regard to what the respective spheres of state and occupational schemes are likely to be in the future.

The remainder of the study will be devoted to a consideration of the aims of public sector schemes and the administrative arrangements necessary to carry them out. This falls into two parts: first, in the rest of this chapter and also in Chapter 9, three issues will be examined which are domestic or internal to the organization of the public sector; then, in the final chapter, a broader view of the pension scene will be taken, and of the place of public sector schemes in it. This consideration of traditional assumptions and methods should put in perspective the problems raised earlier in a way which is rarely possible for those whose main task is day-to-day administration, and should point the way to the future direction which schemes should take.

The three problems to be considered in this and the following chapter are the 'no detriment' rule, the methods of financing schemes and the multiplicity of separate schemes. Both the latter problems are rarely discussed, perhaps because questions about them are unlikely to arise within the context of individual schemes. Yet they have important consequences, not least for the administration of schemes.

The present variety of methods of financing schemes, which were described in Chapter 4, clearly raises issues which go beyond the day-to-day administration of individual schemes. Within each scheme the method of financing is well understood and has led to the elaboration of certain routines of administrative procedure. Questions rarely arise about whether any major change in financing is required; at the same time, to outside observers the fact that some

[1] *Local Government Superannuation, Explanatory Memorandum on the Regulations,* H.M.S.O., 1954, para. 11.

schemes have funds and contributions, some contributions but no funds (or at least no accumulated funds), and some neither funds nor contributions suggests that at least the reasons for this variety need examination.

From the point of view of administration, this variety also appears to have some obvious consequences which ought to be considered. Contributions by employees either as a percentage of wages or salaries or as a fixed amount require additional record-keeping; they also complicate the arrangements when members leave, both in the provisions for refunding contributions and in transfer arrangements; and they raise problems in relation to taxation. Non-contributory schemes therefore offer obvious advantages in administrative terms, and it is necessary to consider whether there are other reasons for keeping contributions.

The position is similar in relation to funding, although a good deal more complicated. There is first the point that the administration of a fund's finances calls for a good deal of time, skill and expert management if the best use is to be made of the investment powers possessed by the fund. But secondly, there is in public sector schemes at the moment a sharp distinction between those, whether funded like local government or non-funded like the teachers', where data and records are maintained so that calculations of the financial position are obtainable at periodical actuarial valuations; and those, such as the police and the Civil Service, where (except in the special case of the Post Office) no regular financial assessment is made. In this second group of schemes, consequently, less work is involved in the maintenance of the present financial arrangements.

These, then, are ways in which pay-as-you-go schemes either are or can be simpler to run than funded schemes. On the other hand, administrative convenience may not be the most important factor to be taken into account in determining the method of financing. The need to fund may be related, for example, to general principles of financing which should apply to pensions as much as to other matters. An assessment of the present situation will therefore need to examine in detail the reasons for the adoption of particular methods in particular schemes. This should reveal the fundamental issues involved in financing public sector schemes, and thus be of relevance for determining whether the present pattern should be followed in future. This is a subject of major importance, and will be considered at length in the next chapter.

The Multiplicity of Schemes

The present multiplicity of schemes in the public sector raises different issues. As was shown in Chapters 1 and 2, historical circumstances have largely determined the present number of schemes in the public sector. Two important influences have been, first, general public policy—e.g. the central government's concern for education was a major factor in the establishment of a separate scheme of teachers' pensions—and, secondly, financial considerations, seen most notably in the case of separate schemes for each of the nationalized industries. The result is that at one end of the scale are the very large schemes, such as that for the Civil Service, and at the other the relatively small schemes for firemen or Atomic Energy Authority staff. But although it is possible to see how the present pattern has been arrived at this does not necessarily indicate the best pattern for the future.

There are two main reasons for raising this question. One is the fairly narrow point that as the links between schemes have grown closer, the administrative disadvantages of differences between them have become more obvious. This point has chiefly arisen from the elaboration of the system of interchange rules in recent years which was described in Chapter 3. This mechanism for preserving pension rights brought additional work both in drawing up the rules in the first place, and in the continuing routine procedures for checking data, calculating transfer payments and so on. A great deal of the work arose because each scheme differed to some degree in its provisions, and, more particularly, because each scheme had its own separate and distinct financial arrangements. For the interchange rules have the dual purpose of providing the transferring member with equivalent rights for his past service in the new scheme, and at the same time of making a fair distribution of the cost between the two schemes. A good example of some of the difficulties which have arisen can be seen by studying the rules for interchange between the Civil Service and local government.[1]

The second reason for examining the present pattern of schemes is the need to consider the general advantages of fewer schemes. In this sense, the difficulties over transfer arrangements have merely called attention to the wider question. The need for transfer arrangements is not an argument either for greater uniformity among schemes or for fewer schemes, but if there were good reasons for bringing them about, both the number of transfers and the complexity of the arrangements would be reduced. The most obvious advantage of fewer schemes is the scope for more economical administration; for example, much more of the clerical labour of detailed calculation could be transferred to machines, and the possibilities of using computers could be more easily explored. Against this, one might argue that the larger the scale of operations the more likely that time-

---

[1] The Superannuation (Transfers Between the Civil Service and Local Government) Rules, 1950, S.I. 1950 No. 145. Among other things, non-contributing service and Local Act provisions have to be translated into civil service terms.

consuming queries would arise; or that administrative economies ought to be weighed against the individual traditions of different parts of the public sector.

But probably the main reasons which would be advanced against fewer schemes would be the lack of uniformity in existing schemes, and the financial considerations which, as already indicated, have been a principal factor in determining the present pattern. On the first point, it must be said not only that a large degree of uniformity already exists, but that where there is lack of uniformity it is either in relatively minor benefits or due to special conditions (e.g. earlier retirement for police and firemen, or continuation of a pre-nationalization scheme as with Railway staff). Moreover, conditions of employment over a large part of the public sector are similar, so that on these grounds there is no serious obstacle to greater uniformity. The existence of the large flat-rate schemes in two of the nationalized industries seems to raise difficulties for this view. However, they serve mainly to draw attention to two major questions of national and not merely public sector pensions policy, that is, whether flat-rate or wage-related pensions are more appropriate to the second half of the twentieth century, and whether there is any justification for continuing to maintain separate schemes for salaried staff and manual workers within the same employment or industry. These questions will therefore be referred to in Chapter 10; here the only comment is that the existence of these schemes limits the scope for reducing the number of schemes.

Finance is also a limiting factor to the extent that as long as separate funds are maintained there are difficulties in amalgamating schemes. Clearly, the important point is to establish first the right method of financing, and this is a major point to be considered in the next chapter. All that can be said here is that if pay-as-you-go schemes were general in the public sector, financial considerations would not be a great obstacle to the amalgamation of schemes, since all that would be necessary would be a reasonable apportionment of costs as they arose. If, on the other hand, funding were to be generally adopted, the number of separate funds would be a determining factor in the extent to which amalgamation could be carried.

At the least, the discussion suggests that the possibilities of amalgamation ought to be seriously considered, the more so since very little attention has been paid to them and there has been no attempt to examine the arguments either for or against such a course.[1] In conclusion, therefore, three possibilities or stages may be outlined for further study:

[1] An exception should be made for the brief article by A. C. Robb, 'The Development of Public Superannuation Schemes', *Journal of the Institute of Actuaries*, Vol. LXXVI, No. 342. This, however, was written in 1949.

(1) amalgamation of closely similar schemes, such as police and firemen;
(2) centralization and mechanization of the routine work of record-keeping in the main groups of schemes (e.g. civil service, local government, teachers and NHS, or the nationalized industries—subject, of course, in both cases to satisfactory financial arrangements being made);
(3) a single public sector scheme.

All or any of these stages have positive advantages and clearly ought to be considered in looking to the future organization of public sector schemes. Nor must it be thought that they imply imposing a rigid uniformity on all those working in the public sector. Variations arising from differences in conditions of employment would remain, just as they arise at present within schemes. Major changes in benefits would apply uniformly, but so they do today, the main differences being that since they have to be negotiated separately for each scheme they do not operate at the same time for everybody. A closer look at the whole question is badly needed.

'No Detriment'

The main reason for looking at the number of schemes is the desire for more efficient administration, but it cannot be claimed that disaster would follow if no reduction were made. 'No detriment' poses a more difficult dilemma. If no change is made in it, not only will the natural development of schemes lead to increasing complexity, but things will be made far worse by a conscious attempt to introduce major improvements and simplification. But to oppose 'no detriment' seems to offend the principle of fair play and gives the appearance of attacking the long-held rights of individuals purely for the sake of administrative convenience.

In considering this dilemma the first point to note is the uniqueness of the situation. When other conditions of service, for example, hours of work, are changed as a result of negotiation between employers and employees, existing employees are rarely given individually the option to continue at their old working hours for the rest of their careers. Admirable as it might seem in theory to preserve the rights of individuals in this way, in practice it is recognized as being quite unworkable.

What is usually held to make pension matters quite distinct from other matters affecting conditions of employment and to justify 'no detriment' is that individuals necessarily have long-term plans and expectations based on the pension terms under which they enter employment. But again, long-term plans are not confined to pension matters; many other factors, such as where he is likely to have to work, will affect a man's plans, and, particularly, where he makes his home. It is true that because pensions generally lie so much in the future when a man starts work, they differ in degree from other conditions of employment in their effect on hopes and expectations, but they cannot be said to differ in kind.

If this is so, it is possible to see how the dilemma might be tackled. For essentially the problem is how to reconcile the reasonable and legitimate claims of individuals for fair treatment with a workable system of administration. This is not simply in the interests of greater administrative convenience; present arrangements seem to go far beyond a reasonable safeguard of individual members' rights and in so doing make nonsense of some changes in schemes. It is sometimes said, for example, that public servants have, since 1948, had their pensions reduced to take account of the state pension, whereas in fact it will not be until the 1980's or later that any appreciable number of those retiring will have any effective reduction in their pensions. It is difficult to believe that in terms of basic principles it could have been claimed that any injustice had been done or long-term expectations harmed if modification had applied at least to all those who from 1948 onwards became entitled to state pensions.

Only a comparatively modest alteration to the rule, so far as members are concerned, is needed to avoid this kind of difficulty. When changes are made in schemes, they should be negotiated in such a way as to bring in existing as well as future members. In other words, the individual would give up his right absolutely to the pension terms which prevailed when he first entered employment, but he would be protected from the arbitrary imposition of much more unfavourable terms by his ability, or the ability of those representing him, to negotiate with his employers for the best terms in prevailing circumstances. This would be no more and no less than happens in the case of salaries and wages or other terms and conditions of employment. 'No detriment' began, it must be remembered, at a time when public servants did not have the protection of highly organized and articulate staff associations. In the second half of the twentieth century, the need for such an absolute rule is less evident, particularly as its consequences have grown far greater than could possibly have been foreseen in 1829, when civil servants first claimed successfully that their pension terms had been unjustly worsened.

For example, whatever view is taken of the different methods of financing schemes, it can scarcely be held that the comparatively low rates of contribution enjoyed by those who are still superannuable under the terms of the Asylum Officers' Superannuation Act of 1909 bear any relation to current ideas of a reasonable apportionment of the total cost of benefits. Nor is it easy to see that it would have been unjust to have brought these officers into the National Health

Service scheme when it started on the terms drawn up for that scheme, since these new terms would have applied only to service after the beginning of the scheme, and their rights under the Asylum Officers' scheme for service up to that point would have been safeguarded. Indeed, so far as the contribution rates are inadequate, it could be held that others and, in particular, taxpayers are being unjustly treated in having to pay more than they need simply because other ideas about meeting the cost happened to prevail in the different circumstances of over fifty years' ago.[1]

Small as the change in the 'no detriment' rule would be, it would require a great difference of attitude in pension negotiations by both employers and members of schemes. There is a tendency at present to treat pension matters in quite a different category from other matters affecting conditions of employment. For example, it would not normally require any argument that nobody can reasonably expect to have his right to particular conditions of service safeguarded for forty or fifty years ahead, whatever happens meanwhile.

Because of this need for a change of attitude and for treating pensions in the same way as and with full regard to other conditions of employment, the proposal to abandon 'no detriment' may seem more revolutionary than it is. For this reason, the greatest difficulty may well be over the initial stage. To abolish 'no detriment', it will probably be argued, would itself be a violation of the rule. It is true that where a practice has become so deep-rooted, to challenge it may seem little short of sacrilege. It would be possible to compromise, and to announce that 'no detriment' would cease to operate at some specified future date, say, in ten years' time. But the question which must be faced is how long we can afford to continue it. It is indisputable that the long-term nature of pension provision coupled with the need to make changes in schemes from time to time inevitably brings a certain amount of complication into the running of schemes. To add to these complications without good cause is to place a further unnecessary burden on administration; but in the long run, it is not in the interests of members either; the difficulties of assessing one's entitlement, the real possibility of errors being made in the calculations and the additional reasons for disagreement and dispute are all likely to grow worse unless some attempt is made at simplification. Abolition of 'no detriment' is a step in this direction, and will not undermine the legitimate rights of individuals. It will destroy a privilege which has long been enjoyed by public servants, but this privilege has no place in present-day conditions.

[1] According to the Government Actuary's Report on the NHS scheme the inadequate contribution rates for 'optants' were one of the main causes of a deficiency at the 1955 valuation (see para. 36 of Report).

CHAPTER 9

Financing Public Sector Schemes:
Funding and Pay-as-you-go

As was indicated in Chapter 4, funding is the generally accepted method of financing pension schemes, but a number of public sector schemes do not have funds. This provides a starting-point for assessing the present situation. Consideration of the reasons for funding, and of their application to public sector schemes, will help to determine what the future method, or methods, of financing should be.

Financial and Psychological Arguments

Foremost among the arguments for funding is the need to safeguard the benefits of the scheme. The money paid into a fund is invested and can serve only the purposes of the pension scheme. Provided, therefore, that the size of the fund which is built up is adequate and the choice of investments is sound, assets are created which will guarantee the pensions both of existing members and of those who have already retired; these assets cannot be used for any other purpose, so that even if the employer goes bankrupt pensions are not put in jeopardy.

Two other reasons in favour of funding may be regarded as subsidiary to this primary purpose. One is that whether the fund is necessary to guarantee security of benefits in a particular case or not, it may help to give the member a feeling of security. The fund is a visible indication that money is in fact being provided to pay pensions. In a similar way a fund may be of value to members as an indication that they now have an entitlement to pension and that their pensions are not simply dependent on the charity of their employers; and it may even be managed by a committee with representatives from both the employers' and the employees' sides.

Another main argument in favour of funding is the argument from financial principles, that if a known liability is being incurred in a particular year, then provision for it should be made from the income for that year. With funding that liability is met, so far as it can be ascertained, in the year in which it is incurred. This reason for funding is particularly appropriate for a body engaged in trading activities, for clearly what is regarded as right to include in the provisions for a particular year is likely to affect the prices charged for the organization's product.

It is important to distinguish this argument, which derives from generally accepted financial principles, from a somewhat similar argument that one of the advantages of funding is that it spreads or evens out the cost of pensions over a period of time. The argument is sometimes put in the form that the burden of pension cost is more equitably divided between present and future generations under a funding system, as compared with pay-as-you-go where future generations may have to bear an increasing and unfair proportion of the cost.

Both these arguments, of proper costing and of equalizing the burden, derive from the peculiar nature of pension costs, and of funding to meet those costs. For not only is it characteristic of pension schemes that the year-by-year cost of pensions starts at a low level and then rises steeply, but the very act of putting more money into the fund in the early years than is currently needed to pay pensions, ensures that an additional source of income, namely that from investments, is increasingly available to meet the commitments of the fund.

A further argument in favour of funding is that it provides the opportunity through skilful investment of the fund's resources to reduce the cost of the scheme, although correspondingly unsuccessful investment may make the scheme more costly than expected. Sometimes, reduced cost will benefit mainly the employer, who will be able to reduce his commitments to the scheme. Nevertheless, it must always be a powerful weapon in the hands of members of a scheme to be able to point to a surplus in the fund to back up a claim to better benefits; and such opportunities are clearly not open in the same way to the members of pay-as-you-go schemes.

The arguments so far considered are all linked to the purposes for which pension schemes exist. But funding has also become the accepted means of securing financial control of schemes. This is largely because the periodical actuarial valuations provide a check on the progress of the scheme's finances and bring out the effects not only of changes in the scheme itself, such as increased benefits, but of external factors also, such as changes in salary or interest rates. The strength of this argument depends on whether funding is the only or the best means of securing proper and effective control of schemes.

A number of the preceding arguments depend to some extent on the method of funding used. There are several possible ways of funding, but in practice the only one which is of importance is the 'new entrant contribution' method which, as described in Chapter 4, is general in the public sector. Its theoretical basis is that of a fund which begins with the first contribution paid in as a new entrant joins the scheme and ends with the last payment of benefit to him (or his widow) by which the fund is reduced to nothing. As was also shown in Chapter 4 this assessment in terms of a fund which is gradually used up is also of importance in providing a criterion of solvency, and hence is closely bound up with the argument for funding as a means of providing security for the benefits. Funding in this chapter is to be understood as this particular form of funding.

Economic Arguments

In considering the national economic implications of financing pensions through a system of funding rather than by means of pay-as-you-go, one difficulty is that a number of factors are involved whose precise effects are not easy to assess. For example, one of the benefits of funding is often said to be that the savings which it creates (or enforces) lead to additional capital investment. But, although it is true that if there is a fund then saving takes place, it is not easy to predict what would happen to that money in the absence of a fund. Probably some but not all of it would continue to be saved and to this extent funding would not contribute to any *additional* capital investment.

But even if not all the money was saved, it would not necessarily follow that the capital investment facilitated through funding would not take place. The money might be found elsewhere, although of course it might not be found so easily, with the result that although no less capital investment took place, it might lead to prices rising higher than they would have done if the money had come through pension funds.[1] Thus, in this example, although it is not possible to say with any precision what the effects of funding are, it is at any rate a probable inference not that funding leads to additional capital investment but that it makes it to some degree easier. This is certainly an advantage but not such a large advantage as the original claim. The same kind of ambiguity perhaps underlies the argument about equalizing the burden of cost between one generation and another. In terms of the effect on the economy as a whole, the physical resources to meet the cost of pensions must be made available at the time when pensions are paid and to this extent the burden of pensions falling on future generations will be the same whether there are funds or not.

[1] Detailed discussion of this point is beyond the scope of this study, but it may be pursued further, e.g. in A. C. L. Day, *An Outline of Monetary Economics*, Oxford University Press, 1957.

Probably the key point in any consideration of the economic effects of funding is the question of savings. It is likely, for example, that at the present time saving through pension schemes represents over 10 per cent of total savings, now running at approximately £5,000 million a year. But the volume of such savings will vary according to the rate at which funds are building up and new funds are being started. Several consequences or possible consequences, some of them necessarily speculative, may follow from this situation. Savings through pension schemes are, from the point of view of the individual member, compulsory savings. Moreover, unlike many forms of personal saving, pension scheme saving cannot be stopped and started again; once a scheme has been started funds must continue to accumulate for a considerable time.

This situation may have advantages; it has been claimed that the fact that pension funds have large sums to invest acts as 'a stabilizing factor in the capital market'.[1] But on the other hand if a situation arose in which from an economic point of view it was desirable to discourage too much saving, the enforced and inflexible nature of pension fund saving would reduce the government's room for manœuvre.

Again, one needs to consider the possible effects of increasingly large amounts of money becoming available for investment. A great deal would depend on whether this money was channelled into certain forms of investment to a greater extent than would have been the case without pension funds. If, for example, pension funds were to concentrate on fixed interest investments, this might result in the lowering of interest rates. If, on the other hand, investment was particularly in equities or property this might lead to a rise in capital values (e.g. land values). Already, pension funds are a significant factor in the market for stock exchange securities.[2] It is clear, therefore, that the development of funded pension schemes is likely to have consequences which may be socially important.

However, for the purposes of this study it seems best to treat the economic significance of funding as secondary to the principal financial arguments. The economic advantages of funding are incidental to its purpose, and they are unlikely to have influenced greatly, if at all, the minds of those who originally introduced funding into public sector schemes. The major question is what the effects of funding are likely to be on the economy as a whole, particularly if certain current trends continue. If, for example, there was a very rapid growth of

[1] J. Enoch Powell, *Saving in a Free Society*, Hutchinson for Institute of Economic Affairs, 1960, p. 76.

[2] For example, private sector self-administered funds already account for 16 per cent of the holdings of company debentures (*Board of Trade Journal*, July 26, 1963).

private sector schemes leading to some of the consequences described in the previous paragraph, this might have repercussions on the public sector. There might be circumstances when the economic interests of the country as a whole compelled consideration of whether some of the present funded schemes in the public sector ought to be unfunded. But at the moment it seems doubtful whether economic arguments tell strongly either for or against funding in the public sector.

FUNDING AND PUBLIC SECTOR SCHEMES

Security of Benefits

In considering the application of the arguments for funding to public sector schemes, the need for security is particularly important. If there were a risk of not being able to meet the obligations to pay pensions, then it is difficult to see how public sector schemes could have avoided instituting funds. This is not only a question of financial prudence; members of schemes would surely have insisted on having their pension rights safeguarded. On the other hand, if the risk is small or entirely absent, it is important to consider what implications this has for future developments.

In the case of the Civil Service, the ability to pay pensions lies in the central government's continuing and permanent powers of taxation. The guarantee that pensions will be paid lies partly in the Acts of Parliament authorizing such payments; but, as has already been pointed out, in strict law the civil servant has no entitlement to pension and probably of more practical importance is the fact that over the years confidence has developed between civil servants and their employers that pensions will be dealt with in a fair and reasonable manner.

At the other extreme are the nationalized industries' schemes. Here there are no powers of taxation, and no guarantee of permanence. Nevertheless, there are some ways in which analogies may be drawn with the central government. Nationalized industries are at present dependent to a greater or lesser degree on the government for their capital; and Parliament, as indicated in Appendix 1, has authorized in legislation the pension schemes of the nationalized industries. To say this, however, is only to call attention to features which distinguish the public from the private sector, and the important point is to assess whether the nationalized industries could pay pensions in the absence of a fund and also what guarantee there is that they would do so.

In between central government schemes and those for the nationalized industries come those which are dependent on the power of local authorities to raise revenue. Here both the power and its continuance seem little if at all less certain than that of the central government, and, as with the Civil Service, Parliament has legislated in great detail for the pensions of those employed in local government.

If, however, the pattern of funding which at present exists in public sector schemes is examined in the light of this analysis, it clearly does not correspond consistently to the need for funds in terms of security. Both the central government schemes (civil service and NHS) are unfunded, and in local government three schemes (teachers, police and firemen) are unfunded and one (the general local government scheme) funded; and in the nationalized industries, although most schemes are funded, those for the Atomic Energy Authority and the Railways (Male Wages Grades) are not. It is clear, therefore, that security of benefits is not the sole criterion which has been applied in deciding whether to fund or not.

The Argument from Financial Principles

It could be argued that if sound financial principles point in the direction of funding, those principles should be applied whatever the actual consequences in particular cases, and hence all public sector schemes ought to be funded. There are several reasons, however, why in considering the public sector it seems reasonable to look at the consequences of adopting these principles.

There is first the point that the principles themselves have been formulated because they led to certain desirable consequences or the avoidance of certain undesirable consequences. It may seem axiomatic that one should make provision in advance for a known future liability, but one very powerful reason for the axiom was that failure to make adequate provision had led to the disastrous experiences of some of the early life assurance offices. What has here been termed security of benefits was in fact a major reason for the formulation of the generally accepted principle behind funding pension schemes.

Secondly, it should be noted how closely the idea of a proper annual charge for pensions which derives from general financial principles is linked to the way in which a fund is built up. This follows quite simply from the fact that the actuary's valuation of a fund, being based on its existing membership, establishes a criterion both for its solvency, and for what is to constitute a proper annual charge for pensions. A deficiency disclosed at valuation means that, if the actuary's assumptions prove reasonably accurate, there is a risk that at some point the fund will not be able to fulfil its obligations, and the amount of the deficiency shows exactly how much must be paid into the fund so that, as far as possible, this risk is removed. But the results of the valuation also determine in effect what annual charge the contributors shall make not only by the assessment of a surplus or a deficiency but also by the calculation (on the same assumptions) of the contribution rate sufficient to support the benefits for a new entrant. The result is that a fund which is established basically to ensure that money to pay pensions is available also establishes a criterion of what is the proper annual charge to make for pensions.

The importance of these two points may be seen by considering the most obvious case where a proper annual charge for pensions is relevant, that is, where it forms an element in the total costs of an undertaking which must be taken into account in fixing charges for goods and services. Here, in considering the public sector, which means effectively the nationalized industries and the Post Office, the consequences of not funding would be that the pension element in, say, the calculation of charges for coal would be on a different basis from that used for cement. What is at issue, therefore, in considering whether the nationalized industries should have funds as a means of making a proper annual charge for pensions is whether in assessing charges they should follow private sector practice in all respects or whether there are cases where they need not or cannot follow such practice.

Both the arguments which have been considered—security and financial principle—are of great importance for assessing how public sector schemes should be financed, and they will need to be examined further later in this chapter. Meanwhile, a number of other arguments will be considered, and first, the argument that without a fund, too great or an unfair burden is put on future contributors.

The Fair Burden Argument

In considering the application of this argument to central government schemes, the main question is whether one ought to charge the taxpayer on any basis other than the normal current cash basis of government finance. The burden of government expenditure must be met as it arises; to establish a pension fund, therefore, and invest it in government stock would not shift the burden but would merely change the manner of accounting for it. The question really turns then on the possibility of setting up a fund with power to invest outside public authorities' stock. Such a course has been advocated, at least for local government schemes, but for political rather than pension reasons.[1] Whether such a method of funding would distribute the burden of paying pensions more fairly between present and

---

[1] For example, as 'a way of bringing capital gains and rising equity incomes into social ownership, not just for the benefit of municipal employees, but of the public services generally'. Douglas Jay, *Socialism in the New Society*, Longmans, 1962, p. 287.

future taxpayers needs to be examined in the light of the points which are discussed below. But certainly it seems doubtful whether use of the fair burden argument alone could justify such a radical departure from normal methods of government financing. Similar considerations apply to the National Health Service scheme, but there the present position is complicated by the notional fund which is used as a means of securing financial control. This subject also is discussed further below.

As far as other public sector schemes are concerned, it will be necessary to consider in a little more detail how in fact the burden of cost is distributed in funded schemes as compared with schemes which are either only partially funded (i.e. which do not aim at maintaining a fund at the level required by actuarial valuation), or which operate on a pay-as-you-go basis. A major difficulty in carrying out such an analysis is that the point has rarely been discussed, and information on it is not readily available. All the more interesting therefore is the record of a case in which arguments for partial funding were put forward.

In 1954 Bedfordshire County Council promoted a Private Bill, the effect of which would have been to make deficiency payments to their superannuation fund optional. The Bill was considered by a Committee of the House of Commons, and in arguments before it, counsel for the County Council claimed that the fund was larger than was necessary. The Bill was opposed by the National and Local Government Officers' Association who feared that it might give less security to future pensioners, and by the Ministry of Housing and Local Government who thought it would be an undesirable precedent to put the liability for pensions on future generations. The Committee rejected the Bill but said that it raised a matter of extreme importance and drew the attention of 'Parliament and the appropriate Ministers to the need for further research and investigation into this problem'. No tangible results have, however, followed from this recommendation. The detailed arguments on the Bill turned mainly on whether the fund would go 'into the red' if no deficiency payments were made and if so when. But the implication of the County Council's argument was that so far from equalizing the burden, the effect of deficiency payments was to put too great a burden, and indeed an unnecessary burden, on the present generation. 'Why', they argued, 'should we be compelled to go on accumulating this enormous reserve of money which will never be wanted?'

The detailed arguments were thus inconclusive in the sense that neither Bedfordshire nor their opponents were able to agree on exactly when, if at all, there was a risk that tomorrow's ratepayers would be called upon to meet a bigger burden than was reasonable. Perhaps one reason why this case was not followed up was that it was thought that funding on the Bedfordshire basis would sooner or later cease to be funding at all. For example, the Hale Committee, which considered the superannuation of university teachers, dealt with arguments for fixing contributions at a lower level than would be the case on the new entrant contribution basis by observing: 'This would result in an inherently unstable condition which in time would inevitably revert to pure assessmentism.'[1] This argument takes to the extreme the arguments put in opposition to the Bedfordshire Bill, but no attempt was made by the Hale Committee to examine in what circumstances and under what conditions such an outcome would result. Rather they rested the case on the fact that since in the long run there would be instability, this alone was sufficient to make such partial funding undesirable.

The point may be taken a stage further by contrasting the effect on spreading the burden of pay-as-you-go as against funding. Here a difficulty is that there are not many funds which have been going for a sufficiently long time to enable a useful comparison to be made. For illustrative purposes, the progress of the London County Council Fund has been examined since it is possible to see the position over a reasonably long period from 1908 (when the fund was established in its present form) to 1961. The table opposite compares in a simplified form (e.g. omitting investment income and relatively unimportant items such as transfer values) the amounts paid into the fund in specified years by employees and by employers (including deficiency payments) with the amounts paid out in benefits.

In the table, column (3) represents the amounts which would have been needed on a pay-as-you-go basis and column (6) the additional amounts which have in fact been raised and paid into the fund. Since the table shows the position only at five-yearly intervals, it would be reasonable to assume that over the whole period of fifty-five years something in the region of £20 million has had to be found to support the fund additional to what would have been needed on a pay-as-you-go basis. The position is complicated by the question of transfer values; over the whole period rather more has been paid out than received in transfer values, but in 1948 there was, in addition to these normal transfer transactions, the very large payment of nearly £6 million for staff transferred to the NHS on its creation. This would serve to reduce the £20 million quoted above to about £15 million, unless one can assume, as indeed is most probable, that in the absence of a fund this particular transfer payment would not have been required. In any case, it can be seen from the table that, except for a relatively small part, the whole of the additional amount needed

[1] See Report of the Committee, H.M.S.O., 1960, para. 18. The Government Actuary was a member of the Committee, as were three representatives of the Treasury.

for funding purposes has been a charge on LCC revenues (rates and Exchequer grant).

There is nothing surprising in this picture; it indicates how, in times of rising membership and salary-rates, funds need constantly to be built up to meet the expected future liability. The consequence

London County Council Fund 1908/9–1961/2

(£000s)

Year	Employees' Contributions	Expenditure on Benefits	Net Charge (—) or Credit (+), i.e. deficiency or excess of col. 2 over col. (3)	Employers' Payments In	Total Gain (+) or Loss (—), i.e. cols. (4) + (5)
(1)	(2)	(3)	(4)	(5)	(6)
1908–9	17	2	+ 15	16	+ 31
1911–12	25	8	+ 17	23	+ 40
1916–17	34	29	+ 5	30	+ 35
1921–22	99	68	+ 31	187	+ 218
1926–27	88	174	− 86	190	+ 104
1931–32	180	335	− 155	322	+ 167
1936–37	251	657	− 406	814	+ 408
1941–42	367	969	− 602	994	+ 392
1946–47	427	1,385	− 958	1,300	+ 342
1951–52	479	1,324	− 845	1,441	+ 596
1956–57	729	1,641	− 912	1,838	+ 926
1961–62	1,096	2,181	−1,085	2,416	+1,331
				TOTAL	4,590

Source: Annual Accounts in Abstract of the London County Council.

is that the burden on past and present ratepayers has been far heavier than on a pay-as-you-go basis, and the investment income of the fund has not yet had to be used. As was indicated in Chapter 4, this situation is paralleled in the local government scheme as a whole where funds are still building up at a considerable rate, of about £50 million a year at present, and now total well over £600 million.

Once more one may compare this actual situation with the theoretical situation described by the Hale Committee. In considering the progress of a fund as compared with a pay-as-you-go scheme, they demonstrated that ultimately 'in the absence of unforeseen changes' the amount to be raised in a pay-as-you-go scheme would be double that in a funded scheme and this situation 'would continue indefinitely'.[1] It is therefore important to try to establish what 'ultimately' and 'in the absence of unforeseen changes' mean in this context, if

[1] See Report of the Committee, para. 17.

one wishes to consider when in fact annual payments on a pay-as-you-go basis would begin to exceed those required for a funded scheme. But in fact it is very difficult to do more than say that it all depends on circumstances; a sharp drop in the membership of a scheme would almost certainly lead quickly to the need for greatly increased payments on a pay-as-you-go basis; but equally if present trends in membership and salaries were to continue indefinitely, there would be an indefinite postponement of the day when pay-as-you-go would become currently more expensive than funding.

One final point may be mentioned; it is sometimes argued that whether it is fair or not to spread the burden in the way in which funds do so, the ultimate cost on a pay-as-you-go basis will be very large indeed, perhaps amounting to the equivalent of an additional 30 per cent on the payroll. As it happens, one pay-as-you-go scheme in the public sector, that for the Civil Service, has operated on this basis for well over 100 years and it ought therefore to be possible to examine the position which this scheme has reached after what, even in pension terms, is a fairly lengthy period. Unfortunately, the available statistics do not permit a precise series of figures to be shown, but the table opposite gives an approximate indication of the position.

Clearly the cost of civil service pensions, although it has tended to rise in recent years in relation to the cost of salaries, has not yet reached anything approaching an additional 30 per cent on the payroll. Two other comments may also be made on the table; one is that over 10 per cent of the cost of pensions is for pensions increase which would not in any case under present arrangements be funded; the other is that if the civil service scheme were contributory, as are all other public sector schemes, the percentage addition to the payroll for pensions would be less.[1] One may also compare the situation in the civil service scheme with that in the funded local government scheme; in the latter in 1960–61, employers had to find nearly £39 million (including deficiency payments and the cost of pensions increase), as against just over £20 million paid in contributions by employees. If this latter figure represents 5 per cent on average of salaries and wages (i.e. allowing for the fact that some pay 6 per cent, some are 'modified', etc.) then the employers' payments of £39 million are equivalent to just under 10 per cent of salaries and wages as against the 13 per cent being paid by civil service employers.

The examination of the fair burden argument seems inevitably to involve two different considerations, theory and practice. In theory,

[1] This is because salaries would undoubtedly be higher if the scheme were contributory, and the net cost to the Exchequer of pensions lower. In other words, the effect of having a non-contributory scheme is to reduce the cost of salaries but increase the cost to the employer of pensions.

partial funding or pay-as-you-go must lead to a situation in which future generations will be asked to meet more than their fair share of the burden of pension costs, but it is a much more difficult

Cost of Civil Service Superannuation in Relation to
Wages and Salaries
(£ million)
(including the Post Office)

(1) Financial year	(2) Gross cost of super- annuation (*excluding* Pensions Increase)	(3) Cost of Pensions Increase	(4) Total Gross Cost (i.e. (2) + (3))	(5) Cost of salaries and wages (*non- industrial only*)	(6) (4) as Percentage of (5)
1929–30	—	—	7	67	10·5
1947–48	—	—	21·5	245	9
1949–50	—	—	22·9	273	8
1950–51	—	—	25·4	298	8·5
1951–52	—	—	27·6	339	8
1952–53	—	—	29·8	350	8·5
1953–54	—	—	31·9	364	9
1954–55	31·6	2·8	34·4	386	9
1955–56	35·6	2·7	38·3	395	10
1956–57	38·0	4·5	42·5	439	10
1957–58	45·6	4·1	49·7	467	11
1958–59	53·8	3·9	57·7	484	12
1959–60	60·0	4·8	64·8	520	12·5
1960–61	62·7	5·6	68·3	552	12
1961–62	66·7	5·2	71·9	590	12
1962–63	70·4	6·5	76·9	620	12
1963–64	76·6	9·4	86·0	650	13

Sources:
Tomlin Commission (1929–30 only).
Parliamentary Question May 11, 1962; adjusted for cost of widows' pensions (cost of superannuation 1947/48–1960/61).
Civil Estimates: Financial Secretary's Memoranda 1955–56 onwards. (Estimated cost of Pensions Increase and Superannuation.)
Whitley Bulletin (cost of salaries and wages).

Notes: Col. (2) includes all payments to or for both industrial and non-industrial civil servants, including gratuities to unestablished staff and marriage gratuities. Col. (5) relates only to non-industrial civil servants: approximately 80 per cent of non-industrial but rather less than half of industrial civil servants are pensionable under the Superannuation Acts. Col. (6) does not therefore purport to give an exact figure of the cost of superannuation in relation to the salaries and wages of those at present covered by it, but for the reasons given above these percentagesare likely to be too high rather than too low.

question to say when in practice such a situation is likely to arise. If one maintains that the theory is valid whether the practical situation arises in ten, a hundred or five hundred years' time, one is faced with exactly the same sort of problem as was discussed earlier in relation to financial principles. Such principles are designed to serve practical situations; in the case of the private sector nobody can tell what the situation of a particular undertaking will be in twenty, much less a hundred years' time, and financial prudence therefore requires that as much of the burden of pensions as may safely and reasonably be borne now should be so. In other words, there is once more a connexion between the fair burden argument and the need for money to be available to pay pensions—the security argument.

If this is so, some doubt may arise how far one ought to go in the public sector in applying the fair burden argument. It has already been shown that it is not an appropriate argument in the case of central government schemes; in the case of other schemes, the extent to which it is justifiable to apply the argument seems to depend on the circumstances of each scheme or group of schemes, and on assessing when and under what conditions there may be a risk of putting too great a burden on the future if funding is not adopted. It is difficult to see how else one can answer the question raised by Bedfordshire and to assert that the right division of the burden has been found. There are, however, still some other arguments for funding to be considered.

Investment Opportunities and Psychological Arguments

Successful investment is a factor in reducing the cost of funded schemes. To the extent that members may benefit from this, e.g. in securing improved benefits, it seems to be equally advantageous to members of funded public sector schemes as to members of private sector schemes. But a number of complicating factors make the picture not at all easy to follow.

In the first place, only local government of the major central and local government schemes is funded, and the circumstances of that scheme are unique, because of the large number of separate funds. Successful investment by one local authority could not secure major improvements for their members, because the terms of the scheme are nationally laid down, although if there was a period of good surpluses in a majority of funds, this would undoubtedly produce pressure for improvements. The second question which therefore arises is how, in the absence of funds, improvements in benefits or reductions in contributions are arrived at. It might be thought that this was part of the function of notional funds but apart from the fact that the vital factor of actual investment earnings is absent from notional funds, at least two schemes, the civil service (except the Post Office) and the police are not assessed at all in these terms.

It seems clear from the history of pensions in the public services that other factors apart from successful investment of funds have played a part in determining changes in schemes. Of these factors, cost in the widest sense and recognition by employers of what is reasonable are probably the most important, the first a limiting factor and the second leading to the extension of schemes. The position differs from that in private sector schemes where the original scale of benefits is largely determined by what it is thought can be afforded, and the success of the fund is pure gain, however the gain may be divided between employers and employees. In the case of the public services, arguments about improved benefits often turn on analogy with other schemes. For example, the improved widows' pensions introduced into the police scheme in 1956 seem to represent a compromise between the proposals put forward by the police (based on the civil service scheme) and those put forward by the local authorities (based on the local government scheme).

In the past, the Civil Service usually took the lead in introducing improved benefits, a clear indication of the importance of factors other than investment opportunities. As the Hale Committee put it: 'the scope for argument about the scale of benefits is limited, since in state-sponsored superannuation schemes the scale of benefits in relation to terminal salary has become largely standardized, and cannot be exceeded without producing inequalities between one occupation and another'.[1] It may be, however, that the existence of the funded nationalized industries' schemes will now tend to disturb the pattern somewhat, since they have more freedom of manœuvre than local government. On the other hand, they clearly have less freedom of manœuvre than private sector schemes; for example, changes in nationalized industries' schemes require Ministerial approval, and this might operate to ensure that no scheme got too far away from the accepted pattern.

On the whole, it seems better, in view of the ambiguity about the practical effect of investment opportunities, to consider the argument largely in terms of its psychological value to members of schemes, together with other similar arguments, such as the feeling of security given by a fund. It is difficult to assess the strength of such arguments. Civil servants, for example, do not have a fund or even contributions to support their benefits, nor can they legally claim their pensions, but this does not mean that there is any movement among civil servants to have a funded scheme instituted either to give them a feeling of added security or because of the possible advantages through successful investment of such a fund.

[1] Report, para. 16.

H

It may well be, of course, that there are other reasons why civil servants do not want a fund; for one thing, they would probably have to pay contributions to it. But it is also true that in the course of time civil servants have grown accustomed to a certain method of settling pension matters, and that in psychological terms this leaves no need for a fund. As was suggested earlier, this is partly to be accounted for by the degree of confidence between employers and employees. Members of other schemes may not be similarly situated and may value a fund more than the actual benefits which they receive from it may warrant. Again, employers may in some cases attach a value to a fund which goes beyond the real need which it serves. But without ignoring the strength of such feelings it is difficult to do more than regard these as arguments which are secondary to the financial arguments already discussed; and it is doubtful whether they played much part in the setting-up of the existing funds.

The Need for Financial Control: Notional Funding

If proper and effective control of schemes can only be secured through funding, then this is at the least a strong reinforcing argument for having funds. It is also the justification for introducing notional funds where, for any reason, funding is on other grounds held to be unnecessary. At present, however, the membership of non-funded public sector schemes is about equally divided between those where notional funding has been introduced and those where it has not. It is therefore a matter of some importance to establish what is meant by financial control and how far notional funding is successful in achieving it.

The two elements in control of most importance, which are achieved through funding, are the periodical check on the progress of the scheme at actuarial valuations, and the assessment of the percentage contribution rate appropriate to a new entrant to meet the cost of all or specific benefits. With these figures, the management of a funded scheme is in a position to determine such questions as whether additional payments into the fund are needed to secure the existing benefits, or whether additional benefits require additional contributions. In a similar way, notional funding was introduced into the teachers' scheme so that, as described in Chapter 4, there should be a 'valid account of liability' so far as the contributors were concerned; the NHS and AEA schemes have followed this pattern.

There is, however, a major difficulty about notional funding. With a true fund one can treat the financial situation of the fund in isolation from the rest of the finances of the particular undertaking; this indeed is what is meant by funding. With a notional fund, however, one cannot ignore the actual cash basis of the finances of the scheme since this may affect what is happening to the scheme, despite what the notional fund assessment shows. For example, as was shown in Chapter 4, the effect of the notional fund in the teachers' scheme, and of the action taken following valuations, has been to postpone indefinitely the day when the Exchequer will have to meet any considerable charge for teachers' pensions. Teachers and their employers have had in the past, and are likely to continue in the future, to meet practically the whole cost of pension benefits despite the fact that in 1925 the Exchequer undertook the heavy obligation of meeting the cost of pre-1922 benefits.

It is because notional funding is not just a theoretical exercise, and because it can have these effects on obligations which have been assumed that doubts are raised about its suitability as an instrument of financial control of pay-as-you-go schemes. Such doubts are not new; as long ago as 1926, the former legal adviser to the Board of Education called the notional fund a 'sterile and expensive imaginary account' which might be dangerous since a valuation 'may give rise to agitation for an increase or diminution of the rates of contribution; but it cannot afford any sure ground for action.'[1] And others have seen in it nothing but 'elaborate make-believe', distorting the true picture of what is happening.[2]

Again, the use of the notional fund creates possibilities of confusion. In 1952, the Public Accounts Committee commented on the Government Actuary's Report, published in the previous year, and described the situation as 'highly unsatisfactory' because of the heavy burdens which the Exchequer would have to bear in future years, and because of the size of the deficiency and its rapid rate of growth. They asked not only for action to be taken on the existing deficiency, but also that Parliament should be kept informed at much more frequent intervals of the estimated deficiency.

Because the Committee were concerned only with the valuation position they did not consider when and in what circumstances this burden would fall on the Exchequer. But since their criticisms were the main factor leading the Government to put the responsibility for meeting future deficiencies on to the local authorities, they have in fact contributed greatly to ensuring not only that the Exchequer does not have to meet future deficiencies but that, as indicated above, it will be unlikely to have to meet its proper share of past obligations.

The criticism that notional funds may be misleading and may distort financial obligations can be generalized; there are occasions

---

[1] W. R. Barker, *The Superannuation of Teachers in England and Wales*, Longmans 1926, p. 40. For an example of agitation (caused by the proposal to increase contributions) see S. E. Finer, *Anonymous Empire*, Pall Mall Press, 1958, pp. 65–66, 89–91.

[2] See John Vaizey, *The Costs of Education*, Allen & Unwin, 1958, p. 175.

when it is useful in administration to see what the effects would be of adopting a certain hypothetical course of action or, more usually, the effects of various alternative courses of action. As applied to pay-as-you-go pension schemes, this would mean attempting to assess the future cost of pensions over a long period ahead on several different assumptions about what is likely to happen to membership, salaries, rates of mortality, etc. But it seems to be a bad principle to adopt a certain course of action quite deliberately for the advantages which it offers and then to superimpose on it a pattern belonging to a quite different course of action, because this can hardly help but cause confusion and make it more difficult to decide questions of future policy.

The distinction between true funding and notional funding as means to financial control can now be seen more clearly. The importance of valuations in funded schemes is that they provide a measure of the progress of the actual fund which has been set up and which represents the only source of pension payments. Such a measure can be achieved in a notional fund valuation only by ignoring how the money for pensions is being found in fact. To regard this as unimportant is to say that what really matters in financial control is not what is happening now or in the immediate future but what is going to happen over the whole life of the scheme, whether fifty, a hundred or an indefinite number of years ahead. One can only regard the situation as paradoxical; if one must pay attention to such long-term effects, it can only be for the kind of reasons mentioned earlier (security of benefits, etc.) which call for the establishment of a true fund, and it is just where the long-term risks are not so important, and where one can dispense with rigid and precise controls that pay-as-you-go schemes are appropriate. Notional funding is an attempt to have the best of both worlds, but it must seriously be doubted whether the results justify the attempt.

One cannot, however, leave the matter there. It may be conceded that notional funding has its drawbacks, but surely, it may be said, it is better to have the teachers' scheme, where at least one can show some evidence that a 12 per cent contribution rate is more appropriate than a 10 per cent, rather than the police scheme where nobody knows just what future obligations are being incurred. It is true that the police scheme is an extreme case of a contributory scheme where no regular information is available, or at least published, which could answer the kind of questions posed earlier as constituting the main elements of financial control. For this the main reason is probably historical, since, as was shown earlier, even when there were funds for the police scheme, no real attempt was made to keep them on a sound financial basis.

The point does, however, emphasize one important fact about pay-as-you-go schemes, which is that financial control of them in the precise way in which funding provides, is impossible without the kind of confusion imposed by notional funds. One of the sacrifices which those who institute pay-as-you-go schemes have to make is the ability to say whether a particular percentage contribution rate is right, or whether the scheme is in deficiency or surplus. Such concepts belong essentially to funding and should have no place in pay-as-you-go schemes. This does not mean that nothing at all need be done about the cost of pay-as-you-go schemes, even though it is true that pay-as-you-go schemes are only possible where cost is not the over-riding factor.

One thing which could be done in pay-as-you-go schemes is to assess the emerging cost of benefits for as far ahead as it is reasonable to make estimates. Clearly such estimates, which would need to be revised at short intervals, could not be as accurate for fifty years ahead as for five, but the point about them is that they would be related to the actual financial arrangements of the scheme, and as such would be more appropriate as a means of financial control than notional funding.

Again, one obviously could not make use of emerging cost estimates in the same way as actuarial valuations. They would not indicate that a certain proposed benefit would require an additional 1 per cent contribution, but only that its cost might rise from £x in five years' time to £5x in twenty years' time, and that this would be equivalent to an extra 5 per cent on the cost of pensions. It might be argued that such statements would be meaningless in terms of financial control. It is true that, for reasons already given, they would not seem as exact as valuation figures, but this would not necessarily make them meaningless. If a small increase in benefits were proposed which seemed reasonable, the fact that it did not seem likely to increase greatly the costs over a period would be an additional reason for accepting it. If a large increase were proposed, then obviously its effect on the costs of the scheme would be carefully examined and might lead to the argument that if the members wanted that benefit, they would have to be prepared to make reductions in cost elsewhere. This was indeed the argument used when death benefits were introduced into the civil service scheme in 1909.

What clearly worries some people about this kind of situation is that it leaves open far more scope for bargaining about pension benefits. If a proposed benefit is going to require an extra 2 per cent contribution, the only argument is about who should pay; if it is going to add 5 per cent, perhaps ultimately 10 per cent to the pension bill, there could be argument in addition over whether it was reasonable to increase the cost of the scheme to this extent. Once again, this difference in precision about costs follows from the nature of funded and non-funded schemes; one cannot expect a pay-as-you-go scheme to behave in the same way as a funded scheme.

The argument presented here, then, is that financial control of schemes does not require funding, but that where, on other grounds, funds are instituted, they have the incidental advantage of providing a means of financial control. In pay-as-you-go schemes the best means of control is an emerging cost assessment.

CONTRIBUTORY VERSUS NON-CONTRIBUTORY SCHEMES IN THE PUBLIC SECTOR

The discussion in the preceding section left one question unresolved, namely, how to assess an appropriate contribution rate for employees in a scheme which is not funded. But such a question ought properly to form part of a larger enquiry into the reasons for having employee contributions at all in the public sector. This issue is considered here.

From the employee's point of view contributions in public sector schemes largely have a psychological value; they seem to give him a greater entitlement to pension, and a greater stake in the scheme, and this may lead to increased interest and participation, as, for example, in the nationalized industries' schemes where representatives of the employees play a part in the management of the scheme. They also have the practical advantage that by convention they enable a benefit to be given on withdrawal; a contributor may also appear to have an advantage over the non-contributor in that, through tax reliefs, he does not have to meet the whole of the cost of his contributions. From the employer's point of view the chief advantage of employee contributions is that they reduce the charge for pensions which would otherwise have to be met by him (unless of course he can pay lower salaries in return for a non-contributory scheme). Of these points, the question of benefit on withdrawal raises wider issues which are discussed in Chapter 10 in connexion with the preservation of pension rights on change of employment. It is enough here to state that from the point of view of the object of pension schemes any benefit on withdrawal (as opposed to transfer or 'freezing' of pension rights) is undesirable, and this advantage of a contributory scheme is therefore accidental and anomalous.

The psychological arguments are, once more, hard to assess. In the only major non-contributory scheme, that for the Civil Service, the absence of contributions does not lead to any lack of interest in the scheme, or weaken the claims of civil servants to receive pensions. But it may be thought that the position of the Civil Service is exceptional, and that in the nationalized industries, for example, lack of contributions would seriously weaken confidence and good relations between employers and employees.

However this may be, it is surely the financial implications of employee contributions which must be the main consideration, their principal object being to spread the cost of pensions between, usually, employer and employee. Here the close connexion between contributions and funding becomes apparent, because the assessment which an actuary makes of the total contribution necessary to support the benefits assumes that the contributions are accumulated in a fund and invested. But how much of the total contribution should be paid by the employee is still a matter for decision in each case. As was seen in Chapter 4, schemes differ greatly on this point, and it is not always easy to see on what principles a particular decision has been made. The words of the Norman Committee which considered local government superannuation in 1919 are still relevant; after remarking that contributions ought to be substantial, they went on: 'There is no division of the burden which can be shown to be just and right to the exclusion of all others, for there is no exact apportionment possible of the advantages consequent on a scheme, but we believe it will be generally felt to be fair that the burden should be borne in equal shares by both parties.'[1]

Whether their view is correct or not it was the one which was adopted for the local government scheme, although it is ironical to reflect that the amounts contributed by the employers to this scheme are now in fact much bigger than those contributed by employees.

The case of the civil service scheme is, perhaps, the most interesting of all. As was shown in Chapter 4, it is impossible to say how the cost of pensions is shared between civil servants and the Exchequer because nobody knows exactly how much their salaries are less than they otherwise would be. It is possible, though perhaps not likely, that the total cost to the Exchequer of pay and pensions is no higher than it would have been if the scheme had been contributory.

It seems then that one cannot say either that there is any specific contribution which employees ought to make or that in a non-contributory scheme they are not making some contribution to the cost of pensions. It follows from this that even in a funded scheme there do not have to be employee contributions; it would be possible, for example, for employers to pay the whole contribution which was required into the fund but (and this is where such a scheme would differ from some private sector non-contributory schemes) to pay rather lower salaries than at present. In other words, from the employee's point of view there would be no difference in terms of what he actually received; and from the employer's point of view the only difference would be an adjustment between two items in his accounts.

The main reason for suggesting such an arrangement is that it

[1] Cmd. 329, 1919, para. 57.

would simplify schemes. The calculation and recording of contributions individually for each employee, for example, or the difficulties over refunds of contributions would be done away with, without in any way impairing the financial arrangements of schemes.

This suggestion also has a bearing on the question raised at the beginning of this section. For if non-funded schemes such as the teachers' were also non-contributory, the question of assessing the right rate of contribution would not arise and the main reason which was originally advanced for instituting a notional fund in the teachers' scheme would no longer apply. If, on the other hand, contributions are retained, they can only be fixed on the analogy of similar contributory funded schemes, since a percentage rate of contribution on this basis is not relevant to pay-as-you-go financing. The alternative, to have an 'assessment' rate of contribution varying over short periods in accordance with the amount needed to meet outgoings (as in National Insurance), would complicate the work of record-keeping and would probably not be acceptable to employees, although it would certainly be more appropriate to a pay-as-you-go scheme.

One may sum up, therefore, by saying that contributions are a traditional, although not an essential part of the financial arrangements of public sector schemes. Because of this it is likely that discussion of whether there should be or should continue to be contributions will tend to centre on the psychological arguments, which ought to be of secondary importance.

FINANCING PUBLIC SECTOR SCHEMES IN THE FUTURE

The main point to which the preceding discussion leads is the need to establish the basic criteria which can be applied to public sector schemes to determine whether they should be funded or not, since the present variety of methods of financing can be explained only by looking at the historical circumstances of each scheme rather than at the intrinsic arguments for funding.

In view of the importance of the security argument, the most obvious criterion is the degree of risk that, in the absence of funding, money would not be available to pay pensions. Here, it is relevant to contrast the position in the public and private sectors. What makes the security argument so important in the private sector is simply that in a world subject to economic pressures and changes, nobody can be sure that a particular undertaking will not decline or even go out of business. By contrast, one of the main characteristics of the public sector is its permanence. This has four principal aspects: first, the functions performed by the public sector are basic functions for which there is almost bound to be a continuing need; secondly, in many cases the public authority has a monopoly of the particular function; thirdly, functions once assumed by the public sector continue to be performed there, even though there may be changes of organization;[1] fourthly, many public sector functions are maintained by the powers of taxation of central and local government, and these have been authorized by Parliament and are longstanding and continuing powers.

The effect of these four factors is that in central and local government the risk of not being able to pay pensions is, for practical purposes, nil. In the case of the nationalized industries, the risk is likely to arise only in two circumstances. One is where exceptionally a decision is made to transfer a function from the public to the private sector; this is unlikely to happen with the industries at present in public ownership, but might happen if a future government were to nationalize an industry which was then de-nationalized by a subsequent government. The second circumstance is of a nationalized industry contracting to such an extent that it would be difficult for it to meet pension commitments out of declining revenue in the absence of a fund. This situation would arise seriously if an industry were to contract rapidly and continuously, e.g. because there was no longer a demand for a particular product or service. But there might also be cases of temporary difficulty, e.g. where contraction was due to reorganization designed to enable an industry which was running at a loss to pay its way.

It does not follow that even in these circumstances a fund is essential for security, but in the absence of a fund there would have to be a firm guarantee that pension obligations would be met. Only the government could give such a guarantee, and in doing so would naturally be concerned to know what additional liability it was incurring. But a guarantee of all nationalized industries' pensions would be likely in practice to impose very little extra burden on the taxpayer, for the following reasons:

(1) on the whole, the nationalized industries are basic industries with considerable revenue-earning capacity;
(2) most of them are almost certain to go on expanding; taken with (1), this means that in most cases the risk of any liability falling on the taxpayer is very small;
(3) in the case of a transfer from the public to the private sector, there would presumably be a sale of assets, and arrangements could be made to include pensions in the terms of the sale;
(4) rapid and continuous contraction of an industry on a scale which would lead to expenditure on pensions forming a sub-

[1] For example, postal services, policing and the maintenance of roads are all public sector functions, but the manner in which they are provided or the means of financing them may change in the course of time.

H*

stantial proportion of the total expenditure of the undertaking is likely to be a rare event;

(5) contraction on any scale would almost certainly not happen to more than one industry at any one time.

The total risk to the government of having to meet large additional burdens for pension commitments to the nationalized industries is thus very small. Despite this small risk, the general policy at present followed by the government and the nationalized industries is to build up sufficient resources to provide a very high degree of security of benefits for every employee in the industries. The result is that very large funds have been and are still being accumulated, although they probably serve little real purpose under present conditions. In any case, as will be indicated later, the funds already accumulated could, if necessary, serve as a reserve or buffer against any emergency which might arise.

It must also be remembered that supplements to pensions, for which there is no contractual obligation and therefore no advance provision, are made from time to time by some of the nationalized industries. Although these payments are small relatively to those for pensions, their continuance depends, strictly speaking, on the ability of the undertakings to pay their way. However, railway pensioners are paid these supplements even though the undertaking is running at a considerable loss. The railways also provide another instructive example; despite the annual deficit, pensions have not ceased to be paid not only in the staff schemes which are funded, although largely invested in the railways themselves, but in the Male Wages Grades' scheme too, which is unfunded. To some extent, the taxpayer rather than the user of railway services may be said to be financing these payments and the railwaymen's security for benefits is dependent on an implicit rather than an explicit government guarantee.

One may sum up, therefore, by saying that use of the degree of risk criterion leads to the conclusion that, given government backing, where necessary, public sector schemes do not need to fund. In terms of degree of risk, pay-as-you-go and not funding is the appropriate method of financing. This leads to consideration of a different criterion. Pay-as-you-go means no more than paying one's bills as they become due. It is the normal method of meeting recurring expenditure unless there are special reasons for departing from it. The importance of degree of risk is that it provides such a reason in the case of private sector but not of public sector schemes. The question to be examined in the case of these latter schemes is therefore whether there are any other reasons in particular schemes which make it justifiable to go to the trouble of accumulating money in a fund, and thus to depart from the usual means of financing.

Before considering the application of this criterion to existing public sector schemes, one general point must be made. It was shown earlier that there is a close link between employee contributions and funding. Such contributions are not, however, essential even in funded schemes, and, in pay-as-you-go schemes, they have few advantages compared with their many disadvantages, particularly in complicating the work of administration. Pay-as-you-go schemes in future ought therefore to be non-contributory.

It is obvious from what has been said that existing pay-as-you-go schemes should be retained. But notional funding ought to be abolished since it is both confusing and unnecessary. Indeed, one of the reasons for introducing it, the desire to demonstrate that contribution rates were fair, will no longer apply. Financial control should in future be exercised through emerging cost assessments.

Of existing funded schemes, the general local government scheme appears to be a special case. Application of the criterion suggested above does not indicate that in local government schemes as a whole there is any reason for departing from pay-as-you-go, and indeed nearly half the employees of local authorities are already in the pay-as-you-go schemes for teachers, police and firemen. But the general scheme is unique in being a single, uniform scheme whose finances are operated through a large number of separate funds. The argument for departing from pay-as-you-go in this way is that funding is necessary because individual local authorities are autonomous bodies and funding is a means by which they can make proper provision for the pensions of those who work for them.

Because a man may, in the course of his career, serve several different local authorities, meeting the cost of pensions does indeed create a problem, but it is essentially a practical problem of how to secure a fair and reasonable apportionment of the cost of pensions between individual local authorities. For clearly if pay-as-you-go meant that the authority with whom a man happened to be serving at the time of retirement had to meet the whole cost of his pension, it might produce an unfair distribution of the cost. This problem is not insuperable and, indeed, two existing non-funded schemes, those for the police and teachers, illustrate ways in which it might be solved. In the police scheme, for example, the cost of pensions is shared between the different authorities with whom a man has served according to his pay and length of service with each; and the teachers' scheme shows how a centralized administration can offer a simpler, though less exact, means of apportioning costs. What must be said, however, is that the existence of this practical problem is no justification for the unnecessary administrative work involved in the maintenance of 500 separate funds. Once this is recognized, the way is

236 PUBLIC SECTOR PENSIONS

open to devising a pay-as-you-go scheme to accord with the particular characteristics of local government.[1]

In the case of the nationalized industries, the justification for accumulating funds is based on the view that they should follow the practice of private sector industries. This view is closely linked with the obligation imposed by statute on the industries requiring them to 'break even', in the sense of raising revenue which is at least sufficient to meet 'outgoings properly chargeable to revenue account, taking one year with another.'[2] To the extent that this view rather than the need for security of benefits has influenced their actions, it seems to have been assumed by the nationalized industries, with few exceptions, that the proper charge for pensions was not the balance of annual cost remaining after employee contributions had been used, but the amount of pension liability incurred in the year. This could only be determined either by establishing a fund or, as in the case of the Post Office, by making a notional fund assessment. Since the pension arrangements of the nationalized industries are subject to Ministerial approval, this must also represent the government's view.

There is, however, nothing in the obligation to break even which necessarily leads to either funding or notional funding. Government policy recognizes that the nationalized industries 'cannot be regarded only as very large commercial concerns which may be judged mainly on their commercial results: all have, although in varying degrees, wider obligations than commercial concerns in the private sector.'[3] These 'obligations of a national and non-commercial kind' place the nationalized industries in a unique position somewhere between a private commercial undertaking and a social service. Examples such as the great extension of rural electrification, the care with which the National Coal Board deals with the problem of uneconomic pits, BEA's provision of air services to the Scottish Highlands and Islands, and the recent refusal of the Minister of Transport to sanction some proposed rail closures (e.g. in central Wales), all point to the influence of social service considerations. And in a number of cases the government has to bear the financial consequences of maintaining such services.

This being so, the unquestioning assumption that pensions must follow normal commercial practice is open to challenge. It has already been suggested that pay-as-you-go is the appropriate method of financing public sector schemes. To use the fact that the nationa-

[1] It should perhaps be pointed out that the convenience to local authorities of being able to borrow from their funds is not an argument for funding, although it may indicate the need for more flexibility in their borrowing powers.

[2] Electricity Act, 1947, s. 36(1)—most of the other nationalization statutes contain similar wording.

[3] *The Financial and Economic Obligations of the Nationalized Industries*, Cmd. 1337, 1961, para. 33; also para. 2.

lized industries are in some ways analogous to private sector industries as an argument for departing in their case from pay-as-you-go is to subject the analogy to too great a strain. In fact, so far as pensions are concerned, present financial obligations on the nationalized industries are irrelevant for determining what is the proper annual charge to make. This can only be determined by first seeing what is the right method of financing pensions; and this, it has been argued, is pay-as-you-go.

Furthermore, the practical consequences of following normal commercial practice must be considered. The effect of using a notional fund assessment of pension charges in the Post Office is that present users of Post Office services pay more than they otherwise would, to the benefit of the general taxpayer, against the theoretical possibility that at some future date the position will be reversed. Funding in the nationalized industries also has the effect that in the present phase of building up funds, additional revenue has to be raised with a consequent tendency towards raising prices; but in this case the additional revenue is set aside against a possible future contingency.

It is generally assumed that funding is the right method of financing pension schemes. This chapter has examined that assumption and shown that it is only correct in certain circumstances, and that those circumstances are largely absent in the public sector. It follows that the main principle to be followed in future is that public sector schemes should operate on a pay-as-you-go basis.

The transition from funded to pay-as-you-go schemes and the accompanying change from contributory to non-contributory schemes will clearly present practical difficulties. Abolition of contributions, like the abolition of 'no detriment', mainly concerns existing members of schemes. Although on rational grounds there may appear to be no difference between receiving a gross salary of £1,000 p.a. with deductions of £60 p.a. for pension contributions, and receiving a salary of £940 p.a. without deductions, in psychological terms many members might feel that they had somehow lost part of their salaries. In addition, difficulties arise because of the tax reliefs on pension contributions, because refunds of contributions would not be possible except on the basis of hypothetical calculations, and because the calculation of pension on a three-year average of salaries would be affected. Most of these points are covered by the discussion of the wider issues of pensions in Chapter 10,[1] and the psychological point could be met by negotiating new terms for existing members at the time of the next two or three salary increases following the introduction of a non-contributory scheme. This would be in keeping with

[1] See, for example, the discussion of whether, if there is universal preservation of pension rights, refunds of contributions are justifiable except in a limited number of circumstances.

the view expressed in the previous chapter that negotiations over pension matters should have regard to other conditions of service, and particularly pay.

The transition from funding to pay-as-you-go would not have the same immediate impact on the members of schemes as the abandonment of contributions. The immediate step would be to stop building up the fund. An important problem would then be what to do with the fund already accumulated, and here there are two possibilities. The first would be to use up the fund's assets until it was finally exhausted; the second, to maintain the fund at its existing level and make use only of the investment income.

The first course would require decisions on the purposes for which the assets were to be used and the period over which the fund was to be run down. On the assumption that the assets should be used exclusively for pension purposes, the primary decision would be whether the fund should be earmarked for a particular group of people, e.g. for paying pensions to existing members of schemes, or whether it should be used up in a given period of time irrespective of which members would receive pensions in that period.

The second course would probably present fewer problems of this kind; it might involve a certain amount of work in looking after the fund's investments, although not to the same extent as with a fund which was actively building up. It would have the advantage not only of reducing the annual charge which would have to be met from other sources, but of making it possible for the fund itself, like the National Insurance Reserve Fund, to serve as a reserve or buffer against certain contingencies; it could, for example, be used if pension payments became relatively heavy as a result of a temporary contraction in a nationalized industry.

The practical difficulties of moving from contributory, funded schemes to non-contributory, pay-as-you-go schemes do not raise any insuperable problems. What is needed is that the principle of pay-as-you-go should be applied to new schemes when they are started, and that suitable means should be devised for applying it to existing schemes. Not only will this do away with the present unsatisfactory variety of methods of financing public sector schemes, but it will also remove one of the obstacles to reducing the present multiplicity of schemes, a point which was discussed in the previous chapter.

The argument of this chapter may therefore be summarized as follows:

(1) Three methods of financing—funding, pay-as-you-go with notional funding, and pay-as-you-go—are found in the public sector, but the reasons for them are historical rather than logical.

(2) The main argument for funding is that it provides security for the benefits, but other arguments are that it spreads the burden of pension costs more fairly and is an effective means of financial control of schemes.

(3) For the majority of schemes in the public sector funding is not essential to provide security, but in some cases a government guarantee is necessary instead.

(4) The argument that funding spreads the burden of costs more fairly is of limited application to public sector schemes.

(5) Whether there is funding or not, financial control is bound to be imperfect because assumptions have to be made about a number of varying factors, e.g. future levels of pay and increases or decreases in the number of staff.

(6) In pay-as-you-go schemes notional funds have little advantage over emerging cost as a means of financial control, and are likely to lead to confusion.

(7) Funding may promote more personal saving which, although usually desirable, may not be so in certain circumstances.

(8) Taking public sector schemes as a whole, there is little advantage in having employee contributions and there are positive administrative disadvantages, e.g. in the very large number of annual calculations which have to be made.

(9) Pay-as-you-go with emerging cost assessment is the most appropriate method of financing public sector schemes, provided that a government guarantee is given where necessary.

(10) The financial autonomy of individual local authorities is not an obstacle to pay-as-you-go as long as there is a reasonable apportionment of the cost of pension payments between different authorities.

(11) The argument that the nationalized industries ought to follow private sector financial practice is not relevant to the question of whether pension schemes should be funded.

(12) Pay-as-you-go should be introduced immediately for new employees in the public sector and for existing employees as soon as the necessary arrangements can be made.

CHAPTER 10

Public Sector Schemes and the Future

THE NEED FOR A NATIONAL PENSIONS POLICY

The major problem for the future of public sector schemes is the part which they should play in the pension arrangements for the nation as a whole. This needs to be viewed from two angles:

(1) The relationship with the state scheme; for example, if pensions are to continue to be provided partly by the State and partly by occupational schemes, satisfactory arrangements must be devised so that they keep in step with one another.

(2) The level of pension in comparison with those in other areas of employment; apart from the fact that the public sector no longer has so marked a pension advantage over the private sector as was once the case, it is still an open question how far divergence should be a conscious aim; for example, it should be considered whether the Priestley Commission's doctrine of fair comparison between the Civil Service and outside employment for purposes of pay ought also to apply to pensions.[1]

To answer these questions satisfactorily requires that there should be a national pensions policy, which accords with the social aims and objectives appropriate to the second half of the twentieth century. The first task of this chapter will be to consider how the need for such a policy arises, before examining how it can be determined.

The need for government policy in general is linked with the accepted view that the State is ultimately responsible for assisting those in extreme poverty. If provision for old age were entirely voluntary and an individual responsibility, there would always be some who were unable or unwilling to make adequate provision, and who would therefore become the responsibility of the State. Broadly the choice open to government is either to make advance arrangements for this situation or to meet it as it arises by relief measures. Advance arrangements may take various forms but, again in broad terms, the choice is between a state system of pensions providing at

---

[1] See *Report of the Royal Commission on the Civil Service 1953–55*, Cmd. 9613, H.M.S.O. 1955, especially paras. 87–111.

least the minimum necessary to prevent destitution, or compulsion on individuals to make their own provision (e.g. through occupational pension schemes).

The basis of present policy is the Beveridge plan of a universal state scheme providing subsistence pensions, leaving supplementary provision to be made either by the individual or through occupational schemes. But for various reasons this now seems inadequate. There is first the fact that subsistence is an elusive concept, and that because there was never unambiguous acceptance of the idea, many state pensioners have in fact had to have recourse to National Assistance.[1]

But of far greater importance are the social and economic changes which have taken place since Beveridge produced his report in 1942. For example, he had very much in mind the severe unemployment of the 1930's, whereas in the last twenty years unemployment has been comparatively slight. Again, the last twenty years have been a period of rapidly rising living standards, and material wealth has been diffused among the population to an extent which was not generally foreseen in 1942. Changes on this scale, particularly if they are likely to continue, call for a re-examination of national policies. But in practice the changes which have been made since 1948 in the state system seem essentially to be short-term and piecemeal adaptations of the Beveridge plan rather than part of the long-term policy which is clearly needed. For example, the most significant development, the graduated pension scheme, was inspired to a large extent by the desire to shift the mounting cost of pensions from the Exchequer to contributors. There has been much discussion of pensions in recent years, and many criticisms of the inadequacy of the Beveridge basis in today's conditions. And both the Labour and Liberal Party plans seek a wider view of pensions. Yet it may be doubted whether criticism of Beveridge has so far produced any generally acceptable alternative.

The only major official inquiry into pensions since Beveridge was that of the Phillips Committee. But this Committee was limited to financial and economic problems, and seems to have been appointed largely because of the fear that the prospective increase in both the number of old people in the population and the proportion in comparison with the working population might lead to a serious financial problem in making adequate provision for them. The problem still exists, although, perhaps in part because of the greater emphasis

---

[1] Cf. the reply of the Parliamentary Secretary of the Ministry of Pensions and National Insurance (Mrs Thatcher) to the question whether anyone could be expected to live on the National Insurance retirement pension: 'The obvious answer is that no one is expected to, because there are other resources available' and she cited private resources or occupational schemes as examples of the other resources (H.C. Deb., March 13, 1962, col. 1161).

now on economic growth, it does not seem quite as serious as was once thought. Certainly the limitations imposed by their terms of reference resulted, as the Committee themselves recognized, in their leaving out of account many human and social problems which are of great importance in any consideration of the provision which can or should be made for old people.

Again, the limitations of the present arrangements for the oversight of occupational schemes from the point of view of the formulation of a coherent national policy were made evident in the chapter on taxation. There is no part of the government machinery which is specifically concerned with the social implications of pensions, in spite of the conspicuous part which pensions, both state and occupational, now play in social and economic life. The Minister of Pensions and National Insurance, despite his title, is chiefly responsible for keeping the National Insurance scheme running smoothly,[1] and the Department of Inland Revenue, which comes most closely into contact with occupational schemes, is by its nature, concerned with a very narrow aspect of pensions policy. Particular assignments, such as the survey of occupational schemes and the collection of statistics about pension fund investments, were entrusted respectively to the Government Actuary's Department and the Board of Trade, but the choice of these departments has not significantly affected the broad policy question.

There is need, then, for a national pensions policy, and for determining the place of public sector schemes within such a policy. The remainder of this chapter will be concerned with seeing what is involved in drawing up such a policy—the questions which must be answered, the factors which need to be taken into account and the general trends which are likely to have a bearing on the situation.

THE AIM OF PENSIONS

In the broadest terms, the most important question to decide is what is the social aim which pensions ought to serve. By posing the question in this form, it is implicitly assumed that however pensions are provided, they are intended to serve a single over-riding aim or purpose. It would be part of the object of formulating policy to examine this assumption, because clearly a good deal else which is relevant to the present and future pension situation turns on this basic point. Central to this point also is a whole group of questions to which we need answers: for example, to what extent should we be aiming to provide pensions as the sole source of income for the elderly? Or should our primary aim be to encourage the old to continue at work, at least for as long as they are able and willing to do

[1] 'Pensions' in his title refers of course only to his responsibilities in connection with war pensions.

so? Alternatively, should there be retirement for all with a pension at a certain age? Or is the main need a flexible approach to these questions? Above all, what are the implications of such questions for the future level of pension provision?

Foremost among the factors which are relevant to these questions is the growth in the number of old people in the population. The number of people over the National Insurance pensionable age has grown from about 6 million twenty years ago to approximately 7½ million now, and is likely to increase to nearly 10 million in twenty years' time. The relative proportion of the elderly to the population of working age is also changing; whereas in 1962 for every 10 elderly people there were 42 of working age, by 1982 it is expected that there will be only 36.[1]

Other social trends which seem likely to continue also point in the direction of greater provision for pensions. Old people may increasingly value an independent life on their own, which can be achieved only with a regular and adequate income. This tendency is likely to be reinforced as more people acquire a stake in material wealth, and consequently feel a greater need for a secure future, particularly in old age.

Trends of this kind do not necessarily imply that pensions will become the only source of income for the old in future. Personal savings or the postponement of retirement until a later age might both be thought to have a part in the future position. It is indeed true that far more people are now in a position to make provision for their future than was the case a hundred years ago when the teachers were faced with this argument against pensions, but the trend to provision for old age through pension schemes (whether state or occupational) is now so well established that it is unlikely that reliance on individual thrift will ever become the primary means of assuring an income in old age. Again, postponing retirement, although it may be advocated for other reasons (e.g. because of the undesirable effects on health of a sudden cessation of work), is hardly likely to do more than provide a partial answer to the problem; at the moment there is little sign of a tendency in this direction.

Another factor which is likely to become increasingly important, is the present trend towards the greater employment of women, and particularly married women. For example, between 1952 and 1962 the proportion of women employees who were married rose from 44 per cent to 53 per cent, and by 1962 married women formed just under one-fifth of the employed population.[2] If this trend continues,

[1] See *Annual Abstract of Statistics, 1963* (No. 100), table 12.
[2] See *Annual Abstract of Statistics, 1963*, Table 133. Figures relate to Great Britain. The proportion of women employees in the total number of employees remained constant in this period at approximately one-third.

there will be a need to assess what effect it will have on pension provision; whether, for example, married women are likely to look more towards their own employment to provide them with a pension, or at least to provide a supplementary pension to any earned by their husbands.

Among the economic trends which are important for the future, an obvious starting point is the increased emphasis on the need for economic growth. If, for example, the National Economic Development Council's growth programme of 4 per cent per annum is attained, real incomes per head could rise by $3\frac{1}{4}$ per cent per annum or 40 per cent in ten years.[1] The significance for pensions of such a rate of growth would be two-fold: first, it would create additional resources which could be used in part to meet any increased demand to provide for the elderly; and, secondly, a rise in real incomes for the working population would be likely to lead to a demand for better pensions, on the grounds that the elderly ought also in fairness to share in growing prosperity.

There are other consequences of economic growth which need to be considered; according to the analysis made by the NEDC, the basis of an increase in real incomes is that prices should either remain stable or rise only slowly.[2] The effects of changes in the value of money are particularly important for pension schemes, since occupational schemes, including those in the public sector, have generally been framed on the basis of stable money-values, and this basis may well seem unrealistic in looking to the future situation. Again, a necessary part of economic growth on the scale indicated by the NEDC is that there should be reasonable mobility of labour, and to the extent that lack of provision for the preservation of pension rights acts as a hindrance to this there will be a need to re-examine the position.

All these points have a bearing on what the level of pension should be, particularly if, as the preceding discussion implies, the aim is a reasonable standard of living for the elderly. This question is also bound up with the type of pension provided and here the experience of the last twenty years points to the fact that flat-rate pensions can never satisfactorily meet the needs of a society in which living standards are rising. The basic questions in relation to the level of pension are therefore how the pension should be related to earnings, and whether, like wages and salaries, it should be designed to serve family rather than individual needs.

Pensions related to earnings throughout working life may well be inadequate in times of falling money-values. But pensions related to

[1] N.E.D.C. *Growth of the United Kingdom Economy to 1966* and *Conditions Favourable to Faster Growth*, H.M.S.O., 1963, para. 214.
[2] *Conditions Favourable to Faster Growth*, paras. 200–213.

earnings just before retirement tend to favour the salaried worker, whose earnings are likely to rise throughout most of his career, as against the wage-earner, who is likely to reach his maximum earnings comparatively early in life. It is possible in either case to make adjustments to overcome these disadvantages; the Labour Party plan for National Superannuation, for example, proposes a series of weightings to adjust earnings at different periods of the working life to take account of changes in the value of money; and in some occupational schemes (e.g. the Electricity Manual Workers) pension may be calculated on the best five consecutive years' earnings in the last twenty before retirement. Any method is likely to involve additional record-keeping and computation. What is needed is a reasonably fair system which does not unduly add to the work of administration. Perhaps the best solution would be an adjusted terminal-salary basis, but there is need for further consideration of the issues involved.

It also seems probable that the pension should be designed, like the salary or wages on which it is based, to provide for the whole of a family's needs although, as suggested earlier, the position of married women in the future must be borne in mind.

Acceptance of this general approach brings certain other problems. A wage-related pension may be less than adequate for the lowest-paid workers whose wages are barely sufficient to provide a reasonable standard of living. It may therefore be necessary to provide for a minimum level below which pensions should not fall. Again, this approach implies the abolition of the distinction between manual workers' schemes (often on a flat-rate basis) and staff schemes (often on a terminal-salary basis); this distinction is frequently found at present and exists in parts of the public sector.

Other questions arise over the determination of the pension; for example, whether, as in the public sector, total pension should vary according to the number of years worked and, if so, on what basis. On the latter point, it may be that a balance should be struck between counting every year worked and the present limitation of occupational schemes to a maximum of forty or, in certain circumstances, forty-five years. One way would be to exclude early years of training and to calculate the pension on the number of years worked after a certain minimum age. This minimum age might be 18 or even 21 in view of the increasing numbers who are likely to receive further education in future; in either case it could happen that pension was calculated on fifty or even more years worked.

This question is closely linked with the subject of retiring ages and the employment policy of individual employers. Perhaps the main question in pension terms is whether there should be a more flexible approach not only in occupational schemes but in the state scheme too. For example, a general minimum retiring age of, say, 60, or even 55, combined with less insistence on compulsory retiring ages would help both those who value leisure even at the cost of a smaller income and those who would like to continue working as long as they are able. There are also lesser problems, e.g. whether different retiring ages for men and women are necessary. The wide implications of any changes in present practice indicate that a great deal of thought will be needed to reach agreement on a generally acceptable policy.

HOW PENSIONS SHOULD BE PROVIDED

The next stage in formulating policy is to decide what means should be used for providing pensions.

Two principal questions are involved: the first is whether there should continue to exist both state and occupational schemes in the future; the second, what the respective spheres of each should be if both are to continue. To a large extent, the issues involved here are political but at least it can be said that all three main parties agree on the need for some kind of state scheme, and that nobody has advocated that occupational schemes should be abandoned. But there is much less unanimity on the answer to the second question. At one extreme, for example, are those who advocate that the State should confine itself to paying pensions only to those who are really in need or who cannot be covered by occupational arrangements,[1] and at the other there is the Labour Party plan under which the state scheme would ultimately provide a pension of about half a man's earnings on retirement so that occupational schemes would be restricted either to schemes providing a better pension than this or to providing supplementary benefits to the state scheme.[2]

The basic dilemma is that the development of occupational schemes has been very uneven. For not only are there many people who are still not members of such schemes, despite the rapid growth of recent years, but the level of pension provided by different schemes varies greatly. It therefore seems unlikely that in the ordinary course of events everybody will be covered by an occupational scheme and still less by an occupational scheme providing a reasonable standard of living, for a very long time to come. Whether the State should step in and fill the gaps left by the growth of occupational schemes or whether every effort should be made to encourage the growth of adequate occupational schemes is likely to prove the central question

[1] See, for example, *Pensions for Prosperity*, Institute of Economic Affairs, 1960, and *Old People in Britain*, Bow Group, 1963. The Conservative Party appears to be moving increasingly towards a selective system of state pensions for those who are in need, but no detailed proposals are yet available (June 1964).

[2] See *National Superannuation*, Labour Party, 1957, and *New Frontiers for Social Security*, Labour Party, 1963.

of political controversy, but there are some consequences which will be of particular relevance to public sector schemes.

In the first place, public sector schemes will need to have closer regard to the fact that, of the total pension, only part will be provided by the public sector scheme and the remainder by the state scheme. But, secondly, in looking to the future, there is at the moment no certain guide to the ways in which the state scheme will develop or consequently to the part which will be played by public sector schemes in the total pension provision.

The most reasonable assumption to make, therefore, is that there will be a need for closer integration of state and public sector schemes and also for greater flexibility in order to meet changes. Clearly this differs from the present situation where integration has not advanced very far and where the arrangements which have been made for modification are too rigid even to meet the changes which have taken place since 1948. Admittedly there are difficulties in integrating schemes which operate on such different bases as the flat-rate National Insurance scheme and the usual salary-related public sector scheme. But although this means that complete integration would not be easy, it still makes possible the kind of arrangement described in Chapter 5 in relation to the 'D' schemes, whereby an automatic adjustment is made in the occupational scheme for every adjustment in the National Insurance scheme.[1] Such an arrangement applied to public sector schemes in place of the present flat-rate modification would not necessarily save much administrative work, although it would certainly be simpler than modification adapted to take account of the various changes in National Insurance pensions since 1948. Its chief merit would be in making intelligible to members a system under which, of the total pension, part was provided by the State and part through the occupational scheme.

THE ADJUSTMENT OF PENSIONS

A further problem of great importance is whether any adjustment should be made to pensions which are in course of payment. There are two distinct questions here; whether pensions should be adjusted in order to maintain the purchasing power which they had when they first began to be paid, and whether they should be adjusted in line with any increase in real incomes which takes place. At present, little is done in the way of regular adjustment on these lines, largely

[1] If the state scheme continues to be contributory (and this is an assumption which needs to be further examined in relation to future policy), difficulties may arise over integration with the non-contributory public sector schemes proposed in the previous chapter, e.g. because increased state contributions will appear to increase the employee's burden. What is needed is an agreement about how to deal with this situation in salary negotiations.

because there is no general acceptance of the principle that there ought to be adjustment. The main question of policy is therefore to determine whether the principle is sound and once more this can only be considered in relation to the fundamental question of the purpose of pensions; for clearly if a pension is designed to provide a certain standard of living, it does not make sense to guarantee that standard only at the moment of retirement.

The question of principle is of more importance than the precise form in which any adjustment is made. There are at least three possible ways of doing this: one is simply to review pensions at regular intervals of, say, one or two years to decide—ex gratia— whether any adjustment is necessary; another is to adjust pensions automatically for changes in the cost of living index; and the third is to raise pensions in line with rises in the average level of wages or earnings. Probably the main practical point which has a bearing on this problem is the increased cost of making adjustments and how that cost is to be met. Here one must stress the importance of the total level of pension generally implied by the preceding discussion; for the cost of improving pensions in payment will depend very much on whether it is entirely an additional cost or whether it can be met in part at least by either reducing other benefits, or limiting increases in them. Furthermore, what seems an excessive cost now may not seem so in ten years' time, and the approach to what constitutes a proper level of pension will need to be flexible enough to allow for possible changes of attitude of this kind.

To illustrate the point at issue: the traditional maximum pension of two-thirds of earnings is now accepted and has the powerful sanction of the income tax rules to make it almost sacrosanct. But it does not necessarily follow that a limit which was arrived at over 100 years ago largely in order to keep down the cost of civil service pensions will be appropriate to today's conditions or those of the next fifty years. Most people would regard 50 per cent of earnings as the minimum level to provide an adequate pension for most of the working population, but it is probably more difficult to be specific about what the desirable aim should be; 80 per cent of final earnings has been advocated,[1] and a theoretical case could be made out for 100 per cent pensions. But the point is to try to arrive at some generally accepted level; it might well be, for example, that most people would be prepared to accept a rather lower rate of pension calculation in return for a guarantee that their pensions would not decline in value or still more if their pensions were linked to a wages index. Naturally any raising of the two-thirds limit would require a

[1] See Michael Fogarty, *The Just Wage*, Geoffrey Chapman, 1961, p. 167. The same author has prepared the Liberal Party plan, *Security in a New Society*, 1963.

revision of the tax rules but in any case the right principle is surely that the tax rules should be adapted to policy requirements rather than vice versa. Some of the suggestions put forward here might well, taken together, mean the abandonment not only of the two-thirds maximum but also of the hallowed sixtieths/eightieths pattern which is general in the public sector; and although such an abandonment should not be undertaken lightly, a case can certainly be made out for it.

PRESERVATION OF PENSION RIGHTS AND OTHER PROBLEMS

Apart from the major policy questions which have been discussed, a number of other issues need to be examined, all of which may have an important bearing on the future shape of pension provision. The first of these is the preservation of pension rights in occupational schemes on change of employment; as was shown in Chapters 3 and 5, the main impetus to action has come from those who, from the national economic point of view, have seen lack of preservation as an obstacle to the mobility of labour. However, not only would many employers be reluctant to introduce preservation, but employees frequently prefer a refund of contributions to preservation; paradoxically, refunds of contributions in many cases provide the greater incentive to mobility.

From the point of view of mobility, therefore, the situation is confused. The problem may indeed not be a large one in terms of the numbers affected. The NEDC's advocacy of preservation is specifically related to the mobility of higher-grade staff who are the people most likely to be deterred from moving by the fact that they will lose their pension rights. In the case of the Civil Service, the provision in the 1949 Act allowing frozen pensions to those who leave at 50 may chiefly have benefited senior civil servants who have been enabled to take posts in the private sector; and indeed the further recent extension of this principle was specifically designed for this purpose.[1]

Important, therefore, as the question of mobility is from the national economic point of view, preservation ought probably to be examined as a pension problem. Here the first point is that if there is preservation it should be adequate; whether a pension is preserved by 'freezing' or by making a transfer payment it ought to form a reasonably proportionate part of the final total pension. This is not so, for example, in a frozen pension at present where no allowance is made for changes in the value of money between the date of freezing and the date of retirement. But, secondly, it is clear that if the object of belonging to a pension scheme is to make provision for a future

[1] See pp. 84–85.

pension, that object is frustrated if transfer to another job results in the loss of pension rights which have been earned up to that point. Equally, of course, the object is frustrated if a man has the choice, which he accepts, of taking a refund of contributions instead of preservation. From the pension point of view, therefore, not only does preservation seem the right policy but it ought to be automatic and not an alternative to a refund of contributions. In practice, there are administrative problems to be considered and there might need to be a short minimum period of service before preservation could operate, to avoid 'freezing' a large number of very small pensions, and in these cases refunds of any contributions paid would continue to be made. Since occupational schemes are unlikely to adopt preservation widely on a voluntary basis, this is probably a case where at least the minimum conditions of preservation would have to be prescribed for all occupational schemes, and this could be done by making it a condition of approval for tax purposes. Such a proposal is not new; it was, for example, considered by the Phillips Committee and rejected by them with reluctance on the grounds that the general climate of opinion was not then in favour of compulsion. But in the ten years since the Committee reported it has become increasingly evident that if something is to be done it must be by compulsion; at the same time, there is scarcely a writer or speaker on pensions who has not advocated preservation.[1]

Problems of an entirely different kind are raised by consideration of the range and type of benefits provided through pension schemes. A lesser problem here is that of lump sums; as described earlier, their introduction into public sector schemes was something of an accident, and in tax terms they have created anomalies and confusion. That some limitation should be put on them seems evident, and recommendations which would achieve this have been lying idle for ten years. All that is needed is for action to be taken.[2]

The provision which should be made for widows is probably the major question which arises in connexion with the range of benefits. As with the pension for retirement, the main point is to establish what the aim of such provision is; but here the question is complicated by the fact that there is not necessarily a single, universal aim. In particular, the needs of a young widow with small children may differ greatly from those of an elderly widow of a man who had

---

[1] Among recent advocates, see especially R. C. Sansom and N. N. B. Ordman, *Preserving Pension Rights for Professional Engineers*, Engineers' Guild Limited, 1964, and John Fryd, *Protect Your Pension*, National Federation of Professional Workers, 1964. Although both are basically concerned with arguing the case for particular professional groups, their arguments have a wider application.

[2] Both the Millard Tucker Committee and the Royal Commission on the Taxation of Profits and Income examined this point (see Appendix 7).

already retired, or of a young widow of such a man. In occupational schemes, and particularly in public sector schemes where widows' pensions are usually found, a pension is paid to the widow until death or re-marriage and is calculated in all circumstances in exactly the same way; in the state scheme, on the other hand, whether a widow receives a continuing pension, and, if so, of what amount depends on her circumstances, for example, her age and whether she has dependent children. A point which also needs to be borne in mind is that widows' pensions at present are relatively so small that there is even more need for them to be adjusted, e.g. for changes in the cost of living.

In considering what the needs of a widow are likely to be, account should also be taken of some of the trends which were referred to earlier, such as the increasing employment of married women, and also the possibility of widows themselves taking up employment. Again, apart from the question of what kind of payment should be made to the widow, it is necessary, as with retirement pensions, to consider the question of how far provision should be made by the State and how far by means of occupational schemes, with its attendant problems of closer integration and greater flexibility. This is particularly a problem for the public sector where widows' pensions are found far more commonly than in the private sector. The net result of a fresh examination of the problem of widows might well be to establish a rather different pattern from the present one; this perhaps is only to be expected in view of the comparatively recent growth of occupational widows' pensions, and of the fact that perhaps too little attention has until now been paid to the problems involved.

CONCLUSION

To a large extent, the problem of the future direction of pensions is most evident in the need for suitable government machinery for determining policy. Three factors are particularly relevant to any decisions which are taken; the first is the importance of the elderly in social and political terms; the second is the economic implications of providing for them; and the third is the political consequences of further government intervention in the field of pensions. Recognition of these factors implies the necessity for a national pensions policy, and yet the means for achieving such a policy are at present lacking.

An essential preliminary is to consider whether pensions policy ought to be kept continuously under review or whether reviews carried out at intervals would be sufficient. This is by no means an easy question because there are no automatic criteria which can be applied. Clearly the decision will depend on the importance of pensions policy in relation to government policy as a whole, and also on whether it is possible to look far enough ahead in pensions to make plans which do not quickly become out of date.

An occasional review of pensions might of course take many different forms. One possibility would be to have a Royal Commission from time to time; this would have the advantage of being able to set out at length all the facts and arguments. Even so, it might not be the most suitable means for formulating policy. Royal Commissions are weighty bodies, but their recommendations do not necessarily compel action. Moreover, although one can readily see that there would be much for a Royal Commission to investigate at the present moment, one could probably not expect another Commission in less than, say, a quarter of a century, and the question then is what happens in the meantime. One might of course have a less formal investigating body or committee than a Royal Commission or it might be that a Committee of the Cabinet could keep pensions policy under review.

If, however, pensions policy is to form a permanent part of government policy, the most obvious means would be by having one Minister who was generally responsible for it, though not necessarily for the whole field of pensions. Perhaps three possibilities need to be considered here. The first is the Chancellor of the Exchequer, in recognition of the economic importance of pensions. The main drawback is that the Chancellor already has many responsibilities. The second possibility is therefore that the Minister of Pensions and National Insurance should indeed live up to his title. Here there is a problem of a rather different kind, that is, how far a Minister who is primarily responsible for administering a state scheme of social security can also take in a wider view of one part of that scheme. A third possibility suggests itself, therefore, of a separate Minister responsible for pensions; it may be doubted, however, whether pensions justify a separate Minister and whether, if they did, the post could attract a man of sufficient calibre to be able to persuade his more powerful colleagues of the necessity for action.

Ministerial responsibility does not of course exclude other arrangements either as supplementary or alternative means for ensuring that pensions policy is kept under review. A recent interesting development has been the growth of independent councils or bodies not directly responsible to Ministers and yet charged with the investigation of matters which have a bearing on government policy. The National Incomes Commission is such a body and might indeed be thought suitable with extended terms of reference for considering pensions too in view of their close connexion with incomes. It may be, however, that the NIC, for political reasons, is an unsuitable body to consider the wider questions of pensions policy, and that a separate Pensions Council or Commission would be better. Here, too, one must consider whether pensions are sufficiently important to justify such a step.

However, the question of government machinery is viewed and decided, the important aim which must be pursued is the determination of general objectives. Here pensions take their place with other aspects of our national life which rapid social and other changes have compelled us to re-examine. Education, traffic in towns and the penal system are or have recently been under scrutiny, not least because, as the Robbins Committee put it, there has been a 'Continued absence of co-ordinating principles and of a general conception of objectives'.[1] For pensions, both nationally and in the public sector, these words ring all too true.

The argument of this chapter may be summarized as follows:

(1) The future of public sector schemes depends on the part they will have to play in the pension arrangements for the nation as a whole.

(2) Government pension policy is at present based on a modified form of the Beveridge plan, despite the great economic and social changes of the last twenty years.

(3) There is a need for a national pensions policy based on aims and objectives appropriate to the second half of the twentieth century.

(4) Political, economic and social trends point to a demand for reasonable living standards for the elderly, largely through the provision of pensions.

(5) Pensions related to wages and salaries will better serve the future purpose of pensions than flat-rate provision.

(6) The future level of pension provision should not necessarily be restricted by existing conventions, e.g. the maximum of two-thirds of salary.

(7) Pensions are likely to continue to be provided by both the state and occupational schemes, but there is political uncertainty about the future relations between them; public sector schemes will need to be more closely integrated with the state scheme and also more flexible to meet possible changes in that scheme.

(8) Arrangements need to be made for adjusting pensions in payment to ensure that they continue to fulfil the aim of providing reasonable living standards.

(9) Preservation of pension rights on change of employment is desirable on pension grounds and should be made compulsory for occupational schemes.

[1] *Report of the Committee on Higher Education*, Cmd. 2154, H.M.S.O., 1963, para. 19.

(10) The provision of benefits for widows needs reviewing to take account of their varying needs.

(11) A national pensions policy requires suitable government machinery not only for current decisions but for keeping the position under review.

(12) The determination of general objectives for pensions is just as vital as for other aspects of our national life, e.g. education.

APPENDIX 1

Occupational Pension Schemes:
The General Picture

The statistical information which is available about pension schemes is, on the whole, scattered and incomplete. This is particularly true of information about the numbers of members of schemes. There are signs, however, that increased interest in the subject may lead to the more regular production of statistics. An attempt is made here to indicate as far as possible the trends in both membership and finances of schemes in recent years.

MEMBERSHIP

(i) *The 1936 Survey*

Mention is made in the text of the study (see p. 42) of the survey of pension schemes in 1936, the first attempt at a comprehensive survey of the whole field. The detailed figures, which were published in the *Ministry of Labour Gazette* for May 1938, give an interesting picture of the situation at the end of 1936, but they deal only with schemes outside the public services.

Such schemes covered 1,617,000 employees or approximately 10 per cent of the employed population outside the public service, but only just over half those covered were classified as manual workers although manual workers formed 80 per cent of the employed population. This disparity is emphasized still more strongly by the fact that more than one-quarter of the manual workers covered by schemes were employed in transport, and less than half in manufacturing industry, although the number of workers in manufacturing industry outnumbered those in transport by about 6 to 1; if it had not been for the transport schemes, and particularly those for the railways, manual workers would have appeared even worse off relatively to administrative and clerical workers.

Of the latter, a high proportion (over one-quarter) were employed in insurance, but other large groups covered were in Co-operative Societies and transport.

If, finally, allowance is made for the members of public service schemes (including the Armed Forces) who were not included in the Ministry of Labour survey, the total number of employees covered by schemes at that date was probably in the region of 2½ million, or perhaps about one-seventh of the total employed population.

(ii) *The Institute of Actuaries' Figures*

Nothing quite on the lines of the Ministry of Labour's pre-war survey has been attempted since. In particular, the detailed classification of schemes by industry and according to the status of the employees covered has not been repeated.[1] But there have been a number of attempts in recent years to estimate the total coverage of pension schemes.

The first of these estimates was that made by the authors of the survey carried out jointly by the Institute of Actuaries and the Faculty of Actuaries between 1952 and 1954.[2] They concluded that at the beginning of this period there were approximately 6¼ million members of schemes and 600,000 pensioners in the following categories:

Members (thousands)		Pensioners (thousands)
1,837	Central and local government	341
2,500	Privately administered (inc. nationalized industries)	200
1,400	Life office	46
540	Mineworkers	10
6,277		597

Although, in the absence of much of the basic data, these estimates depended on a number of untested assumptions, this was a pioneer work in trying to cover the whole field of pension provision, and the overall picture which it presents may be compared with that of the 1936 survey. This shows that in fifteen years the number of members of schemes had more than doubled; of more significance is the fact that instead of 14–15 per cent of the employed population being covered, by 1951 the figure was nearer 30 per cent.[3]

The Phillips Committee on the Economic and Financial Problems of the Provision for Old Age, which reported in 1954 (Cmd. 9333), asked the Institute of Actuaries (and the Faculty) for up-to-date figures. The results, presented in a rather different form, were as follows:

Members (thousands)		Pensioners (thousands)
2,500	Public services	600
1,500	Nationalized industries	100
1,400	Internally administered	150
1,700	Life office	50 (tentative)
7,100		900

[1] A limited analysis of a small number of industrial schemes will be found in William Durham, *Industrial Pension Schemes*, Industrial Welfare Society, 1956.

[2] F. W. Bacon, M. D. W. Elphinstone, B. Benjamin, 'The Growth of Pension Rights and their Impact on the National Economy', *Journal of the Institute of Actuaries*, Vol. 80, Part II, No. 355.

[3] The authors relate their figures of members to the 'gainfully occupied' population as returned at the 1951 census. This and the fact that they include some allowance for ex gratia pensions means that their figures slightly overstate the proportions of employed people in schemes; these show about one-third of men and one-fifth of women in schemes.

These statistics were compiled partly from returns made by members of the Institute and Faculty (and the Government Actuary) and partly from information published by the Life Offices Association and the Associated Scottish Life Offices. They are of particular interest in that an attempt was made to estimate roughly the division of members of the first three groups (i.e. all except those in life office schemes) according to whether they were staff or workpeople. The results (in Appendix V of the Report) although 'subject to many limitations' are as follows:

	Staff	Workpeople	Not known
Men	1,403,000	2,349,000	259,504
Women	716,000	177,000	78,653
	2,119,000	2,526,000	338,157

(For reasons not explained in the Report these figures do not add up to the 5,400,000 shown in the previous paragraph.)

It is tempting to compare these figures with those of the 1936 survey to show that the proportion of the total number of members of schemes who are manual workers has not changed greatly. It would be unwise, however, to draw this inference, if only for the following reasons: (i) the 1954 figures *include* the public services where staff employees are greatly in preponderance; (ii) the 'not known' and, more importantly, the 1,700,000 members of life office schemes, might conceivably alter the total picture if information had been available about them.

(iii) *The Government Actuary's Survey*

One of the recommendations of the Phillips Committee was that in view of the great and increasing importance of pension schemes in the national economy, there ought to be a series of regular statistics collected and published by a central official agency. The first step in this direction was a survey of the position in 1956 carried out by the Government Actuary and published in 1958.

This is the most comprehensive survey of occupational pension schemes yet to be carried out in this country; it has not, however, been followed up or made into a regular series, as recommended by the Phillips Committee, and for total membership of all schemes it remains the only recent source of information.[1]

The Government Actuary estimated the membership of schemes in three categories, and added tentative estimates for 1958 as shown on p. 258.

Direct comparison of these figures with earlier surveys is not possible because of the different bases on which the calculations have been made, but the most striking fact about recent years has been the steady growth of private sector schemes; at the same time membership of public sector schemes has remained fairly steady. The main reason for the contrast is

[1] The Institute of Actuaries announced in June 1963 that it was to conduct a statistical inquiry into pension provision in the private sector. For Life Office figures see 'Private Sector Schemes' below.

I

	Members (thousands)		Pensioners (thousands)
1956	1958		1956
2,300		Public service (including Armed Forces)	
	3,750		800
1,500		Nationalized industries	
4,300	5,000	Private schemes	300
8,100	8,750		1,100

simply that with the inauguration of the large new schemes for the nationalized industries after 1945, there was little scope for further expansion of membership in the public sector except by the growth of employment.

The contrasting position of the private sector is well brought out in some further figures quoted in the Government Actuary's survey.[1] These show that less than half the 10 million employees of those firms which had pension schemes were members of those schemes. The percentages in the different categories were:

	% in pension schemes			% in pension schemes
Men: salaried	71	*Women:* salaried		34
wage-earnings	38	wage-earning		23
	—			—
Total	49	Total		27
	—			—

		% in pension schemes
Men and Women: salaried		60
wage-earning		34
		—
Total		42
		—

(iv) *The Position in 1963*

Of the 8¾ million estimated by the Government Actuary to be members of pension schemes in 1958, 7 million were men, representing nearly one-half of employed men, but as the figures in the previous paragraph indicate, salaried staff, particularly men, still enjoyed the benefits of a pension scheme much more commonly than wage-earners. Professor Titmuss estimated, presumably on the basis of these figures, that 86 per cent of male salaried staff in the private sector but only 20 per cent of wage-earners were in schemes.[2]

[1] Occupational Pension Schemes, H.M.S.O. 1958, para. 13.
[2] See Pilch & Wood, *Pension Schemes*, Hutchinson, 1960, p. 141.

Unfortunately, it is impossible to say what the trends have been since 1958, because, as was said above, no further inquiry on this scale has since been undertaken. In what follows, various items of information have been pieced together to try to form a picture of the number of employees covered by schemes in 1963, but the information gives no guide for estimating a break-down according to sex and status.

Public Sector Schemes (including the Armed Forces). The figures in Appendix 5 have been compiled for the most part from published data for each scheme or from information supplied by the particular government department or nationalized industry concerned. These figures are therefore reasonably accurate and indicate that by 1963 approximately 3,800,000 public sector employees were members of pension schemes. Because of difficulties of definition and other reasons, an exact figure is not easy to obtain; the point is well illustrated by comparing these figures with those compiled by the Government Actuary's Department and published in the May 1964 issue of *Economic Trends*.

Private Sector Schemes. Perhaps the hardest figure to estimate is the total membership of private self-administered funds until the results of the Institute of Actuaries' survey (footnote 1, p. 257) are known. In 1956 the Government Actuary calculated that rather less than half the membership of private sector schemes was in self-administered, that is, non-insured schemes; in terms of the 1958 figures this would indicate approximately 2¼ million members of non-insured schemes against 2¾ million of insured schemes. It can be assumed that there has been some increase in membership since 1958, but perhaps not to the extent indicated by the figures for insured schemes discussed below. A reasonable guess (it can be no more in the circumstances) would be to assess membership of non-insured schemes at around 2¾ million in 1963.

Figures published jointly by the Life Offices' Association and the Associated Scottish Life Offices show that, excluding overseas business, the number of employees covered by occupational pension and life assurance schemes organized through life offices rose from 2,850,000 at the end of 1957 to 4,200,000 at the end of 1962, but these figures include some duplication, as well as including some pensioners and employees with 'frozen' pension rights.[1] A noticeable feature of these life office figures is that the number of employees covered by schemes for the first time rose sharply from an annual average of about 500,000 in the period 1957–60 to nearly 840,000 in 1961 but fell back to about 600,000 in 1962. This increase in 1961 is attributed to the fact that 'many new pension schemes were set up with a view to contracting out of the state scheme'. If this is so, then it is likely that the figure for 1961 will prove to have been exceptionally high, as indeed seems to be indicated by the 1962 figures. Taking these various factors into account, a reasonable estimate for insured schemes would be 3¾ million employees covered by 1963.

---

[1] See *British Life Assurance*, 1958–1962 and, on the limitations of these figures, Richard M. Titmuss, *Income Distribution and Social Change*, George Allen & Unwin, 1962, p. 157.

The total number of employees covered by pension schemes in 1963 probably does not exceed 10½ million made up as follows:

	Members (thousands)
Public service (including Armed Forces)	2,450
Nationalized industries	1,350
Private sector { non-insured	2,750
insured	3,750
	10,300

The number of pensioners is even more difficult to estimate with accuracy but may be in the region of 1¾ million, of whom approximately 1,100,000 are in the public sector.

If the figures quoted in the preceding paragraph are approximately accurate, they indicate that nearly half the present employed population have a prospect of an occupational pension, but only 20 per cent of those who are at present of pensionable age are receiving an occupational pension (about 80 per cent are receiving National Insurance pensions). About one-third of those who are in employment are women and if past trends are any indication of the present position, it is possible that by now rather more than half the employed men but possibly only about one-quarter of the women are in occupational schemes.

FINANCES

Reference may be made more briefly to the financial position of pension funds. Here perhaps the two most important points are the size of the accumulated funds of pension schemes and the rate at which they are growing. It has to be remembered in this context that in a large part of the public sector there are no funds (notional funds are excluded from the present analysis), so that the total of funds is a good deal less than it would be if all schemes were funded.

Once again, the Actuaries' survey of 1952 is an invaluable pioneering work and may conveniently be taken as the starting-point for an investigation of the position in recent years. Their figures may be summarized as follows:

Position at the end of 1951
(£ millions)

	Accumulated Funds	Annual Increase of Funds
Privately administered schemes (including nationalized industries)	910	100
Life Office schemes	336	48
Local government	265	25
Total	1,511	173

In 1958 the Radcliffe Committee estimated the latest position, and for self-administered funds (including both local government and the nationalized industries) put the total of funds at £2,500 million, increasing at an annual rate of approximately £250 million.[1] Unfortunately, there is a fundamental difficulty about making similar estimates for life office schemes. Generally speaking, for most purposes for which financial statistics are required, it is not important to distinguish between the funds accumulated by life offices for ordinary life business and those for pension scheme business. This is true of the statistics published by the Life Offices' Association and of estimates made by the Radcliffe Committee. For example, the total of life office ordinary funds was just over £3,000 million in 1957, but what proportion of these funds represented pension business is impossible to say with accuracy; perhaps between one-third and one-half or £1,000–£1,500 million would be a reasonable figure.

One of the recommendations of the Radcliffe Committee was that more statistical information should be published about the assets of both insurance companies and pension funds, not so much in relation to the totals of those assets as to the amount and type of investment undertaken. In accordance with this recommendation, the Board of Trade in 1963 published further detailed information of the position in 1962 and began a series of regular surveys of transactions in the assets of private pension funds.[2]

From these new figures it appears that the total of self-administered funds in 1962 was approximately £4,000 million, and thus that the increase in these funds during the period 1958–62 was approximately at the rate of £350–£400 million a year. The total of life office funds, from the published figures of the Life Offices' Association, increased in the same period from £3,000 million to approximately £5,000 million, and of this latter figure perhaps something approaching £2,000 million represents pension scheme business. Thus in round figures, pension funds amount to getting on for £6,000 million, approximately three-quarters of this figure being accounted for by private sector pension schemes; furthermore, these funds are still increasing at a considerable rate, partly through the extension of pension business and partly through the natural growth of existing funds. This increase may be in the region of £500 million a year at present.

Although the figures quoted in the preceding paragraph cannot, for the reasons given (and for the further reasons given by the Board of Trade, e.g. the lack of a uniform basis for quoting the value of assets), be regarded as precise, they indicate the magnitude of the funds involved. But probably of more significance is the relation of these assets to the market for securities as a whole. The Board of Trade has analysed the value of the holdings of private self-administered pension funds at the end of 1962 amounting to £1,860 million or approximately 5 per cent of the market value of all quoted securities. Within this total figure, however, the analysis shows that there are wide variations in the holdings of different

[1] Committee on the Working of the Monetary System, Cmnd. 827, H.M.S.O. 1959, para. 252.

[2] See *Board of Trade Journal*, July 19 and July 26, 1963; also December 13, 1963.

types of securities. Thus, these funds held only 4 per cent of the total of British Government Securities and of ordinary shares, but 8 per cent of local authority securities and 16 per cent of company debentures. To get the full picture, however, one would need to look also at the holdings of public sector funds,[1] and also of life office pension funds. It is likely, therefore, that, in total, pension funds hold at least 10 per cent, and possibly more, of all quoted securities.

[1] According to the Board of Trade they held another 3 per cent to 4 per cent of government securities and around 1 per cent or 2 per cent of company securities.

APPENDIX 2

Public Sector Pension Schemes

The precise boundaries of the public sector may be drawn differently for different purposes. In this study, description and comment is primarily concerned with schemes for those employed in central and local government, the National Health Service and the nationalized industries. Brief notes on these schemes are given below. There are, however, other schemes which ought to be included in any description of the public sector, particularly the scheme for the Armed Forces. Because of the unique character of service in the Armed Forces, their pension arrangements have no exact counterpart in the rest of the public sector and are not considered in the text of the study. Nevertheless, in view of the importance of those arrangements, a separate note on them is included in Appendix 3. A further group of public sector schemes not directly considered in the text is referred to below under the not very exact heading of 'Other Public Boards'. On the whole, these are smaller schemes than those considered in detail in the text of the study, and what is said there must be taken as applying to these schemes with necessary modifications. Finally, mention should be made of the Federated Superannuation System for Universities (FSSU), which is referred to in Chapter 5. In view of the heavy dependence of universities on public funds,[1] it could be argued that FSSU ought to be treated as a public sector scheme. On the other hand, universities do still have other sources of finance, and, perhaps equally important, have a strong tradition of independence in other matters. It seems best for these reasons to treat FSSU here as part of the private sector.

CENTRAL AND LOCAL GOVERNMENT, THE NATIONAL HEALTH SERVICE AND THE NATIONALIZED INDUSTRIES

Civil Service

For practical purposes, all whole-time established civil servants in Great Britain are covered by a single scheme. Unestablished civil servants may also, under certain conditions, receive limited benefits. Although certain groups, notably prison officers, receive special terms, it is probably true to

---

[1] Parliamentary grants alone account for 70 per cent of university income (excluding college income at Oxford and Cambridge), and there are in addition non-recurrent grants for capital expenditure on buildings, etc. See University Grants Committee, *Returns from Universities and University Colleges in receipt of Treasury Grant, 1961–62*, Cmnd. 2135, H.M.S.O., 1963.

say that this is the largest homogeneous scheme not only in the public sector but in the country as a whole. No distinction is made between staff and manual workers.

Source of Rules, etc.

Mainly in Acts of Parliament, Orders in Council and Regulations. Not consolidated, but collections of current provisions in force published at intervals by H.M. Treasury: latest—*Digest of Pension Law and Regulations of the Civil Service* published in 1952.

Chief Acts still in force in whole or part

Superannuation Acts of 1834, 1859, 1909, 1935 and 1949.

Local Government

The local government scheme covers those who are employed by local authorities in England, Wales and Scotland, except for teachers, police and firemen for whom there are separate schemes. Apart from counties, county boroughs, metropolitan boroughs and county districts, other bodies either must or may come into the scheme; this covers, for example, employees of River Boards and the Metropolitan Water Board. A few authorities (7 in England and 2 in Scotland) still maintain schemes under powers given by local Acts, and these schemes differ in detail from the general scheme. Manual workers are not automatically covered, but the decision whether to include all or particular groups rests with each authority. Apart from this, manual workers receive the same benefits as other employees. As with the civil service scheme, certain specified groups (for example, female nurses) receive special terms.

Source of Rules, etc.

The general outline of the scheme is contained in Acts of Parliament, but much of the detail will be found in a series of Regulations. These are not consolidated, but the Ministry of Housing and Local Government have issued a volume, *Local Government Superannuation (England and Wales): Principal Statutes and Regulations as in force on 1st January, 1955* (H.M.S.O. 1955); they have also issued explanatory memoranda on the Regulations.

Chief Acts still in force in whole or in part

Local Government Superannuation Act, 1937
Local Government Superannuation (Scotland) Act, 1937
Local Government Superannuation Act, 1953

Principal Regulations

Local Government Superannuation (Benefits) Regulations, 1954. (S.I. 1954, No. 1048)
Local Government Superannuation (Administration) Regulations, 1954 (S.I. 1954, No. 1192)
Local Government Superannuation (Reckoning of Service on Transfer) Regulations, 1954 (S.I. 1954, No. 1211)

Local Government Superannuation (Transfer Value) Regulations, 1954 (S.I. 1954, No. 1212)

Local Government Superannuation (Actuarial Valuations) Regulations, 1954 (S.I. 1954, No. 1224)

(There are corresponding Regulations for Scotland)

Teachers

For practical purposes, all full-time teachers in schools (except independent schools for whom there is a separate voluntary scheme) are covered by a single scheme with a central administration. There are, however, differences in detail between the provisions affecting teachers in England and Wales and those in Scotland. Because of this and because of the long-standing difference in educational traditions and administration between England and Scotland, the central administration for teachers in schools in England and Wales is in the hands of the Department of Education and Science, and, for teachers in Scotland, of the Scottish Education Department.

Source of Rules, etc.

The principal provisions are contained in Acts of Parliament, supplemented in detail by a series of Regulations. No attempt has been made to consolidate the various provisions, although both Departments issue brief explanatory memoranda outlining the scheme.

Chief Acts still in force in whole or in part

Teachers (Superannuation) Act, 1925

Education (Scotland) Act, 1946 (sections 99–108 and Third and Fourth Schedules)

Teachers (Superannuation) Act, 1956

Principal Regulations

The Teachers Superannuation Rules, 1926 (S.R. & O. 1926, No. 415 as amended by S.R. & O. 1930, No. 219; 1937, No. 808 and 1941, No. 599)

The Teachers Superannuation Amending Rules, 1947 (S.R. & O. 1947, No. 493)

The Teachers (Superannuation) (Scotland) Regulations, 1957 (S.I. 1957, No. 356)

The Teachers (Superannuation) (Scotland) Rules, 1957 (S.I. 1957, No. 583)

Police

The scheme covers regular policemen and policewomen (but not auxiliary policemen), and all ranks from constable to chief constable, including the Commissioners of the Metropolitan Police. Clerical and other civilian staff come into the general local government scheme, except for those in the Metropolitan Police area who are in a separate scheme which is similar to that for civil servants. Administration is in the hands of the local police authorities, the Home Office (and Scottish Home and Health Department) exercising general guidance and supervision.

I*

Source of Rules, etc.

Statutory authority for the Home Secretary to draw up rules is given by Act of Parliament, but the details of the scheme are in Regulations. Consolidated Regulations are issued at intervals, but a notable step forward was taken in 1962 when consolidated Regulations covering Scotland as well as England and Wales were issued.

Principal Act

Police Pensions Act, 1948

Principal Regulations

Police Pensions Regulations, 1962 (S.I. 1962, No. 2756)

Fire Services

Separate schemes for firemen date only from the Fire Brigade Pensions Act of 1925. The present scheme applies for the most part only to regular firemen, that is, whole-time members of brigades engaged on fire-fighting duties. A single scheme applies to England, Wales and Scotland and is administered locally by the individual fire authorities; general guidance and supervision is given by the Home Office.

Source of Rules, etc.

Statutory authority for the Home Secretary to draw up a scheme is given by Act of Parliament, but the details are set out in Regulations. Consolidated regulations are made at intervals.

Principal Acts

Fire Services Act, 1947, section 26
Fire Services Act, 1951

Principal Regulations

The Firemen's Pension Scheme Order, 1956 (S.I. 1956, No. 1022) brought into force the Firemen's Pension Scheme, 1956, which is set out as an Appendix to the Order.

National Health Service

There is a single scheme for all those who are employed whole-time in the National Health Service, and for certain part-time staff. Thus doctors and dentists, both in hospital and general practice, clerks and manual workers all come into the scheme. The scheme is administered centrally, by the Ministry of Health in England and Wales, and by the Scottish Home and Health Department in Scotland. An important minority of NHS employees remain subject to the conditions of schemes of which they were already members when the NHS was created. The NHS scheme provides special terms for certain groups, such as women nurses and those employed in psychiatric hospitals.

Source of Rules, etc.

Statutory authority for the Minister of Health (Secretary of State in Scotland) to draw up rules is given by Act of Parliament, but the details of the scheme are in Regulations. Consolidated Regulations are issued at intervals.

Principal Acts

National Health Service Act, 1946, section 67
National Health Service (Scotland) Act, 1947, section 66

Principal Regulations

National Health Service (Superannuation) Regulations, 1961 (S.I. 1961, No. 1441)
National Health Service (Superannuation) (Scotland) Regulations, 1961 (S.I. 1961, No. 1398)

Nationalized Industries

For the purposes of the study, the nationalized industries have been taken as Coal, Electricity, Gas, Transport, Airways and Atomic Energy. The Post Office has been included in the civil service scheme. Details of the arrangements for superannuation in each of these industries since nationalization are indicated below, but the general pattern is that the Act creating the nationalized industry provided for the appropriate Minister to make Regulations establishing pension schemes. The following extract from the Electricity Act, 1947, may be regarded as typical:

'54 (1) The Minister and the Secretary of State [i.e. for Scotland] may make joint regulations for all or any of the following purposes, that is to say—

(a) for providing pensions to or in respect of persons who are or have been in the employment of an Electricity Board or a Consultative Council . . .

(b) for the establishment and administration of pension schemes and pension funds for the purposes of the foregoing paragraph, for the continuance, amendment, repeal or revocation of existing pension schemes. . . .'

Regulations made under the statutory provisions generally delegate to the Boards of the nationalized industries the power to draw up and run schemes subject to the Minister's approval. Again taking Electricity as an example, the Regulations (S.I. 1948, No. 226) provide:

'1. Any Electricity Board may, for the purposes of paragraph (a) of subsection (1) of section fifty-four of the Act establish and administer any pension scheme which has been approved by the Minister . . . or participate in any such approved scheme established by another Electricity Board; and may for the purposes of any such scheme as aforesaid contribute to any pension fund or execute or maintain any policy of insurance, bond, indemnity or other similar instrument.'

The detailed rules of the various schemes are then contained in booklets issued by the Boards for the benefit of members. Where other arrangements apply, this is indicated in the notes on individual industries' schemes. A distinct problem with most nationalized industries has been the safeguarding of the pension rights of those who were already working in the industries at the time of nationalization. This problem is not considered in detail here, but it is worth noting that the Acts and Regulations made under them make full provision for ensuring that such people are at least no worse off because of nationalization than they would otherwise have been. In the cases particularly of Gas and Transport many of the existing pension schemes have been continued, though closed to new members. (See below the special note on Transport schemes.)

Coal

Two schemes cover employees in the coal industry. The National Coal Board Principal scheme covers all non-industrial staff and industrial staff in the supervisory grades; the Mineworkers' Pension scheme covers the remaining industrial staff. The former was approved by the Minister on July 31, 1947, and established on January 1, 1947; the latter has operated since January 1, 1952, and, as explained in Appendix 4, the two schemes are on entirely different bases.

Statutory Authority and Regulations

Coal Industry Nationalization Act, 1946, Section 37 (and Coal Industry Act, 1949, section 4)
The Coal Industry Nationalization (Superannuation) Regulations, 1950 (S.I. 1950, No. 376)

Electricity

Two schemes cover employees of the Electricity Council, the Central Electricity Generating Board and Area Boards in England and Wales. The Electricity Supply (Staff) Superannuation scheme which was approved on August 8, 1949, and has operated since August 15, 1947, covers staff on administrative, professional, technical, commercial or clerical work; the Electricity Supply (Manual Workers) Superannuation scheme, which was approved on April 7, 1955, and has operated since April 1, 1948, covers all other staff. (For the position in Scotland, see 'Other Public Boards' below.)

Statutory Authority and Regulations

Electricity Act, 1947, section 54
The Electricity (Pension Scheme) Regulations, 1948 (S.I. 1948, No. 226)

Gas

The position is similar to Electricity, except that in the case of both staff and manual workers there are thirteen separate but identical schemes, one for the Gas Council and one for each of the Area Boards (including Scotland). The Gas Council Staff Pension scheme was approved on

September 19, 1952, and has operated since May 1, 1949; the Gas Council Manual Workers Pension scheme was established and came into operation on June 1, 1958. The schemes of the 12 Area Boards have followed the same pattern:

Statutory Authority and Regulations

Gas Act, 1948, section 58
The Gas (Pension Scheme) Regulations, 1949 (S.I. 1949, No. 744)

Transport

The arrangements are rather complicated and are set out in a separate note at the end of this Appendix, but the basic position is the same as for other nationalized industries.

Statutory Authority and Regulations

Transport Act, 1947, section 98, later replaced by Transport Act, 1962, section 74
The British Transport Commission (Male Wages Grades Pensions) Regulations, 1954 (S.I. 1954, No. 898) contains the detailed rules of the scheme for the Male Wages Grades
Following the Transport Act, 1962, there was a considerable reorganization of pension responsibilities. See especially The British Transport Reorganization (Pensions of Employees) (No. 3) Order, 1962 (S.I. 1962, No. 2758)
The rules of the present railway staff scheme are set out in the Schedule to the London and North Eastern Railway (Superannuation Fund) Act, 1939, as amended in June 1946, June 1957 and June 1961

Airways

There is a joint pension scheme covering all employees of BEA and BOAC. The original scheme which came into force in 1948 covered only general staff, that is, broadly, excluding pilots and other flying crew; further provisions extending the scheme to cover Pilots were made in 1951, and to cover Radio, Navigating and Engineer Officers in 1953. From April 1, 1957, the scheme was revised; in the original scheme the amount of pension was based on the amount of contributions paid ('money purchase'), but the 1957 revision put the scheme on to a terminal-salary basis. A further revision of the scheme was made from June 18, 1963, the main change being the introduction of widows' and children's pensions. The revised scheme applies compulsorily to all new employees of BEA and BOAC from June 19, 1963, and there is provision for those who were already in service on that date to transfer to the new basis. Two points of detail may be noticed:

(i) the statutory provisions specify that any scheme shall provide for benefits in the case of injury or death; it is unusual to find such a specific provision in the statutes, and this no doubt reflects in this case the particular circumstances of employment in civil aviation;

(ii) as in the case of the BTC Male Wages Grades scheme, the rules of the Airways' scheme are set out in the form of a Schedule to the Regulations.

Statutory Authority and Principal Regulations

Civil Aviation Act, 1946, section 20, as later consolidated in Air Corporations Act, 1949, section 21

Original Scheme	The Airways Corporations (General Staff Pensions) Regulations, 1948 (S.I. 1948, No. 2361)
	The Airways Corporations (Pilots Pensions) Regulations, 1951 (S.I. 1951, No. 527)
	The Airways Corporations (Radio, Navigating and Engineer Officers Pensions) Regulations, 1953 (S.I. 1953, No. 1296)
1957 Scheme	The Airways Corporations (General Staff, Pilots and Officers Pensions) (Amendment) Regulations, 1957 (S.I. 1957, No. 87)
1963 Scheme	The Air Corporations (General Staff, Pilots and Officers Pensions) (Amendment) (No. 2) Regulations, 1963 (S.I. 1963, No. 1108)

Atomic Energy

Three schemes cover all the staff of the U.K. Atomic Energy Authority (with the exception of a few people under other arrangements such as the Federated Superannuation System for Universities). The Principal Non-industrial Superannuation scheme has operated since August 1, 1954, and was approved by the Minister (then the Lord President of the Council) on December 17, 1954; it covers broadly the same groups of staff as the staff schemes of the Gas and Electricity industries. The Industrial Superannuation scheme has also operated since August 1, 1954, and was approved (by the Prime Minister) on September 25, 1958; it is compulsory for industrial employees joining the Authority from January 1, 1959. The third scheme, known as the Protected Persons Superannuation scheme, is designed to provide the benefits of civil service superannuation to certain civil servants who enter the Authority's employment, particularly those who were industrial civil servants in the Department of Atomic Energy immediately before the Authority was set up on August 1, 1954. The statutory provisions differ from those of other nationalized industries in that they provide simply for the Authority, with the approval of the Minister (originally the Lord President of the Council, now the Minister for Science), to set up pension schemes for their employees.

Statutory Authority

Atomic Energy Authority Act, 1954, section 1 (9), and first Schedule, para. 7 (2)

OTHER PUBLIC BOARDS

Several groups may be distinguished, as follows:

(1) *Pension Arrangements on the Analogy of the Civil Service.* Some public bodies, whose employees are not civil servants, follow the civil service superannuation pattern closely. Perhaps the most important of these are the Forestry Commission and the Nature Conservancy. The Metropolitan Police Staff, as already noted, also come into this category.

(2) *Scottish Electricity.* The North of Scotland Hydro-Electric Board was set up in 1943 and under the Hydro-Electric Development (Scotland) Act of that year was empowered to pay pensions to its employees and to adopt the local government scheme for that purpose if it wished. Under the Electricity Act, 1947, Area Boards were set up for South West and South East Scotland and both they and the North of Scotland Board were Electricity Boards for the purpose of section 54 of that Act.

In 1954, under the Electricity Reorganization (Scotland) Act, the South West and South East Boards were abolished and a South of Scotland Electricity Board established. A separate superannuation scheme (the South of Scotland Electricity Board's Superannuation scheme) was, with the approval of the Secretary of State for Scotland, then introduced and was effective from December 1, 1954. Both the Hydro-Electric Board and South of Scotland schemes follow broadly the pattern of the English schemes, except that both staff and manual workers are covered in each case by a single scheme.

(3) *British Broadcasting Corporation.* The Corporation operates five separate schemes for different categories of staff, but the main current scheme (known as the New Pension scheme), which covers both salaried and manual staff, is on broadly similar lines to the main public sector schemes described earlier.

(4) *British Council.* A single scheme for all staff, with benefits very similar to those in the civil service scheme, was introduced on September 1, 1957. Before that, the Council's staff were pensionable under insurance-type schemes.

(5) *Commonwealth War Graves Commission.* Although not strictly a Public Board since the Commission is a Commonwealth Organization incorporated by Royal Charter, it is useful to include it here as an example of a body which is definitely in the public rather than the private sector. A single scheme covers all staff and the benefits are similar to those provided under the civil service scheme.

All the above are sizeable schemes, even though they do not compare with the very large schemes of, for example, the Civil Service or the National Health Service. At the other end of the scale are to be found such schemes as those for employees of the Sugar Board or the General Optical Council. Again, the difficulty of drawing a precise boundary between the public and private sectors may be illustrated by the schemes for the staff of the Commonwealth Institute or the Royal College of Art, both of which may from some points of view be regarded as coming within the public sector; for example, transfer arrangements may be made between them and other public sector schemes.

THE BACKGROUND AND PRESENT POSITION OF
BRITISH TRANSPORT SCHEMES

As described in Chapter 1, the railways were among the earliest commercial undertakings to institute pension schemes for their staff.[1] After the 1921 reorganization existing schemes were continued until the four new main line companies had established their own schemes. At nationalization, there were four main schemes for salaried staff, on the whole following much the same pattern, but in addition a great variety of other arrangements both for salaried and wage-paid employees, including provident and benevolent funds and ex gratia payments as well as formal pension schemes. Some employees in other undertakings which were nationalized under the 1947 Act were also covered by pension arrangements. Existing schemes were continued after nationalization until the establishment of new schemes, when they became closed to new members. At the time of the 1962 reorganization there were still in existence over 150 of these closed schemes.

For railway salaried staff a new scheme has not been introduced since nationalization; instead, in 1957 the LMS, GWR, and SR staff schemes were closed to new members, and a new section of the LNER scheme was instituted as the scheme for new entrants from June 1, 1957. Salaried staff belonging to other parts of the British Transport Commission's activities, such as docks and hotels (but excluding those specifically covered in schemes described below) were also brought into this new section of the LNER scheme, which was a modification of the old LNER scheme. For the wage-paid staff, a completely new scheme was introduced from October 1, 1954, known as the British Transport Commission (Male Wages Grades) Pension scheme; as the title implies, it did not cover women employees, but, unlike the LNER Staff scheme, it did cover London Transport employees. The scheme was compulsory for new entrants to BTC service from October 1, 1954, but voluntary for existing employees.

The other main schemes open to new members at the end of 1962, when the British Transport Commission was dissolved, were:

London Transport Staff. Revised in 1954 and similar to the LNER Staff scheme.
British Road Services Staff. New scheme, compulsory for new staff from April 1, 1957, similar to LNER Staff scheme;
British Road Services Male Wages Grades. New scheme, compulsory for new employees from July 1, 1957, closely following corresponding BTC scheme.

There were also schemes for the salaried staff, but not the wages grades, of the Tilling Group and Scottish Omnibuses.

The Transport Act, 1962, has not so far affected the number of schemes in the various transport undertakings, although the Act gives the Minister of Transport wide powers to regulate the provision of pensions by the

[1] A good deal of information about these early schemes will be found in the report of the Departmental Committee set up by the President of the Board of Trade in 1908. (Cd. 5349, 1910.)

Boards set up under the Act, including 're-arranging, amalgamating, simplifying and assimilating pension schemes'. Responsibility for the various existing schemes, whether open or closed, has been assigned to the various Boards according to their functions; for example, the BRS, Scottish Omnibuses and Tilling schemes are now the responsibility of the Transport Holding Company, but the majority of schemes now come under the British Railways Board, the largest part of what previously constituted the British Transport Commission.

One effect of the situation described above is that the membership of closed schemes is still comparatively large. The new section of the LNER scheme, whose provisions are considered in detail in the study, contain only a minority of the salaried staff of British Railways, although in course of time it will become the major staff scheme. The same situation exists to some degree in other nationalized industries, but is generally on a much smaller scale. For this reason, the following statistics relating to both current (i.e. open to new members) and closed schemes are presented here, to supplement the figures given later in Appendix 5.

These statistics relate generally to the position at the end of 1962.

Membership

(a) Closed schemes	Members	Pensioners
LMS Superannuation Fund	25,500	15,000
LNER Superannuation Fund (old section)	20,000	10,000
GWR Superannuation Fund	10,500	4,000
SR Superannuation Fund	8,000	4,000
London Transport Staff (old section, i.e. up to 1954)	2,000	850
	66,000	33,850

To these must be added the smaller staff schemes and the wages grades schemes, bringing the total number of members to about 90,000 and of pensioners to nearly 50,000.

(b) *Current schemes*

As indicated in Appendix 5, membership is approximately 310,000, together with 33,000 pensioners. In all, therefore, the nationalized transport undertakings have approximately 400,000 pensionable employees, and rather more than 80,000 pensioners.

Finances

The method of financing described in the text as applying to the LNER scheme (new section) also applies to the closed LMS, GWR, and SR schemes and the whole of the surplus of these funds has been used for the capital purposes of the railways. This is in fact the method which was recommended by the Departmental Committee of 1908 to which reference has already been made. Of current schemes, other than the LNER, the London Transport Staff scheme is funded and the Railways' Male Wages Grades not funded. In the case of the two British Road Services' schemes, the surplus of income over expenditure in a particular year is deposited with the company who issue debentures and guarantee interest on the amounts.

Thus the most important schemes, both current and closed, are either not funded or have the bulk of their assets invested in the transport undertakings themselves. The position was indicated until the end of 1962 in two tables (V—13 and V—14) published in the annual accounts of the British Transport Commission (from 1963 onwards there will be separate accounts for the British Railways and each of the other Boards established under the 1962 Act). Table V—13 showed the Balances of Staff Superannuation Funds, that is, it represented the total amounts used for the capital purposes of the transport undertakings from the various funds; 23 such funds were listed (together with 'sundry funds') totalling £127 million at the end of 1960 and £143 million at the end of 1962, the bulk (£124 million at the end of 1962) being in the four schemes for salaried staffs of the pre-nationalization railway companies.

Table V—14 showed the annual provision for pensions, in the form of an account to which were credited the amounts charged to working expenses, together with interest and members' contributions to the unfunded Male Wages Grades scheme. Payments into superannuation funds (including deficiency payments) and direct payments of benefits (e.g. in the Male Wages Grades scheme) were debited to this account which at the end of 1962 stood at just over £117 million. In 1962 nearly £13 million was charged to working expenses for pensions, together with nearly £4 million for interest, but, as a note in the accounts explains, although the charge to revenue each year is regarded as a fair and reasonable amount in relation to the Commission's pension responsibilities, the balance in the account 'does not purport to cover the full amount which would be required if the Commission's pension responsibilities were assessed on an actuarial basis'.

APPENDIX 3

Pensions for the Armed Forces

The subject is complicated first by the fact that provision has developed in different ways for officers on the one hand and 'other ranks' on the other, and, secondly, because it has always been closely associated with other subjects, particularly pay and promotion. Before describing in out-line the present arrangements, something will be said about the back-ground, and, in particular, the nineteenth-century background.

Before the nineteenth century such provision as there was for the super-annuation of officers and men of the army and navy was irregular and unsystematic. This is hardly surprising since there was no regular standing army or navy until after the Napoleonic Wars. In the case of officers, however, this lack of system was to some extent counterbalanced by the arrangements for the purchase of commissions. The sale and purchase of commissions continued until well into the nineteenth century and was not finally abolished until the Regulation of the Forces Act of 1871 was passed. As long as it continued no regular system of retirement pensions for officers was possible, in the way that such provision had developed in the Civil Service. Various attempts were made by the Crown to make some provision for superannuated officers, particularly by creating a half-pay list. One such example is an Order in Council of 1747 which refers to the discontent among old captains in the navy at having junior captains pro-moted over their heads and proposed that 'all such captains . . . should be appointed rear-admirals . . . and that they should be esteemed as super-annuated sea officers, and have for the rest of their lives a pension equal to the half-pay of a rear-admiral'. Again, a Royal Warrant of 1830 pro-posed that in order to make some provision for 'worn-out and disabled officers' in the army 'a limited number of officers on retired full pay shall be kept up'.

Such arrangements could only touch part of the problem, since, as the earlier Order in Council indicates, much of the trouble arose from poor promotion prospects. The expedients of half-pay or even full pay proved to be only expedients as long as there were no set rules governing retire-ment, and indeed retirement policy was largely governed by promotion policy. As a Select Committee of 1863 put it: 'The Active Lists were so crowded, promotion so obstructed . . . that large retirements became a necessity.'[1]

Already in 1860 steps had been taken so far as the navy was concerned to introduce some regularity into retirement by having age retirement (at 60) for Commanders and Lieutenants, but it was not until 1876 that a

[1] Report from the Select Committee on Navy (Promotion and Retirement), H.C. 501, July 24, 1863, p. x.

Royal Commission on Army Promotion and Retirement concluded that with the purchase of commissions abolished 'retirements will have to be brought about in the lower as well as the upper ranks, and this can only be done in the main by means of a pension or sum of money on retiring, whether by compulsion or choice'.[1] Effectively, one may date the beginning of the modern system of officers' pension in the army from the time of this Report of the Penzance Commission.

Pensions for men who had served in either the army or the navy, as opposed to officers, were also subject to a variety of arrangements. Again, nothing which could truly be said to be a regular system of pensions existed before the nineteenth century, although some provision was made.[2] Perhaps the nearest approach to a systematic provision was the establishment, in the eighteenth century, of various hospitals for pensioners, of which the best known are the Greenwich and Chelsea Hospitals. Although primarily intended for disabled and invalid soldiers and sailors, they also served to some extent to provide for those who were discharged after long and faithful service.

Formally, there is still a difference between the manner in which pensions are provided for officers and the manner in which they are provided for men. Officers' pensions depend on the exercise of the Royal Prerogative, those for men have as their basis specific statutory authority. The statutory authority for naval pensions is the Naval and Marine Pay and Pensions Act of 1865 and, for military and air force pensions, the Pensions and Yeomanry Pay Act of 1884; both Acts were concerned with putting the provision for pensions on a regular basis.

THE PRESENT SYSTEM

Service pensions differ from the normal pattern of civilian public sector schemes in not being directly related to pay at the time of retirement. Thus increases in pay do not automatically lead to increases in prospective pensions as happens in terminal-salary schemes. When, therefore, either because of inflation or for some other reason, a change in pension rates is thought desirable, a new scale or 'code' is drawn up in place of the existing one. Hence at any one time there may be several codes in existence, and the pension received by any individual pensioner will depend on the code which was in force at the time he retired. Before 1958 there was no regular system of review of pensions and new codes were introduced at irregular intervals; there were, for example, new codes in 1945, 1950 and 1956. But in 1958 important changes were made in this and other aspects of pension matters following the Report of a Committee set up by the government to advise on recruiting.[3] Reviews of pay and pensions are now

[1] Report of the Royal Commission on Army Promotion and Retirement (Chairman: Lord Penzance), C. 1569, 1876, p. x.

[2] For example, in 1764, one man in every fifty of those who had served with good character for thirty years as an artificer in the naval dockyards was made entitled to a pension of £20 a year (W. L. Clowes, *The Royal Navy*, Vol. III, p. 342).

[3] See Report of the Advisory Committee on Recruiting (Grigg Committee), Cmnd. 545, 1958, especially paras. 112, 113, 116, 119 and 120.

held every two years, and although a review does not necessarily imply change, under present conditions increases in both pay and pensions are almost bound to occur, as indeed has been the case at each review since 1958.

The main characteristics of the present system of pensions may be summarized as follows: the amount of pension varies according to rank at the time of retirement and the total length of service; in addition, lump sums (known as 'terminal grants') are payable, the amount being three times the annual pension; widows' pensions are one-third of the husband's pension. The manner of calculation of the pension is thus the most distinctive way in which Armed Forces' pensions differ from civilian public sector schemes, but allied to this is the generally much lower age of retirement. Retirement commonly takes place when a man is in his forties and when, consequently, he is likely to have done less than thirty years' service. Hence, in the case of officers, for example, the minimum rate of pension is for sixteen years' service and the maximum for thirty-four years' service. It should also be noted that pensions in payment are not affected by the biennial review, but increases are applied to them in line with those under the Pensions (Increase) Acts. A further difference between service and civilian pensions is that members of the women's services are paid less and receive smaller pensions than men.

The way in which pensions vary with rank and length of service may be illustrated from the following figures taken from the two latest pension codes, those of 1962 and 1964, applying respectively to men retiring between February 1962 and January 1964, and between February 1964 and January 1966:[1]

Examples of Pension Rates
(Army ranks only given for convenience)

Officers	Captain and Below		Major		General	
	1962–64	1964–66	1962–64	1964–66	1962–64	1964–66
16 years' service	£485 p.a.	£520 p.a.	£545 p.a.	£585 p.a.	—	—
22 years' service	£600 p.a.	£640 p.a.	£705 p.a.	£755 p.a.	—	—
30 years' service	£685 p.a.	£735 p.a.	£870 p.a.	£930 p.a.	£2,440 p.a.	£2,880 p.a.
34 years' service	£725 p.a.	£775 p.a.	£930 p.a.	£995 p.a.	£2,800 p.a.	£3,305 p.a.

Other Ranks

Corporal	1962–64	3s 0d per week for each of first 22 years' service plus 6s 0d per week for each additional year's service.
	1964–66	3s 3d per week . . . plus 6s 6d per week
Sergeant	1962–64	3s 10d per week . . plus 7s 8d per week
	1964–66	4s 1d per week . . . plus 8s 2d per week
Warrant Officer I	1962–64	5s 0d per week . . . plus 10s 0d per week
	1964–66	5s 4d per week . . . plus 10s 8d per week

N.B. Members of the women's services receive pensions calculated as 85 per cent of the corresponding rates for men.

[1] See the White Papers, Service Pay and Pensions, Cmnd. 1666, March 1962, and Cmnd. 2268, February 1964.

It is noticeable how service beyond the minimum length sharply increases the pension. In the case of other ranks this operates quite simply to double the basic rate of pension for each year's service over 22, giving a somewhat similar effect to that in the police scheme for service over twenty years. In the case of officers, the position is more complicated, and not the same for each rank. For example, a Captain under the 1962 code received 25 per cent more than his basic (16-year) pension for twenty-two years' service, and 40 per cent more for thirty years' service, but the corresponding percentages for a Major were 29 per cent and 60 per cent (the same situation applies to the 1964 code although the percentages vary slightly).

These points reflect clearly the different approach to service, as opposed to civilian pensions; service in the Armed Forces is usually for a fixed term of years which is only a part of the total working life. The amount of pension and how it is determined in relation to years of service may therefore be an important factor both in attracting men and women into the services for a fixed term and in influencing their decision whether to remain for a further period at the end of that term. Hence it is not surprising that major changes in the system of pensions for the Armed Forces should have followed the report of a committee concerned with recruiting, nor that that report should have made some forthright comments on the system as it then existed; for example, they regarded the level of other ranks' pensions as a serious deterrent to men re-engaging, and dismissed the widows' pensions as 'derisory'.[1]

For similar reasons, it is not perhaps very rewarding to attempt comparisons with civilian schemes on a terminal-salary basis. Indeed, it is not easy to relate Armed Forces' pensions to pay at the time of retirement. Pensions vary only according to rank at the time of retirement and total length of service; pay can vary according to qualifications, status and length of service in the particular rank, so that the basic pay of a sergeant, for example, may be as little as £1 11s 6d per day or as much as £2 12s 0d. But in addition to pay, there are allowances which are paid to all (e.g. ration allowance) or most men (e.g. marriage allowance) to form the total emoluments received by those serving in the Armed Forces. It is possible to calculate average or general figures of the 'terminal emoluments' received by different ranks, but for the reasons given these could only be regarded as approximations, and the relationship between emoluments and pension could in particular cases show wide variations.

One other major point needs to be considered—the financing of Armed Forces' pensions. As in the Civil Service, the scheme is non-contributory and non-funded. But, unlike the Civil Service, there are no contributions for widows' pensions; the point was considered by the Grigg Committee in recommending better widows' pensions. They argued against contributions because they thought, like the 1857 commissioners on the civil service scheme, that contributions without a fund did not make sense, and that contributions with a fund would be too complicated.[2] Underlying these arguments was the feeling that contributions would (or would seem) to

[1] Cmnd. 545, paras. 51, 119.
[2] Cmnd. 545, para. 121.

worsen the conditions of service, an important point in view of their primary concern with recruiting. Thus the whole cost of pension benefits falls on the Exchequer, the amounts in recent years having been as follows:

The Cost of Armed Forces Pensions
(£ millions)

		1962–63	1963–64	1964–65
Pensions	Officers	22	24	25
	Other Ranks	24	25	26
Terminal	Officers	8	7	7
Grants	Other Ranks	4	4	4
Widows and	Officers	2	3	3
Dependants	Other Ranks	1	1	1
Other		5	7	7
	Total	66	71	73

Note: These figures have been taken from the Defence Estimates and actual expenditure may differ slightly.

The figures in the table may be compared with the cost of pay for the Armed Forces which during the same period rose from nearly £350 million to almost £400 million, indicating the relatively high cost of pensions. It should perhaps also be noted that the cost of war pensions is not included in the figures, but is borne on the vote of the Ministry of Pensions and National Insurance and amounts to about £100 million a year at present.

APPENDIX 4
Main Provisions of Twelve Public Sector Schemes

	Civil Service	Local Government	Teachers	National Health Service	Police	Firemen
1. Contributions by (a) Employee	(a) None, except for widows' and children's allowances	(a) 6% (manual workers 5%)	(a) 6%	(a) 6% (manual workers 5%)	(a) 6¼% (women 4½%)	(a) 5%
(b) Employer	(b) —	(b) 6% (manual workers 5%)	(b) 6%	(b) 8% (manual workers 6%)	(b) —	(b) —
2. Benefit on retirement on age grounds	After 10 years' service: annual pension of 1/80th of final salary for each year's established service, together with a lump sum payment of 3/80ths of final salary for each year, payable from age 60: maximum pension 45/80ths, but at age 60 maximum is 40/80ths (and similarly with lump sum). (N.B.—Lump sum payable after 2 years' service)	As for Civil Service, but (i) calculation is based on contributing, not established service; (ii) benefit payable at age 65, or from age 60 if 40 years' service; (iii) non-contributing service counts as half; (iv) lump sum payable at age 65 after 5 years' service	After 30 years' service (of which 10 pensionable): as for Civil Service, but calculation is based on contributing, not established service. (N.B.—The 30 years' qualifying service does not have to be continuous)	As for Civil Service but (i) contributing and non-contributing service as for local government; (ii) lump sum payable at age 60 after 5 years' service. (N.B.—For general medical and dental practitioners pension is calculated at 1½% of total remuneration during service, and similarly for lump sum)	After 25 years' service: annual pension of ½ (30/60ths) of final pay; additional 1/60th for each half-year of service beyond 25, with maximum of 2/3rds (40/60ths), i.e. after 30 years' service; pension payable from age 50. (N.B. — Compulsory retiring ages at 55 and later according to rank, and pension payable in these cases provided at least 10 years' service — see Note 3)	As for Police
3. Benefit on retirement because of permanent ill-health	After 1 year's service: lump sum of 1/12th of final salary for each year's service supplemented after 2 years' service with a lump sum of 3/80ths calculated in the same way.	After 5 years' service: lump sum equal in amount to final salary (or refund of contributions if greater)	After 3 years' service: lump sum of 1/12th of final salary for each year of service	As for local government	After 1 year's service: lump sum of 1/12th of final pay for each year's service (or refund of contributions if greater)	As for Police

4. Death benefit	*After 10 years' service:* annual pension and lump sum calculated in the same way as for retirement on age grounds, but generally with a minimum based on 20 years' service	*After 5 years' service:* lump sum equal in amount to final salary or, if greater, lump sum of 3/80ths of final salary for each year of service. (N.B. —If death occurs after retirement, payment is limited to cases where pension payments actually made to the deceased have been less than his final salary, and the amount is then the *difference* between these two)	Generally similar to the Civil Service, but the amount of the lump sum is equal to the total of contributions paid (with compound interest) if this is greater than either of the other two possibilities	*After 10 years' service:* as for Civil Service, but there is no minimum payment for the lump sum	Generally similar to local government	No specific benefit (*see* Note 3)	*After 10 years' service:* annual pension of 1/60th of final pay for each year's service up to 20, and for each half-year beyond 20. Maximum 40/60ths, 30 years' service	As for Police
5. Widows' and children's pensions		*After 10 years' service:* *Widows:* 1/3rd of husband's pension (if death occurs in service, pension is calculated as though he had retired on ill-health grounds on the day of death). Minimum £26 p.a. *Children:* pensions calculated as fraction of mother's pension, the fractions varying according to the number of children	*Widows:* as for Civil Service, but no minimum amount *Children:* none	None None	As for local government	*Widows: after 3 years' service:* either 1/3rd of husband's pension or a flat rate pension varying according to his rank. (A widow not entitled to a pension gets a lump sum of 1/12th of final pay for each year's service) *Children:* no benefit if widow chooses first alternative for her pension; if second alternative, flat rate pensions varying according to father's rank	*After 3 years' service:* flat rate pension varying according to husband's rank or percentage of final pay varying according to years of service (lump sum as for Police)	Flat rate pension as for Police (*see* Note 3)

[Continued

APPENDIX 4—continued

Main Provisions of Twelve Public Sector Schemes

	National Coal Board Principal	Electricity Supply (Staff) (England and Wales)	Gas Industry (Staff)	British Railways (Staff) (L.N.E.R. Scheme)	Airways' Corporation (General Staff)	Atomic Energy Authority (Non-Industrial)
1. Contributions by (a) Employee	(a) 4% + optional 1% for widows' and children's benefits	(a) 5% + optional 1% for widows' and children's benefits	(a) 5% on first £425 of annual salary, 6¼% on remainder (women pay 4% and 5¼% respectively)	(a) Varies according to age on joining scheme, i.e. 5% at ages under 23, rising to 8½% at age 51 or over	(a) 6¼% (women 5%)	(a) 6%
(b) Employer	(b) 8% + optional 2%	(b) 10% + optional 2%	(b) Balance of cost as determined by the actuary	(b) Amount equal to employees' contributions	(b) balance of cost as determined by the actuary	(b) 8%
2. Benefit on retirement on age grounds	After 10 years' service: annual pension of 1/80th of final salary for each year of service with a lump sum of 3/80ths, payable from age 65 (women 60): maximum pension 45/80ths but at age 65 (women 60) maximum is 40/80 (and similarly with lump sum)	As for National Coal Board	After 10 years' service: annual pension of 1/80th of first £425 of final salary and 1/60th of remainder of final salary for each year's service. Payable from age 65 (women 60): maximum pension 2/3rds of final salary at these ages, but an additional 1¼% is added for each quarter of a year of service beyond these ages	After 10 years' service: annual pension calculated in two parts, (a) 1/120th of average salary throughout *total* years of service, plus (b) 1/120th of *final* salary, for each year of service, together with lump sum of 1/40th of salary at date of retirement for each year of service, payable from age 62 (women 57): maximum pension and lump sum after 40 years' service	After 10 years' service: annual pension calculated of 1/60th of final salary for each year's service. Payable from age 63 (women 60): maximum pension 2/3rds (40/60ths) at age 63 (women 60)	As for National Coal Board
3. Benefit on retirement because of permanent ill-health	After 10 years' service: annual pension and lump sum calculated in the same way as for retirement on age grounds, but with a minimum based on half the years of service which could have been counted if service	As for National Coal Board, but minimum pension is based either on 20 years' service or on years of possible service to age 65 (60 women), whichever is less	After 10 years' service: annual pension calculated in the same way as for retirement on age grounds. Minimum pension based on half the years of possible service to age 65 (60 women)	After 10 years' service: annual pension and lump sum calculated in the same way as for retirement on age grounds. Specified minimum amounts according to years of service	Annual pension calculated in the same way as for retirement on age grounds but after 10 years' service, minimum pension of 1/6th of salary at date of leaving	After 5 years' service: lump sum equal to amount of final salary

	had continued until age 65 (women 60). Minimum amount, £52 p.a.					*After 10 years' service:* as for Civil Service
4. Death benefit	*After 5 years' service:* lump sum *either* 3/80ths of final salary for each year's service *or* equal to the amount of final salary or equal to total of contributions paid (with compound interest, whichever is highest. (N.B.—Where death occurs after retirement amount payable is limited to any balance needed to make up 5 years' pension payments)	As for National Coal Board	No specific benefit (*see* Note 4)	Lump sum, *either* 1/30th of salary at date of death for each year's service *or* half of salary at date of death *or* equal to total of contributions paid plus 2¼% of total salary, whichever is highest. (N.B.—For death in retirement amount is what is needed (if anything) to make up lump sum and lump sum actually paid to death benefit calculated as above)	Lump sum equal to annual salary at date of death (minimum £500) (doubled if death due to an air accident). Minimum amount equal to total of contributions paid plus compound interest. (Where death occurs in retirement, benefit paid only, if no widow's pension, equal to amount by which pension actually paid less than minimum amount above)	*After 5 years' service:* as for ill-health retirement. *After 10 years' service:* as for National Coal Board. (N.B. — For death in retirement, after 10 years' service, amount paid is equal to what is needed to make up pension and lump sum actually paid to death benefit calculated as above)
5. Widows' and children's pensions	*After 10 years' service:* as for Civil Service (*see* Note 4)	As for Civil Service but no minimum amount specified (*see* Note 4)	*After 10 years' service:* half of husband's pension (if death occurs in service, pension is calculated as though he had retired on ill-health grounds on the day of death) (*see* Note 4)	None	*After 10 years' service:* half of husband's pension (if death occurs in service, husband's pension is calculated as though he had continued in service until age 63) (*see* Note 4)	*After 10 years' service:* as for Civil Service
	Annual pensions of fixed amounts or, if greater, as a percentage of mother's pension; in either case pensions vary according to the number of children	Annual pensions of fixed amounts, varying according to the number of children	Quarter of mother's pension if one child, otherwise half	None	Quarter of mother's pension for each child (maximum, four children)	As for Airways' Corporation

NOTES TO TABLE

N.B. The aim of the table is to set out in summary form the main provisions of the twelve schemes as they affect the average new entrant in 1964. No attempt has been made to list the numerous variations (e.g. earlier retiring ages for certain classes of members). The following notes are intended to amplify the essential information about these schemes.

(1) *Final Salary.* The term most often means the average of the three years' remuneration immediately before retirement, but, especially in the nationalized industries, there are variations, either a different basis (e.g. the average of the highest paid 3 consecutive years in the last 6 in the Airways) or an alternative (e.g. the average of the highest paid 4 consecutive years in the last twenty or of the last 3 years, whichever is the higher, in NCB).

(2) *Refunds of Contributions.* All contributory schemes provide for a refund of an amount equal to the total of contributions paid by the employee, with or without interest, where no other benefit is payable. This point should be borne in mind especially in cases where no specific benefit is shown in the table. Sometimes, as indicated in the table, the amount of a refund of contributions is specified as an alternative to another method of calculation of benefit and it may even be one of three alternatives (cf. death benefit in NCB).

(3) *Pensions for Police and Firemen.* Although half pension is payable after 25 years' service, a pension is not payable before the age of 50 except in the comparatively few cases where 30 years' service has been achieved before that age. Where the compulsory retiring ages are reached after 10 but with less than 25 years' service, pension is calculated at 1/60th for each year up to 20 years' service and for each half-year beyond. If retirement is caused by injury received in the course of duty, ill-health pension is payable even with less than 10 years' service, and may be supplemented. There are special pensions for widows and children if death results from injury. (N.B. Under new (1964) Regulations, a widow's pension scheme for firemen is being introduced similar to that for the police.)

(4) *Widows' Pensions (NCB, Electricity, Gas and Airways' Schemes).* In NCB and Electricity further contributions may be paid at the option of members (at present waived in NCB) to raise the widow's pension from $\frac{1}{3}$ to $\frac{1}{2}$. In Gas and Airways, where widows' pensions are an integral part of the scheme, if a man dies and no widow's pension is payable, a refund of that part of the contributions which covers widows' benefits is made in addition to any other death benefit.

(5) *Children's Pensions.* These are generally paid for dependent children, i.e. while receiving full-time education, and the amounts are usually doubled if the mother is dead or if she subsequently dies.

(6) *Other Benefits.* In most schemes it is possible to allocate part of the pension to provide, after the death of the pensioner, a pension of equivalent value for a wife, husband or dependant. Commutation of pension is permitted in some schemes (notably police and firemen); conversion of lump sum into additional pension is found more commonly. A few schemes, apart from the special cases of police and firemen, make additional lump sum payments if retirement or death is caused by an injury received during the course of duty. There is also a great variety of provisions relating to what service is to count and how, as well as a number of lesser benefits.

(7) *Staff and Manual Workers.* In the six central and local government schemes, manual workers generally have the same benefits on the same terms as staff members, except that as noted, they pay lower rates of contribution in the local government and NHS schemes. In the nationalized industries, except the Airways, there are separate schemes for staff and manual workers (in NCB the separate scheme is for Mineworkers and other manual staff are included in the Principal scheme). The AEA industrial scheme differs from the staff scheme only in that

contributions are 4¼ per cent instead of 6 per cent. In Electricity there are also some variations in the benefits as well as a lower rate of contribution (5 per cent instead of 6 per cent, including family benefits), and in Gas a smaller pension is payable (1/100th of final salary instead of 1/60th) for lower contributions (roughly equivalent to 2/3rds of those in the staff scheme). The Mineworkers' scheme and the Railways' Male Wages Grades scheme are quite different from the corresponding staff schemes, being on a flat rate and not a terminal-salary basis. In view of the importance of these two schemes, brief details of them are appended below.

	Mineworkers	* Railways' Male Wages Grades
1. Membership	Compulsory for new entrants from April 3, 1961.	Compulsory for new entrants from October 1, 1954.
2. Maximum years of membership	From date of entering employment until age 65 (women 60).	From age 21 to age 65.
3. Contributions	Employee: 3s 2d a week (before January 6, 1964, 2s 3d). Employer: 3s 8d a week (2s 9d).	Employee: 1s 8d–2s 5d a week according to age (employees in higher grades pay 8d–11d a week extra).
4. Age Pension	1s 4d a week for each year of service payable from age 65 (women 60) (10¼d a week for service before January 6, 1964). Minimum pension (after 10 years' service): £1 a week.	*After 10 years' service*: 9d a week for each year of service. *Maximum pension*: £1 10s 0d a week after 40 years' service (higher grades get approximately 3½d a week extra for each year of extra contributions with maximum additional pension of 10s 0d a week after 35 years' service).
5. Ill-health pension	*After 10 years' service*: 7d a week for each year of service. Minimum: £1 a week.	As for age retirement.
6. Death Benefit	No specific benefit.	Specified amounts varying according to number of years' service (contributions refunded if greater).
7. Widows	Pension of 10s 0d a week or a lump sum according to length of service.	None.
8. Children	Pension of 5s 0d a week for each child (6s 0d if the mother is not alive).	None.
9. National Insurance	Not modified. Contracted out. (Hence changes in contributions and pension in 1964.)	Not modified. Not contracted out.
10. Finances	Funded. Employer meets deficiencies.	Not funded, but provision is made in the accounts of the British Railways Board.

* The Railways (former British Transport Commission) Scheme covers all male wage earners on British Railways, London Transport and the nationalized docks, canals and waterways. (See Appendix 2.)

Membership and Finances of Public Sector Schemes[1]

Table 1. Membership

Scheme	Number of members (thousands)	Number of Pensioners (including widow pensioners) (thousands)
Civil Service	700	244
Local Government	600	120
Teachers (England and Wales)	330	82
Teachers (Scotland)	40	11
National Health Service (England and Wales)	350	41
National Health Service (Scotland)	50	3
Police	90	69
Firemen	25	10
TOTAL (Central and Local Government)	2,185	580
National Coal Board, Principal	95	22
National Coal Board, Mineworkers	520	144
Electricity Supply Staff (England and Wales)	59	4
Electricity Supply Manual Workers (England and Wales)	75	3
Gas, Staff	34	3
Gas, Manual Workers	31	2
Transport, Staff (LNER Scheme)	24	—
Transport, Male Wages Grades	256	30
Transport, Other Current Schemes	30	3
Airways Corporations	30	2
Atomic Energy Authority, Non-Industrial	20	—
Atomic Energy Authority, Industrial	10	—
Other Public Boards	60	4
TOTAL (Nationalized Industries and Public Boards)	1,244	217
Armed Forces	230	200
TOTAL (Public Sector Schemes)	3,659	997

N.B. — indicates less than 500 in the category.

Notes:

(1) Information relates to the latest available year (generally 1962–63). For the coverage of schemes and 'Other Public Boards', see Appendix 2.

(2) Schemes closed to new members are not included, except in the case of the National Health Service, whose membership includes approximately 25,000 'optants' pensionable under the terms of schemes before the creation of the NHS (e.g. the Asylum Officers' Superannuation Act of 1909). Closed schemes are chiefly of importance in the nationalized industries, particularly Transport (on which see Appendix 2), but it is not easy to estimate their total membership. It is probable that an additional 150,000 members and 90,000 pensioners should be added to the figures given in Table 1, making a total of just over 3,800,000 members of schemes and nearly 1,100,000 pensioners.

(3) 'Transport, Other Current Schemes' includes mainly the Staff and Male Wages Grades schemes of British Road Services, and the London Transport Staff scheme.

[1] For the difficulties of assembling accurate information and for an analysis covering both the public services and the nationalized industries over the past ten years, see *Economic Trends*, May 1964, *Growth of Pension Schemes in the Public Sector of the British Economy, 1953–1962*.

Table 2. Finances (£000's)

| Scheme | Year | INCOME | | | | Expenditure | Pensions (Increase) | Amount of Fund |
		Employees' Contributions	Employers' Contributions	Investment and other Income	Total			
Civil Service	1960–61	2,400	—	—	2,400	62,200	5,600	—
	1962–63	2,450	—	—	2,450	70,400	6,500	—
Local Government (United Kingdom)	1960–61	20,400	32,900	26,700	80,000	33,200	5,600	586,000
	1961–62 (See Note 1)	21,300	34,300	30,300	85,900	36,800	5,600	635,000
Teachers (England and Wales)	1960–61	20,000	20,000	200	40,200	26,500	5,500	—
	1962–63	23,300	23,300	300	46,900	30,200	5,300	—
Teachers (Scotland)	1960–61	2,500	2,500	—	5,000	3,900	600	—
	1962–63	3,000	3,000	—	6,000	4,400	800	—
National Health Service (England and Wales)	1960–61	17,000	26,300	1,000	44,300	13,700	500	—
	1962–63	17,100	28,100	1,500	46,700	17,000	700	—
National Health Service (Scotland)	1960–61	2,200	3,400	500	6,100	1,700	40	—
	1962–63	2,200	3,600	500	6,300	2,000	50	—
Police and Firemen	1960–61	4,600	—	—	4,600	18,800	3,200	—
	1962–63	6,000	—	—	6,000	19,100	4,000	—
National Coal Board (Principal)	1960–61	4,100	8,200	7,500	19,800	7,100	—	133,500
	1962–63	4,300	8,700	8,400	21,400	8,800	—	159,300

National Coal Board (Mineworkers) 1960–61 (See Note 1)	2,000	6,800	3,300	12,100	7,300	—	57,000
1962–63	3,700	10,900	5,900	20,500	11,800	—	72,200
Electricity Supply Staff (England and Wales) 1960–61	2,800	5,500	5,500	13,800	2,200	—	85,700
1962–63	3,500	6,400	6,700	16,600	3,200	—	110,200
Electricity Supply Manual Workers (England and Wales) 1960–61	1,600	1,600	3,300	6,500	1,000	—	31,000
1962–63	2,100	2,900	1,900	6,900	1,300	—	40,300
Gas Staff 1960–61	1,200	2,200	2,300	5,700	900	—	31,300
1962–63	1,600	3,000	4,600	9,200	1,400	—	44,500
Gas Manual Workers 1960–61	400	300	200	900	300	—	1,900
1962–63	500	500	400	1,400	500	—	4,100
Transport 1960–61	3,000	1,500	1,000	5,500	1,300	—	16,500
1962–63	3,500	1,900	1,000	6,400	1,800	—	24,000
Airways Corporations 1960–61	1,100	2,600	2,000	5,700	900	—	33,700
1962–63	1,500	3,500	3,800	8,800	800	—	48,400
Atomic Energy Authority and other Public Boards 1960–61				14,000	5,000	—	30,000
1962–63				17,000	6,000	—	40,000
Armed Forces 1960–61	—	—	—	—	65,000	—	—
1962–63	—	—	—	—	66,000	—	—

[Notes—see overleaf]

K

SUMMARY INFORMATION

Income of *Funded* schemes was approximately £156 million in 1960–61 (£178 million in 1962–63), of which £38 million (£45 million in 1962–63) was contributed by employees.

Expenditure of *Civilian* schemes (excluding Pensions Increase) was £185 million in 1960–61 (£213 million in 1962–63) and of this £127 million in 1960–61 (£147 million in 1962–63) was of *non-funded* schemes.

Pensions (Increase) was £21 million in 1960–61 (£23 million in 1962–63).

Total funds were £1,000 million in 1960–61 (£1,200 million in 1962–63).

NOTES

(1) Figures relate to Great Britain, except where otherwise stated, and to the two financial years 1960–61 and 1962–63; in a few schemes whose accounts do not cover financial years the nearest available years have been used instead. (N.B. for local government the latest available year is 1961–62 and for the Mineworkers' Scheme 1962–63 figures cover a period of eighteen months.)

(2) Employers' contributions include any deficiency payments.

(3) Expenditure includes all expenditure falling on the fund or in non-funded schemes, the actual cost of benefits, etc.; in either case, the major part of this item is for pensions (or pensions and lump sums) on age or ill-health retirement.

(4) Pensions (Increase) refers to amounts expended under the Pensions (Increase) Acts and is therefore additional to what is shown in the expenditure column; analogous arrangements in some nationalized industries are not shown in the table. (N.B. expenditure figures for the Armed Forces *include* the equivalent of Pensions (Increase).)

(5) Amounts of funds are at the end of each year. (N.B. if allowance is made for closed schemes, etc., the total of funds was approximately £1,200 million in 1960–61 and nearly £1,400 million in 1962–63.)

(6) Civil Service includes the Post Office and no account is taken of transactions between the Post Office Fund and the Exchequer.

(7) Transport: information relates only to schemes open to new members (see note in Appendix 2). Comparable information for closed schemes (approximate figures):

	Employees' Contributions	Employers' Contributions	Other Income	Total Income	Expenditure	Fund
1960–61	3,700	9,100	5,700	18,500	12,100	140,000
1962–63	3,600	11,500	6,200	21,300	13,800	150,000

National Insurance Retirement Pensions

A sketch of the history of the provision of pensions by the State has been given in Chapter 1. This note is concerned with developments from 1946 onwards so far as they affect retirement pensions.

National Insurance Act, 1946

The essential elements in this Act were that in return for weekly contributions everybody was entitled to a flat-rate pension on retiring at or after the minimum retiring ages of 65 for men and 60 for women. The following points may be noted:

(a) different rates of contribution applied to different types of contributor, but for the purpose of this study only the rates for employed persons are considered (they in any case form about 90 per cent of the total);

(b) in the case of employed persons, contributions were paid by both employers and employees and there were lower rates of contribution for women than for men;

(c) a man who continued working beyond the age of 65 (or a woman beyond age 60) did not receive a pension until he finally retired from regular employment, or else reached the age of 70 (65 women) whichever was the earlier, but his pension would be increased according to the number of extra contributions paid;

(d) on the other hand, a man who had retired and taken his pension and then took up work again between the ages of 65 and 70 (or 60 and 65 in the case of a woman) had his pension reduced if his earnings were more than a certain minimum;[1] at age 70 (65 for women), however, the full pension was payable whether the man was earning or not;

(e) the pension was 16s a week higher for a married couple than for a single person; however, strictly speaking what happened was that if the wife of a retirement pensioner was over 60 and herself retired she was granted a separate pension of 16s by virtue of his insurance whereas if she was under 60 he claimed an extra 16s for her as a dependant, and this was subject to the usual National Insurance conditions for dependants' benefits.

[1] By 1s a week for each 1s of earnings after the first 20s in the original provisions.

Although the contribution was for all National Insurance benefits, retirement pensions were the most important single item in the benefits accounting for nearly half the total contribution.[1] Contributions were divided between the employed person, the employer and the Exchequer in the following way (excluding the National Health Service and Industrial Injuries contribution):

	Men		Women	
	s	d	s	d
Employee	3	10½	3	0½
Employer	3	8½	2	10½
Exchequer	2	1	1	7
Total	9	8	7	6

Changes 1946–1958

The essential nature of the National Insurance scheme was not changed but many of the details were changed more than once. The original 1946 Act had provided for increases in contributions to be made in 1951, but in fact when 1951 came most retirement pensions and some other benefits were also increased, and at the same time the Exchequer supplements were reduced to about 1/7 of the total contributions.

Further increases in contributions were made in October 1952, June 1955 and February 1958 raising the total contribution by the employed person, employer and Exchequer (again excluding the National Health Service and Industrial Injuries contributions) from the original 9s 8d per week (7s 6d for women) to 16s 10d (14s 0d for women).

Increases were also made in the rates of retirement pension in September 1952, April 1955 and January 1958 so that the original 1948 rate of £1 6s 0d per week for a single person (£2 2s 0d for a married couple) became £2 10s 0d and £4 0s 0d respectively under the 1958 provisions.

There were also changes in the earnings limit and in the rates of extra pension which could be earned by continuing to contribute between the ages of 65 and 70 (or 60 and 65 for women).

National Insurance Acts 1959 and 1960

The 1959 Act made no change in the flat rate of retirement pension but did alter the rates of weekly contribution by providing for a reduction for those who took part in the graduated scheme which was to operate from April 3, 1961. However, before that date a further Act, the National Insurance Act, 1960, was passed which increased both benefits and contributions, except for the graduated part of the scheme. The 1958 rates of contribution and pension may therefore be compared with those in operation from April 1961, as follows:

[1] See, for example, Table V (page 13) of Government Actuary's First Quinquennial Review (HC 1, 1954).

Weekly Contributions (flat rate)

		Employee		Employer		Exchequer		Total	
		s	d	s	d	s	d	s	d
February 1958	Men	7	4½	7	0½	2	5	16	10
	Women	6	2½	5	9½	2	0	14	0
April 1961	Men	7	3½	7	3½	3	8	18	3
('Participating')	Women	6	3½	6	3½	3	2	15	9
April 1961	Men	8	10½	8	6½	3	8	21	1
('Non-Participating' or 'Contracted Out')	Women	7	1½	6	8½	3	2	17	0

Weekly Retirement Pensions (flat rate)

	Single person			Married couple		
	£	s	d	£	s	d
January 1958	2	10	0	4	0	0
April 1961	2	17	6	4	12	6

The effect of the 1959 and 1960 Acts was thus, that those who took part in the graduated scheme (and their employers) paid approximately the same contribution as under the existing scheme in return for increased flat-rate pensions, but those who did not take part paid higher contributions for the same benefit.

National Insurance Act 1963

Apart from changes made in the graduated scheme (discussed below), increases in flat-rate contributions and benefits were made under the National Insurance Act, 1963, resulting in the following new rates:

Weekly contributions (flat rate)

		Employee		Employer		Exchequer		Total	
		s	d	s	d	s	d	s	d
June 1963	Men	8	3½	8	3½	4	2	20	9
('Participating')	Women	7	2½	7	2½	3	7	18	0
June 1963 ('Non-participating')	Men	10	8½	10	8½	4	2	25	7
	Women	8	8½	8	8½	3	7	21	0

Weekly Retirement Pensions (flat rate)

	Single	Married
May 1963	£3 7s 6d	£5 9s 0d

Graduated Scheme

The 1959 Act provided that those who were earning over £9 a week should pay extra contributions in return for increased pensions unless they were in 'non-participating employment'. These extra contributions amounted to 4¼ per cent on earnings between £9 and £15 a week, and the employer was to pay a similar amount, making 8½ per cent in all. The increased pension was 6d a week for every £7 10s 0d of graduated contributions paid by a man (or every £9 paid by a woman). The Act also specified maximum increases to be made both in flat-rate and graduated contributions in 1965, 1970, 1975 and 1980. The 1963 Act increased the range of earnings on which graduated contributions at 4¼ per cent a side were to be paid by making the maximum £18 week instead of £15.

Contracting Out

The 1959 Act and Regulations specify the conditions under which an employment can be treated as non-participating (the procedure is usually referred to more simply as 'contracting out'). To do this the employer must obtain a 'certificate of non-participation' which states the groups of employees covered by it. The Certificates are issued by the Registrar of Non-participating Employments after he has made sure that the employees to be covered by it are entitled to equivalent pension benefits under a superannuation scheme. This means primarily that the following conditions must be fulfilled:

    (i) the superannuation scheme must be financially sound and guarantee the benefits, e.g. by being set up 'by irrevocable trust';

    (ii) the employee must be entitled to a pension for life beginning not later than the age of 65 (or 60 for women);

    (iii) the pension (excluding any part which can be surrendered, commuted or assigned) must be equivalent at least to the maximum which could be earned under the graduated scheme, i.e. 46s 2d a year for each year of non-participating service (38s 6d in the case of women), under the 1959 Act, but increased under the 1963 Act to 69s 7d a year (58s for women).

Equivalent Pension Benefits

A further important feature of contracting out was the obligation imposed on employers to assure equivalent pension benefits for any employee who left after a period of non-participating service. A prominent feature of these arrangements was that the employee was to be assured of a pension at least equivalent to the maximum graduated pension which he could have earned under the graduated scheme; in other words, the assumed basis for calculating equivalent pension benefits was earnings of £15 a week (£18 a week under the 1963 Act), irrespective of the employee's actual earnings during his period of contracted-out service. This equivalent pension could be assured in one of three ways:

    (i) by giving the employee a legally enforceable right to the equivalent pension payable either immediately or not later than age 65 (60 for women). The pension must be payable for life with no provision for surrender, commutation or assignment, and its amount was to be as stated above under (iii) of the conditions for contracting out;

(ii) by means of a transfer to another contracted-out employment with the second employer undertaking to assure equivalent pension rights for the earlier contracted-out period as well as for any periods during which the employee was in his service;

(iii) if neither of these means was employed, by making a 'payment in lieu' to the National Insurance Fund, which would ensure the maximum graduated pension for the employee for the period of his contracted-out service; the amount of this payment was therefore calculated as the difference between the contracted-out rate of contribution and the maximum graduated contribution, i.e. 7s 4d per week (8s 11d for women) under the 1959 Act and 10s 6d per week (12s 4d for women) under the 1963 Act. Since the employer in fact paid the total contribution in this way (i.e. both his own and the employee's share of the graduated contribution) he was given the right to recover up to half the payment in lieu from any return of contributions under the occupational scheme.[1]

Effect on Contributions and Benefits of Graduated Schemes

For simplicity, the contribution rates quoted earlier have excluded the amounts paid to the National Health Service and for Industrial Injuries, both of which are included in the single stamp payment applied weekly to the employee's contribution card,[2] and both of which have also been varied several times since 1948. At present (1964) the employee pays 8d a week for Industrial Injuries and 2s 8½d a week for the National Health Service (5d and 2s 0½d in the case of women), the employer paying different amounts for these items. The total flat-rate contributions including these payments are therefore:

		Employee		Employer		Total	
		s	d	s	d	s	d
'Participating'	Men	11	8	9	8	21	4
	Women	9	8	8	4	18	0
'Non-participating'	Men	14	1	12	1	26	2
	Women	11	2	9	10	21	0

To these must be added in the case of those participating, the graduated contributions:

[1] Further points to note about equivalent pension benefits are that the 1959 Act rates operated for periods of contracted out service from April 6, 1961, but the 1963 Act rates did not come into force until January 5, 1964; that there are elaborate arrangements for determining at what point contracted out employment comes to an end; and that the employee must be notified on a special form by the employer of his preserved pension rights except where a payment in lieu is made.

[2] Graduated contributions are, however, not included in the weekly stamp, but collected under the PAYE income-tax system.

Graduated Contribution	Weekly Earnings	Total Contribution Paid			
		Men		Women	
		Employee	Employer	Employee	Employer
s d		s d	s d	s d	s d
—	£9 or less	11 8	9 8	9 8	8 4
11	£10	12 7	10 7	10 7	9 3
1 10	£11	13 6	11 6	11 6	10 2
2 8	£12	14 4	12 4	12 4	11 0
3 6	£13	15 2	13 2	13 2	11 10
4 4	£14	16 0	14 0	14 0	12 8
5 2	£15	16 10	14 10	14 10	13 6
6 1	£16	17 9	15 9	15 9	14 5
6 11	£17	18 7	16 7	16 7	15 3
7 8	£18 or more	19 4	17 4	17 4	16 0

These are the figures which count so far as the employee or employer are concerned since these are the amounts which they have to pay, but it must always be remembered that a good part of these contributions does not go to finance National Insurance benefits.

The graduated pension will depend on the total of graduated contributions paid, which will in turn depend on the amount of earnings. Thus a man earning £10 a week regularly would have to contribute for over three years before earning an extra 6d a week on his pension. In other words, if he contributed for 45 years and his earnings were constant at £10 a week his extra pension would be 7s 6d a week. The *maximum* pension under the original graduated scheme of 1959, i.e. for 47 years' contributions from 18 to 65 at the highest rate would have been £2 1s 6d, but no pension as big as this would be payable before the year 2008. Under the 1963 Act, a maximum graduated pension of just over £3 a week is possible.

If and when increases are made in the contributions in 1965 and later years, there will be no increases in pensions because the object of the provision is to meet an expected increase in the cost of pensions. Thus greater amounts of contributions will be needed to earn 6d on the pension, and it will still be necessary to contribute for over 3 years on earnings of £10 a week to gain the extra 6d a week.

The Financing of National Insurance Retirement Pensions

Since the contributions paid under the National Insurance Acts cover the whole range of benefits, it is not possible to deal with the financing of retirement benefits in isolation from the financing of National Insurance as a whole. Although there is a National Insurance Fund, whose function is considered below, the present system of financing is on an 'assessment' basis, that is, 'the aim is to achieve a balance between income and expenditure over relatively short periods'. This system dates only from the 1959 Act, however, and before then the contribution rate was assessed, not in terms of what was needed to meet current expenditure, but, broadly on the basis of what was sufficient over a normal working life to meet the cost of benefits; it was, therefore, termed an 'actuarial contribution', although as in the case of public sector notional funds, it was not in fact accumulated in a true fund.

There has, however, always been a third main source of income in the National Insurance scheme, apart from the contributions paid by those in employment, and by employers, namely, the Exchequer. Apart from a specific Exchequer contribution (which has been varied from time to time), the importance of the Exchequer's role lay in the fact that it had to meet the gap in any particular year when total income was insufficient to meet total expenditure. Such a gap might arise chiefly for two reasons: many people become entitled to benefits, and particularly retirement pensions, long before sufficient actuarial contributions had been paid; and the increases paid since 1948 have increased immediate costs and liabilities far more than the increased revenue from contributions could meet. The first point was explicitly recognized in the Beveridge Report which recommended reducing part of the heavy liability for pensions by introducing them gradually over a period of years; this proposal was rejected by the Government in introducing the 1946 Act. The second point has, however, largely been a consequence of inflation, although some of the more recent increases in pensions and other benefits have been designed to do more than merely keep pace with the cost of living.

National Insurance Funds

The 1946 Act established a National Insurance Fund and a National Insurance (Reserve) Fund. The National Insurance Fund is not a fund in the sense in which the term is used in relation to occupational pension schemes. It is rather an account showing the current income and expenditure of the scheme; any surplus of income over expenditure in a particular year is invested and securities corresponding to the amount of these accumulated balances are held by the National Debt Commissioners, and total rather less than £300 million. The Reserve Fund, also invested for the most part in gilt-edged securities, consists mainly of assets inherited from the pre-1948 unemployment insurance and similar schemes; it now stands at £1,168 million (at cost price of securities). Its purpose is to serve as an emergency reserve (e.g. it might be useful if there were a sudden sharp rise in unemployment), and meanwhile the interest on its investments is used as an additional source of income for the National Insurance scheme. But in relation to the large sums involved in current National Insurance transactions, neither the accumulated £300 million of the National Insurance Fund nor the total of investment income from these investments and those of the Reserve Fund makes or is intended to make much contribution to the financing of the scheme.

The position may be illustrated from the figures on page 298 taken from the Government Actuary's Interim Reports for the financial years 1961–62 and 1962–63:[1]

The heavy cost of retirement pensions has always been a main feature of the accounts of the scheme. In the first full year (1949–50) they accounted for nearly two-thirds of total expenditure, and have maintained roughly

[1] H.C. 246, 1962–63, H.M.S.O. 1963; H.C. 173, 1963–64, H.M.S.O. 1964.

K*

	£ Millions	
	1961–62	1962–63
National Insurance (Reserve) Fund at March 31	1,168	1,168
National Insurance Fund	278	268

Income

(1) Contributions	915	952
(2) Exchequer Supplement to Contributions	187	189
(3) Interest on Investments	53	54
Total	1,155	1,195

Expenditure
(1) Benefits

(a) retirement pensions	784		807	
(b) other benefits	302		343	
	—	1,086	—	1,150
(2) Cost of administration		43		48
(3) Other		13		10
Total		1,142		1,208

that proportion ever since. Largely because of this heavy cost, total expenditure began to exceed income in 1958–59, and it was estimated that this deficit would, on the basis of the scheme as it then was, have reached an annual figure of about £400 million in twenty years' time.[1] The situation, although not necessarily the extent of it, was inherent in both the method of financing and in the decision which had been taken on the qualifications for the original and the increased benefits; at some point either the Exchequer, that is, the taxpayer, would have to increase its share of the cost or contributions would have to be increased far beyond the strict actuarial contribution.

Effect of the Graduated Pension Scheme on Financing

In effect, the graduated scheme changed the first situation, that of an increasing cost falling on the Exchequer, into the second, with the rising cost of benefits being met by increased income from contributions. It is true that the extra graduated contributions qualify for increased pensions, but, unlike the situation with the flat-rate scheme, there is a fixed ratio between the amount of contributions paid and the ultimate amount of pension, so that although the income from contributions is made available immediately, the cost of graduated pensions will not become heavy for many years, and when it does, there should be an increased yield from contributions to meet it. In the words of the 1958 White Paper (paragraph 31): 'in a buoyant and expanding economy contributions related to earnings will expand, and so make additional resources available to meet the growing pensions bill'. In the first year of the graduated scheme (1961–62)

[1] See *Provision for Old Age*, Cmnd. 538, 1958, para. 13.

graduated contributions of £147 million were paid (about 16 per cent of the total of contributions) and this sum was almost exactly equal to the deficit which would have occurred on the flat-rate scheme as it existed before the 1959 Act, and which would therefore have had to be met by the Exchequer.

Perhaps the best way of conveying the changed financial picture is to compare the projected situation as it would have been under the pre-1959 Act scheme (column (1) in the following table); as it was proposed in the 1958 White Paper (column (2)); and as it was estimated as a result of the 1963 proposals (column (3)).[1]

Estimated National Insurance Income and Expenditure
(£ millions)

	1971–72			1981–82		
	(1)	(2)	(3)	(1)	(2)	(3)
Income						
Contributions {graduated	—	{1,015	344	—	{1,219	504
{flat-rate	714		1,044	723		1,196
Exchequer Supplements	126	170	245	128	170	280
Interest	50	50	53	50	50	53
Total Income	890	1,235	1,686	901	1,439	2,033
Expenditure						
Retirement {graduated	—	{878	15	—	{1,053	73
pensions {flat-rate	862		1,173	990		1,356
Other benefits	311	{349	432	306	{344	432
Administration	33		50	33		50
	1,206	1,227	1,670	1,329	1,397	1,911
Excess of income over expenditure (+) or of expenditure over income (−)	−316	+ 8	+ 16	−428	+ 42	+122

The table demonstrates how even after twenty years the cost of graduated pensions is likely to form only a modest part of the total cost of retirement pensions, although the Government Actuary has pointed out (in his report on the 1963 Bill) that ultimately it will form a good part of that cost. Also demonstrated in the table is the large annual deficit which was in prospect on the pre-1959 Act flat-rate scheme, so that by 1981–82 the cost of retirement pensions alone would have exceeded total income, and the Exchequer would have had to find £428 million in addition to the £128 million supplement under the scheme; total Exchequer payments would therefore have gone to meet about 40 per cent of the expenditure.

If it is misleading to talk of a 'fund' in relation to National Insurance,

[1] See Cmnd. 538, 1958, para. 13, and Appendix II, and Cmnd. 1935, 1963, Appendix Table I and II.

it is probably almost as misleading to talk of 'insurance'; since the scheme 'is compulsory and there is no adjustment of premiums to risk; it is, in fact, a social service financed by a poll-tax, by an indirect tax on employers and by general taxation levied by the Government'.[1] If this is the position, the main significance of the 1959 Act in terms of the financing of National Insurance lies in the limitation it imposed on the obligations of the third party, that is the general tax-payer, and correspondingly, in the increased obligations it put on the other two parties, the contributors, for meeting the annual cost of the scheme.

[1] Alan T. Peacock, *The Economics of National Insurance*, Hodge, 1952, p. 42.

The History and Purpose of Tax Reliefs

Chapter 7 considered some of the ways in which tax law and practice affect the administration of superannuation schemes. It is the purpose of this Appendix to indicate how the present situation has arisen and to draw attention to the controversy which surrounds the reasons for tax reliefs for pension schemes.

The starting-point is a tax relief which seems to have little connexion with the provision of pensions. It has, however, influenced later developments and is still part of the tax law affecting schemes. This is the tax relief on premiums paid for life assurance, which has existed in some form for most of the time since the Income Tax Act of 1799, and now, broadly speaking, means that a man who insures his own (or his wife's) life has two-fifths of the premiums allowed for income tax purposes in much the same way as a personal allowance. Legislation in 1916 placed certain restrictions on these reliefs, but continued to allow relief on policies which were effected: 'In connexion with any superannuation or bona fide pension scheme for the benefit of the employees of any employer, or of persons engaged in a particular profession, vocation, trade or business.'[1]

The significant point about this provision is that the legislation did not define what constituted a superannuation or bona fide pension scheme, and this was therefore left to be determined by the tax authorities. This may therefore be regarded as the first point at which the Inland Revenue Department began to exercise detailed surveillance over pension schemes. The 1916 legislation was, however, limited in scope and probably at the time did not seem of great importance for the future. But a further stage was reached with the Finance Act of 1921.

THE 1921 LEGISLATION

First, there are two preliminary points to be mentioned. One is that the 1921 legislation was the first specifically designed to deal with the taxation position of pension funds. Secondly, certain features of pension scheme arrangements come within the scope of the laws relating generally to income tax; in particular, the payment of a pension by an employer out

---

[1] Finance Act, 1916, s. 36. For the history of these reliefs see the Report of the Committee on the Taxation Treatment of Provisions for Retirement (Millard Tucker Report), Cmd. 9063, H.M.S.O., 1954, especially paras. 20–31 and 61; also the note by Tony Lynes in Richard M. Titmuss, *Income Distribution and Social Change*, George Allen & Unwin, 1962, pp. 212–16.

of the resources of the business or the regular payment of contributions to a pension fund are treated as business expenses.

The 1921 legislation, following a recommendation of the Royal Commission on the Income Tax in 1920, laid down that under certain conditions a pension fund could be approved by the Board of Inland Revenue and gain a number of advantages, the chief of them being that ordinary contributions made by an employee could qualify for expenses relief and that no income tax would be payable on the income of the fund from investments. No reasons were given by the Royal Commission for this recommendation, and this has caused some difficulty to later investigators. The point will be considered later in this Appendix, and it is sufficient to note here that there seem to be two elements in present government policy on this question: the desire to encourage provision for retirement, at least in certain ways and within certain limits, and the element of equity, the desire to avoid taxing twice what is in some sense the same income.[1]

The main effect of the 1921 legislation was that it provided an incentive for an employer who wished to establish a pension scheme to frame it in such a way that it would conform to the requirements of the Inland Revenue. It was in this way that taxation affected the provision for superannuation, and also, to the extent that employers were positively encouraged to set up funds by the 1921 Act, led to the growth and development of pension schemes. The latter point must not, however, be exaggerated; as was shown in Appendix 1, there had been a steady growth of schemes by 1936, but not all of this growth was due to the 1921 Act. Perhaps it would be nearer the truth to say that the taxation position after 1921 made it easier in financial terms for those employers who wished to set up pension funds to do so.

TAX-FREE LUMP SUMS AND THE 1947 ACT

The main principle on which tax reliefs are based is that ultimately some tax will be paid, since the pension will be subject to tax in the normal way. But at the time of the 1921 legislation two important schemes, those for the Civil Service and for teachers, provided, in addition to a taxable pension, a lump sum on retirement which under general income tax law was not taxable. The 1921 Act was quite consistent in providing that one condition which a superannuation fund must satisfy to gain approval was that its sole object was to provide pensions. Clearly neither the civil service nor the teachers' scheme would have satisfied this condition but, as at that date they were non-contributory and not funded, the point was of little practical importance and no specific reference was made to public service schemes in the 1921 Act. This still left open the position of those employees, such as poor law officers under the 1896 Act, who were paying contributions but were not in a funded scheme. This, and the fact that in 1922 the teachers' scheme became contributory, may have led to a reconsideration of the problem.

---

[1] See, for example, the speech of the Economic Secretary to the Treasury, in an adjournment debate on 'Pension Schemes (Treasury Control)', January 24, 1962 (H.C. Deb., 652, col. 372).

At all events the Finance Act of 1922 (section 31) made specific provision for the exemption from tax of compulsory contributions by employees who could receive superannuation payments 'in pursuance of any public general Act of Parliament'. This distinction between 'statutory superannuation schemes' and others at once produced an anomaly in the taxation treatment of pension schemes. No doubt there were good practical reasons for making such a distinction; clearly, a scheme set up under Act of Parliament was both more susceptible to scrutiny by the Inland Revenue in advance than a private scheme and less in danger of being a vehicle of tax avoidance. It is also true that the question of tax free lump sums may not have seemed of great importance at that time. But it is as well to note that the 1922 Act did what the 1921 Act had not done; that is, it gave statutory sanction to tax concessions on contributions which might ultimately emerge in the form of a tax-free benefit. This has had important consequences for the subsequent history of tax reliefs.

Tax-free lump sums came into prominence as the level of taxation rose. For example, an employer could put aside money regularly to provide for a future retirement benefit of his employees, or could simply promise as part of the terms of employment to pay such a benefit on retirement, without requiring any contributions to be made by the employee; the payments by the employer in either case would rank for expenses relief. But the benefit might take the form of a lump sum which would be tax-free as far as the recipient was concerned. To those who were subject to surtax, arrangements on these lines could be a very convenient means of avoiding the payment of heavy sums in taxation.[1] Such 'schemes' were not really concerned with superannuation at all and the only point of mentioning them here is that they led, in the interests of equity and because of the considerable loss of revenue arising from them, to further legislation in 1947 which, although its main purpose was to check an abuse of the general income tax law, led in practice to further intervention and surveillance by the Inland Revenue of pension schemes.

This arose primarily because the Finance Act, 1947, provided that payments made by an employer in the type of case mentioned above should be treated as income of the employee, except where the arrangements were genuinely intended to provide reasonable superannuation benefits and were not merely a device to avoid paying tax. To qualify for this exemption, schemes had to be approved by the Board of Inland Revenue who were thus again in the position of determining whether in detail a scheme conformed with the particular conditions of approval. The statutory conditions governing the taxation position of the approval of such schemes are now contained in section 388 of the Income Tax Act, 1952; these schemes are therefore frequently referred to as 'Section 388' schemes to distinguish them from the 'Section 379' schemes approved under the earlier arrangements. It is important, however, to make quite clear that the abuses which the 1947 legislation was designed to check arose from provisions of the general income tax law and that the position might have developed very differently if, for example, lump sums had been taxable. It should also be noted that schemes which were in operation before April 6, 1944, are not

[1] See Millard Tucker Report, para. 89, for an example of this.

required to be approved, provided that the main benefit is a pension for life, and such schemes can even continue to receive new members.

APPROVAL UNDER SECTION 379

Thus the need to secure approval has become a major factor in the involvement of pension schemes with tax matters. For 'Section 379' schemes (i.e. those coming within the terms of the original 1921 Act provisions now incorporated in Section 379 of the Income Tax Act, 1952), the basic conditions for approval are laid down partly in the Act and partly in Regulations. The main conditions are that there should be a fund set up under trust (indeed for taxation purposes it is the approval of 'funds' which is in question rather than schemes); that the fund should be concerned only with providing pensions and not also, for example, lump sums; that the employer should contribute to the fund; and that both employers and employees should recognize the fund. One may sum this up by saying that the tax reliefs are designed only for genuine pension schemes which are funded. But in two ways the position was likely to lead to complications: first, there was the difficulty of establishing what was a genuine pension scheme; secondly, it was part of the original arrangements and indeed a necessary part of providing flexibility to meet a wide variety of cases, that the Board of Inland Revenue could approve a fund in whole or in part even if it did not entirely meet the basic conditions, for example, if it did not only provide pensions. A further important factor was added by the Regulations which provided that in the first place any alteration in the 'rules, constitution, objects, or conditions of the fund' was to be notified to the Inland Revenue Inspector of Taxes and, secondly, that the Commissioners might withdraw their approval of a fund if they thought the facts warranted it.[1]

The effect of all this was to give the Commissioners very wide powers of inquiring into those funds which were submitted for their approval and of determining what should or should not be approvable. This led to the elaboration of working rules dealing with almost every conceivable type of provision which might be found in schemes, and to secure full approval these rules had to be followed. Even so, this is not now the only method by which schemes can get tax relief, and rather different conditions apply to what have come to be known as Section 388 schemes.

SECTION 388 SCHEMES

The point was made in Chapter 2 that private sector pension schemes could be divided into those which were set up under trust deeds with separate, self-administered funds and those where the benefits were insured with an insurance company, in which case the policy or policies agreed between the firm and the insurance company formed the basis of the scheme instead of a trust deed.[2] The position of these latter schemes for taxation purposes

[1] S.R. & O. 1921, No. 1699, Regs. 2 and 3.
[2] In some cases, benefits are assured with an insurance company, even though a fund has been established.

is, generally speaking, that contributions by employees only qualify for life assurance relief and there is no specific tax relief on the investment income of the insurance companies, although they do secure some relief under the general tax laws. Before the 1947 legislation, control of contributory insured schemes was exercised by the Inland Revenue through the fact that this life assurance relief was restricted by the 1916 legislation, but this control did not extend to non-contributory schemes.

The method of approval introduced by the 1947 Act affected chiefly insured schemes but it differed in significant manner from that which was already in being for funds coming under the earlier legislation. The main difference is that whereas full approval of a fund under the 1921 legislation could only be secured by a fund providing pensions (and not pensions together with lump sums), approval under the 1947 legislation was possible for schemes whose main benefit was a pension but which also provided lump sums, provided that the lump sum did not constitute more than one-quarter of the total benefit. Apart from this main condition, approval under Section 388 (as it now is) was intended to be automatic if the scheme conformed to six other specified conditions, and was at the discretion of the Board if any of the conditions was not completely fulfilled. In particular the main benefit was to be payable only on retirement at a specified age (although exceptions were permitted, e.g. for retirement at an earlier age because of ill-health), and the total benefits of the scheme were to be reasonably comparable with those of statutory superannuation schemes.

It follows that after 1947 any scheme which did not gain approval by one of the two methods which were then open, was, from the point of view of taxation, put at a great disadvantage. As one author puts it, 'taxation is so important that it is no overstatement to say that unless reasonable taxation privileges are obtained, a scheme may be quite impracticable'.[1] Here then is the great importance of the 1947 legislation, which for the first time ensured that all pension schemes, practically speaking, should come under the detailed scrutiny of the Board of Inland Revenue.

It is perhaps not surprising, in view of the piecemeal way in which taxation law and practice have developed in this field, that the 1947 legislation led to certain anomalies. The most important of these was certainly the fact that there could be two separate ways in which schemes might be approved, but corresponding to this was the different consequences which followed from each method of approval. The first point was due in part to the differences in types of schemes which had developed, but is also due to the different intentions of the 1921 and the 1947 legislative provisions, the first concessive, the second restrictive. But the second point illustrates the difficulties of trying to adapt to a changing situation rather than making a fresh start. For whereas Section 379 approval carried with it relief for both the employer's and the employee's contributions and relief on the investment income of the fund, an employee in a scheme approved under Section 388 was still in the position of being able to claim only life assurance relief. On its investment income a Section 388 scheme was liable to tax, as indeed was all the investment income of insurance companies;

[1] Gordon A. Hosking, *Pension Schemes and Retirement Benefits*, Sweet & Maxwell, 2nd ed. 1960, p. 12.

this led to the position that a Section 379 fund could gain exemption from tax if it made its own investments, but not if it used the money of the fund to buy deferred annuities through an insurance company. Before considering what action was taken to deal with these anomalies, a further complicating point must be noted.

For simplicity, 1921 Act (i.e. Section 379) funds have been discussed chiefly in terms of full approval, but from the start the Board of Inland Revenue have had the power to approve a fund in part if it did not meet all the conditions of full approval. Partial approval under Section 379 is chiefly of importance in the case of schemes where the main benefit is not simply a pension but, as in many public sector schemes, a combination of pension and a lump sum; provided that the lump sum does not exceed the normal limit of public service schemes, that is approximately one-quarter of the total benefit, that part of the scheme would be approved which provided pensions. Some of the complications of this situation are described later.

THE MILLARD TUCKER REPORT AND THE FINANCE ACT, 1956

In 1950 the Millard Tucker Committee was appointed to review the law on the subject. They found the complexity and inconsistencies particularly striking, and, among other things, put forward recommendations designed to remove the inconsistency in treatment between self-administered funds approved under Section 379 and funds and schemes based on insurance policies, by having only one channel of approval under which, for all approved schemes whether insured or not, there would be full 'expenses relief' on employees' contributions, investment income would be free of tax, and lump sums, in addition to pensions, would be permissible. They also endorsed the general principle on which taxation reliefs were based, that is, that the 'build-up' should be exempt from taxation but the benefits should be taxed, but were then faced with the difficulty that by long tradition, dating as far back as 1909 in the case of the Civil Service, lump sums had been untaxed. The Committee thought that they should remain untaxed, even though this conflicted with the principle which they had endorsed, but for new schemes they wanted an upper limit of £10,000. On the other hand the majority of the Royal Commission on the Taxation of Profits and Income, in their final report of 1955, considered that the £10,000 limit should apply to existing schemes and that for new entrants to schemes the maximum should be £2,000. A minority of the Commission wanted to go further and abolish lump sums altogether for future entrants to schemes. These conflicting recommendations are no doubt one of the reasons why, for the moment at least, the problem has been shelved. When, in 1956, legislation was introduced, in what became the Finance Act, 1956, to carry out some of the recommendations of the Millard Tucker Report, the main point covered, so far as employee pension schemes were concerned, was the position of the funds of insurance companies transacting pension business.

It will be evident from what has already been said that, because of the way in which pension schemes have developed and tax law and practice have been adapted to the changing development, schemes in which the benefits were assured by means of policies with insurance companies were at a disadvantage compared with self-administered fund schemes in that the investment income of the former was, and that of the latter was not, subject to tax. The point was most obvious in relation to schemes set up under a trust deed, since of two schemes in most respects similar, one might be relieved of tax on its investment income and the other having re-insured its income would gain no advantage, although both might be Section 379 schemes. The Finance Act, 1956, put all Section 379 schemes in the same position by exempting from tax part of the annuity funds of life assurance companies, that is to the extent that they represented invested premiums arising from deferred annuity business either for the self-employed or for Section 379 funds.

This removed one obvious anomaly, but did not of course go anything like as far as the Millard Tucker Report had recommended. Nor is it difficult to see the dilemma with which the government were faced; and once again the problem centres on lump sums. Short of making a clean sweep and abolishing the tax-free privilege of lump sums, perhaps in the way advocated by the minority of the Royal Commission, the government would have found it difficult not to accept the logic of the Millard Tucker recommendations and to have permitted Section 379 funds to pay lump sums in the same way as Section 388 if there was to be only one channel of approval. But to do so would have added to the already considerable cost of tax reliefs to pension schemes; moreover, the 1956 Act was already making a further concession costing £7 million, but rising to an estimated £30–£50 million, and one which was generally admitted to be fair, to enable the self-employed and employed people not in a pension scheme to get relief on premiums paid to provide a deferred annuity on retirement.

However, one consequence of making all Section 379 investment income free of tax must be mentioned: life offices were able to quote lower premiums for this type of business than for similar policies for schemes approved under Section 388. As a result there was a certain amount of re-drawing of Section 388 schemes so that they could be re-approved under Section 379 and take advantage of the better terms; and this in turn brought extra work to the life offices and the Inland Revenue. It is not easy to say how much of this conversion work took place, but there is no doubt of the irritation felt by insurance people at what they regarded as unnecessary work. Among recent and comparatively mild comments is the following: 'The work involved in carrying out this conversion operation is still going on, five years later. . . . While this improvement did result in the more economical provision of retirement benefits, it did absorb the time and energy of many people in pension business who were thereby prevented from increasing the numbers covered by private Pension Schemes.'[1] This result was not entirely unforeseen. A number of M.P.s connected with insurance companies raised the matter in the debates on the 1956 Bill, but the government spokesman (Mr Henry Brooke) argued that it would be unwise for employers to be too anxious to change from Section 388 to Section 379 in view of the uncertainty about the future of the law relating

[1] C. W. T. Philpot, *Pensions in Britain, 1962*, Metropolitan Pensions Association Limited, p. 12.

to pension schemes; he did not think that in any case there would be much switching in view of the difficulty and expense of changing schemes. That in spite of this, many employers did decide to change is an interesting commentary on the power of taxation provisions to influence pension schemes, a power which seemingly surprised even the Inland Revenue Department.

'TOP-HAT' SCHEMES

As was indicated in Chapter 7, the level of benefits in both public and private sector schemes is likely to be held in check because of the taxation position. This arises because indirectly in the case of Section 379 schemes and directly in the case of Section 388, the level of benefits in private schemes is limited to what is reasonably comparable with 'statutory superannuation schemes'. Section 388 specifically lays down this criterion both in relation to the proportion of benefits which is in pension form and to the aggregate value of all benefits. In spite of this, there is one important way in which the upper limit of benefits is still left open.

Under the 1921 Act, it will be remembered, one of the essential conditions to be fulfilled by a fund was that it should have as its sole purpose the provision of pensions. But there can be few if any contributory funds which do not provide that, in certain circumstances, the employee should receive a return of his contributions. A contributory fund therefore does not have as its sole purpose the provision of pensions and in these circumstances it is in the Board of Inland Revenue's discretion whether to approve the whole or part of the fund, and to attach conditions to such approval. In fact one important condition attached to approval is that the pension should not exceed £3,000 per annum (£2,000 before April 1961). This seems effectively to limit pension schemes so that nobody earning more than £4,500 a year can get a maximum, i.e. two-thirds pension. However, this is not the case, because no monetary limit is imposed for approval under Section 388, but only the two-thirds limit. It is therefore possible for a man earning, say, £18,000 a year to belong to a second pension scheme, approved under Section 388 and providing him with the 'balance' of his pension of £6,000 a year together with a lump sum of £27,000 the whole being equivalent to a two-thirds pension of £12,000, with one-quarter taken in the form of a lump sum.

Schemes of this kind have come to be known as 'Top-Hat'; they are non-contributory (because if the employee contributed he would get only life assurance relief for income tax purposes and no relief for surtax purposes), usually additional to the employers' normal staff scheme, and often (unlike the example quoted above) of an amount determined not according to a precise formula but according to the amount of premium paid. For suppose that in the example the employee concerned had agreed to take a salary not of £18,000 a year but of £17,000 and that the employer had agreed to apply £1,000 a year towards his retirement benefits. The employee would be comparatively little worse off in terms of current remuneration because of the high rate of tax on incomes of that level; the employer would not suffer, and at retirement the employee could enjoy not only a good pension but a large tax-free lump sum. It is this element of deferred remuneration which has attracted most attention to 'Top-Hat' schemes, coupled with the realization that, admittedly in exceptional cases, very large sums indeed could be gained on retirement; even ten years ago the Millard Tucker Committee were told of cases in which the tax-free lump sum might be as much as £40,000. Of course, senior employees earning, say, £15,000 a year or more are rare; but even at lower levels there is considerable advantage to be gained in tax reliefs, even if not quite to the same extent as before the recent reduction in liability for surtax. It may be, as a recent writer has said,[1] that 'while some of the attraction has been taken out of Top-Hat schemes if regarded as devices whereby executives could defer compensation to retirement age, they will still retain their popularity, especially as there is a stronger trend towards the provision of these benefits without salary sacrifice'.

SOME EXAMPLES OF COMPLICATION IN THE TAX LAWS

Widows' Pensions

Briefly, a *compulsory* contribution by an employee for a pension for his widow (or his children after his death) attracts, under the Income Tax Acts, a similar relief as the payment of premiums for life assurance, that is, there is, within certain limits, a relief of tax paid. When these provisions were introduced (in part they date back to 1853), widows' pensions did not form part of pension schemes and the object was to cater for certain specific funds providing benefits for widows (and orphans). But now schemes often provide widows' pensions and such provision is allowed by the Inland Revenue for the purposes of approval under the specific legislation relating to schemes.

Since approval by the Inland Revenue (at least for funded Section 379 schemes) carries with it 'expenses relief' for contributions, and those contributions do not necessarily have to be compulsory, it follows that there may be two different ways of getting tax relief, and two different kinds of relief, according to whether the contributions are compulsory or voluntary. But what happens if the contributions to the approved fund are compulsory? Here the law steps in and says that 'expenses relief' can only be given on contributions which do not qualify for the life assurance relief. It seems, then, that we are left with the position that compulsory contributions can only get life assurance relief, whereas voluntary contributions may secure expenses relief.

This is just the kind of odd situation which naturally arises when fresh legislation is superimposed on existing and when unforeseen developments take place. But this is not quite the end of the story: in the words of the Millard Tucker Report (para. 58): 'In practice, however, the whole contribution is given expenses relief, unless the part relating to widows' and children's benefits exceeds a quarter of the whole.' Thus, in addition to what ought to happen those who run pension funds need also to know what does happen.

An example of how expert knowledge of the tax situation in relation to widows' pensions may influence practical proposals may be found in the

[1] C. W. T. Philpot, op. cit. p. 12. Cf. also Richard Titmuss, op. cit. pp. 148–50.

report from the Scottish Education Department on *Pensions for Teachers'
Widows* (H.M.S.O. Edinburgh, 1962). The problem was how to find a
method of financing widows' pensions which would be acceptable both to
teachers and the local education authorities (and, indeed, to the government as well). One suggestion would have taken maximum advantage of
tax reliefs in order to reduce the net contribution required, but would have
led to the additional complication of instituting a true and not a notional
fund simply to provide widows' pensions (see Report, paras, 38–44).

Refunds of Contributions under the Local Government Scheme

The general position of refunds of contributions for Section 379 funds is
that tax must be paid on them. This is in accordance with the general
principle, but, no doubt for administrative convenience, a special rate of
tax is charged at one-quarter of the standard rate. This was the position
in local government before the introduction of the 1953 Act, and still
applies to those who have chosen to remain subject to the 1937 Act
provisions.

The introduction of lump sums in 1954 (under the 1953 Act) has complicated the position in the following way. Tax reliefs for contributions so
far as they relate to the provision of pensions are given under Section 379,
but so far as they relate to the provision of lump sums, under the specific
provisions for statutory schemes. It is, however, a feature of the latter
that when contributions are returned the tax payable is assessed not at the
conventional rate (one-quarter standard rate) but according to the tax
position of the employee in the individual years in which he paid the
contributions. This is no doubt fairer than charging a fixed rate under
which some people pay less and some more tax than the relief which they
have received; but it does mean that extra work is created, particularly
where the contributions have been paid over a number of years.

There are further complications for those who were in service before the
1953 Act came into force and who then changed over to the 1953 provisions.
Their contributions are then split into three:

(*a*) pre-1953 Act, taxed at one-quarter of the standard rate;
(*b*) post-1953 Act, related to pensions (conventionally taken at 92½ per
cent of a man's contribution and 85 per cent of a woman's), taxed
at one-quarter of the standard rate;
(*c*) post-1953 Act, related to lump sums, i.e. the remaining 7½ per cent
or 15 per cent taxed according to H.M. Inspector of Taxes' assessment.

Thus there are three main groups of contributors:

(i) 1937 Act, refunds taxed at one-quarter standard rate;
(ii) 1937 Act, changing to 1953 Act, as above;
(iii) 1953 Act, refunds taxed on the split basis.

Thus those responsible for running local government funds need to
be very careful when questions of refunding contributions arise.

This does not exhaust the possibilities even in the single instance of a
return of contributions under the local government scheme. Nothing, for
example, has been said about the return of contributions paid to a local

Act fund, or to the position about payments in lieu of contributions under the National Insurance Act, 1959. Then there are such comparatively abstruse matters as the position of a return of contributions to an employee for whom a transfer value had been paid in the past by a statutory but non-funded scheme, or the position of an employee who repays contributions which had been returned to him, when he again takes up local authority employment.

THE REASON FOR TAX RELIEFS

A general question of great importance is raised by the tax treatment of pension schemes. Since the tax reliefs granted to these schemes are also capable of being used as a convenient means of paying less tax than would otherwise be the case, doubts have been raised about the fairness of the system of tax reliefs. Naturally these doubts are particularly concentrated on the question of tax-free lump sums. This is one reason why the Millard Tucker Committee wanted to limit the amount of these benefits and not merely their proportion to the total. As they put it: 'The benefits will have been provided free of tax out of an untaxed build-up (so far as contributions are concerned) and the amount of the build-up is bound to have been substantial. Consequently the tax foregone by the Revenue will have been considerable. We do not think it either reasonable or fair to the general body of taxpayers that such large lump sum benefits should be tax-free.'[1] The majority of the Royal Commission on the Taxation of Profits and Income also agreed that it was impossible to recommend the continuance of the tax reliefs and at the same time to approve schemes which allowed a good part of that relief to be converted into a tax-free capital sum; and the Memorandum of Dissent (signed by Mr George Woodcock, Mr H. L. Bullock and Mr Nicholas Kaldor) went to the further stage of saying 'the only satisfactory way of dealing with a concession that is admitted to be anomalous is to abolish it altogether'.[2]

But even if there were not the anomaly of tax-free lump sums, some question might still be raised about the purpose of tax reliefs. Admitting that it can be argued that it is only fair and reasonable that income should only be taxed once, the fact that this principle is not applied uniformly to all forms of savings has the effect of putting savings for retirement through approved pension schemes in a more favourable tax position. It is also true that because tax is deferred and therefore ultimately paid on a generally lower income, there may be a net reduction in the total amount of tax collected. A difficulty in considering this point is that it is not entirely clear what the motive was behind the introduction of the original tax reliefs in 1921.

Beyond the recommendation by the Royal Commission of 1920, there seems to have been little discussion of the question.[3] The Millard Tucker

[1] Cmd. 9063, para. 161.

[2] See Final Report, Cmd. 9474, 1955, paras. 72 and 73, and Memorandum of Dissent, para. 199.

[3] The Clause dealing with these tax reliefs was introduced at a late stage of the discussions on the Finance Bill, 1921, and no debate took place on it. (See H.C. Deb., July 18, 1921, col. 1848.)

Committee suggested (para. 338) that the Royal Commission may have had in mind that the reliefs would chiefly benefit 'only the less well paid'. If this is true, it suggests that one of the motives behind the acceptance of the Royal Commission's recommendation by the government of the day may have been a desire to encourage the provision of occupational pension schemes for such employees as a means ultimately of relieving the cost of Old Age Pensions.

The main point was taken up by the Royal Commission on the Taxation of Profits and Income who stated 'there is a difference between saving in general and saving that is ascertainably related to the object of obtaining for the saver and his dependants a reasonable provision in the case of retirement, death or emergency'.[1] This emphasis on the social desirability of encouraging one distinct form of saving has also been stressed by government spokesmen,[2] but no very precise reasons for singling out this particular form of it are generally advanced. Rather it has become part of the established system of taxation in much the same way as life assurance relief. On the analogy of occupational pension schemes, too, contributions to National Insurance, so far as they relate to the long-term benefits such as retirement pensions receive tax reliefs; a deduction (at present of £22 irrespective of whether contributions are being paid to the graduated scheme or not) is made from the contributor's income for tax purposes.

The question of saving has another aspect; granted that contributions to a pension fund represent compulsory savings, do they even so lead to additional savings? For it might be true of any individual contributor, as the Royal Commission said,[3] that: 'his net disinvestment for the year is as great as the amount of the premium that he has paid'. They considered whether this fact might not mean that the whole system was wrong but concluded: 'On the whole we are content to accept the presumption that those expenditures upon which the existing allowances depend do represent a true saving of income . . . (and these allowances) can amount to an encouragement of genuine saving, even though in certain cases they may be claimed by persons who have made no such saving'. They therefore concluded that superannuation relief was 'unexceptionable' and 'its justi-fication seems to us to lie in the fact that the man whose income is derived from his personal earnings must in effect regard some provision for his retirement and the care of his dependants as a charge upon those earnings'.

Thus any attempt to establish the precise reasons for these tax reliefs (as opposed to the general proposition that income should not be taxed twice) is rather inconclusive. And this is very largely because, as long as some reasonable control is exercised over them, most people would accept the position. It may be argued that there is some injustice in the present system to the extent that some tax-payers have to pay more to balance the reliefs granted to those who are fortunate enough to be in approved schemes. But this argument really amounts to a plea for a proper system of reasonable pension provision for everybody, and to some extent the

[1] Cmd. 9474, para. 63.
[2] E.g. Mr Anthony Barber (then Economic Secretary to the Treasury), H.C. Deb., January 24, 1962, col. 372.
[3] Cmd. 9474, paras. 65, 66 and 70.

tax position is an accidental factor. Indeed it might not have been of any great importance nor have led to this amount of attention if it had not been for the size of tax reliefs, and this in turn arises both from the growth in the number of schemes and from the general increase in the level of taxation. The factors which made 'Top-Hat' schemes so attractive also ensured that attention would be drawn to the implications of tax reliefs for pension schemes.

THE COST OF TAX RELIEFS

Reference has been made elsewhere to the survey by the Institute of Actuaries and the Faculty of Actuaries on *The Growth of Pension Rights and their Impact on the National Economy*. The authors in the course of the survey made what was perhaps the first comprehensive attempt to assess such factors as the contribution of pension funds to the national savings. The subject is complicated by many factors, not least among them being the effect of tax reliefs. Even to estimate the amount of tax reliefs on employers' and employees' contributions and on the interest income of funds is no easy task because of such factors as the different reliefs for employees' contributions on Section 379 and Section 388 schemes, and the different rates of tax payable by those who are liable to income tax. The results, expressed in terms of the 1953–54 situation showed that estimated tax reliefs amounted to £84 million; to some extent this figure was offset by, for example, the tax paid on pensions, so that the final estimate amounted to £81 million.[1] This figure related only to funded pension schemes and compared with gross savings on these schemes (i.e. the excess of income over expenditure in the year) of £170 million. If the tax reliefs on contributions to unfunded schemes are included the total reliefs may have been in the region of £100 million.[2] No comparable figures in the same amount of detail have been estimated for more recent years, but figures supplied by the Inland Revenue indicate that the £100 million of 1953–54 may have grown to about £160 million by 1958–59 and to about £235 million by 1961–62.

One interesting point suggested by these figures is what the effect would be of removing these reliefs. The Exchequer would benefit by the exact amount of the reliefs only on the unlikely assumption that the money would be laid out in exactly the same way as at present. But, to take only one example, if there were no Section 379 reliefs it seems certain that more would be spent on endowment assurances and other forms of policy attracting life assurance relief. In other words, perhaps the most interesting question is how far tax reliefs have the effect of diverting into this particular channel money which would otherwise have been saved in any case but in some other way. Unfortunately, this question is not one to which a very definite answer can be given. The authors of the report of the Institute of Actuaries, probably wisely, made no attempt to assess in quantitative terms the extent to which the tax reliefs had had this effect, but reached

[1] See *Journal of the Institute of Actuaries*, Vol. 80, Part II, No. 355, pp. 160–65.
[2] This was the tentative figure suggested by the Phillip's Committee, no doubt mainly on the basis of the Institute of Actuaries' Survey (Cmd. 9333, para. 230.)

the broad conclusion that 'Pension fund saving is considerably facilitated by tax reliefs and to a substantial extent may simply replace other forms of saving'.

Finally, to give some idea of the volume of business represented by the approval of schemes, the following figures may be noted:

New Applications for Approval

Year	Section 379	Section 388
1957	1,845	7,248
1958	1,766	6,290
1959	1,425	5,796
1960	2,350	7,034
1961	5,307	9,743

(Figures supplied by Inland Revenue Department)

The sharp rise in 1961 is particularly noticeable, and is no doubt connected with the introduction of the state graduated scheme.

INDEX

Abel-Smith, Brian, 188 n
Acland, Rev John, 32
Acts of Parliament:
  Asylum Officers' Superannuation (1909), 210
  Electricity (1947), 236
  Local Government and other Officers' Superannuation (1922), 56, 57
  Local Government Superannuation (1937), 57
  National Insurance (1946), 39, 158, 180, 291
  National Insurance (1959), 39, 158, 168, 171, 180, 185, 186, 292
  National Insurance (1963), 172, 185, 186, 293
  Old Age Pensions (1908), 35–6, 37
  Pensions (Increase) Acts, 88–9, 122, 123, 149
  Police Pensions (1890), 60–1
  Police Pensions (1921), 61
  Superannuation, see Superannuation Acts
  Superannuation (Miscellaneous Provisions) (1948), 83–4
  Teachers' Superannuation (1925), 110
  Teachers' Superannuation (1956), 79, 113–14
  Trustee Investments (1961), 98
  Widows', Orphans' and Old Age Contributory Pensions (1925), 38
  Widows', Orphans' and Old Age Contributory Pensions (1936), 160 n
Actuarial valuations, 95, 100–2, 147
  civil service scheme, 108 n
Actuary:
  assessment of cost by, 93–5
  assumptions made by, 100–1
Addison, Dr, 56
Administration, complexity of, see Complexity
  cost of in public sector, 118–21
  cost of in private sector, 147–8
Age of retirement, 47, 51, 53, 57, 61, 75–6, 245–6
  in private sector, 132
Airways Corporations' pension scheme, 63, 78, 85, 102, 118, 124, 200, 269–70
  modification, 162–4
  provisions of, 282–3
  statistics, 286, 289

Amalgamation of public sector schemes, 208–9
Amory, D. Heathcote, 88
Anonymous Empire, 113 n, 227 n
Approved employment, 83
Armed Forces' pensions, 60, 72
  description of, 275–9
Assessmentism, 91 n
Association of Chief Financial Officers (NHS), 119 n
Atomic Energy Authority pension schemes, 72, 77, 83, 270
  modification, 163–4
  notional funds, 108–9, 114
  provisions of, 282–3
  statistics, 286, 289

Bacon, F. W., 140, 255–6, 313
Barker, W. R., 227 n
Bedfordshire County Council:
  Bill to abolish deficiency payments, 219–20
  Superannuation Fund, 99
Benjamin, B., 255–6, 313
Berkshire County Council, 119
Beveridge, Sir William, 39, 159, 175, 188, 241
Bismarck, 35
Blackley, Rev William, 34–5
Board of Trade Journal, 215 n, 261–2
Booth, Charles, 33, 34, 35, 40
Bow Group, 246 n
Boyd-Carpenter, John, 87
Brabrook, E. W., 21, 34
British Broadcasting Corporation, 271
British Council, 271
British European Airways, see Airways Corporations
British Institute of Management, 183 n
British Overseas Airways Corporation, see Airways Corporations
British Railways, see Railways
British Transport Reorganization (Pensions of Employees) (No. 3) Order, 1962, 203 n
Bromfield, A. E., 140
Brown, E. H. Phelps, 40 n
Bruce, Maurice, 31
Bullock, A., 36
Butterworth, A. Kaye, 41

Century of Revolution, The, 30 n
Chamberlain, Joseph, 34
Chamberlain, Neville, 38
Charles Booth: Social Scientist, 33 n

Chartered Accountants, employees' pension scheme, 143
Civil service pension scheme, 225, 263–4
  cost of, 106–7
  1810 scheme, 46–7
  1834 scheme, 49–50
  1856 inquiry, 18, 19, 50–1
  growth, 20–2
  modification, 163
  nominally non-contributory, 80, 104–5, 231
  origins, 15–17
  pensions increase, 124
  preservation of benefits, 81–8, 249
  provisions of, 280–1
  security of benefits, 216
  statistics, 223, 286, 288
Civil Service Staff Side, 89
Closed schemes, 69
Coming of the Welfare State, The, 31
Committees of management, nationalized industries' schemes, 102–3
Commonwealth War Graves Commission, 271
Complexity of administration, feature of public sector schemes, 199
  modification arrangements, 166–7, 173–5
  need to examine, 204–5
  reasons for, 200–3
  taxation, 191–2, 196
Conservative Party, 188, 246 n
Contracting-out, see Graduated Pension Scheme
Contributions:
  modified, 162–4, 169–70
  in private sector, 65–6, 134, 145–6
  in public sector, 75, 96–7, 102, 230–2
  refunds of, 85, 310
Costs of Education, The, 114 n, 227 n

Dalton, Hugh, 160 n, 178 n
Death benefits, 51, 78–9
Deficiencies:
  in funded schemes, 95, 101–2
  in teachers' scheme, 112–14
Desborough Committee (Police), 61
Digest of Pension Law and Regulations of the Civil Service, 201 n

Eccles, Lord, 114 n
Economic and Financial Problems of the Provision for Old Age, Committee on (Phillips), 241, 250, 256–7
Economic growth and future of pensions, 244
Economic importance of pension funds, 146–7, 214–15

Economics of National Insurance, The, 300
Eden, John, 188 n
Electricity supply industry pension schemes, 72, 83, 85, 92, 268
  modification, 163–4
  provisions of, 282–3
  statistics, 286, 289
Ellis, Kenneth, 16
Elphinstone, M. D. W., 255–6, 313
Engineers, Amalgamated Society of, 35 n
Engineers, pensions for, 143–4
Estimates Committee, House of Commons, 84 n

Faculty of Actuaries (Scotland), 140, 188 n, 256–7
Fair burden argument, 213
  Bedfordshire C.C. Bill, 219–20
  LCC Fund, 220–2
Farr, Dr William, 59
Federated Superannuation Scheme for Nurses and Hospital Officers, 143
Federated Superannuation System for Universities, 74, 83 n, 131, 263
  provision of, 135–6
  preservation of pension rights, 142–3
Financial and Economic Obligations of the Nationalized Industries, 236 n
Financial control, argument for funding, 213, 226–30
Financial principles, argument for funding, 212–13, 217–18
  relevance to nationalized industries' schemes, 236–7
Finer, S. E., 113 n, 227 n
Firemen's pension scheme, 74, 266
  financial arrangements, 115–16
  modification, 163
  provisions of, 280–1
  under 1925 Act, 62–3
Fogarty, Michael, 248 n
Forster, George H., 169 n, 173 n, 185 n
Friendly Societies, 31–2
'Frozen' pensions, 82–3, 140, 249–50. See also Preservation of pension benefits
Fryd, John, 250 n
Funding, 57, 64
  appropriateness to public sector, 216–39
  arguments for, 212–16
  in public sector, 96–104
  meaning of, 90–1
Funds:
  local government, 92, 104, 235
  police, 59–61, 115
  private sector, 146–7
  size of, 104, 147, 221
  statistics, 260–2

Gas industry pension schemes, 72, 76–7, 78, 92, 102, 268–9
  modification, 162–4
  provisions of, 282–3
  statistics, 286, 289
Geddes Committee, 116
George, Lloyd, 35–6
Government Actuary, 167, 257, 259
  reports on NHS scheme, 203 n, 211 n
  reports on teachers' scheme, 111 n, 112–14, 227
  survey of occupational pension schemes, 43 n, 128–30, 136, 140, 146, 148, 175–6, 257–8
Government Pension Scheme 1961, 183 n
Graduated National Pensions as affecting Local Authorities, 169 n, 173 n, 185 n
Graduated pension scheme, 138
  assurance of equivalent pension benefits, 184, 294–5
  description, 293–6, 298–9
  effect on local government and NHS schemes, 68–75
  and occupational pension schemes, 187–9
  problem of contracting-out, 180–6
Great Eastern Railway New Pension Fund, 203
Group Life and Pension Scheme, 67
Growth of British Industrial Relations, The, 40 n
'Growth of Pension Rights and their Impact on the National Economy, The', 255–6, 313
Growth of Pension Schemes in the Public Sector of the British Economy, 1953–62, 287

Hale Committee, *see* Superannuation of University Teachers
Halévy, Elie, 35 n
Henderson, Sir Hubert, 188 n
Higher Education, Committee on (Robbins), 253
Hill, Christopher, 30 n
History of the English People in the Nineteenth Century, 35 n
History of Unilever, 41 n
Horserace Betting Levy Board, 143
Hosking, Gordon A., 42 n, 145 n, 147, 305 n
Houghton, Douglas, 89, 202 n

Ill-health retirement:
  in private sector, 136
  in public sector, 77–8
Income Distribution and Social Change, 259 n, 301 n, 309 n

Ind Coope, 183 n, 185 n, 204 n
Inflation:
  effect on public sector schemes, 88–9, 122–6
  in private sector, 148
Inland Revenue Department, 135, 136, 191
  approval of pension schemes, 192–5, 196, 301–14
Institute of Actuaries, 140, 188, 208 n
  surveys of pension schemes, 255–6, 257 n, 313
Institute of Municipal Treasurers and Accountants, 119, 199 n
Insured pension schemes, 66–7, 128–9, 131
Integration with National Insurance, 138–40, 247
Interest rates:
  funded schemes, 95
  notional funds, 107, 111, 114
Investment, 214
  private sector schemes, 146–7
  public sector schemes, 98–9
  to reduce costs, 213, 224–5

James, H. R., 119
Jay, Douglas, 218 n
Just Wage, The, 248 n

Kaye-Shuttleworth, Sir James, 26
Kekewich, G. W., 27

Labour Party, 37, 188, 202, 241
  National Superannuation, 43 n, 45, 245, 246
Level of pension, 244–9
Liberal Party, 241, 246, 248 n
Liberal Tradition, The, 36
Life Officers' Association, 184, 257
  British Life Assurance, 259 n, 261
Local Act schemes, 55
Local government pension scheme, 79, 92, 200, 264–5
  funding in, 103, 224, 235–6
  modification, 163–7, 168–75
  1922 Act, 57
  provisions of, 280–1
  statistics, 286, 288
Local Government Superannuation, 119
London County Council pension scheme, 203
  progress of fund, 220–1
London Transport Staff pension scheme, 118, 272–3
Lump sums, 51, 77, 130, 131, 132, 136
  tax treatment of, 191, 195, 302–4
Lynes, Tony, 301 n

McDougall, R. S., 199 n
MacKay, G. S., 34–5

MacLeod, Iain, 201 n
MacPherson, Niall, 186 n
Manual workers' schemes, 65, 70–1, 130, 284–5
Massey, J., 119
Merchant Navy, 143
Mineworkers' pension scheme, 71, 72, 118, 268
  investments, 99 n
  provisions of, 285
  statistics, 286, 289
Ministry of Housing and Local Government, 175, 204–5, 219
Ministry of Labour:
  inquiry into pension schemes (1936), 42–3, 255 n
Modification of pension schemes for National Insurance, 76, 138, 247
  limitations of, 164–7
  in local government and NHS schemes, 168–75
  in private sector, 176
  in public sector, 158–64, 177–80
Mond, Sir Alfred, 56
Monetary System, Working of, Committee on (Radcliffe), 261
Mosely, Rev H., 23
Mowatt, Frank, 20
Multiplicity of schemes in public sector, 206–8

Namier, Sir Lewis, 15
National and Local Government Officers' Association, 219
National Association of Pension Funds, 131
  Journal of, 149 n
National Coal Board Principal scheme, 73 n, 79–80, 85–6, 125
  modification, 163–4
  provisions of, 282–3
  statistics, 286, 288
National Economic Development Council, 101, 144, 244, 249
National Farmers' Union, 143
National Health Service pension scheme, 68, 83, 200, 203, 210–11, 266–7
  cost of administration, 118–19
  modification, 163, 168–75
  notional fund, 108–9, 114
  provisions of, 280–1
  Regulations, 201
  statistics, 286, 288
National Incomes Commission, 252
National Insurance scheme, 39, 70, 91 n, 137–40, 150, 159
  description of, 291–300
  funds, 297–8
  future of, 246–7
  and public sector schemes, 160–80

National Insurance scheme, relation with occupational schemes, 187–9, 246–7
  see also Graduated pension scheme
National pensions policy, need for, 240–2
  factors affecting, 242–4
  how achieved, 251–3
  preservation of pension rights, 249–50
  problems of, 244–9, 250–1
National Union of Teachers, 88, 113 n
Nationalized industries' schemes, 102–3, 145, 200, 216, 267–8
  and funding, 232–4
  and pay-as-you-go, 236–7
  see also under individual schemes
New Trends in Pensions, 130 n
Nield, Sir Herbert, 56
'No detriment':
  abolition of, 201–11
  contribution to complexity, 202–3
  meaning, 69
  origin, 49
  problem of, 166, 179, 205, 209
Non-contributory schemes:
  in private sector, 130
  in public sector, 230–2, 235
  see also civil service pension scheme
Norman Committee, see Superannuation of Persons Employed by Local Authorities
Northcote–Trevelyan Report, 18–19
Notional funds, 224–5, 226
  abolition of advocated, 235
  contributions to, 108–9
  disadvantages of, 227–8
  financial arrangements in teachers' scheme, 110–15
  in Post Office, 107–8, 145, 237

Oaksey Committee, 116
Occupational pension schemes, see Pension schemes
Old Age Pensions, 34–5
Old Age pensions, 35, 158
  cost of, 36, 38
Old People in Britain, 246 n
Old people, numbers, 243
Ordman, N. N. B., 141 n, 144 n, 250 n
Owen, A. S., 188 n

Parity, 88, 125
Pay-as-you-go, 91
  advocated for public sector, 232–4
  in Civil Service, 104–7, 222–3
  and fair burden argument, 220–4
  financial control, 229–30
  notional funding, 107–15
Peacock, Alan T., 300

Pension:
  aims of, 242–6
  meaning of, 14–15
Pension Schemes, 40 n, 43 n, 182, 258 n
Pension schemes:
  definition, 13 n
  membership of, 42–3, 255–60
  reasons for, 16, 19, 26, 27, 29, 41, 43
*Pension Schemes and Retirement Bene-
  fits*, 42 n, 145 n, 147, 305 n
'Pension Schemes at the Crossroads',
  188 n
Pensions in Britain 1962, 307 n, 309 n
Pensions (Increase) Acts, 88–9, 122, 149
  provisions of, 123
Pensions for Prosperity, 45, 188 n, 246 n
'Pensions, Public and Private', 142 n
Percy, Lord Eustace, 110 n
Philpot, C. W. T., 307 n, 309 n
Pilch, M., 40 n, 43 n, 130 n, 182, 258 n
Police Council, Working Party on
  Widows' Pension, 116–17
Police pension scheme, 28, 74, 225, 266
  early arrangements, 58–9
  1890 scheme, 60–1
  financial arrangements, 115–17
  modification, 163
  provisions of, 280–1
  statistics, 286, 288
Police Superannuation Funds, Select
  Committee, 59
Poor law officers, 28
  pension scheme, 52–4
Port Employers' and Registered Dock-
  workers' Pension Scheme, 143
Post Office, *see* Notional funds
*Post Office in the Eighteenth Century,
  The*, 16
Poverty and old age, 30–5
Powell, J. Enoch, 105, 215
Preservation of pension benefits, 150
  future policy, 249–50
  in private sector, 140–4
  in public sector, 81–7
Preservation of Pension Rights, 140
*Preserving Pension Rights for Profes-
  sional Engineers*, 141 n, 144 n, 250 n
Prison officers, 70, 200
Private sector pension schemes, 40, 63,
  126, 129
  compared with public sector, 131–7
  financial arrangements, 144–9
  variety of, 64–8, 128–9
Protect your Pension, 250 n
Provision for Old Age, White Paper,
  39, 187
Public Accounts Committee, 227
Public boards, 84, 271

Railway pensioners, 125 n
Railway Superannuation Funds, Departmental Committee, 41–2

Railways' pension schemes, 41–2, 63,
  71, 76, 78–9, 269, 272–4
  investments, 99
  Male Wages Grades scheme, 72,
    269, 272, 274, 285
  modification, 163–4
  provisions of, 282–3
  statistics, 286, 289–90
Religion and the Rise of Capitalism, 30
Robb, A. C., 203 n, 208 n. *See also
  Shaw's Guide to Superannuation*
Royal Commissions:
  Civil Establishments (Ridley), 19, 51
  Civil Service (Priestley), 80 n, 81 n,
    86 n, 105 n, 107 n
  Civil Service (Tomlin), 51
  Friendly Societies, 32
  Poor Law, 34, 35 n
  Popular Education, 25, 27
  Superannuation Act (1834), 18, 19,
    50–1
  Superannuation in the Civil Service
    (Courtney), 20, 21–2
  Taxation of Profits and Income, 190,
    196, 250 n, 306, 307, 311–12

Sansom, R. C., 141 n, 144 n, 250 n
Saving in a Free Society, 105, 215
Saving, pension fund, 214–15, 311–14
Scottish Electricity pension schemes,
  271
Security argument for funding, 212,
  216–17, 232–4
Seldon, Arthur, 45, 142 n, 188 n, 246 n,
'Self-administered' schemes, 66, 128–9,
  131
Senior, Nassau, 31
Sharpness and Gloucester Dock Com-
  pany scheme, 203
*Shaw's Guide to Superannuation for
  Local Authorities*, 173, 177, 199 n,
  200, 203 n
Shock, M., 36
Simey, M. B., 33 n
Simey, T. S., 33 n
Social Insurance and Allied Services,
  39, 159, 175, 188, 241
Social workers pension scheme, 143
Socialism in the New Society, 218 n
Spratling, F. H., 140
State pensions, 13 n. *See* National
  Insurance
*Structure of Politics at the Accession of
  George III, The*, 15
Superannuation Acts:
  (1834), 17, 18, 49–50
  (1857), 51
  (1859), 21, 51
  (1909), 51
  (1914), 83
  (1935), 79
  (1949), 51, 70

Superannuation of Persons Employed by Local Authorities in England and Wales, Departmental Committee (Norman), 29 n, 56, 231

Superannuation of School Teachers, Departmental Committee (1923), 27

Superannuation of Teachers in England and Wales, The, 227 n

Superannuation of University Teachers, Committee (Hale), 136 n, 137, 220, 221, 225

Superannuation Schemes, 14. *See* Pension Schemes

Surplus, in funded schemes, 95, 102

Tawney, R. H., 30

Taxation, 150, 190

Taxation Treatment of Provisions for Retirement Committee (Millard Tucker), 194 n, 196, 250 n, 301 n, 303 n, 306–7, 309, 311

Tax reliefs for pension schemes, 190–7
cost of, 313–14
history of, 301–9
reasons for, 311–13

Teachers' pension scheme, 85, 265
history of, 22–7, 62
modification, 163
notional fund, 108–14, 227
provisions of, 280–1
statistics, 286, 288
widows' pensions, 79, 310

Teachers' Superannuation, Select Committees:
(1872), 25
(1892), 26

Terminal-salary schemes, 72, 132
comparison with, FFSU, 136–7
development of, 46–52

Thatcher, Mrs M., 241 n

Titmuss, R. M., 45, 258, 259 n, 301 n, 309 n

'Top Hat' schemes, 145, 195, 308–9

Transferability, *see* Preservation of pension benefits

Transfer values, 84, 141, 167, 220

Transport schemes, 269, 272–4, 286, 289–90. *See also* Railways

United Kingdom Atomic Energy Authority, *see* Atomic Energy Authority

University Grants Committee, 137, 263 n

University teachers' pensions, *see* Federated Superannuation System for Universities

Vaizey, John, 114 n, 227 n

Widows' pensions, 130, 132
airways' scheme, 200
civil service, 51–2
local government, 58
police, 61–2, 116–17, 225
policy for, 250–1
in public sector schemes, 79–80
tax position, 309–10
teachers' scheme, 79, 310

Wilson, Sir Arnold, 34–5

Wilson, C., 41 n

Women, increased employment of, 243–4

Wood, V., 40 n, 43 n, 130 n, 182, 258 n